The Demon Pr

The Demon Profession

Michael Laws

HarperCollins*Publishers* New Zealand Limited

First published 1998
HarperCollins*Publishers (New Zealand) Limited*
P.O. Box 1, Auckland

ISBN 1 86950 257 4

Designed and typeset by Chris O'Brien
Cover design by Dexter Fry
Cover photo by Sally Tagg
Printed by Publishing Press Limited, Auckland

To my wife, Karen,
who is far too good for me!

ACKNOWLEDGEMENTS

My thanks to those of my family and friends forced to endure my out-loud readings of sections of this book and for their silent suffering.

To Darius Consultants for providing me with the wherewithal to indulge myself in completing this tome; and to HarperCollins' Ian Watt for both his unflappable optimism and cheery encouragement. Even in suffering the author's occasional Vesuvian outburst he continued to smile. I want some of that drug.

To all those staff who worked with me when I was an MP and gathered the resource material for this book — Anne, Louise, Lisa, Kathy, Jo and Tania. Only you know how bad and how good it could really get.

To Greg Jones, Simon Penlington and Bruce Gray — who kept me sane, solvent and stoic in 1997.

To the cartoonists whose work features in this book — only too glad to have been a target for your undoubted skill and wit — Brockie, Crimp, Doyle, Greenall, Klarc and especially Tom Scott. One day I'll get my revenge.

Finally to my parents and my wife, who allowed me to delve into domestic history and justify my past misdeeds. Thank God you have never been tempted to write.

CONTENTS

Preface

I have always been the black sheep of my family. I confess to this infamy now rather than attempt any justification of my later behaviour.

Of course my parents would be scandalised if it was ever proven that any of their son's wayward actions had been inspired by genetic predisposition. If pushed they tend to advance the 'swapped at birth' theory, although patient records at Wairoa's maternity hospital have never been properly investigated; perhaps for fear of having this hypothesis disproven.

It is not as if I have ever cultivated any eccentricity of character; indeed, my sole childhood ambition was to be 'normal'. Sadly, I lacked both the chromosomal talent and the internal discipline to satisfy even this first inkling of self-awareness. I wanted to fit in — it is just that no one else perceived this as a viable possibility.

I guess I have always been an instinctive frontier dweller, although my family pooh-pooh even this attempt at self-justification. According to their experiential wisdom, I wantonly chose non-conformity and embraced anarchic viewpoints through sheer devilishness.

There are two other characteristics that I should admit to now rather than have to establish later. I was always a loner, and I was always in trouble. One reinforced the other.

As a child and a teenager such isolation could be alternately devastating and welcome. Certainly it induced melancholic bouts of self-pity and sullen anger, but at least such disappointment trained me for a lifetime of supporting the New Zealand cricket team. Looking back now I am not quite sure what came first — whether others perceived me as 'not fitting in', or whether I resolved to choose independence over peer acceptance. It matters little — that's just the way it was.

11

For all that, I admit to a historic difficulty in accepting that any of my actions should ever be governed by the conventions and expectations of others. Being the prisoner of others' prejudice rather defeats the whole purpose of existence. I have always regarded moral collectivism as a refuge for the unthinking.

In writing this book I have been forced to confront such truths, and also been required to revive memories that had been stealthily buried by a guilty conscience. However, this book is not about absorptive self-analysis; that terrain is far too terrifying. NASA would refuse to go there. My autobiography can wait until my memory completely fails and I can blame other persons, safely dead, for all my vices.

Instead this is an attempt to share my political experiences of the past decade or so. The hope is that through looking at the New Zealand scene via my eyes and my consciousness some light might be cast upon its turgid operation. Sure this book will highlight the incompetence, the banality and the caprice, but that is only because they exist.

Having witnessed or experienced virtually every political vice and virtue during the past thirteen years, perhaps I could have preached a moral fable. Except that I am not the parliamentary equivalent of a reformed alcoholic; each reader can draw their own conclusions. I make no apology if the vantage I provide is sometimes skewed, insensitive, difficult or even disturbing. It is a personal perspective after all.

And generally, individual lives are neither good nor evil; rather, they hover between the petty foothills of each. Thus there are no heroes or villains in this book; merely a group of very ordinary people entwined within an extraordinary profession. That profession is politics — the 'Demon Profession' of the title.

Politics is a world of both illusion and self-delusion. By its very nature it seeks control and influence over the lives of others. In parading its motivations as beneficent, politics also blinds its own practitioners to the consequences of their meddling. For human society is constantly evolving, only to be restrained by those very political institutions that pledge to make us free. I have little doubt that most politicians really do believe that the country is a better place for their involvement. That is where the self-delusion comes in.

Like most professions, politics jealously guards its secrets. In doing so it retains a mystique that defies rational comprehension. At a time when politicians are among the most distrusted, disliked and even despised group on this planet, we accord them untoward respect and allow them continued influence over our personal lives.

This book is my personal journey through the maze. I profess to no great intelligence or insight. But if we do learn through the experiences of others then there is a truth in every life. This is mine.

Michael Laws
21 March 1998

– Chapter 1 –

ORIGINS

FAMILY

Manifest as my deficiencies may be, I cannot claim any mitigation on the basis of family background.

My father Keith is an unabashed romantic, despite being born in the Napier of the 1930s. Perhaps in a later life he will become the soaring Italian tenor who is entrapped within. All my tendencies toward dreaminess, to imaginative flight, even to a hint of creativity, I ascribe to my father.

Despite his sentimentalism my father's innate character was muted by the more dominant strictures of self-discipline and self-denial — qualities well beyond my ken no matter how intense the paternal preaching. I never quite understood how this inherently kind man could daily metamorphose into a disciplinarian schoolmaster with illiberal standards. It was just a mite too spooky — like Ulysses and the Lotus-eaters occupying the same consciousness.

My mother Helen was also born in Hawke's Bay, in the then small township of Taradale. She was the first-born and wantonly assertive, with the ability to be both stroppy and charming in the same moment — characteristics that my two younger sisters, Diane and Susan, have inherited, with sufficient of the second quality to get away with it. Whereas my father could forgive and forget, my mother deemed such charity imprudent. As a consequence, my mother was very definitely the dominant partner in the marriage; it is impossible to compromise with truly implacable individuals who possess searing memories. I should have learned this lesson earlier and applied it elsewhere — it is the reason why conservatives ultimately thrash liberals.

The death of Mum's younger brother and only sibling from leukemia at the age of eleven traumatised her family. They grieve still. My mother assimilated this pain, and her primary aim on marrying was to produce a male child in an attempt to fill this aching void in her parents' lives. Thus I was born in Wairoa, in June 1957, and named Michael Brian — in memory of an uncle I had never known but whose parents would love me as their own for the next forty years. This was particularly true of Grandma Robinson, whose cautious manner and abhorrence of public spectacle was always abandoned whenever I came to visit.

I was doubly blessed. Nana Laws also regarded her first-born grandchild as special. Although I proved a constant source of disappointment no child ever possessed such staunch champions. As I began to develop my wayward reputation within the Laws and Robinson clans I could always rely on my grandmothers to play the twin roles of comforter and advocate.

My father had always wanted to be a schoolteacher, and consciously abandoned any pursuit of a greater personal destiny in making this career choice. However, he compensated for Shaw's famous dictum by pursuing the ambition of having 'his own school', although only if it came with a decent rugby fifteen. The art of teaching itself he regarded as no special feat — the real prize lay in climbing the promotion rungs, and as principal of Waitaki Boys' High School and the private Scot's College he clearly fulfilled these imperial ambitions. He also excelled as a secondary school rugby coach and clearly had aspirations that his son might possess the modicum of talent necessary to succeed at this sport — a source of later disquiet for me.

Ambition within teaching circles is an invitation to a peripatetic lifestyle. Dad's first posting was to the northern Hawke's Bay township of Wairoa, and thence to the new coeducational high school in Wanganui to teach social studies, history and geography.

My family moved to a new state housing subdivision in Gonville — a half-formed suburban wilderness where cars and bikes went to die and there be cannibalised — their rusting remains strewn over front lawns as a warning to other errant vehicles. Domestic animals were either quick or dead — sometimes both if we neighbourhood kids caught up with them during the annual Guy Fawke's pillage, a diversion from the ceaseless games of street cricket and bulrush that occupied our non-school hours.

I attended the local Tawhero Primary School and excelled at little apart from a unique ability to break wind and project vomit at roughly the same instant. This skill was discovered while being force-fed half-pints of compulsory school milk which daily curdled in the morning sun. Such feats had a startling effect on my classmates, who would eagerly await this ritual and gaze on with a mixture of awe and revulsion.

Academically I was given a significant head start by my parents, who introduced me to the rudiments of learning from the earliest age. Our education path had been pre-planned and was inculcated from the first instant — Dad's alma mater of Otago University the final destination. Such parental emphasis put me at a distinct advantage over most of my classmates — many of whom had had only a fleeting association with their father's TAB form guide. As a consequence I was pushed ahead a schooling year by the authorities and thence required to contend with older children who were larger, more socially aware and duly resentful of the brainy little snot who made dramatic 'pick me' gestures whenever the teacher asked for class participation.

I retained this foolhardy streak no matter what faces were pulled and despite the pointed blindness of the teacher to my pleadings. Looking back I can see that I already had the vital skills to be a politician — an absurd desire to impress strangers matched by an unsubstantiated belief in my own abilities. It was either Parliament or driving a taxi.

For all my competitiveness, I lacked even the faintest degree of physical self-confidence. No, that is too kind a summary. I was a complete coward. In the normal hurly-burly of Tawhero there was always a fair measure of pushing, prodding and punching as social pecking orders were established. My place in this order was to be the most pecked.

This handicap may also have been linked to my childhood physical appearance — a shock of unruly curly hair, protruding front teeth, a scrubbed complexion, an immaculately ironed school uniform, and a buffed sheen that had been applied courtesy of my mother's obsession with hygiene. It was as if Dettol had come to life. And for that I blame the sand.

Our homes had all been posited on black ironsands, so the local state housing wallahs did their best to disguise this oversight with a thick matting of tough buffalo grass. It was about the only organic material that would grow, and the traditional Saturday morning encounter with the two-stroke motor mower assumed epic proportions as a consequence. Anybody harbouring the remotest of gardening ambitions found it necessary to import truckloads of topsoil and, given the general poverty of our suburb, the annual Jaycees 'manure drive' proved exceedingly popular. Then the whole of Harper Street would reek of chicken shit for weeks. It made little discernible difference — the surrounds to our suburb were regularly whipped by westerly gales straight off the Tasman which at least removed the need to visit the nearby Castlecliff beach. It came to us.

My mother loathed the stuff. As a result, cleanliness supplanted godliness in our household; a religion all of its own with Mum the high priestess. This reached the ridiculous extreme of our being banned entry to the house if the linoleum floors had just been scrubbed and waxed. Such order extended to our personal appearance and each Laws child was cleaned and groomed to a standard that would have done us credit at Crufts. My sisters got away with such treatment but at Tawhero my appearance could only provoke wonder and derision in roughly equal proportions.

Despite this I did my best to fit in and enthusiastically participated in the schoolground demolition derbies of rugby, bulrush and a particularly violent game of tag that involved large stones and metres of sticking plaster. I was particularly useless at rugby, displaying a generous tackle that essentially escorted opposing players to the tryline. Each wintry Saturday morning my father was forced to abandon anew any hope that his son might become an All Black or even a passable sportsman. Hell, it would be a miracle if I survived through to adulthood.

In turn, I was becoming increasingly suspicious of my father's intentions now that it was obvious I would not be a future source of free test tickets to Athletic Park. For Dad had acquired a disturbing medicinal cure-all when it came to his son's many ills and accidents — the much-feared 'good night's sleep'. All the world's problems could be solved, my father frequently opined, by everyone having a good night's sleep. This even extended to physical injury when such somnolent faith-healing was prescribed for a badly broken right arm acquired in one of the neighbourhood bulrush epics. I remember stoically bearing this injury with O'Rorke's Drift heroism — my mother insists she could hear my screaming from a block away.

Dad would reapply this infamous remedy later the same year when severe stomach cramps were similarly prescribed the 'good night's sleep' cure. Acute appendicitis threatened to flare into peritonitis and only the intervention of Nana forestalled such an eventuality. As I recovered in hospital, on Christmas Day no less, there seemed only two possible explanations. Either my father was grossly fallible (always a shock discovery in childhood) or he had taken out a very large insurance policy on my life.

By the end of my Standard Four year my timid idiosyncrasies had become so well understood as to be finally tolerated. For all that I was a solitary and sensitive child, much given to the dawdle of distant daydreaming and a sullen brooding if denied. My family accepted this emotional aloofness as a defined personal trait, perhaps misinterpreting total insecurity as deliberate conviction.

It was particularly devastating then to learn that I would be required to attend a distant and different intermediate school from my classmates the next year. Despite tearful petitioning my parents were unmoved. The family was departing Mum's dreaded Gonville, my father having gained promotion to Head of History at Wanganui Boys' College and also being appointed resident Senior Housemaster of the school's boarding establishment.

Whatever the excuse I could not fathom the rationale that forced me to depart Tawhero for a two-year sojourn in the educational limbo of Wanganui Intermediate — a bizarre interregnum within which my age group could be pubertally detonated without causing too much damage to the surrounding buildings. This then was the season of personal sexual awareness, to which we were duly alerted by a special showing of cartoon health slides, accompanied by an embarrassed commentary from the teacher. I am afraid it was all totally beyond me and the only hint that something unusual was occurring amongst my peer group was when the headmaster held a series of 'special assemblies' with the common theme that some sort of moral danger lurked behind the bikesheds. Still not detonated, I was herded off down the road to secondary school.

Wanganui Boys' College was far more than just a shock to the system — it was the equivalent of a full-scale lightning strike. The school was a dishevelled mix of aggressive and destructive personalities who plundered any and all attempts at the slightest sensitivity. An implacable macho order pervaded the place from its teaching staff, who instinctively accepted that to spare the rod was to spoil the child, to the hierarchy of bullying that accompanied social progress through the various forms.

Third formers were the lowest of the low — mere 'turds' who were routinely harassed simply for being the junior inmates in this tribal madness. But pity the poor kid who suffered either physical or intellectual disability. They were separated out and attacked with all the merciless precision of a hyena troop.

Having one's father teach at the same school was a clear invitation to join the victimhood. When that same father possessed a notoriety among the students for his imposition of strict and unpopular discipline, then membership was mandatory. It was a measure of my emotional distance from the family that I never confided this bullying hell to my parents. Instead I responded with further lengthy periods of sullen silence punctuated only by petty outbursts of frustrated petulance. I was marked as 'a difficult child' and retreated further into a self-imposed teenage isolation. It was but one small step to alienation.

For all that, it was not in my nature to suffer such peer predations without demur. The domination of the meek by the brutish came to offend every sensibility within me, if only because I was so often the chosen target. The only recourse available was one that had somehow been gifted to me at birth — a quick tongue, which was now trained to lash back at the instant of provocation. It was faintly reassuring to see how the tormentors suffered when any of their own characteristics were amplified and mocked. In the perverse environment of Boys' College such verbal cruelty even earned a certain respect.

But such fleeting retribution could not remove the emotional insularity and insecurity, that oppression of aloneness, that bedevilled my adolescence.

This process was further accelerated by my family's relocation to Hamilton, where my father had gained a deputy principal's job at Hamilton Boys'. Perhaps cognisant of the Wanganui experience, my parents sent me to the coeducational Fairfield College, which I loathed from the first day. It loathed me right back. By mid-year I was wagging complete periods and then days, and I had become adept at forging my mother's signature and faking a succession of flu-like symptoms.

Finally that toxic combination of complete isolation from both family and peers induced a drastic determination. Such an existence could be tolerated no longer. In the timeless tradition of adolescent rebels everywhere I undertook my own intensely private odyssey. I literally ran away from home.

This is not the time to recount all that occurred in that month of independence and personal freedom. The experiences, the personalities, the frank awareness of self marked a clear turning point in my young life. At fifteen years of age, I substituted my wringing concern for the opinions and expectations of others for an aggressive self-reliance.

By the time I had hitchhiked to Wellington and caught the inter-island ferry across Cook Strait a new identity had been invented and adopted — though my modest and plausible tale was somewhat compromised by front-page news stories of a runaway child, distraught parents and an accompanying school photograph. I had become living proof of Andy Warhol's curse — and thus plunged further southwards in an attempt to outrun such unwelcome attention.

I found the required isolation in the remote Mackenzie Country and the tiny township of Lake Tekapo. The surrounding scenery was eerily breathtaking — sheer mountain peaks rising from a sapphire-coloured glacier-fed lake in turn framed by the parched landscape. A swanky new motor inn had been constructed for the tourist trade — American and Japanese bus tours in the main travelling on budget package tours. The proprietor had just fired half his kitchen staff after a particularly roisterous gathering at the staff quarters and I was employed as a kitchenhand, although I soon assumed responsibility as the breakfast cook. Lake Tekapo was a perfect refuge and since every other staff member was either a foreigner or involved in their own psychosis I fitted in perfectly.

However, those newspaper headlines lingered and I was sufficiently concerned to write a brief letter of guileless reassurance to my parents advising them of my general health. The police duly deciphered the postmark, made the appropriate enquiries and a month after I had departed Hamilton my relieved parents arrived at Lake Tekapo, wholly unsure as to their reception. It was a curious meeting — as if we were all very wary strangers trying to negotiate an armistice.

There would be no happy ending. If anything the estrangement between my parents and me widened beyond any possible rapprochement. I was now, officially and publicly, the black sheep within the family. There was unanimous agreement that forced repatriation would cause only further upset and so it was determined that my secondary schooling should be completed back at Wanganui Boys'.

After the relative freedom and independence that had accompanied my southern sojourn, the College's hostel seemed a detention centre. And, in a sense, that is exactly what it was. Stifling regulations governed every aspect of student activity — ranging from the banning of all multi-coloured undergarments to the confiscation of my Solzhenitsyn poster on the grounds that it was 'patently subversive'. Clearly the housemasters considered all Russians with facial hair to be a menace to western society regardless of their philosophical background.

Transgression of any of the hostel's myriad rules was met with a stiff caning, which consisted of a lethal bamboo rod being dashed repeatedly and with great vigour on the transgressor's upraised backside. The resident housemasters were a curious collection of social outcasts and humourless bullies, some of whom took peculiar pleasure in administering such floggings particularly if the recipient was attired in the flimsiest of pyjama bottoms. We were thence alerted to the fact that more than mere punishment occupied the minds of our persecutors; sadly confirmed when the police were required to investigate the paedophiliac tendencies of one particular master.

Only two things bothered any of the inmates — acne and sex. Or rather the prospect of sex. The two were perceived as irretrievably interconnected, which produced the dormitory mantra that 'you can't get a screw with a screwed-up face' — our equivalent of the Nicene Creed.

We were thus compelled to wage continual battle against our disloyal visages, with all pimples and blackheads ruthlessly hunted and destroyed — a battle that was often Pyrrhic in its consequences. Acne was the common enemy for it robbed us of that rarest of teenage commodities — self-confidence. Thus we became driven in a joint pursuit for the holy grail of an instant cure, with no shortage of volunteers for scientific experimentation.

The most bizarre remedy involved smearing one's face with a concoction of soap, baking soda and cigarette ash; another involved an oral paste composed of sulphur and honey. Initially this latter combination proved promising, if only because a couple of the guinea pigs discovered its ability to induce retching after a combined 'dump' within the school buildings. The perpetrators themselves seemed immune to the olfactory carnage and became instant legends. The concoction — whose odour was likened to a putrid, decomposing horse at the height of summer — was never used prior to school socials but was insanely popular prior to internal school examinations. This craze withered somewhat when the acne splotches remained stubbornly immune to either the chemical properties of the mixture or the smell.

But nothing, and I mean nothing, occupied our fetid minds like the folk myths and mysteries of fornication.

There were various attempts to break the pattern of failure. Three drooling sixth-formers pooled their weekly pocket money and other meagre financial resources for an end-of-term foray to the local massage parlour. Sadly, this transaction was ruined when the prospective vendor turned out to be one of the boys' sisters. When the other two insisted that this need not hinder their enjoyment a nasty scene ensued. A similar event was marred when the first participant rather overdid his arousal and suffered a violent fit during the coupling. It became much harder to procure after that incident; the word about the hostel boys was out.

In the end, impetuous gropings and fumblings were left to staged 'socials' in the hostel's Common Room with equally desperate girls from sister boarding schools. For some reason I always ended up with girls who had much larger brothers resident at the hostel and subsequently had the most chaste of evenings.

The school itself suffered from a gross inferiority complex. For decades, Wanganui Boys' (previously Wanganui Technical) had compared itself to the private and posh Wanganui Collegiate up the road and been found seriously wanting. One school was a thorough-bred in terms of academic and sporting pedigree; the other a mongrel which revelled in such a stigma because it had no alternative. The most unfortunate side effect of this status, or rather its lack, was that it dissuaded most sensible young girls from social contact with the school's inmates. It became a schoolgirl status symbol in Wanganui not to have a Boys' College boyfriend.

My experiences with the teaching staff were no more successful. Despite the best efforts of the school's career adviser to have me leave school and attempt an apprenticeship ('Laws, make it easy on yourself. Leave now before you're expelled.') I managed to successfully complete University Entrance and Bursary examinations. Such were the teaching standards that the handicap of being banned entirely from my seventh-form English class actually assisted my studies, although similar suspension from my accounting and economics classes made rather a dent in the rest of the school day. 'Insubordination' was the most common charge, although spontaneous student protests over hostel food and haircut regulations presented flashpoints for a little demagoguery. I soon found myself accused of being the ringleader for any and all such insurrections, which was wholly untrue. As the slowest runner I was simply the first caught.

It was not that I was uniformly evil or unnecessarily disruptive. Rather my attitude of continually demanding justification for the perceived pettiness of school rules drew me into a constant battle with the authorities. In questioning the arbitrary decisions that passed for measured authority, I had been alerted to the first maxim of the powerful. Never justify your decisions: otherwise they will know you are an idiot. Blind acceptance of authority and tradition was abhorrent to me at the tender age of sixteen years but I consoled myself that my boarding school career would soon be over. Little did I realise that such absurd and unthinking traditions dwelled comfortably within both party caucuses when elected to Parliament some sixteen years later.

I left school under suspension — a return to the hostel precincts at three in the morning being the principal crime. Headmaster Colin Noall was a family friend and refrained from the normal expulsion, choosing instead to append my end of year testimonial with the portentous warning: 'Michael is maturing … slowly.'

In truth, I agreed. Pronouncing myself unready for tertiary studies I strayed only as far as my grandmothers' cooking and decided on a year's sabbatical in Napier while I determined the barest rudiments of what to do with tomorrow.

I ended up working at the massive and foreboding Whakatu freezing works, with its seven chains and workforce of over 2500 people. I became a trimmer on the beef chain, which was the least skilled job at Whakatu, but incompetence was easy to hide in this vast workforce — a point later made more obvious by the directors of the company. There are still sufficient scars on my hands to suggest that my knife-work represented a clear danger to everyone within feet of my work station but most especially me. My colleagues noted my skills and awarded me the nickname d'Artagnan.

As well as being gratuitously repetitive the work was bloody, smelly and wet — a constant spray of cattle viscera coagulating with the beef hair, fat and ever more blood. The monotony numbed all sensibilities. Workers simply turned their brains to 'off'; some never turned them on again. They became the trade union officials.

By now I was flatting in Napier with a couple of older guys and through their female associates being introduced randomly to sex, drugs and rock 'n' roll — in reverse order as it transpired. To complete the image of a teenage dissolute I had grown my curly hair into a gravity-defying Afro, attempted a sparse beard in an effort to escape the licensing laws, and complemented these affectations with a pair of round-framed, orange-tinted John Lennon spectacles. Nana said I looked like a stoned, albino Fijian.

But I had the time of my life. The casual pub social scene was friendly and non-judgemental, the drugs freely available, the girls uncomplicated and the works' wages sufficient to just last until the next payday. For a repressed kid straight out of a single-sex boarding school and choked by inadequate interpersonal skills Napier was a hedonistic heaven.

This alcohol–cannabis idyll was rudely shattered one languid summer night. My father had mailed me the Otago University handbook for the next year in the rather forlorn hope that I might consider resuming academic studies. That same evening I attended one of the usual Friday evening gatherings with the dope smoke an acrid haze, the real 'heads' engaged in their latest LSD adventure, Pink Floyd thumping out of the speakers — another cruisy evening of personal dissolution.

Then a startling screech of car tyres, doors being slammed shut, angry voices raised in confrontation, barking dogs, heavy boots ascending the stairs, the scraping of a stereo needle across a now ruined LP — a police bust!

A man I recognised as the flat's supplier burst out from the corridor and took flight over the verandah railings, tumbling through the bush hedge below — a police dog followed in effortless pursuit. All manner of plastic bags and envelopes were being heaved out into the night air; disrobed and dishevelled couples were herded out of bedrooms and ushered downstairs, snarling Alsatians menacing each step. Miraculously, I escaped attention — an extinguished joint secreted in my palm.

That evening a good number of my associates were arrested for possession of a varied assortment of mind-altering substances — marijuana, cannabis resin, LSD tablets, Abba records. I had been but a policeman's glance away from a similar fate — arrest, conviction and the possible compromise of any professional career. Suitably chastened, I strolled somewhat briskly back to my flat, flushed my meagre stash down the toilet and completed the pre-enrolment forms for Otago University.

UNIVERSITY

Otago University in 1976 was simply an excuse to party.

The taxpayer provided generous and universal student bursaries; holiday jobs were plentiful, with a fully subsidised student holiday programme for the truly lazy; and long skiing weekends in the

Remarkables or Treble Cone routinely undermined those few student politicians pleading campus poverty. Their real grievance seemed to be that they personally could not afford the ruinous expense of such social jaunts to the snowline. Another lesson. The politics of envy always starts with the middle-class aspiring to nouveau riche pretensions.

My undergraduate years were little different from many others — turbulent, anarchic, boozy, intense and selfish. If there was one vice that I absorbed exclusively from my tertiary days it was selfishness. Universities instil this attribute into all their charges via a bizarre osmosis. It is their enduring legacy to society. No social group is as mercenary as the educated upwardly mobile.

To its credit Dunedin had solved the problem of what to do with its student population and constructed enough bars and taverns in the tertiary quarter that a routine visit to the dairy or the hairdresser could take days. Alcoholic temptation filled in any personal void that might exist around the occasional lecture, tutorial or term test. For some the temptation was too severe, with their oases transforming themselves into great black holes from which there could be no escape. We lost one flatmate in late March to such an attack and he finally surfaced in the middle of June apologising for missing his night of washing the dishes and asking what was for tea.

Although cannabis was in plentiful supply, Speights Draught was the favoured fuel of oblivion. There were those who had more exotic tastes — nitrous oxide canisters stolen from chemistry laboratories proved trendy for a while, as did experimentation with the hallucinatory datura plant. My sole dabble with the latter proved suitably salutary with various parts of my anatomy dissembling themselves completely from the rest of my body. To this day I am still not convinced that they have all come home.

Of course, the more refined among us were also beginning to appreciate New Zealand's fledgling wine industry, particularly if it was priced at $1.99 and located in the bargain bin. Cold Duck, Brother Dominic and Velluto Rosso were names that would mask a student generation of epicurean abuse.

My first days at Otago began poorly. No student residential hall would accept my application despite glowing character references from people who did not know me. Eventually I was informed that Arana Hall had accepted my application but this correspondence possessed a twilight character considering that I had neither applied to nor

25

even heard of the place. Later it became apparent that this dwelling was the dumping ground for all the troublemakers, refugees and rejects that every other residential hall had declined.

Arana Hall was the Animal House of Otago University — of the entire New Zealand university system I suspect. An all-male hostel of 160 twitchy, sex-starved, destructive, boozy, borderline sociopaths. In retrospect, it was my kind of place. This Hogarthian madness was presided over by a perpetually harassed, stooped and unblinking warden with the pallor of a month-old cadaver and a penchant for 'moral rearmament' crusades. In quixotic fashion these were launched each term in the vain attempt to save our souls — or at least those female souls who had strayed inside the compound.

There were many incongruities within the hostel, most notably the smattering of south-east Asian students who had ended up at Arana because of some derelict Colombo Plan official. They were studious, polite, scrupulously honest and meticulously hygienic; ergo, they did not belong and soon knew it. I shudder now to think of the collective Malaysian impression of New Zealand as a consequence of these experiences with the barbarian hordes.

The debauched excess, appalling social snobbery, the obvious racism directed against Asian students on campus and the indifferent teaching standards of the lecturers soon convinced me that I had entered no portal of sophisticated excellence. Far from it. Any protestation of academic freedom seemed a convenient excuse to mask substandard instruction and petty regulation. At one of my first English lessons the lecturer lurched in from his latest visit to the void, burped and then stumbled out again. It was the most brilliant insight of the year.

I was both disappointed and strangely relieved. Disappointed that my intellectual mettle would not be challenged but relieved that this dreaded confrontation had been forestalled. The quickest way to destroy vanity is to have one's inadequacies brutally highlighted at an impressionable age. If they are not exposed by the age of twenty then one is generally afflicted for life; hence the enormous popularity of tertiary education and its calculated failure to challenge.

Otago University abounded with specialist schools — the legacy of its historical traditions as New Zealand's oldest tertiary institution. The premier faculty was undoubtedly Medicine. Its students were the supposed apogee of academic excellence, although once admitted into its hallowed halls it was like Hotel California — impossible to leave.

The trick was to get accepted in the first place.

As a consequence the campus teemed with beastly swots known as med intermediates — over a thousand obsessional nerds measuring their latest grade average with a calculator and keeping a hostile eye on all potential competition.

There was a booby prize for the med int failures. A word of warning: never venture this observation to your dentist. Dental school students bitterly resented this slur against their intellectual capabilities. They had deliberately sought those B and B-plus gradings so that they could spend a professional lifetime looking down other people's throats for a living. Sure.

My undergraduate academic record was thoroughly undistinguished. I performed competently in my first year, being invited to study for honours in History and somehow fluking a pass in the Legal Systems paper. This pass provoked the unfortunate and foolish suspicion that I was harbouring a dormant and untapped legal bent — a conceit wholly excised a year later when I failed every one of my law papers. Along with any prospect of a legal career went my student bursary — stripped by way of my failure to pass the required number of units.

I returned to Dunedin, procured a job as a barman in the great void and started to attend the odd lecture. By year's end I had scraped sufficient grades to be invited back into the final-year History honours/postgraduate class. History was the only subject that really interested me during all this time, or rather, it was the only subject that appreciated any hint of my endeavour.

Which was a skill particularly ill-suited to imminent parenthood. In a moment of madness a local Dunedin lass had misread my immature confusion as innocent charm, and by the time she realised this vast misjudgment the lady was carrying our child. A pretty and gentle redhead, Rachel Elizabeth, would be born in October 1979 — a tender testimony to the fact that children need not inherit the sins of their fathers.

Fortunately, Rachel's mother recovered her emotional poise and quite rightly determined that no permanent relationship should be even remotely contemplated.

In my final undergraduate year I applied myself with the tangible ambition of gaining a First, but still had no idea as to what I would do with such a degree. When the department informed me that I had achieved this petty ambition and been awarded a postgraduate

27

scholarship into the bargain, I was duly tempted to return and begin doctoral studies. When they sweetened the reward with a contract to tutor first-year students, the prospect of pursuing a PhD took on considerable appeal.

BEATING THE BOKS

The 1981 Springbok rugby team landed in New Zealand at the exact moment I realised my marooning on the desert island of doctoral research. Dusty church minute-books, discarded pamphlets, congregational registers, religious tracts, unread sermons, contemporary newspapers and church magazines comprised the weighty and arid source material for my studies. An eclectic interest in theology had seduced me into believing that the relationship between church and society in New Zealand (from the passage of the 1877 Education Act to the end of the First World War) would prove personally intriguing and historically important. From where these thoughts emanated I know not … possibly that first heady flush of postgraduate arrogance. I just had to choose a topic that was worthy … and sweeping … and impossible.

My initial visits to Dunedin's archival Hocken and Knox Libraries produced Freudian sneezing fits as the powdery detritus of yellowed papers and long-dead books repelled investigation. The feeling became mutual. I lacked the required masochism to imprison myself in small airless rooms and there research and record the vain resistance of minor antipodean churchmen to the onslaught of post-Darwinian and colonial secularism. But it would require three years of constant diversion before I admitted to my failure of will.

The Springbok Tour represented the first diversion, although it was something much more than that. It was my first real experience of politics, if only on the periphery — and a university campus down in Dunedin is a fairly extreme perimeter. It would also provide my first political experience of the mercurial media, of strategy and gambit, of seeking to convert others' opinion to a personal viewpoint. I could recount a dead past or take part in a vibrant present; it was a no-contest.

The events of 1981 also forced me to define my understanding of the world — what I believed, how I perceived my role and responsibilities to the society in which I lived. This was a hard one. I had deliberately avoided such introspection and equally cursed the NZ

Rugby Football Union, HART and Prime Minister Muldoon for forcing the confrontation of such issues. In short, the Springbok Tour made me aware of the strange, new world of politics; of personal choice and societal decision-making. Previously I had simply been an un-thinking spectator to the aspirations of others.

The nature of experience is that changes only become apparent after they have occurred. With politics it is usually a little more dramatic — like an alien embryo punching out through one's ribcage. If I had known what I was about to experience I would have gone on a course of antibiotics — the last thing I was looking for in 1981 was self-awareness. It was hard enough finding a steady girlfriend.

Like most rugby followers I was looking forward to the South African rugby tour, primarily so that we could beat the snot out of the Afrikaners after enduring their crooked hometown referees in 1976. In addition, the prospect of getting rat-faced on the terraces of Carisbrook in a southerly gale while watching such contests had its charms. All the hoopla that surrounded the proposed tour skimmed across my horizon like fleeing clouds.

I had absolutely no difficulty with the protests of those who opposed the Tour on the ostensible grounds that South Africa's racist regime should be isolated. That was an understandable reaction; it was just not mine. I was of the 'if we boycott South Africa where do we stop?' school, although the equally valid 'if we don't play the Boks which decent teams will be left?' school also had strong appeal.

I appreciated that apartheid was morally wrong. I also appreciated the liberal consciousness that such discrimination was even more heinous if practised by a white man. The reality of one African tribe discriminating against another — or one darker race isolating another — was not quite as evil. To me the most insidious racism in New Zealand lay in the patronising and vicarious guilt that Pakeha liberals felt for the actions of white fascists half a world away. The obvious disparities of race at home, and the blind eye to black racism elsewhere, left me cold.

What I failed to realise at the time was that middle-class liberal consciousness divides its morality into 'fashionable' and 'unfash-ionable'. The anti-apartheid fight was a fashionable middle-class cause in 1981 deserving of concern and effort. The Chinese genocide against the Tibetans, the ceaseless Hutu and Tutsi massacres, the Nigerian state's active discrimination against non-Ibo tribal groups, even the corrupt and openly racist Fijian government — these apparently could be excused or ignored because they were 'unfashionable'.

As was to be expected there existed a strong anti-Tour element on Otago's middle-class liberal campus comprising staff and students alike. The mainstream HART branch was considered a little too respectable and restrictive so a more active, anarchic student derivative, SATT (Students Against The Tour), was formed to take 'direct action'. This 'action' primarily consisted of dominating sparsely attended student forums and chanting 'Amand-la' at bemused Dunedin residents who assumed this was some kind of faddish lament for a past girlfriend. Troop bleatings of an extended 'Amand-la Ngawhe-tu' were also popular — which was Zulu or Xhosa or something for 'power to the people' — and a dead giveaway that the 1960s still had a solid grip on the leading activists.

Such activism was officially fanned by the Otago University Students Association (OUSA) executive, much reviled by its compulsory membership as the preserve of all those not bright enough to be in a specialist school or too disturbed to 'make it in the real world' — a pejorative term of abuse used to condemn all those exhibiting the fatal symptoms of a pseudo-socialist political conscience.

OUSA funded its own weekly newspaper, *Critic*, edited by that patron saint of lost left-wing causes Chris Trotter. No fashionable protest was complete until Chris had arrived with his guitar and clutch of Irish protest songs — an act which sadly nipped many promising movements in the bud. Like many middle-class student radicals Chris cursed those cruel fates that forced him to lead a life of comfort in the peaceful tranquillity of a country on the edge of nowhere and in the relative comfort of the late twentieth century. Not a Marxist revolution in sight; no huddled and tortured masses yearning to be free; no police beatings in the dead of night — it was sheer hell. Chris also had one other activist flaw; he was a thoroughly decent human being with the talent of appreciating if not agreeing with opposite viewpoints. In some radical quarters such decency was tantamount to betrayal.

By contrast I assumed the more pathetic role of the indifferent spectator.

After the cancelled Waikato match — when a Gordian knot of protesters thoughtfully provided alternative entertainment for 30,000 baying rugby fans — the mercury on Otago's campus rose perceptibly. A delegation of campus conservatives led by roly-poly roisterer Mike

Greenslade and his phlegmatic alter-ego, Dean Tobin, sought to interest me in supporting their efforts to overturn OUSA's anti-Tour policies. They had failed to convince the policy-making Students' Council despite startling allegations that SATT was considering a bombing campaign against Dunedin landmarks — the unfortunate result of misheard remarks about someone detonating a thunderflash in the Octagon's public toilet to scare the literal living crap out of nearby cubicle dwellers. It was the Greenslade/Tobin view that someone else should present their pro-tour case to the next Student Council. Such refreshing candour mixed with the Hamilton debacle and a nascent belief that sport and politics should never mix, not even socially, finally persuaded me. There was something else. These guys were unfashionable underdogs — these were my kind of odds.

The first step was to form a campus organisation that might rival SATT and attain a modicum of respectability. All planning to achieve this end was rather undone when the inaugural meeting attracted over three hundred largely Commerce students who generated an impassioned debate over the naming of our disparate group — SCRUM being narrowly preferred to BEER, although GETTING PISSED proved a serious contender.

I was elected an unwilling chairman — my first task to try and find five words to justify the acronym. All manner of rationalisations were attempted with a conspicuous lack of success. Our HART/SATT opponents thoughtfully suggested that if we removed the R from our title then the organisation would be more accurately described. I settled on the unconvincing Students Civil Rights: University Movement which meant, well, absolutely nothing really.

It soon became clear that SCRUM had a dual purpose mixed with a universal and chronic drinking problem. As chairman my job was to act as public apologist and private urologist, while the committee's task was to neutralise, annoy and harass the anti-Tour crowd on campus. For every silliness perpetrated by SATT there was corresponding stupidity from SCRUM. A subgroup named LIVER (Lively Individuals Very Expectant of Rugby) performed all manner of questionable activities — breaking into the HART offices to xerox any relevant file, ordering truckloads of coal for the homes of anti-Tour leaders, or getting cheap deals from sympathetic liquor outlets for the repeated social occasions that masqueraded as committee meetings.

We were taken seriously enough for the local SATT branch to

send along a 'spy' to the inaugural meeting; he thoughtfully identified himself by wearing a HART badge. Instead of ejecting him we elected him to SCRUM's executive and openly discussed our links with other pro-Tour groups, the South African embassy and finally the CIA. At the conclusion he dashed from the room in pant-wetting excitement, eyes brimming with revelation, while we got down to the real and serious business of conning free test tickets out of the Otago Rugby Union.

Ultimately SCRUM was victorious on campus because we pursued a deliberately non-combative public line while launching all manner of private subterfuges. My strategy was simple — we could overturn OUSA's anti-Tour policy by observing the deep divisions within the student body and suggesting a compromise of no policy on the Tour whatsoever. Individual students could take their conscientious concerns to the relevant anti- or pro- organisation but there should be no official sanction of protest activities.

It was a useful hook which had the added advantage of working. A good number of the anti-Tour protesters even accepted this rationale themselves and the motion to have no official OUSA student policy on the Springbok Tour was passed overwhelmingly. The reverberations were immediate.

The New Zealand University Students Association sent a 'flying squad' down to Otago to upbraid SATT and the OUSA leadership for this humiliating policy U-turn. NZUSA was mortally embarrassed. The bastion of support for fashionable and/or liberal causes had always been provided by student campuses and now those same campuses were withdrawing from the greatest moral struggle of the time. General Westmoreland's quotation on the Vietnam domino effect suddenly assumed an uncharacteristic student currency.

The arrogance of all politicians, student politicians included, is that the reasoned choice of the people can never be accepted if it is contrary to their own. It can only be explained as the furtive manipulation of opposing forces. Elements within NZUSA convinced themselves that Otago students could not possibly have reached their 'no policy' decision by democratic means — rather that they were confronted with some sort of fascist-inspired, counter-revolutionary force. They made the cardinal error of committing such paranoia to paper and then instructed their associate bodies to begin an active intelligence-gathering operation on 'all right-wing personalities on campus'.

One of our members had strayed across the NZUSA correspondence during his nightly snooping through the OUSA offices as
a part-time cleaner but it was my decision that the information should
be held back until an opportune moment. The decision of NZUSA
to organise a special Student Council meeting to overturn the 'no
policy' policy brought just such an opportunity.

The media bit like a pack of rabid dogs; from their reaction you
would have thought they had stumbled on the tertiary equivalent of
the Ems telegram. Breathless front-page treatment was complemented
by radio and television coverage in a frenzy of superficial sensation.
Confronted with such dastardly perversions — 'NZUSA spying on
students' gushed the headlines — the campus council voted overwhelmingly to retain the 'no policy' stance and roundly censured the
national body for their tactics. It was the perfect rout and my first
experience of the dark art of 'spinning'; I had proved a natural. It was
the kind of audacious stunt so beloved of undergraduates. I had no
excuse. It was pure devilment; the kind where you light the blue
touchpaper and stand well clear.

From that point on the campus battle descended into stalemate.
To the chagrin of the protest movement the University Union catered
for the much reviled Red and Blue police squads when they were in
Dunedin — unencumbered now by previous political constraints. In
turn, SCRUM reduced its role to acting as a gargoyle for the status
quo. The rest of the student year dissolved into an unsatisfying verbal
wasteland, with SATT gaining a measure of revenge by organising
one of their own into the OUSA presidency.

The prettiest conclusion though was reserved for the emotions.
SCRUM's vice-president ended up in a relationship with one of
HART's publicity officers — proving that sex will always be a far
more powerful beast with the middle class than political conviction.

DIVERSION BLUES

The doctoral thesis returned to haunt me for my woeful inconstancy.
I dutifully returned to the draughty libraries and church vestries,
burying myself in the religious and social controversies of another
age and hoping that some form of self-discipline might finally triumph.
From my readings New Zealand's fledgling church seemed to be
engaged in the same struggle for relevance. At least it possessed an
excuse — unhappily grafted onto this frontier society among a

pioneering people who equated its stern overtures with unending boredom and the class distinctions of a distant land.

In addition, it had to contend with a revolution in thought presided over by the luminaries Marx and Voltaire and clinically supported by the iconoclastic science of Darwin and Haeckel. It was an uneven and forlorn struggle with church leaders required to enter the political domain to justify their relevance against the encroachments and demands of respectable secularism. The political controversies that provoked the clergy's ire fascinated me — in the main issues of public morality including divorce, prohibition, gambling and dancing, mixing unhappily with the struggle for denominational identity that marked the education and Bible-in-schools debates. The curse of the nineteenth-century Christian church seemed as relevant and as depressingly familiar to me as it remains today — a confused and disparate message that satisfies neither the soul nor the senses. Matched with a general mediocrity of leadership it seemed no wonder that the church eventually lost virtually every moral cause that it championed.

The research was proving of occasional interest and clearly provoked my own religious consciousness. But as I sifted through each long-deceased social movement and each interminable politico-religious drama of the age, I was forced to admit that such historical research was of increasing irrelevance to my world of the early 1980s. If anything the Springbok Tour had further highlighted my desire to be a participant rather than a recorder. And yet to withdraw would be to admit to academic weakness — my vain and silly pride refused capitulation.

Another distraction was required, and quick. The unlikely commercial possibilities surrounding the recreation of competitive debating provided the next release. Debating is an unpopular verbal bloodsport peopled with often manic personalities — the ostensible goal being to win a structured and logical argument. In reality, the aim is to orally eviscerate your opponents until they run gibbering from the room begging for psychotherapy. It is a smart-aleck, petty and vindictive pastime which attracts enormous numbers of like-minded individuals and thus is littered with aspirant lawyers and politicians. There are also far too many schoolteachers involved for me to feel truly confident about the future of the education sector.

Otago University had its fair share of such characters although most found more satisfying release for their personality disorders in the drama club or student politics. For all its quirkiness, the Otago University debating club did attract some speakers of keen intellect and rare verbal ability. Banking guru Rod Carr — the original architect of National's health reforms — was a brilliant and incisive debater; Bankers Trust economist Craig Stobo excelled, as did young legal tyros like Vicky Casey and Liam Kennedy.

My sister Diane had organised the first 'festival' style debate in Dunedin in a brave attempt to present an evening of erudite wit without the attendant wankers. Some hope. In this kind of combat minor celebrities are provided with an excuse to parade their grossly inflated egos while resurrecting dead jokes under the guise of sophisticated entertainment. It is one step removed from indecently exposing oneself in a public place but perhaps lacks the frisson.

Diane's innovation was rather marred by the notorious performance of then youthful comedian Jon Gadsby, who recounted, in stunning and obscene anatomical detail, the two-inch difference between the average male sexual organ and its accompanying female receptacle. The chairman valiantly tried to intervene in justifiable fear of the conclusion but Gadsby was in irresistible flight, executing the punchline '…and that's why there is over 2000 miles of unused c— in the world!' to eye-popping shock and audible gasps. The mass walkout of half the audience rather obliterated the memory of anything else — a seat-sliding embarrassment made much worse when Gadsby then invited the rest of the paying audience to 'Piss off then. Go on — fuckin' piss off.'

The students loved it and Gadsby became a living legend on campus if a social leper off it. The whole incident rather tarnished any immediate attempt to promote festival debating in Dunedin — or, I suspect, anywhere in the English-speaking world.

When the fallout from this verbal Chernobyl had been reduced to an acceptable half-life we revisited the site to prepare for a secondary launch. We persevered with the concept of public figures attempting to be funny, which proved a 'no lose' scenario because if they succeeded then people were amused, and if they failed there was a macabre entertainment in watching a celebrity's self-respect dissolve in front of you. Thus was born this country's most prestigious and successful debate — the BNZ Festival Debate series.

The initial debate in 1982 was stunningly successful. We employed a 'Media versus Politicians' theme, which allowed the MPs a chance to savage those who daily savaged them. They duly relished the opportunity and were chosen for their comedic value — my old history lecturer and now Labour deputy, Michael Cullen, legal raconteur and ACT convert Trevor de Cleene, and that unique Invercargill personality Norm Jones.

Unwittingly Norm Jones was the stand-out performer with a scathing parody of simpering Cabinet ministers who crawled to the ninth floor of the Beehive as if they had just evolved from the primeval swamp. How else did one explain Colin McLachlan? The evening's special guest, Prime Minister Rob Muldoon himself, lapped it up. At the post-debate function he continued the gag by not so tenderly commenting on the invertebrate qualities of these same colleagues. One received the impression that a Muldoon Cabinet was little more than a sheltered workshop for the politically bewildered.

The rest of the function became a contest between the BNZ's head office staff and local dignitaries over who could fawn, ingratiate and generally slobber the longest over the PM and laugh the loudest at his jokes. It was a fascinating relationship — not so much that of master–servant as of monopoly drug supplier and a hat full of addicts.

After the success of the first year the festival debate boomed. There were five more years of packed-out theatres, hour-long primetime telecast highlights, and an array of media and political celebrities who regarded our invitation to appear as a singular honour. Such was the success of this venture that we had to relocate the event to the Dunedin Town Hall, which seated 2500 people, but even then all tickets were sold out five weeks in advance. We had created a monster. Most top politicians and media celebrities participated over that period — Muldoon, deputy Prime Minister Jim McLay, Labour leader David Lange, Bob Jones, Doug Graham, Annette King, Jim Hopkins, David McPhail, Brian Edwards, Judith Fyfe and the like.

Eventually all the key organising students graduated and departed Otago for northern weather and employment. Finally there was no one left to organise it and the event simply expired. But the organisational skills, the media and marketing ploys, the entrée to top politicians and media celebrities alike had all been learned, absorbed and stored away. There would come a time.

PARTY TIME

During this time both my lecturers and my bank manager had begun to make insistent demands that some straight answers be given to the question of my career prospects. My lecturers observed the uninterest of their doctoral student; my bank manager observed the reverse spiral of my overdraft and the final instalment of the scholarship.

I was now aware of talents in marketing and event organisation. Helpful colleagues suggested that irregular and fertile minds like my own were best harvested in advertising or public relations — the occult arts of the commercial world. I rejected them as trivial. In truth, Dunedin indulged my lack of discipline; the reality of the workplace would not.

My two former SCRUM associates, Mike Greenslade and Dean Tobin, had by now joined an increasingly febrile National Party and invited me to share their experiences of the local Dunedin North electorate executive meetings. I was wholly unready for such a surreal encounter, not then realising that dedicated political party workers are a breed apart. Actually an entire species.

Stoked with an enthusiasm that can only suggest a delusional disorder of the greatest magnitude, such individuals toil with no prospect of reward or encouragement for their party's cause. Their activities are the political equivalent of digging a hole, filling it in again, then repeating this process until mortal release. I had obviously come to the wrong place; this was a geriatric ward on hallucinogens — my first upfront experience of the National Party at work. I had crossed over into the Twilight Zone.

Rather than scare me off, the whole experience proved both infinitely entertaining and illuminating. It was obvious — even from this bizarre assortment of oddball characters — that the National Party's activist membership had been decimated; a point dramatically reinforced when I undertook renewal canvassing for the electorate and discovered most of my target names affixed to bronze plaques at the crematorium.

It was now 1984 and there was no Springbok Tour in the offing to secure the provincial marginal seats to National's side. Which was just as well because the '84 All Blacks were not a strong team. A simple election year rule: if the All Blacks lose, so does the government. The election of David Lange as Labour's leader had brought a relative unity to the Opposition ranks, while the public behaviour of Muldoon became ever more erratic. The final desertion of many metropolitan liberals to Bob Jones' New Zealand Party made the 1984 general election a formality. It was all over — you could smell the coming change as if it was summer rain.

The combination of these experiences and pressures had, as yet, hewn no obvious path to a political future. But of one thing I was naively convinced and for that I can blame my studies: a quality life is spent in the service of others — that was the noble ideal grafted onto me by my ignoble study of the past. I was motivated by neither money nor social status — that much was obvious from all my previous endeavours. Equally plainly I had no desire to conform to the 40-hour-a-week routine of the established workplace, lacking the essential discipline ever to rise before eight in the morning or to perform allotted tasks within the confines of an air-conditioned office.

Those then were the parameters for my career choice — public service, ability to use your own initiative, as little external discipline as possible, set your own hours. There were only two possibilities: prostitution or politics. Actually there was a realistic third option. The church. The money was appalling and there were set Sunday services but at least you were assisting others and, if I chose the Anglican church, I could pacify the external discipline with a good-sized whisky decanter.

There was just the one problem. Irrelevance.

Both politicians and prostitutes have a much greater capacity to practically assist large numbers of people than the average clergy. The days of the warrior-priest or the crusading cleric were over — with the possible exception of those who practised liberation theology in central America. And that was too hot, too distant, too dangerous. After much internal struggle politics narrowly edged out the other as the profession of greater societal benefit. It was the wrong choice of course, but I was young and naive.

OK, so now I had decided on the destination, but what would be my mode of transport? Here Bob Jones proved more than useful. I was endeavouring to secure his attendance at the year's festival debate when he propounded in conversation that 'you buy a company's shares at their lowest point'. The observation assumed metaphorical proportions for one considering a political career. Labour was approaching its zenith — National its nadir. Those in the military often desire a good war for promotion; in politics a good defeat procures the same advantage. In addition, a good southern winter might just open up vistas of opportunity in the Dunedin electorates — electoral loss or not.

My motivations then for entering Parliament were relatively pure. In retrospect, they were puerile. I had this damned-fool notion that I could make the country a better place through my input and influence, and that people might regard my assistance as welcome and worthy. This was no mere display of self-delusion — it was an act of psychotic proportions.

But this is an affliction shared, I suspect, by every candidate, every aspirant, every dreamer of political office. We really do want to help people. No bull. The real problem is that to help others we must first help ourselves. Therein lie the seeds of our eventual corruption. National and personal interest intertwined from the first instant.

My basic problem in executing this ambition tripped another Bob Jones maxim. Location. The National Party and Dunedin were two mutually exclusive bodies dwelling in wholly different ages and galaxies. Even if that cold southern snap did arrive and wither the remaining activist membership there would be nothing left to inherit. Instead I joined the party's prat brigade, the Young Nationals, who at least possessed the twin virtues of a social life and their own teeth.

Young Nationals in 1984 had assumed a schizoid social demeanour. It was irrevocably split between the beer-drinking larrikin student types and the champagne-quaffing Sloane Ranger set. There seemed no earthly reason why these two vastly different and antipathetic social forces should ever be seen at the same place at the same time, but there we were. In Young Nationals.

Within months I was the division's new chairman, my university colleagues had assumed all other executive responsibilities, and this minor coup even provided a place on that organisational holy of holies — the party's Dominion Council. This caused a great deal of jealous resentment from more senior members who had worked in the party's service for over two decades and never glimpsed this inner chamber. Suddenly a dope-smoking 'scarfie' pluck full of arrogance and with a gaggle of anarchic supporters had found his way to 'their' chosen place. Was there no justice?

They need not have worried. Organisational politics in the National Party was built on the time-honoured illusion that those higher on the totem pole were gifted the luxury of information. I soon worked out why the grassroots membership were told nothing about Council's inner workings — nothing of real consequence ever happened. Fifty of the party's top activists would be flown to Wellington, accommodated in the then swanky James Cook Hotel, receive a series of hectoring lectures from party president Sue Wood, meet a few MPs at the obligatory cocktail party and then quake in terror as

Muldoon told them to work harder. The only interesting information — the state of the party's finances or the planning for the election campaign — was hidden away within an inner Council executive. Even the Council could not be trusted with such information. For councillors to admit their impotence would be to rob themselves of their party standing. Best to say nothing and be thought of as mysterious and powerful — a trick many back-bench MPs still employ with regard to their constituencies.

The National Party organisation was like a Russian doll. As you opened each outside layer another image confronted you. But there was a difference. When the final doll was opened in the National Party organisation … it was also empty. Because real power lay in the parliamentary wing. This secret was hidden by the party's apparatchiks for a good reason. It lessened their prestige. And without that prestige they were nothing more than ordinary people involved on the distant periphery of an extraordinary profession.

Strangely enough the Young Nats understood this. Maybe it was their youthful cynicism or maybe it was just plain old-fashioned common sense. But no bright Young Nat ever aspired to be an electorate or divisional chairman or a party president or a Dominion Councillor. They wanted to be an MP. Full stop. Anything less was just wasting political ambition and good partying time.

Muldoon's sudden, swaying and shock announcement of a snap general election banished all such immediate thoughts. I watched this drama implode while at a student flat — the gathering hooting with derision at the entire event. Interestingly most of the contempt was directed at the simpering courtiers who surrounded their tired and emotional leader — Sue Wood, Jim McLay, Bill Birch, Don McKinnon. No amount of historical self-justification would ever excuse such fawning behaviour.

The 1984 general election was the rout that all expected. Muldoon's leadership style had alienated the vast majority of New Zealanders and the wage/price freeze and legislated interest rates had offended the last of the private enterprisers. Bob Jones' New Zealand Party harried National on its Right; the Social Crediters still had a rural constituency; and a reinvigorated Labour looked capable of forming a stable and progressive administration. With 35 per cent of the popular vote National plunged to its worst-ever vote since the party's formation.

To make matters worse just about every bright young thing had deserted National's membership. Except a host of ambitious Young Nats who understood perfectly the military truism that a bad battle is followed by rapid promotion.

Around this time a host of people of similar age if differing personalities flooded into the Young Nats. Current ministers Nick Smith, Bill English, Tony Ryall and Roger Sowry were prominent personalities; tyros like millionairess publisher Jaqui Lane, Auckland lawyer Mark Lowndes, Sky Casino PR manager Heather Shotter, DB media supremo Wayne Eagleson and INL director Phil O'Reilly assumed leadership roles. There was enough ego, ambition and ruthless determination within that group to run any number of African dictatorships but for now it was contained within the so-called youth wing of the party.

Meanwhile the National Party hierarchy was still coming to terms with its electoral humiliation. Wood, her chief executive, Barrie Leay, the party's public relations strategist, Michelle Boag, and most of the Dominion Council laid the blame definitively at the door of Muldoon. In turn, Muldoon blamed the party's organisation — no rapprochement was possible. In an effort to win the peace Wood and Leay launched a post-election review of the party even if their clear targets were Muldoon and the Caucus that had failed to rein him in.

They wanted the party to act as an effective disciplinary brake on Caucus, veto the leadership if necessary and oversee all policy development. The past excesses of Muldoonism must never be allowed to repeat themselves. National had evolved into a socialist dictatorship. Control of the party's heritage and destiny must be wrested back.

At the same time the Otago Young Nationals had embarked on a provocative series of Leadership Dinners. Supposing that Muldoon's reign was now over, I had invited all the potential leadership contenders to dinner meetings, sold tickets to the party faithful, and then invited the media. These evenings were staggering successes, with the Otago University Young Nats, under Lisa Futschek, Malcolm Wright and Deborah Russell, displaying the fearlessness of youth in effectively announcing that Muldoon's term as leader of the National Party was over and 'here are the new heavyweight contenders'.

Jim McLay, George Gair, Bill Birch, Jim Bolger and John Falloon all attended the respective functions. McLay was the stand-out performer, while Bill Birch used his speech to suggest that he could be McLay's deputy — or anybody else's if they won. Then we received a call from Sir Robert's secretary enquiring when his invitation would be despatched. We were staggered — 'But your boss is retiring,' I stammered. Not so. A day later the great man defiantly announced that he would be seeking a further term. He was not dead yet.

There would be a mini-drama associated with each dinner. We were forced to give tickets away to hungry varsity students because no one would pay to listen to Jim Bolger, although, just to cap off that disastrous evening, these same students noisily departed directly after the last serving of dessert but before the startled Bolger's speech. Having three-quarters of his audience vanish before he had even uttered a word was bound to unsettle. A drunken senior Nat rudely interrupted Jim McLay in full flight and told him to 'piss off… you're not half the man of our Rob', whilst Muldoon himself decided to eschew any hint of audience empathy and meander through an excruciating exposition on superannuation — ice ages had taken less time. Thankfully Lisa leavened this Stygian gloom by crunching into an apple and walnut roll despite being hyperallergic to nuts and was carted off to Dunedin Hospital to recover. She earned our everlasting gratutide.

At about this time I was approached by National's research director, David Lloyd, and offered employment within the party's parliamentary unit. Dunedin still retained a seductive torpor. A similar affection was not reciprocated by my bank manager, however. He wished me to have a job … he wanted me to have a job … he demanded that I get a job. Now. His usual generosity had been dulled by my ever-burgeoning overdraft and a Visa balance that had taken on trade deficit proportions.

Lloyd offered a salary package of $25,000 a year and free toll calls. To an impoverished student with $15,000 of debt, political ambition, and the prospect of having every finger broken should I ever write another cheque, the offer was irresistible.

And thus, like hundreds of thousands of Otago students before me, I embarked upon the Great Northern Postgraduate Migration. It was a journey undertaken with enormous reluctance because it signalled the final rite of passage to adulthood and responsibility. My days of carefree behaviour and procrastination were over. Driven from my southern lair by cold harsh fiscal considerations and the vague promise of excitement, I resolved to demonstrate that all my supposed potential could now find a suitable outlet.

The intoxicating draught of Parliament — with its beguiling promise of power and influence — loomed before me. It would take a long decade to be rid of its spell.

Chapter 2

RESEARCH UNIT

My introduction to the august and hallowed chambers of Parliament was inauspicious. David Lloyd welcomed me to the ground floor quarters of the National Research Unit, introduced me to its various and varied inhabitants, and then directed me to my new office — a room little bigger than a toilet cubicle. Judging by the smell of it this also appeared to be its prime function. By the end of the first week I had located the cause of this sickly stench, pushed to the back drawers of a dusty and unused filing cabinet — the decaying leftovers of a Chinese takeaway meal, upended wine glasses and a soiled condom.

When one of the researchers commented that my room had previously been used for an affair between a senior MP and their predecessor, the image of the brothel hovel was complete. I came to regard all office furniture as unclean; all stains as suspect.

Unfortunately, before making this climactic discovery, I had been visited by that lurking back-bench Quasimodo Sir Robert Muldoon, who sniffed the air with regal disdain. I stammered out that a rat had probably died under the floorboards.

'That'll be McLay,' he half grimaced, half cackled.

Despite being the ex-leader and clearly past his prime, Muldoon still possessed the unsettling charisma of an axe murderer — you instinctively sensed a simmering potential for violence lurking under the poker expression. Holding a conversation with the great man was the equivalent of a verbal bungy jump except that you were never sure if the safety harness was properly attached.

I often tried to analyse just why Muldoon made people feel so uncomfortable and reached the conclusion that his small talk and body language broke all conventional rules. The staccato sentences lacked normal beginnings, his stance was pointed just over your right shoulder, and his too-large face betrayed little or no emotion — an unsettling visage made even more so by piercing blue eyes that fixed on a spot six inches beyond the back of your neck. Muldoon's voice had such a range of subtle nuances, from mere disdain to outright contempt, that time and space could freeze at the precise moment he opened his mouth. The unit collectively held its breath and jumped whenever he passed through its doors. For all his familiarity, David Lloyd's attempts at badinage were swotted away as an irritant — God knows what he could have done to the rest of us had he been of the mind.

Lloyd had been the unit's director for many years now and in the first zeal of opposition his tenure appeared to be reaching a solid horizon. With the succession of Jim McLay as Leader of the Opposition, Michelle Boag as McLay's senior press secretary and chief adviser, Sue Wood in the presidency and her mentor, Barrie Leay (now grandiloquently titled 'secretary-general'), imposing like a bloated toad over party affairs, the research unit director was regarded as superfluous and placed distinctly on the outer.

Lloyd was an inoffensive soul with a solid academic background and the nervous laugh of a furtive clergyman at a strip show. But the powers that be considered him too close to the *ancien régime* and lacking in that spirit of regeneration so beloved of the post-Muldoon hierarchy. They wanted action, excitement, glamour — instead they had an earnest, bespectacled, balding functionary who hitched his trousers up near his chest.

My limited experience of both Wood and Leay suggested that all the sins of the party could generally be pinned to a strange amalgam of Muldoon, the brattish Young Nats and a languid research unit. Great — I was involved with all three. But it did teach me the one great principle of the National Party organisation: whenever anything goes wrong it is always the tea lady's fault.

With few obvious exceptions the 1984–87 National Opposition lacked balls and brains in equal measure. Typically the only non-eunuch was a woman — Ruth Richardson — who possessed enough political testosterone to impregnate half the dairy herds of Taranaki. The rest of Caucus divided into two major groups — those who adored the new Rogernomics revolution and those who despised it. Get a coherent strategy out of that mess.

In addition National now possessed a leader in Jim McLay who was well groomed, well behaved and knew how to wear a tailored suit. But for all his undoubted intelligence McLay had that deadly political defect — the brittle personality of a meringue. Politics can forgive every vice bar weakness.

The incompetence of National in opposition cannot simply be ascribed to the breathtaking and breakneck progress of Roger Douglas and his New Right cohorts or to McLay's inability to galvanise and lead his depleted parliamentary team. Rather, the failure was one of philosophy, of party personality, of political principle. Simply, National had no defined reason for being — neither an alternative vision nor a set of policies that might provoke and capture public attention.

Amazingly, none of these frailties were considered fatal nor even cause for real parliamentary alarm. The greatest mindset that this young researcher encountered in 1985 was the preternatural belief, an unholy faith no less, that electoral victory would be delivered two years hence as if ordained. National had been in power for 21 of the past 24 years. Within its ranks there existed a quasi-religious determinism that Labour could be relied on to botch it all up again and that the New Zealand public would come to their collective senses. Then the party would resume its rightful heritage as the nation's secular steward and the beastly bolsheviks would be put to flight.

That consciousness permeated the parliamentary Opposition to an unfathomable depth and astounded me with its limpet-like hold on the party's front bench. Now that Muldoon had been replaced as party leader Caucus saw no need to rejuvenate — just to wait out the inevitable Labour interregnum before resuming the Treasury benches. That imposed its own frustrations of course — how to fill in all the time was one. Some took up jogging; others pursued secretaries, Hansard reporters and anything in a skirt with indecent abandon; Merv Wellington would throw his office furniture through parliamentary windows … boys were boys.

Thus my entrance into National's parliamentary research unit found both party and Caucus confused, divided and finally bewildered by the scale and breadth of reform being rushed through the House by the zealots of the New Right. Which was just as well, because I did not have the slightest clue as to what my responsibilities or duties were; no understanding of the arcane rituals and practices of the House; nor even the merest hint of direction from my distracted director.

To compound matters, I now learned that my job itself was under threat. Lloyd called me into his room within days of my arrival to warn me that the party president was demanding my dismissal from the unit's employ. Apparently, as a result of the BNZ Festival Debate series I was considered 'too close' to prominent Labour Party figures, with Leay allegedly uttering the belief that I was 'a communist or worse … a very dangerous young man'.

Keenly aware of the similar disfavour with which he was regarded within the party leadership, Lloyd saw criticism of my appointment as both a direct attack on his authority and, opportunely, a way to twit his detractors. For such a mild-mannered individual I could only thank the respective political gods that Lloyd's sense of offence had been so honed that he was prepared to protect my appointment. In the end, the dark forces became distracted and lost interest. That, and the fact that I was effectively a civil servant — an employee of the Legislative Department with my salary paid by the taxpayer and not the National Party. One of the curious incongruities of being a party political researcher — the taxpayer rewards your obvious political bias.

I need not have worried. The Empire was striking back.

There were more compelling distractions than some junior researcher's mixed loyalties. Muldoon had convinced his old ministerial mate Bert Walker to launch a series of Sunday Club rallies with the express purpose of undermining McLay, Wood and Leay in equal measure. The Caucus itself was becoming impatient with the attempts of the organisation to elbow itself into Caucus discussions and deliberations. The party's finances were under considerable strain and the aura of secrecy around Leay's salary package and responsibilities rankled with elements in Caucus and the grassroots. I could now safely explore my parliamentary surroundings.

But the spectre of Labour Party fraternisation was not shaken so easily. Fellow jogger Warren Cooper — surmising that all runners shared collegial loyalties — pulled me into his parliamentary office one afternoon 'for a word'.

'The word is "Don't".' The southern drawl of this eccentric MP emphasised the negative. 'Don't ever have anything to do, socially, with the other side. We're at war here, son. War.'

For the first time I received an inkling of comprehension as to why politicians never subsume their party interests for national considerations. Their collective culture of conflict, of implacable and hostile battle, is inculcated into every new recruit — be they MP, press secretary, researcher or secretary. There must be no admission of partisan mistake or failure, for to admit such is to hand victory to opposing forces who will only seek to prolong the humiliation.

LEARNING THE ROPES

The only researcher ever to have made the transition from the research unit to the House debating chamber was Marilyn Waring — a precedent which had made the party duly phobic about researchers with similar ambitions. They need not have worried. The apparent lack of political hunger in my new colleagues mystified me because I assumed that an activist background was mandatory. I assumed wrong.

The deathly pallor of the civil service hovered within our offices but there were other more immediate difficulties that created equal confusion and consternation for this novitiate. My duties had no definition, the lines of accountability were haphazard, and the jargon that passed for intelligible conversation remained impregnable. This was not my fault.

Parliament has a language all its own — its Black Rod, Whips and private members' bills falsely proclaiming something both exciting and exotic. There were select committees and Caucus committees; first readings, second readings, third readings (none of which were ever read); Estimates, Financial Reviews and Annual Reports; Address and Reply debates, general debates, snap debates — and questions. Question time, oral questions, written questions, questions of the day, urgent questions, questions without notice — it was Telebingo on speed.

This plethora of institutional inquisitions would ordinarily signal that MPs were either inordinately inquisitive or extremely thick. To a degree both observations were valid — but the real aim of the multi-hued parliamentary question is to expose information that will embarrass the hell out of the other side. It was the political equivalent of the game of Battleship — you call out a speculative number and hope there is a passing scandal lurking underneath. Boom. Gotcha.

The only problem is that the government are prewarned of this query and have a few hours or even a few days to either prepare a suitably bland response or move the offending cruiser out of harm's way. This unending process does possess the relative virtue of keeping scores of civil servants in jobs tracking down the most arcane of facts or the most obscure of statistics. The side effect is a little more deleterious — the process wastes literally millions of dollars of taxpayers' funds every year. All these questions and replies are then transcribed for posterity — a practice that has devastated more forests than a plague of tussock moths could ever dream of.

Lloyd had assigned me the policy areas of education, industrial relations and science as my primary research responsibilities, which, in turn, made me accountable to Ruth Richardson, George Gair and Simon Upton respectively. Later Bill Birch would assume the shadow labour portfolio and I would learn my political trade at the feet of the technocratic master.

Much of my early energy was expended upon the various projects of Opposition education spokesperson Ruth Richardson, who attacked her shadow portfolio with the ferocity of a tropical cyclone, lifting every rock, tree and dwelling in the merciless quest for a quality and 'accountable' sector. Academics and teacher unions, always the most precious of pressure groups, ran screaming.

Ruth was an entirely self-ordered individual with a smattering of teutonic graces, but best admired from a safe distance. Stray too close and a vortex of tasks and deadlines would sweep you away — I hid behind my competing responsibilities to other MPs. Yet she was also capable of great tenderness — the rural background from Waitotara would surface and a childish sense of humour would brush away the seriousness. The pity was that as she assumed each new responsibility her humour was squeezed out by a self-imposed pursuit of clinical perfection and a careless regard for the frailties of the human condition.

For all her fervour Richardson possessed just the one political drawback. She scared the living crap out of just about everyone.

Her full frontal attacks upon meandering Caucus policy made her as popular as a rogue parking warden. Social welfare spokesman Venn Young once complained to me that he felt as if he had been marauded by a troop of army ants after a Richardson inquisition into the sustainability of his proposed superannuation policy. Intolerant of her slower Caucus colleagues (of which the National Party seemed to have an untapped supply) she would officiously hector them into submission rather than patiently convert them, and acquired a reputation as the policy nanny from Hell.

Deputy leader Jim Bolger regarded her with especial distaste. This may have been due to Ruth's undiluted embrace of the New Right or her obvious ambition to succeed McLay, but it may also have been a character assessment — Bolger loathed ostentatious intelligence in any form, especially from one who never shared a drink with the boys or told dirty jokes and lacked even the alternative virtue of a large cleavage. Any Opposition social gathering had an air of the rugby aftermatch about it and Richardson rarely ventured into such assemblies.

After one party policy forum at which Richardso
contradicted and bested him, Bolger marched upon h
adversary with scarcely suppressed anger. He would figh
policy ideas 'to the ends of the earth'. Various versions ᴏ ᴛᴛᴜ ᴜᴜᴜ,
percolated through Caucus and the research unit but they all ended
on the same note — Ruth sniffing the air contemptuously. Her
intellectual regard for Bolger equalled that of a feminist for a flasher.

Richardson's social aloofness contributed to the Boadicea quality
she brought to all her political relationships. Only the similarly asocial
Simon Upton had the academic mettle to appreciate Ruth but even
he exhibited occasional discomfort when confronted by this tiny ball
of kinetic energy with the pudding haircut. The rest of Caucus
derisively tagged them Hansel and Gretel, suggesting some symbiotic
cloning. There were similarities admittedly — proximity to the
ground, the same barber and the snub nose. Oh, and one other thing
— an IQ 30 points higher than any of their colleagues'.

Simon possessed a much keener and more discerning intellect than
Richardson but lacked her ruthless drive. This is not a criticism —
Ruth would have been drilled from the Waffen SS for overeagerness.
There was a wonderful naivete about the youthful Waipa MP that I
only began to appreciate fully on a trip to Christchurch, when the
strange subject of oral sex entered a conversation. Simon simply
refused to believe that anyone could possibly use their mouths for
such a foul purpose — his body and face contorting at the mere
prospect, as if someone was noisily sucking a lemon in his immediate
vicinity. 'I eat with this mouth,' was his shocked observation. I pointed
out that that was precisely what oral sex was all about.

He got his own back though. After a solid week of touring DSIR
stations we had discovered a shared affinity for jogging. I surmised
that he could easily be beaten in any running race and wagered upon
my abilities. Simon insisted on choosing the location — a vertical
ascent of Victoria Hill on a disused track that no self-respecting
mountain goat would have considered. I was totally humiliated in
less than five minutes of upward progress. By the time I breathlessly
arrived on top of the windblown ridge Simon was already inspecting
the flora and reciting their Latin names.

My other major source of parliamentary work was the Hon. George
Gair — a delightful if pedantic gentleman — a refugee from the age
of manners. George had been posited as Muldoon's great rival in the
late 1970s but seemed to lack both the ambition and the sheer devilry

to market himself as leadership material. By 1985 there was an air of the amiable duffer about him although I was later to be firmly disabused of this impression.

He had one distracting flaw — an obsession with minutiae. George believed that the key to effective opposition was to win a series of small skirmishes rather than risk an uncertain battle. Piles of written questions would be delivered to the Clerk of the House requesting ministers to 'amplify and explain' the most minuscule of policy details. Then the replies would be carefully sifted for incongruities or the slightest of contradictions. Further 'amplifications' would be requested — he kept one question on the go for seven months. It was turgid stuff.

Unwittingly, Gair also provided me with the necessary understanding that political decisions have human consequences — a self-evident truth except within Parliament. A particular tragedy emphasised this chilling lesson.

It also taught me something else; never admit to the minutest portion of responsibility for fear of its escalation to the entire blame. A small plane had been sliced open by high-tension wires strung across the Marlborough Sounds and eight passengers and crew killed. The only survivor was a small child whose immediate family were among the dead, and Gair found himself in the firing line. He had been Civil Aviation Minister in the last National government and resisted attempts to remove the wires entirely from the channel. Despite the imposition of a strict no-fly zone the pilot had flown below the prescribed heights in an attempt to provide a better view of the Sounds for his passengers. Kind thoughts had produced a horrific end.

The next morning I found George at his parliamentary desk with his head buried in his forearms, the morning newspaper splattered with tears and convulsive sobs wracking his body. There appeared a strong element of private guilt in such bitter grief — deserved or not. A firestorm of criticism instantly flamed, demanding a political sacrifice to match the senseless deaths of those eight innocents.

Yet to admit any doubt, omission or oversight was a sign of simpering weakness. The venom of one's political opponents and the simplistic black-and-white reporting of the Press Gallery demanded no backward steps. It was better to be thought a fool than confess to even a hint of wrong-doing. It was like the Battle of the Somme on an endless loop.

As with all war the first casualty in politics is the complete truth. The full facts paint varying shades of grey — it is the human condition. Politics demands absolutes. Black or white. Right or wrong. And the second casualty is the individual member trapped in this ritualistic conflict which allows no admission of either indecision or error. These were regarded as weaknesses and weakness is politics' cardinal sin. This same mentality would extend nine years later to Conservation Minister Denis Marshall and the Cave Creek tragedy.

Bill Birch was the master of this technique. As former Energy Minister he refused to admit that there could be any legitimate questioning of Think Big, even in private conversation, and repeatedly sought to convince McLay to marshal a cogent defence of its lavish blunders. The Leader's office lacked such a will, surmising that scarce party funds would be wasted seeking to defend the indefensible. There was much Russian eye-rolling at even the prospect. In late 1985, Birch had already been written off (not for the last time) as 'yesterday's man'. But rust never sleeps. A change in leadership would produce the apologia. The defence itself was irrelevant — it was the political necessity to provide one that drove this personal quest.

There was always a touch of vanity about Bill that I found incongruous. He rightly prided himself on being someone who did not panic under political attack — years of practice I suppose — and extended this reputation throughout Caucus. If an MP had a problem then Bill could be relied on for a considered strategic response.

There must have been some self-doubt though, because I was hushed to secrecy by his secretary Liz when I discovered that he was being provided with elocution lessons by the party. Bill had the kind of voice that sounded as if it was trapped in an overturned 44-gallon drum. It also had a light and monotonal aspect that could glaze the eyes then deaden the lids until sleep was a mercy.

However, these lessons had a curious effect. Obviously he had been coached to put the accent on certain words and syllables so as to break up the usual white noise. Unfortunately, Bill lacked a sense of rhythm. He began to emphasise the wrong words or syllables, with the result that his speeches sounded like a long-distance shortwave broadcast — the clarity flicking in and out at irregular intervals. Finally he abandoned this late quest for a RADA accent but I was intrigued that he recognised his limitation. A politician who knows his weaknesses is a rare and dangerous beast.

LEADERSHIP COUP

By late 1985 there were dark mutterings within the research unit about plots, counterplots and clandestine meetings taking place in MPs' offices. The tension at Caucus committee meetings, at which we researchers acted as minute-keepers, had quickened appreciably. A tangible leadership challenge was in the offing. Of course it always had been — since the Caucus vote in late 1984 when the new deputy leader convinced himself that the Chief Whip was clearly dyslexic and had misread the voting results.

Jim McLay's personal approval ratings were plummeting, squeezed by a variety of forces — the destructive Sunday Club campaign, the breathtaking zeal of the Labour Government, ceaseless and ever upward sharemarket speculation, and his own weak and distant image.

In addition, McLay's deputy was undermining him both publicly and in private. In public Bolger refused to support his leader, relying on tacit signals of filial duty. In private he was receiving delegations of MPs who urged him to provoke the inevitable. Bolger's response was typically cautious. He would not hazard any showdown without absolute assurances as to Caucus numbers. McLay's staff knew Bolger's game precisely. They began to put pressure on erring MPs via the party machine.

McLay then decided on bold and decisive action. Buoyed by a rapprochement with the pathetic remnants of the New Zealand Party, all three of them, McLay launched a pre-emptive strike to stamp his mark upon the Caucus. Removing the last vestiges of Muldoonism from his front bench he dumped Birch and Gair, while promoting those MPs who had strong centre-right credentials. Ruth Richardson, Simon Upton, Michael Cox and Ian McLean got the call-up, their elevation enthusiastically endorsed by the party's organisational leadership.

The dumping of Gair and Birch proved the catalyst. For the first time it welded Bolger, Birch and Gair with the Salamanca Road cowboy quartet of Don McKinnon, Paul East, Winston Peters and Philip Burdon — a team that could manoeuvre McLay's dumping and agree on Bolger as the successor. By now Peters and Burdon had started a 'second front' by attacking Sue Wood and Barrie Leay for perceived organisational mistakes and weaknesses, and they linked with Muldoon to garner their ammunition, thus provoking the old tusker's backing for Bolger's push.

Burdon's rationale for a leadership change contair
dient — an intense and implacable loathing for McLa
favourite, Ruth Richardson. Philip's personal antip
Richardson knew few bounds, and his distaste was h
rocated. God knows the circumstances that underlay th
hate someone that much usually meant a torrid love affa.. gone bad
but even that extenuating circumstance was absent.

The mere mention of one was a tripwire for the other. Ruth would
bemoan the unwholesome stench that surrounded Burdon's Lincoln
mushroom farm and suggest that the taint of manure had permanently
addled the multi-millionaire's senses. Burdon, in turn, would openly
wonder at the accuracy of Richardson's parliamentary expenses claim
sheets, hinting at some strange calumny. I was not immune to the
temptation of teasing Philip with Ruth's latest public foray and then
awaiting the monsoon as spittles of foam were expelled in spluttering
condemnation.

For a humble researcher, the personality dynamics were both
startling and entertaining. Watching the supposed leaders-in-waiting
of one's country engage in petty backbiting and errant behaviour
quickly made me realise that personality not policy was a critical
determinant of parliamentary action. Policy differences were simply
used as an excuse to mask selfish motivation.

Birch and Gair's demotion signalled McLay's end. They were the
two senior pros who brought stability and a rudimentary organisational prowess to the plotters. After Birch's front-bench demotion I
went in to see him in his offices to offer genuine sympathy. Whatever
his political faults he had always been kind and courteous to me —
the commiseration was sincere. I proffered the thought that the
demotion was 'crazy'. With him was George Gair. There was a
conspiratorial atmosphere in the room.

Birch glanced quizzically at Gair then turned toward me.

'How well do you know Michelle Boag?'

Michelle was the dragon lady of the National Party. Acutely able,
with an in-your-face, take-no-prisoners approach to parliamentary
politics, she always wore too much make-up, dresses that were too
tight, and the kind of strappy heeled footwear that both excites and
frightens middle-aged men. Her dominatrix looks, direct manner and
closeness to party leader Jim McLay had most of National's Caucus
in a quiver. There were party rumours that she was 'too close' to the
recently married McLay, but then there were Caucus rumours that

Michelle was involved with anyone with a pulse, which ruled out a good number of them. The former lover and campaign manager of party tyro Murray McCully, Michelle had also impressed as a researcher and speech writer for Prime Minister Muldoon. The Wood/Leay set greatly admired her formidable skills and regarded Boag's ruthlessness and experience as critical to McLay's longevity. In the end, even she could not save him.

There was something else about Michelle. She possessed neither artifice nor pretence. She played hardball politics, she partied hard and there were never any excuses. I had come to admire her as an uncompromising and complete individualist. So when these two vengeful veterans enquired as to the ease of my working relationship with Michelle I was pricked with much the same sensation as a randy teenager at a wet T-shirt contest. No, in hindsight, I was less subtle.

'You're going to roll McLay!' I blurted with sufficient megaphonic volume to provoke an equally loud shushing response and uncomfortable glances at the open window. Birch motioned me to a nearby chair and into the conspiracy. I was to be given a task: to throw Michelle off the scent. It was her twitchy nose that had ferreted out an earlier attempt when Kaimai MP Bruce Townshend had openly wondered where his new office might be after the coup — and her equally swift work that had garnered the organisational veto.

Birch and I were due to attend a lunch meeting in Dunedin that Thursday — the day of the next Caucus meeting. His speech contained essential ingredients of the party's employment policy, thus the Leader's office was interested in the employer audience's reaction. I invited Michelle to dinner so that we might work through the policy details and ensure that Birch's utterances matched the symbolism and intent of the Leader's recent pronouncements. To add lustre to this ruse, I also made travel arrangements for both Bill Birch and myself in case Birch's travel plans were checked by McLay's staff.

Were her staff to get wind of the challenge then the universal fear was that divisional chairpersons, electorate chairpersons, the president, the secretary-general — Uncle Tom Cobbley and all — would pressure individual MPs to withdraw their support for a leadership change. The plotters' aim was to present McLay with the *fait accompli* of committed Caucus numbers and then let him announce his resignation with as much dignity as being sacked would allow. In that way the Leader might still be knifed in the back but the mortal wound would be swiftly cauterised and the blood confined to inconsequential blotches.

For these reasons secrecy was considered absolutely essential. The media were not to catch so much as a passing whiff, the dwindling band of McLay loyalists were to be either misled or avoided, and Bruce Townshend was to be bound and gagged and kept in the boot of a car.

Early that Thursday morning Michelle's nostrils twitched. She telephoned me at my flat even before the first nagging sparrow had realised the new dawn. Was I still going to Dunedin with Birch this morning? Later she would check again, with an urgent message awaiting me at Wellington airport. I returned the call then caught the early flight to Dunedin as instructed. By the time the Leader's office had its first tangible proof that a plot was afoot it was all too late. Michelle later told me that McLay walked into the Caucus Room confident that he could face the plotters down. But when a letter was immediately handed to him by the Senior Whip, Don McKinnon, containing the signatures of over three-quarters of the Caucus and requesting his resignation such bravado was put to flight.

Angry words were exchanged, with McLay storming from the Caucus Room in seething fury and marching toward the Press Gallery to declaim the treachery of his deputy leader and the other con-spirators. It was Michelle who trailed after him pleading that this was not the way to go out — not the public exit that he deserved.

'The others might be pricks, Jim. But you don't have to descend to their level.' It was a measure of the man that he could be counselled to go quietly despite the treacherous actions of a deputy who had undermined him from the first instant of his tenure.

With a strange mixture of approval and resentment Michelle later telephoned me in Dunedin to acknowledge the successful ruse and my petty role in the Bolger coup. Apparently McLay had caught a whiff of unstable testosterone the evening before but Michelle had convinced him, as a consequence of our discussions, that he was being overly sensitive. Despite my furtive conduct she forgave me and we forged a friendship based on the upcoming political operator success-fully stiffing the incumbent.

'You'll go a long way in this business,' she flattered me. 'Just the right mix of sincerity and cunning.' It was a remark that was appro-priately mortifying and gratifying in equal measure.

The question now arose as to Michelle's position in this new order. Bolger regarded her as a stroppy painted lady and had previously exhibited a palpable discomfort in her presence. In turn she regarded him as a rural plodder, while recognising that dogged plodding had delivered him the Leader's role. Bolger was smart enough to recognise Boag's political abilities and she, in turn, was smart enough to recognise that no one else was offering alternative employment. They both held their noses long enough for a mutual respect to bridge their differences — a construction intensely resented by some in the party, who felt she should have thrown herself on her stilettos.

A different culture now inhabited the Opposition. Bolger rewarded the formerly destructive Muldoon with a front-bench role, promoted chief plotter and new deputy George Gair to the finance portfolio, and upgraded Bill Birch to place his now loyal ally in charge of election policy development within the party. As Birch's senior aide and researcher (in fact his only aide and researcher), I gained slightly more prominence within the wider party.

The demise of McLay was soon followed by the retirement of Sue Wood as party president, while Barrie Leay saw the proverbial writing on the wall and scarpered. Meanwhile the Caucus resumed all development of both policy and political strategy, ending previous hopes of sharing this with the organisational wing. Bolger, Gair and Birch knew that the majority of the National Executive had rested their sympathies with McLay, and thus they distrusted the acumen and loyalty of the party's upper hierarchy. Birch regarded the party's new divisional policy committees as strictly cosmetic. Any policy paper or conference remit was welcomed with the same paternalistic smile that greets a finger painting brought home from kindergarten. It was then assigned to the appropriate researcher, who had the onerous task of transferring the ideas it contained to Parliament's favourite filing cabinet — the round green rubbish bins at the foot of our desks. This process was euphemistically described as 'active consideration', which seemed sufficient encouragement for electorate policy committees to begin the yearly lemming remit rush all over again. We could have saved the parliamentary cleaners much work had we simply sent each electorate a box of matches.

It was an important lesson. The party were mere cannon fodder marching at the behest of the parliamentary wing. Useful for organising public meetings, raising money from door-to-door canvassing, delivering election year pamphlets and leaflets, but not much else. Conversely, the organisational wing continued to delude itself that it had some influence over parliamentary events. Under Jim Bolger's leadership such influence was reduced from anorexic to amoebic. The failed 1987 election campaign ended even that pretence.

The relatively graceful exit of McLay absorbed many of the factional tensions and even Muldoon's conflagrations lessened, his spite satiated by this sacrifice. The party now turned its attention outwards for the first time since its election defeat two years earlier. The finalisation of policy, the selection of candidates and the planning of a winning campaign took precedence over all else.

But I was a political virgin no more. I had tasted the elixir of involvement and actively connived on the Caucus sidelines. Original ideas and concepts had been grafted into policy papers and then been endorsed by the party and Caucus alike. I had made contacts with those who both created the political news and with those who reported it. Powerful outsiders sought my advice on who to approach and enlisted my assistance to advance their lobby group's activities.

It was heady stuff. I had infused a new drug and the high was not wearing off. As they say, this was the most fun you could experience sober and with your clothes on. But as with all such reality suspenders, I now required a stronger dosage.

PRETENSIONS

The change in National's leadership provided only a brief revival in the Opposition's fortunes. McLay's demise exposed King Country farmer James Brendan Bolger to the political glitterati and the glitterati were not impressed.

By now Labour's free-market reforms had become distinctly trendy. Neighbourhood share clubs replaced suburban Tupperware parties as the second favourite after-hours mischief of the middle class; nauseous personalised number plates became the new social currency.

Public debt might have doubled, inflation and interest rates escalated to record double-digit highs, tens of thousands of redundancies may have swollen the dole queues, but — hey — the sharemarket was booming, the Press Gallery were blindly and unquestionably supportive, and David Lange's beatific anti-nuclear stance was wowing international audiences. New Zealanders began to perceive themselves as world visionaries in a style peculiarly unique to the very insecure or the very stupid. Roger Douglas and his drinking buddies hallucinated that the agrarian sector could be discarded now that New Zealand was en route to restyling itself as the 'Switzerland of the South Pacific', though without the clocks, the seven centuries of armed neutrality or the mass market of Europe being just a yodel away. Minor details.

An unfortunate mix of self-righteous anti-nuclear sensibilities and selfish laissez-faire attitudes predominated. This was the time for yuppie values, plastic consciences and the knighting of property speculators. Barren metal did not just breed — it cavorted and copulated in public. Shylock was in his element.

Against such sentiments National did not stand a chance. They were political bogans — uncool and sad dudes. The dread prospect of a re-elected Labour Government loomed.

Meanwhile the party organisation was putting the destructive internecine conflict of the past two years aside. Wood's retirement produced a contest for the presidency between the old forces and the new. Incredibly, neither won. Gregarious Christchurch lawyer and arch pragmatist Neville Young slipped through the middle to defeat the Wood/Leay protégé Hamish Kynoch and the arch-conservative Brian Shackel. Young's expansive hotel drinks cabinet proved the winning hit of the conference, demonstrating that a stiff gin and tonic can beat a cogent argument any day.

Candidate selection now dominated the party's thinking. There was a general view that the party's choices should be selected as early as possible, particularly in the marginal electorates, with the idea that an elongated preparation militated against the natural advantage of an MP's incumbency. This strategy had quite the reverse effect. Candidates became bored (and penniless) after twelve or more months of ceaseless campaigning, while the locals got to know their National candidates so well that all their personality defects became common knowledge.

It was my judgement that Labour would be re-elected in 1987 with a diminished parliamentary majority. A host of previously 'safe' National provincial seats would presumably return to the fold — East Cape, Hawke's Bay, Wairarapa — solid rural/provincial seats feeling the pinch of the reform process and possessing unspectacular first-term Labour MPs. I mulled over the prospect of winning a marginal seat yet remaining in opposition. Selfishly, that would be the best of both worlds — three years to create a favourable impression and then straight into an executive role should the party win in 1990.

It was a lovely theory. There were just a few problems. When, where and how?

I made the great mistake of confiding these thoughts to Michelle over dinner one night at Bellamy's. Perhaps it was her sense of exquisite personal revenge, or even a parting legacy for Bolger, but Michelle dissected and dismissed all my anxieties about contesting a candidacy selection. She rightly noted the lack of quality nominations, with early selection dates frightening off the family-oriented and an MP's salary scaring the truly talented. There was also a general desire among electorates for young, fresh faces to mask the party's relative torpor.

I was still unconvinced. Michelle assumed another tack and ran through a checklist of current MPs — Neil Austin, Derek Angus, Jim Gerard, Roger Maxwell. What particular abilities did they possess that were not within me? This was a dirty trick — anyone breathing could qualify against that standard. But then the clincher.

'I'll run your campaign for the nomination.'

The greatest hurdle to a parliamentary career is self-imposed. Any number of individuals have the requisite experience, education and ego to make the step from citizen to politician. It is simple fear that holds them back — a fear of the unfamiliar, a fear of losing, a fear of public elevation and interest, a fear of the more difficult path.

On the basis that the worst that could happen was humiliating defeat (and had not my whole life prepared me for such an outcome?) and fortified by a second bottle of chardonnay, I accepted Michelle's offer. We clinked glasses and celebrated this momentous step. Now just the one problem remained ... umm ... what unsuspecting electorate should I inflict myself on?

There was just one possibility: Hawke's Bay. It was one of those rural marginal seats that supposedly 'belonged' to National but had been lost in the '84 landslide, the aged Speaker, Sir Richard Harrison, losing his 22-year grip to a Labour candidate who had only arrived in the district one month prior to election day. The conventional Wellington wisdom was that this late arrival was just as well. Labour's Bill Sutton had a prickly personal manner coupled with the kind of egregious dress sense you might expect from a nudist in a hurry, the mixing of brown suits, socks and sandals confirming his dysfunctional fashion sense. As with most conventional parliamentary wisdom this impression proved only half right.

Despite his eccentric personal habits and occasional intemperate language Sutton was no moron, and he possessed a modern and able electorate organisation. In addition he had proven a willing and public champion of the Rogernomics revolution, exhibiting a deft cunning by blaming all its deleterious side effects on the previous National administration.

In contrast the National Party in Hawke's Bay had a refined sense of taste and dress but no idea about how to run and win an election campaign. Worse, it had allowed Sutton and his team unchallenged supremacy in the local media. All these factors remained firmly out of sight as I contemplated my nomination. But I had no real choice. Hawke's Bay was the only electorate with which I could claim any association, with my maternal grandparents residing in Taradale and my paternal grandparents in the neighbouring seat of Napier.

Yes, but would my previous profligate days in the area be recalled? I took refuge in the cliché about the 1960s — if you could remember them you were not there. Besides, I no longer had an Afro hairstyle and full beard so my current facial characteristics were relatively unknown. Of course what I failed to appreciate was that Hawke's Bay was an ideal home for Otago graduates, who had later and lasting memories of my excesses down south. Now I was seeking to be their Member of Parliament, I could only hope they had also destroyed sufficient brain cells to wipe out those parts of their memory in which I appeared. No such luck.

Fortunately no one took my nomination seriously. Nine other nominations were received, with three party stalwarts declaring themselves the frontrunner and the smart money being laid on Waipawa farmer and deputy Harbour Board chairman Ewan McGregor. McGregor was in his early forties, a respected leader within Federated Farmers and strongly supported by 'progressive' elements within the party's hierarchy. He was the logical successor to Harrison.

Conservative, keen, well-respected and with proven local body experience, he had only one defect — he was boring.

There is an old adage about boredom and excitement in political parties. Most electorates err toward selecting the former, employing the same logic that is used by NASA with the space shuttle programme. Two thousand boring widgets doing their job are distinctly preferable to nineteen hundred and ninety nine boring ones and one exciting widget. It is the exciting widget that tends to spectacular conflagration — which makes for epic TV viewing but is slightly contrary to Mission Control's objective. The National Party ignored this rule for the 1987 election in Hawke's Bay. Boredom lost them the seat in 1984 — if they were going to lose again they wanted the big bang as well.

There were other favourites — Harrison's electorate chairman and fellow farmer, Harvey Boyden, the party's previous Napier candidate and holy roller, Kevin Rose, and the highly regarded local canvasser and CWI stalwart Jean Hill. As it transpired I had one great virtue with regard to the Hawke's Bay nomination, apart from the potential for excitement. I was none of the above. Each had successfully alienated elements within the electorate organisation during their mad rush for the Harrison succession — classic proof that familiarity not only breeds contempt but contrariness as well.

For the moment I had a much more fundamental problem. I did not know a single soul in the membership of the Hawke's Bay National Party and nominations closed on Friday. This was Wednesday.

At that point Ruth Richardson came to the rescue. Ironic in retrospect. She knew someone in the area — a member of the local Education Board and a keen party supporter. Maybe she could help me. Help — now that is an understatement. This lady, a widowed farmer from Marekakaho near Hastings, delivered me the candidacy.

Jan Graham was a remarkable woman in her late fifties, who had that unfailing tolerance and humanity that only great personal heartache seems to produce. Her husband had gradually succumbed to an insidious cancer and Jan had nursed him through this enervating experience while raising their large family and running their varied horticultural and farming interests. Her partner, Dick Black, was a typically guileless Kiwi sheepfarmer with a wonderful dry wit and a sentimental regard for all living things. For some reason such beneficence also extended to me.

Looking back it seems quite bizarre to think that, unannounced, I would drive to Jan's place in my grandparents' car, introduce myself as 'Ruth's researcher', ask for her help in winning the party's nomination, and receive absolute support all in the course of one afternoon. But that is exactly how it happened — a snap judgement — and by the time I was driving home Jan was already on the telephone to her friends and neighbours extolling my virtues. By Friday night I had the requisite fifteen party members' signatures.

And then another stroke of good fortune. The key urban heart to the electorate was Taradale, where the party's branch chairman was Dr Brian Woodhouse, a retired medical specialist whose son Brendan and I had shared a few dissolute moments during our undergraduate days at Otago. Again it was introduction, discussion, total support and, as with Jan and Dick, a friendship that would last through the good times and the bad to the present.

I was completely bemused — was I exuding some irresistible pheromone (and if so why were attractive young women immune?)

or were these people on something? Sadly, neither. The answer was spectacularly prosaic — I had a pulse and I was none of the other candidates. These were the outstanding qualities for this particular contest.

The first hurdle for prospective National Party candidates is the preselection meeting. A mixture of electorate and divisional figures probe the personal philosophies, preferred policies and private lives of those nominated, then compose a short list of nominees for the wider attention of the party's voting delegates. The theory is that those with shady business backgrounds and Ku Klux Klan sensibilities will be rooted out before exposure to party and public. It rarely works in practice because nominees are relied upon to furnish their own CVs and the time factor prohibits discussion of their recent encounter with Elvis in the alien mothership. A simple declaration that the nominee is neither a bankrupt nor a triad gang member is generally sufficient to pass preselection muster.

The Hawke's Bay preselection panel had the relatively simple task of whittling down nine prospects to five contenders after a half-hour interview with each. Having watched far too many Le Carré dramatisations, the panel arrayed themselves in an inquisitorial semi-circle and adopted the impassive expressions of the recently lobotomised. This stern collective demeanour was such that I instantly regretted not bringing a solicitor and hoped that I might at least be granted the 'one phone call prior to questioning'. No such luck.

I need not have concerned myself; the preselection panel were relieved to see me principally because I was the last of the nominees and by now they were bored, hungry and in desperate need of a drink. Any alcohol would do — anything to blot out the self-congratulatory worthiness of my predecessors. Unbeknown to me the panel had attempted to break this tedium by designating one of their number 'the bad cop'. This individual would pursue an aggressive line of questioning and concentrate on any perceived deficiencies in the nominee.

My 'bad cop' was Neil Kirton — a youthful orchard manager and another bloody Otago graduate, who had obviously psyched himself up for the role with a De Niro method-acting course. At any moment I was expecting an arc light in my face, electrodes to be attached to my genitals, and a length of rubber hose applied to the rest of my body. Kirton steepled his hands and glared over them.

'Mr Laws, it is my impression that you don't suffer fools gladly.'

'Oh, I don't know Mr Kirton. I seem to be doing a pretty good job at the moment.'

The panel erupted — some in mirth, others in outrage. I was hastily escorted from the room by the party's divisional secretary, James Austin, who touchingly reassured me that mine had been the briefest session of the day — by about 25 minutes.

Later that evening the panel announced their short list, which featured my name but included no Jean Hill. Any relief I felt was quickly tempered by local newspaper grumblings that something underhand had occurred, the hard-working local activist being ditched to make way for the brash young interloper from the big smoke. I was thus introduced to the idiosyncrasies of the Hawke's Bay media, an unusual mixture of young, ambitious itinerants and detached, jaded 'lifers' worn out by years of chasing ambulances, fire trucks and that ever-elusive promotion.

Surprisingly, this adverse attention generated considerable sympathy from within the electorate organisation. Jan marshalled a supportive vanguard of mostly rural married women, who adopted me like a stray puppy. Special supper meetings were hosted and the 160 voting delegates plied with home-cooked delights and enough liquor to satisfy a one-day cricket embankment crowd. I spoke only at the conclusion of these gatherings, by which time my manifest inadequacies were able to be hidden behind an all-consuming fog of folksy bonhomie.

I was thus taught an abiding political lesson. If you want something done properly, give the responsibility to a woman. It is just not part of a man's genetic make-up to do anything without a self-congratulatory fuss. Men talk, posture, dispute, procrastinate. Women do. The other candidates had male-dominated campaign teams — it was a no-contest.

Meanwhile Michelle was co-ordinating all my campaign literature, while Ruth Richardson and Bill Birch had granted me the necessary three weeks' leave to lobby the delegates full time. Michelle skilfully reinterpreted this consent as explicit support and spun this story with the local media. Delegates were now under the impression that my candidacy had strong Caucus backing — a considerable stretching of the truth but one never contradicted. The Hawke's Bay papers possessed another great asset — they were not read in Wellington.

The selection night meeting was held at the Taradale High School assembly hall and bulged to overflowing with the delegates, their partners, the various support teams and a mass of curious party members who had foresworn the television for a slightly more dramatic evening's entertainment. Individually the nominees gave their set ten-minute speeches and answered questions prepared by the party leader and the president, the undoubted drama being provided by Kevin Rose with his hallelujah special, alternately singing, pleading and praying for the audience to deliver him the nomination.

Finally a surprised Neville Young announced the verdict: a victory on the first ballot to the young researcher from Wellington. Any immediate exhilaration was tempered by the reaction of my fellow contestants, ranging from undistilled relief to unsparing hostility. As I noted their various expressions amid the hand-pumping and back-slappings of wider congratulation, just two words flashed through my mind. Uh oh.

CAMPAIGN BLUES

There is an apocryphal proverb that Hell hath no fury like a woman scorned. The truth is that Hell hath no fury like ambition thwarted. For the next twelve months I was to encounter a parade of salacious gossip based on fantasies of my wrongdoings and concocted by a gaggle of defeated nominees and their supporters. By year's end the popular wisdom was that I had fathered half the gannet colony at Cape Kidnappers and knew the Medellin cocaine cartel on a first-name basis. If only. The Colombians' fearsome reputation for dispensing retributive justice would have proven very handy. Even the most charitable stories suggested that the party delegates had selected a cross between Julian Clary and Superfly.

This subterranean whispering campaign proved highly effective by tying an inexperienced campaign team and a wholly inexperienced candidate into emotional knots. For every moment we spent fighting another rumour or allegation was a debilitating moment robbed from our efforts elsewhere. By Christmas 1986 I was ready to throw it all in. If this was politics, forget it.

My unease was exaggerated by the decision of the boundary-setting Representation Commission to shave three more rural wards from the electorate. I was now looking at a Sutton paper majority of 1500 votes, and that was at my most optimistic.

The festive break, a family Christmas and a long heart-to-heart with Michelle calmed my frazzled nerves. Michelle produced the startling intelligence that a good number of other National Party candidates were facing the same distractions from similarly venomous ex-nominees with unrequited ambitions. One candidate had been accused of illiteracy, another of fiddling his company's books, another of blatant homosexuality — as each instance of alleged infamy was detailed I progressively relaxed. Being a nature lover with a crack habit was not so bad after all.

Rejuvenated by the misfortune of others and opinion polls that showed National only marginally behind Labour, I began to explore both my electorate and the Hawke's Bay region in general. After careful thought I decided to live in neglected Flaxmere, which I surmised would be vulnerable to an anti-Labour message in the wake of the Whakatu closure. Party canvassers considered any trip into the interior of the suburb as missionary work. In contrast I felt at home, well prepared by my childhood experiences in Gonville. I joined the local Flaxmere Club, began coaching one of the rugby club's junior teams and generally introduced myself to the wider community. In turn they enjoyed the novelty of a Tory in their midst even if they had no intention of voting for him!

This move was not universally appreciated within the party and I was visited by a delegation who tried to persuade me to reside in Havelock North or Taradale — anywhere other than working-class Flaxmere. The party's image was at risk. When this approach drew a stony glare they changed tack. At least stop living here — in this house.

The problem this time was that I shared a flat with another who had the dubious moral distinction of being single and female. The fact that my flatmate had a steady boyfriend and that ours was a strictly platonic relationship was neither here nor there. Again, it was 'image'. I shook my head in disbelief. Nothing had prepared me for provincial morality. Of course I refused to either admit or submit to such perceptions, scoffing at the very notion that untoward references might be drawn. A month later a Labour Party rumour had me 'shacking up' with a heavily pregnant unmarried partner in my Flaxmere love nest.

It was rapidly becoming apparent that Hawke's Bay was neither Wellington nor the student quarters of Dunedin. There is something about provincial New Zealand that is at once comforting and unsafe — a nostalgic familiarity mixed with an unsettling intolerance. Hawke's Bay had rarefied all these qualities to such a degree that you felt instinctively safe in the roughest public bar but in mortal peril at an upmarket cocktail party.

In addition Hawke's Bay's self-described elite appeared to take great pride in their blind and unthinking snobbery, which permeated every aspect of the region's commercial and social infrastructure. The white gentry were perched on the heights of either Havelock North or the Napier Hill and looked down, both literally and figuratively, on the darker classes of Flaxmere or Maraenui. Social status and envy rippled the remaining suburbs. Hastings had been divided into two types of people — those who lived in Havelock North and those who wanted to. It was the kind of place where, darling, you screwed the tennis pro but you never took them to lunch.

This provincial duality was amplified by the economic environment that dominated in late 1986. For decades Hawke's Bay had been a synonym for rural wealth. The sons and daughters were sent away to the exclusive boarding schools of Wanganui Collegiate or Woodford House, while the export receipts and the SMPs procured an annual replacement for the latest saloon and any number of shopping expeditions to Sydney, Hong Kong or 'home'. Hastings prospered amid this rural plenty until the twin shocks of declining meat and wool prices and the stripping away of all agricultural subsidies. With the decline of the rural sector a social revolution took place in Hawke's Bay during the mid-eighties — the rise of a professional and financial provincial elite, a gaudy nouveau riche addicted to light opera and four-wheel-drives that never strayed from the tarseal.

By a strange set of coincidences Hawke's Bay had also developed a healthy appetite for the burgeoning sharemarket. A maze of transfer deals in the 1970s allied with the local prominence of Brierley director Selwyn Cushing and his Hastings accountancy firm, Esam Cushing, produced the greatest number of Brierley stockholders outside the metropolitan cities. A good portion of the region's blue blood was perplexed — on the one hand their productive labour was declining in value with each passing day; on the other, their speculative interests were returning boom profits.

As for the financial, commercial and professional classes, things had never been better. The stock exchange was in overdrive, every new business venture produced handsome book profits, and a new mood of sophisticated optimism drowned out the conservatives and the Jeremiahs. It was yuppie heaven.

As a counterpoint to such excessive enthusiasm there were a significant number of struggling farmers and nervous orchardists who, sadly, did not possess buoyant stock portfolios. They were watching their returns decline at the converse exponential rate of the Barclays share index. Declining overseas prices, the cessation of SMPs and fertiliser subsidies, ruinous bank interest charges and then a killer drought catapulted many a farmer's equity into irretrievable reverse. As bankruptcies spiralled and stock numbers dramatically declined Hastings caught cold. The massive Whakatu freezing works shut its doors with over two thousand jobs lost. Flaxmere caught pneumonia.

Therein lay the contradiction. The numbers of yuppies and beneficiaries were growing at roughly equal rates and both owed their new status to Labour's pursuit of the free market.

Despite all the obstacles — inflammatory rumours, woeful inexperience, indurate disdain from the business community, infrequent media attention and insalubrious electoral boundaries — I was still in with a chance. Hawke's Bay's position on the electoral pendulum required just under a 3-per-cent two-party swing. The public opinion polls continued to assure me that this movement would happen.

ADIEU HAWKE'S BAY

Personally, I blame Sitiveni Rabuka.

Until the Fijian military coup National was trailing at a sufficiently close distance to open a parliamentary door to their Hawke's Bay candidate. Then, in an instant, the political landscape transformed itself as a consequence of a much more startling transformation elsewhere.

The Indians had won an election in Fiji for the first time ever. It was the South Pacific equivalent of the Berlin Wall collapsing as the Fijian Labour Party, with their titular native head, Dr Bavadra, triumphed despite outrageous official interference and long decades of constitutional impediment. A horrified indigenous Taukei movement — horrified at the prospect of having to work for a living — linked up with a sympathetic military and launched the first of two effective blows against democracy.

Prime Minister Lange wet himself. Here was the perfect excuse to appear nightly on the TV screens with a torrent of self-indulgent waffle that would upset no-one. As the Fijian saga went through each new twist and turn Lange was offered gratuitous media coverage. The polls suddenly widened to a chasm.

Just why the New Zealand public should be so vitally concerned with the internal problems of a literal banana republic bemused me. Maybe it was the prospect that their cut-price winter holidays to the South Pacific sun would be jeopardised, or the more immediate threat that every Auckland taxi driver would turn out to be a Fijian Indian. Whatever the excuse Jim Bolger and the National Opposition disappeared from view.

Of course the other external factor to so cruelly dash my political hopes was the All Blacks. By winning the inaugural World Cup within sight of election day the All Blacks provided just the right ambience for a Labour victory. The political cliché that governments lose elections rather than oppositions win them was nevertheless true. If people feel good about themselves they reflect this in their political judgements. Sport has always contained a wonderful measure of social control and the World Cup, plus the subsequent Bledisloe Cup revenge over the Wallabies, ensured a beneficent ballot box for the incumbent administration. If only Grant Fox had missed a few of those kicks.

Of course most political candidates refuse to admit to themselves that their fate is decided by events and personalities way beyond their tiny ambit. Under the first-past-the-post system a new candidate had no prospect of repelling national trends. The old adage that a good candidate is worth five hundred votes but a bad one can lose a thousand was all too depressing. If all your frenetic efforts are for such inconsequential reward then what is the point? Such thinking was best avoided for it pinpointed the futility of an individual candidate trying to restrain the national mood.

It took me some months to appreciate that none of us — neither those on the campaign team nor those at National Headquarters in Wellington — had a blind clue about what we were meant to be doing. In the absence of an alternative vision the party chanced upon an American political convention/party/hoop-la theme. This usually works in the United States because the staging is immaculate, the supporting cast are professional entertainers and the political candidate is trained to appear urbane and intelligent — usually through a mixture of plastic surgery and electric shock treatment. The glitz is intended to distract from the vacuum of substance in the same way that illusionists employ near naked women to distract cynical eyes from extraneous hand movements.

The only problem with National's campaign in 1987 was that they imported the lack of substance all right but left the glamour and glitz back in the States. The polystyrene boaters and blue-and-white streamers promised a party — instead they delivered the Labour-voting Yandall Sisters and a tuneless Lockwood Smith, who would have preferred a Gang Show gig for any number of reasons. The climactic appearance of party leader Jim Bolger was supposed to excite the party faithful to orgasmic frenzy. They should have stuck with the naked women.

National were in such disarray that we candidates were left to stumble through our campaigns as if blind drunk. It was inevitable that innocent bystanders had their toes mashed by rampaging and insensitive aspirants — we knew no better. The grand prize went to Gisborne candidate Georgina Tattersfield, who managed to hijack an army vehicle during a military parade in an attempt to raise her public profile. It worked. The howls of censure lasted for weeks.

The conventional wisdom was that a candidate could be most effective if they engaged in a frenzy of systematic neighbourhood door-knocking. Introduce yourself, smile, make favourable comments about the garden, the kids, the Rottweiler's bite marks, leave your card and voila — the homeowner would be sufficiently impressed by your charm, teeth and friendly manner that they would vote for you on election day. Yeah, right.

Far from being impressed by this Mormon clone rapping on their front door most people deeply resented the intrusion into their activity of the moment — be it hanging out the washing, preparing the tea or getting up from the loo. By the end of the first week I had interrupted a copulating couple in their back yard, been chased by numerous dogs (on one occasion an enraged goat), and told to perform a wide range of anatomical impossibilities. Alternately I had been invited inside for a coffee, a beer and a joint. It was my considered opinion that not one person was now more inclined to vote National as a result of my interruption, except perhaps the frisky back-yard cavorters, who seemed to enjoy the audience.

These visits were not as random as might first appear. The electorate had provided me with numerous street addresses as a result of their much prized canvassing system. This activity was based on the theory that a smiling stranger with a blue rosette on their lapel could convince any number of cynical, uninterested individuals into parting with cold, hard cash and buying a worthless membership in the National Party. There may be a sucker born every minute but not in our immediate vicinity. Either that or they were off being farmed by Amway salespeople when our canvassers called.

This system of directly asking for a financial donation relied on the same logic as those men who ask every woman to sleep with them. You might get your face slapped nineteen times but the twentieth success supposedly justifies the effort. Excited canvassers would typically return from a full morning's effort, numerous insults and a guard-dog attack with one new membership receipt and five dollars — that one success blotting out the pain of six stitches and a tetanus shot.

There was another similarly mad excuse for these door-to-door sweeps — they rendered invaluable 'intelligence' to the campaign team. This 'blue dot' system was much beloved by the party. It was also a complete disaster. Like most human folly it resulted from trusting a professional task to well-meaning amateurs. Scores of untrained party canvassers descended upon unsuspecting neighbourhoods and made snap personal judgements on the basis of one brief doorstep conversation. Subjective evaluations abounded. Bill Sutton's campaign manager was awarded a blue dot on the basis that he knew a lot about politics and asked the canvasser how our campaign was going. Another judged anyone who answered the door unshaven and poorly dressed to be 'adverse'; yet another reasoned that a polite smile proved good manners and deserved the benefit of the doubt. On that basis, my first list of 'swingers' included Labour's Flaxmere chairman and the local Democrat Party candidate.

The only good thing about losing in 1987 was that I was not alone. If misery loves company it had enough recruits on election night for the millennium. The supposedly safe National seats of Manawatu and New Plymouth were also lost to Labour — a quite amazing feat of political incompetence by the incumbents Cox and Friedlander. It is almost impossible for an incumbent to lose an electorate when in opposition but somehow these two managed it.

Despite all this a truly dreadful scene was played out at the Taradale Red Cross Hall on election night. Previously eager and expectant faces that had crammed around the television sets, laughing and quaffing champagne, slowly adjusted to the reality of the booth results as they were transcribed onto the large whiteboard. The initial results from Flaxmere suggested that we had done enough to win and prompted political sage Colin James to declare Hawke's Bay a National

Party gain. But as the evening wore on it became plain that the middle-class suburbs of Taradale and Greenmeadows had swung strongly behind Labour. Sutton's paper majority had been cut to 850 — close but no cigar.

It is my nature to shrug off, disregard, even ignore personal failure. A fleeting 'Yeah, so what?', a hollow insouciance, an unthinking pursuit of tomorrow's goal — these are my reactions to defeat and disappointment. They come too easily at times — sometimes before the race is even run — but that's me. Those are my defence mechanisms, learned from all the bumps and bunglings of childhood and adolescence. I am not a dogged individual.

One thing had been made certain. I had been cured of parliamentary ambition.

Not of politics — but of being an MP. After a year of campaigning, a year of observing the minimal public respect for politicians, a year of recognising the futility of wanting to be a glorified social worker — I was cured. And even should I reconsider, Hawke's Bay was not an option — the rapidly shrinking electoral boundaries would shape the seat into the tightest of urban marginals, bending to whichever electoral wind from whatever direction. I did not want my political fate decided by the actions and mistakes of others.

And, in truth, there was something else — something I could scarcely admit to myself. I never ever wanted to confront again the pain of defeat I had seen etched on the faces of my family, friends and supporters that election night. The agony was too intense for me to consider placing these people at risk a second or third time. They had evolved from mere party workers to supporters to friends, and I had failed them.

As I drove back to Wellington, and a senior position within the research unit, there was a permanent adieu to Hawke's Bay in my wave. It had been an adventure, but a once-in-a-lifetime adventure. There would be no repeat. The hunger was gone.

Chapter 3

AMBITION

PREAMBLE TO PETERS

Like that of many female restaurant and bar staff, my first impression of Winston Peters was distinctly unfavourable. During my first year in the research unit Peters had launched an audacious attack under parliamentary privilege against High Court Justice Maurice Casey and his decision to grant an injunction against the proposed 1986 All Black tour of South Africa.

Included in Peters' parliamentary denunciation was the claim that Casey's wife, Stella, had been prominent at a recent anti-Tour demonstration in Christchurch. The plain inference was that her strong anti-apartheid opinions had influenced the granting of the injunction. These railings offended on a number of levels — the attack on the courts; the suggestion of judicial bias; the inability of Casey to defend himself — but the most wounding charge seemed to be that this justiciary was a henpecked individual at the mercy of a spousal harridan. But these were minor criticisms. Peters just happened to be dead wrong.

I knew this because one of the Casey daughters, Vicky, had been an Otago debating colleague and fellow campus prankster. I had met both her parents and no two people had ever struck me as more pathologically responsible or proper in their public and private conduct — which possibly accounted for their unease in my presence. This joint respectability was later emphasised when each was knighted by the Queen in 1991 — surely a unique family honour.

I made this observation, trenchantly, to David Lloyd. These comments garbled their way to Peters in the debating chamber and he raced downstairs to the research unit expecting the good oil on the Casey family and further innuendo to support his most recent ramblings. I quickly disabused him of such conspiratorial notions.

Peters would later apologise in a private missive to the judge, although in a public voice so quiet that one suspected laryngitis. The whole episode did give me an inkling as to Peters' favourite flaw.

Winston could will gossip into gospel in an instant.

However, I was not yet ready for such personality analysis — all I knew was that this ill-disciplined backbencher had publicly attacked the family of a friend over a fiction. During the next two years Peters maintained this penchant for speculative oral dabbling — allegations with regard to the sunken Soviet liner *Mikhail Lermontov* and its linkage to foreign powers; claims of 'rack renting' against sundry Cabinet ministers; and even a close encounter between a Cook Strait ferry keel and the ocean floor grabbing similar headlines. He was National's unruly back-bench cowboy with a 'shoot-first-and-stuff-the-questions' attitude to parliamentary propriety — an adolescent Richard Prebble although with more obvious hormones and better hair.

That was my first and last encounter with Peters prior to being selected as National's Hawke's Bay candidate. At the start of that election year my perception of Peters softened for purely selfish reasons. He had struck political pay dirt — and at the height of the summer media desert. The Maori loans affair.

Like most observers, like the public at large I suspect, I did not have the foggiest as to what the whole affair was about — apart from the fact that various figures within Maoridom, aided and abetted by the Department of Maori Affairs and its Minister Koro Wetere, had sought to procure a $600-million loan for 'Maori development' in contravention of the Public Finance Act. A cast of shadowy figures — mostly failed entrepreneurs and international financiers at the far fringes of commercial decency — were similarly involved. Not surprisingly, given these vast leagues of collective incompetence, the attempt had failed ingloriously.

One of the disgruntled parties in this ill-fated adventure had taken umbrage and deposited various papers and documents with Winston Peters. In turn, Peters provided fragments of this dossier to the media, outlining a sorry saga of foolishness and suggesting a New Zealand Watergate. When shadowy CIA operatives were rumoured to be involved, a surreal character overtook the whole affair.

Prime Minister Lange could handle the embarrassment — being squeezed into a small family sedan and trailing the field at every petrolhead circuit in the country had long conditioned him to ridicule. Nope, he had worked his emotions into a state well beyond embarrassment — Lange was livid. Not only had one of his ministers attempted to contravene the law of the land, but Wetere's behaviour had allowed the Opposition to score its only palpable hit during the entire first parliamentary term. There were tense and secret meetings, first to discuss damage control, and then resignation. Finally, though, Wetere stayed — saved by his tribal associations with the Maori Queen and perhaps the prospect that either Whetu Tirikatene-Sullivan or Bruce Gregory would be his successor. That realisation alone must have sent shudders through the rest of the Labour Cabinet.

After weeks of intrigue and innuendo the issue eventually died. There were no more papers to drip-feed to the breathless media, no new revelations to report, and no resignation to climax proceedings. But this struggling parliamentary candidate still blessed Peters for, at the very least, removing the media focus from National's lack of an election-year vision, leadership or policy. The circus had done its job — it had distracted the populace.

Then, as previously explained, Sitiveni Rabuka went troppo. And Koro was nowhere near him at the time.

THE OPPOSITION TAKES SHAPE

I arrived back in the unit, after the '87 defeat, to promotion and a new research director. David Lloyd had resigned after his similar failure to win Ohariu-Belmont and been replaced by a youngish ex-army colonel, Lindsay Scott, who had the added distinction of appearing in TV car commercials. He was very kind. He left me well alone, imposing his gentle discipline on the rest of the unit but only if that was okay by them.

By now the unit had assumed a more permanent rigour and consequently enjoyed a closer relationship with the Leader's office. A fellow Otago history graduate, Rob Eaddy, had been made the Leader's chief of staff — we Otago grads were everywhere. Eaddy had a great love of all things military (especially ANZUS — I think it was the sailors) and possessed the kind of conservative views that would have been fashionable during the war — the Boer War. These earned him both the trust and the respect of the Leader — after all, like all good politicians, Bolger always liked and respected people who agreed with him. Rob had a gaunt Uriah Heep physique offset by a wiry mane of prematurely greying hair that extended to a full beard — a decent haircut and a shave and he would have been blown away by any average Wellington gale. But Eaddy possessed the saving grace of a sharp intellect and a cynical sense of humour — he could take the piss out of both himself and his boss about one second before the rest of us.

Eaddy's great mate was Wayne Eagleson — a young, trusted Bolger confidant — much loved in the party for his youth, good humour and delightful naivete. Wayne was also a true conservative — on some issues he could make the RSA look like raving commies. But his personality was an endearing cross between Clutch Cargo and Bambi and there was not a mean bone in his body — much to his regret. Eagleson had graduated from Victoria with a good law degree but rightly regarded practising the law as a gross abuse of a decent education and instead had been seconded as the Leader's personal researcher.

Wayne also had a very strong personal friendship with the outspoken Whangarei MP John Banks — so strong that they referred to each other as 'brother' and acted like any normal pair of siblings. Regular lunchtime running expeditions around the Wellington waterfront with Eagleson, Banks and fellow northern MP Ross Meurant allowed me to glean an entertaining if warped back-bench view of the leadership, Caucus, party structure, research unit and so on. As researchers we were chiefly confined to assisting front-bench spokespeople — backbenchers were regarded as annoying pests and resolutely ignored. It was thus difficult to know what the Opposition back bench was thinking — if anything. All I could hope was that their collective neuroses were vastly different from those displayed by these two macho types from the Far North.

The other notable in this Leader's office/research unit bratpack was the outrageously heterosexual Paul Sherriff, a part-time male model and great favourite of any number of Opposition secretaries for all the obvious reasons. (There was some degree of consternation when Paul later announced his homosexuality.) Paul followed one uncomplicated philosophy — a completely unrestrained hedonism that would have made Hugh Hefner blush. He also had a relationship with the sun which was uncovered by many an MP as they trooped into the research quarters and found Sheriff shirtless, perched on the windowsill, arms outstretched, absorbing the ultraviolet rays like a human satellite dish. When he began instructing aerobic classes at the trendy, narcissistic, inner-city Les Mills gym our envy was complete.

This staffers' bratpack got along famously — exchanging parliamentary gossip and confidences, working out which MP was sleeping with which secretary, protecting each other's flanks, and generally exuding the arrogant disdain so common of ambitious young men recently graduated from university. Such an interrelationship also gave each of us the ability to appreciate the various factions and philosophies that continued to haunt the Opposition ranks.

Despite the lack of Caucus unanimity, Jim Bolger had been generally heartened by his first campaign experience as party leader. The conventional party wisdom was that Labour had been unbeatable, its election theme of needing another term to 'finish the job' proving irresistible. If anything, the party kidded itself, Bolger had 'done a Dunkirk' and rescued the Opposition from total electoral annihilation. The loss of Michael Cox and Tony Friedlander was seen as no great talent tragedy — rather a useful culling of the inept.

George Gair did the decent thing and resigned his deputy's role in a vain bid to inject some excitement into the Opposition leadership. There were only two nominations — senior whip Don McKinnon and the restless tyro Ruth Richardson. Michelle Boag had been given the task of preparing media résumés of both contenders but had been stumped by Press Gallery requests to describe McKinnon's personality. Eventually she settled on the word 'deep' — laughing at her inventiveness and knowing that the description could explain any number of defects.

The deputy contest sparked a frenzy of Caucus lobbying made even more intense when Bolger let it be known that he found the very idea of a Richardson candidacy anathematic. The last thing he needed was a deputy like himself who would covet the top job, undermine the Leader and plan a premature succession. On the other hand, a McKinnon candidacy would deliver a decent drinking buddy and political torpor — the ideal deputy really — someone so bland and dumb that even the boss looks good. But to win, McKinnon desperately required Bolger's imprimatur, especially as the 1987 Caucus intake had ushered in a new breed of MPs in Jenny Shipley, Murray McCully, John Luxton and Maurice Williamson who adhered to strong free enterprise principles. Ruth Richardson was their ideologue.

I was not averse to a Richardson win myself. This was a purely personal wish based on our past working relationship and my gratitude for her initial support in Hawke's Bay. In addition, a male/female pairing of Bolger/Richardson had an obvious political synergy — the balance of gender, geography, tertiary education, oratorical ability, youth and even intellect all being provided by the Selwyn MP.

Richardson lost. Just. After the Caucus vote I went to her office to offer my sympathies and any clichéd sporting analogies that strayed close. For my pains I was dished the most telling of rebukes.

'I don't want your sympathy, I wanted your vote,' Ruth snapped in an obvious reference to my failure to win Hawke's Bay. I beat a hasty retreat.

Such misdirected anger signified a real problem for Bolger and he knew it, for Richardson's unrequited ambitions were now amplified by her awareness of his direct intervention in the contest. It was the cold fury of a bird of prey after you have just robbed the nest of its eggs — you could sense the winged revenge long before you heard the final shriek.

Bolger's bold reply to this slow fuse was to appoint Richardson his finance spokesperson, thus providing her with sufficient mana to appease the strained ego while also providing sufficient reason for her Caucus supporters to be bound to the common cause. At first glance it seemed a very clever stratagem.

At first glance. Especially when Eaddy and other Bolger staffers began privately suggesting that Richardson would have no automatic entry to the Finance Minister's job should National win the next general election. Wayne Eagleson was commanded to start researching the role of the Australian Treasurer, thus providing the clear impression that even if Richardson was to be made Minister of Finance it would be a ranking on the Cabinet totem junior to Bolger's chief political aide Bill Birch, the suggested Treasurer-designate.

But like most clever stratagems conceived in haste, Bolger's second prize of the finance portfolio had its subterranean perils. For a start he underestimated both Richardson's personal distaste for him and her knowledge of the proposed Treasurer ruse. Thus she began to shore up her defences by taking newer MPs into her confidence and winning powerful business allies to the National Party cause. They soon made it clear, to both Caucus and the party organisation, that their political and financial support was dependent upon Richardson's post-election elevation to the senior finance role in any National administration. Birch was clearly regarded as suspect given his former role as a Muldoon handmaiden and the depressing proof that his Think Big phase of chameleon political development had a multi-billion-dollar debt tag.

Little by little, meeting by meeting, Richardson pinned Bolger into delivering first private and then public assurances as to her post-election portfolio. In return, the private sector matched its entreaties with cold, hard cash. Strongly pro-market businesses provided direct funding to the National Party to allow Richardson access to 'independent' commercial and economic advice. This included the appointment of tinder-dry National Bank economist Martin Hames as Richardson's full-time policy adviser.

Hames was an unusual character, with his nervous head-rolling and permanent frowning, offset by an unfortunate lisp — it was the image of someone in the midst of electroconvulsive shock therapy. That would certainly have explained his great love of von Hayek, Friedman and the other social Darwinists. Hames' social skills always had a whiff of anthrax about them but despite this (or perhaps because of it) he singularly devoted himself to Richardson with an almost unseemly loyalty that made him the butt of much bratpack humour. Of course, we were just jealous — no one else could quite envisage the amalgam of Cleopatra, Maggie Thatcher and the *Penthouse* Pet of the Month that Martin seemed to see in Ruth. We all marked him as a very strange young man.

If there is one memory of Martin's misshapen devotion to Richardson that will remain permanently imprinted in my mind, it was an incident after the announcement of her resignation after being jettisoned from the finance portfolio in the wake of the 1993 election result. Ruth made her announcement with just the right amount of stern pathos, rose and marched briskly towards the door. Overcome by the emotion of the moment Hames lurched toward her with a presumed kiss of staffer affection — and missed. He was left groping in midair with his lips beating an unanswered tattoo — like an elderly uncle at Christmas who wants to share his festive bonhomie despite having the breath of an oxidation pond.

Hames' work colleague was a Treasury secondment, Iain Rennie, who possessed a slightly greater range of interpersonal skills but gave the impression that something had crawled up his nostrils and died there. It was not until later that I discovered virtually all Treasury employees had this same head-lifting, sneering arrogance and, presumably, the same wasteland of a social life. We bratpackers would ruminate over a Bellamy's beer that perhaps the best way to put a human face on these fiscal Jesuits was to get them all laid one night — this would be a unique pleasure for most of them, we were sure.

Not all of Richardson's supporters were mollified by her appointment to the finance portfolio. In an extraordinary and rather courageous outburst, Simon Upton angrily denounced Bolger's meddling to his face with such vehemence that the echoes could be heard throughout the Leader's suite and most of the adjacent corridors. This exchange may have produced smirking entertainment for all those within earshot (half of Wellington I suspect) but it also provided a clear sign that there would be no burying of the hatchet — except in someone else's scone.

The ironic upshot of this verbal stoush was that Upton refused to accept the now vacant education portfolio — miffed at both Bolger's alleged treachery and that Richardson had already blazed the true and righteous path in this policy sector. Bolger now had to find another spokesperson — and fast. As Eaddy recounted to me, the Leader looked down his Caucus list, saw that the inexperienced and ponderous Lockwood Smith had a doctorate, and promptly decided that a PhD in the sex lives of pigs was just the kind of prerequisite necessary for an education spokesman. Taupo MP and former primary school headmaster Roger McClay was singularly unimpressed — an attitude that he retained and often displayed through the next two terms as Lockwood's associate. You got the feeling that the jovial McClay was just marking time until Jim worked out what a dreadful mistake he had made.

Fortunately, National's post-election internal friction was dwarfed and then overwhelmed by the civil war that had broken out in Labour's ranks in the wake of the sharemarket collapse of 'black October'.

In the blink of an eye the middle class lost faith in both the Labour government and the high priests of the commercial world — a process hastened further by a string of spectacular business failures and Prime Minister Lange's vain and rather public attempt to rediscover a social conscience on the various racetracks of New Zealand. Having realised that the Treasury juggernaut possessed no brakes the Prime Minister began to exhibit an almost Freudian fondness for racing ever faster cars and crashing them into concrete barriers.

It became the conventional wisdom in Opposition quarters that Labour was finished, that it could not survive the twin body blows of a rapidly declining economy and internecine insurrection. The more important issue now was the shape National's Caucus and policy would be in when it assumed the Treasury benches. That speculation included the leadership of the party — a process far from settled by McKinnon's elevation.

National's party organisation was having its own problems. The financial members were dying of old age, which made renewal canvassing all the more difficult — no party canvasser likes to loiter around rest-homes. The days of mass membership parties were coming to an end, squeezed by both the range of alternative entertainments and the supposed irrelevance of the political process to younger generations. In addition, activist party members were being urged to work harder to take up this slack — the kind of exhortation that demands a pressing engagement elsewhere.

Even the Young Nationals had changed their alcohol-fuelled, sex-crazed characteristics of yesteryear. Now their membership seemed to be entirely composed of dwindling and isolated pockets of nerdy munchkins who perpetually dressed in collar and tie and complained that the senior Nats were way too liberal for them. Never have I seen a group of people in more desperate need of a blow job.

Meanwhile secretary-general Max Bradford was desperately trying to modernise the party's administration and update the antiquated technology in the wake of the 1987 defeat. Labour's relative sophistication, with their up-to-the-minute professional polling, personalised mail, interest-group targeting, computer literacy and direct policy communication, had blitzed National during the campaign. Bradford accepted these lessons and determined not to be outmanoeuvred again. Max was a well-paid professional administrator trying to introduce order to an organisation of well-meaning voluntary amateurs — it was all destined to end in tears, and it did. Within a year the voluble personality of president Neville Young and the edgy psyche of Bradford had reached the stage where someone had to go. It would be Bradford — to a plumb party nomination for the Tarawera seat. Poor old Neville Young won the battle to lose the war — unseated later in the year by his Auckland challenger, John Collinge. There was a double whammy to this loss as Collinge was later appointed High Commissioner to London and there proceeded to delight the tabloid press by demonstrating novel ways in which to rearrange the dining room furniture.

A similar paralysis was accompanying the policy-making process within Caucus. Richardson had reached the conclusion that the only problem with Douglas' monetarist revolution was that it had not gone far enough — the body-count was way too low for any self-respecting revolutionary. Ruth was determined to stamp out such namby-pamby wimpishness, and the complete deregulation of the labour market was provided as a classic illustration of where Labour had failed and where an incoming National government would take no prisoners.

The artful pragmatist Birch was determined not to frighten the horses without good reason. It became my responsibility to arrange various seminars, policy meetings and sector group discussions to indicate an evenhanded reform of the labour markets. Explicit deregulation and the move to an individual-contract-based industrial relations system were policy tenets vigorously advocated by many large industrial concerns — Alan Jones from Fletcher Challenge and Roger Kerr from the Business Roundtable being particularly prominent. But Birch's stated aim was to get through the 1990 election with as little fuss as possible, which involved pacifying large union groups as well. All the necessary noises were made — awards structures could stay if that was the workers' choice, there would be no end to penal or overtime rates, additional resources would be provided for the overworked mediation services — even the concept of worker shareholding in companies and worker representation on company boards was promoted. I often travelled with Birch during this period and drafted many of his speeches and press releases, the key theme being moderation.

The Employment Contracts Bill, introduced into Parliament within the first few weeks of the new National Government in December 1990, would bear no resemblance to those discussions or public promises. The horses had now become irrelevant — they were to be herded off to the abattoir and reconstituted into Jellimeat.

WORKING WITH WINSTON

Bolger's reshuffling of Caucus responsibilities had its attendant consequences for the unit, and eager researchers crowded around Lindsay Scott's desk to discover who their new masters were, greeting the news with smiles or groans. In my case it was a grimace. Winston Peters had been allocated the key employment portfolio, which was my secondary research responsibility after industrial relations, and would obviously be a central political pivot for the next three years. Within minutes of the public announcement Peters telephoned and asked to see me in his ground-floor office.

I remember walking into a dense blue haze and wondering if the sofa cushions were on fire. Instead I had just been introduced to the omnipresent calling card of my new boss. Winston did not just smoke

— his lungs smouldered like an underground peat blaze. These attempts at self-immolation were offset by his appearance — a relatively short man, with a dapper dress sense that always appreciated the fine line between fad and fashion. He had just taken to wearing his trademark double-breasted, navy pinstripe suits, but lightened their sombreness with a range of brilliant neckties that would alternate from red to gold to emerald green — a legacy of his wife, Louise, and her new cottage industry.

This day Peters was in a thoughtful mood. He wanted a short oral briefing on the employment portfolio, the key issues, the trends, and the possible policy options, to which he sat back and listened without question. After I had finished a relatively lengthy exposition he leaned forward, elbows propped on the desk, his eyes on the cigarette rolling through his fingers.

'Laws — I'll do you a deal.'

The last person to utter such words to me had been my friendly neighbourhood dope peddler in Napier. I should have seen the warning in that precedent.

'You look after me and I'll look after you. You find the issues — and I'll put them on the front page.'

And then with added spice, and perhaps already realising the political ambition that lay within me, 'And where I go, I'll take you with me.'

This was an extraordinary, if premature, offer of political partnership. However, Peters was no mug. No matter how brilliant any of my research or how insightful the policy prescriptions, Winston would automatically take the lion's share of the media attention and hence the public reward. In addition Winston was an early believer in the American principle of political management — surround yourself with smart advisers, distil their best advice, then pray to the heavens you choose the right option. Sadly, Peters had no galaxy of intellectual luminaries — he just had me.

Within weeks Maori affairs had been added to my research tasks to further align my efforts to Peters' portfolio responsibilities. The one great lesson I learned very early here was that when discussing Maori politics it is critical to realise that there is no such thing as 'Maoridom' — rather a shifting pattern of intertribal rivalries and loyalties that owe as much to historical grievance as they do to contemporary personalities. That and the incessant hierarchical garbage that masquerades as 'mana'.

Ambition

At about this time Jim Bolger let it be known that
for a press secretary to replace the retiring Michel'
suggestion of Eaddy and Eagleson I tendered my sp
and was surprised to find myself on a short list of two despi
no previous media or publicity experience — something o
commentary on the paucity of interested talent.

I soon discovered that my job interview with the Leader was merely
an excuse to probe my personal concepts on image-building and their
relationship to the world of politics — a topic that had often been
canvassed within the bratpack. Eaddy and Eagleson had sympathy
for my breakfast theorem of political management, and this job
interview was an excuse for their boss to listen to it.

In short, I put to Bolger, he was Weetbix competing against the
toasted muesli of David Lange, the Rice Bubbles of Jim Anderton
and the Coco Pops of Roger Douglas. Weetbix might be good for you
but it has been around for a long time and toasted muesli tastes better,
has novelty value and shamelessly advertises its dietary fibre. The
key, I argued, was not to change the basic Weetbix formula but to add
dried apricots and then package the revamped product in a racy new
technicolour box.

A couple of hours later Eaddy popped around to the research unit
to inform me that middle-aged Canadian broadcaster Hazel Whiteoak
had been appointed Bolger's chief press secretary '…but he liked your
idea about the Weetbix. He said that Richardson would be the All
Bran.'

Bolger may have heard my exposition but he had not listened.
Within weeks there were widespread moans within the Leader's office
that their new press secretary lacked marketing skills and was not
'selling the message' effectively to the Gallery hacks. Meanwhile I
was putting my breakfast theorem into action. Winston Peters was
not just toasted muesli — his physical gifts and mannerisms suggested
a new taste sensation.

Enough cereal imagery. Yet the concept of politicians as competing
breakfast brands appealed to me as a self-evident truth. No matter
how intelligent, genuine, able or warm the individual, a politician
had to be properly packaged, marketed and promoted to be effective.
Only in that way could the policy ideas and principles attached to
the individual be properly delivered.

The theme of my first few weeks with Winston was to relegate the
message to secondary importance. I would market the messenger first

- the rest would follow. Which was just as well because Winston did not possess one solitary creative thought on the employment portfolio and only a scattered understanding of Maori issues at best. He had, instinctively, opposed the amendment to the Treaty of Waitangi Tribunal Act allowing Maori claims prior to 1984, supported Muldoon in opposition to the Bastion Point settlement, and privately regarded the Treaty itself as a chimera that distracted Maori from focusing on more immediate concerns. One detected an unease within Winston over all things Maori. Others within Parliament were less charitable, suggesting that he was embarrassed by his Maori background and had attempted to pass himself off as a swarthy Italian in his university days. This discomfort was exemplified by his inability to speak the language and thus feel relaxed on the marae. Early gibes from Maori critics at these relative cultural inadequacies wounded him deeply and there were sporadic attempts to remedy these deficiencies through language tapes and even private lessons.

Such efforts were, at best, half-hearted. Peters was too much of a social animal to graft away for hours without immediate reward and could easily be dragged away for a whisky, a wine, a meal and a chat — usually all four. Often he would simply vanish and could not be found in any of his favourite haunts. This could induce intense personal frustration, particularly if one of our stories was developing or the media were seeking his comment on a breaking issue.

Very early on in our relationship, and before the widespread and lamentable advent of the yuppie phone or pager, I made a cheeky bid to bridge these periods of Peters-imposed isolation. I began to manufacture press releases in Winston's name and then distribute them to whichever frustrated media outlet required satisfaction, refusing any follow-up interview with the excuse that Winston was 'tied up in a very important meeting and cannot be interrupted'.

Far from being upset at such initiative, Peters loved the idea and would later complain if I had failed to reply to a criticism or missed a particular opportunity. Often he would telephone me in the research unit and laugh that he had just listened to himself on 'Morning Report', '…and Laws, I was brilliant!' Our partnership autopilot was working.

Within weeks we had established a very close rapport that involved a large element of trust on Peters' part and vast acres of research analysis on mine. But Peters well appreciated the character weaknesses of his researcher — each time he allowed me to use my initiative he bound the invisible cords of personal loyalty ever tighter. My psyche worked on positive reinforcement — it was the only external stimulus that could influence me — and Peters was the first and only political master to understand this craven and pathetic need within me. I might have been faintly aware of Peters' weaknesses — he was fully attuned to mine. His offer of political partnership had now strayed into Deadly Sin territory and I had a nagging image of Mephistopheles and Faustus, with an even nastier feeling that the climax would remain true to Marlowe's moral fable. Faustus never did get to bonk Helen of Troy.

DIVINING A PATH

One insight that I could bring to Peters was the recent experience of a losing election campaign in a marginal seat and the painful lessons learned therein. It is my firm conviction that MPs and candidates in marginal seats have a rarefied understanding of public mood because their very survival is dependent on adjusting to it. In contrast, safe-seat MPs turn off their guidance systems in the secure knowledge that it has no relevance anyway — which goes some way to explaining why Cabinet ministers impose policies so out of touch with practical human experience.

Similarly, I had come to believe that the Hawke's Bay electorate was a social microcosm of the rest of the country, for the reasons already explained, and that what worked in the Bay would work elsewhere. What failed in the Bay would similarly belly-flop every-where else too. Along with my cereal approach to political promotion, the Hawke's Bay experience proved invaluable in detecting the twisting skeins that began to metamorphose in the body politic. By a curious coincidence the issues of unemployment and race relations had started to surface during my candidacy.

Through trial and error, usually the latter, I had also absorbed the art of the press statement and thus chanced upon the general inadequacies and indolence of the news media. Reporters preferred not to think — they were not paid enough to rush their synapses on a daily basis and the tyranny of the deadline sabotaged any latent enthusiasm to do so. All they wanted was the same tasty bite-size chunks of information demanded by breakfast consumers. Rather than lecture and hector these same journalists for their appalling lack of investigative ability or analysis, I worked on the Barnum and Bailey theory of gratification — best give them what they want. In practice that meant a press statement edited for spicy sensation, the 'hook' line in the first sentence, a careful summation of any supporting documentation and just the right balance of titillation and titivation. In essence, a Winston Peters press release became the political equivalent of a chesty page-three model, complete with gleaming smile, flowing locks and extremely large tits.

In addition, my failed candidature had made me acutely aware of the political potential lurking within the Official Information Act. I had learned, for example, that not all government departments had standardised processes for dealing with requests under the Act, and that many were answered without reference to the relevant minister or even departmental head. As a consequence, it was entirely possible that a simple request could elicit politically sensitive information completely unbeknown to the government of the day.

Better still, these official papers would often suffer the most amateur of censorship, with large felt pens used to cross out any paragraphs that might legitimately be excised under the various provisos of the Act. It was then a simple case of holding the page up to the light and reading the censored paragraphs in the reverse. These sections might be thoroughly innocuous but the very fact that departmental discretion had been exercised always made for a good yarn.

Another flaw in the system was that papers were provided under request without any notification that the Official Information Act had generated their disclosure. This opened up vast acres of media intrigue because it was then possible to give the impression that the document had been leaked — a suggestion that would excite press hacks in the same way that catnip suspends feline judgement. Numerous members of the Press Gallery would fall for this ruse time after time. Pavlov's dogs were smarter.

Of course, I had also learned that most journalists hate wading through pages and pages of official reports and that these also needed to be summarised, enumerated, highlighted and otherwise served up in the same bite-size chunks as the original release. I came to one unalterable conclusion — reporters were lazy. If I was to achieve good media coverage for Winston I would need to do more than just basic research — I would need to package the information, summarise it, distil any controversy, and then 'sell' the story in person to the Gallery.

Though I didn't know this at the time, this nursery technique is known as 'spinning' and has developed into a va-va-voom industry in the States. This dark art now infects all Western parliamentary democracies and is practised by press secretaries, party strategists, lobby groups, the public relations industry (which is mostly composed of ex-hacks anyway) and even sections of the media themselves.

My spinning role for Winston was unique within the Opposition of the late eighties. There was no daily Opposition attempt to link with the all-important electronic media staff nor those younger print reporters who made up the bulk of the Press Gallery. Only later, when ex-*Listener* editor David Beatson arrived, would there be the first preliminary attempts at a positive marketing strategy from the Leader's office.

The Labour Party had no such deficiencies. They had observed this American corruption at first hand and adapted the general principles to their party's advantage. Ross Vintiner led the Prime Minister's press staff and Bevan Burgess spun on behalf of his revolutionary Finance Minister Roger Douglas — it was a wholly unequal contest.

What savage irony then that these two teams should later find their greatest competition coming from each other. As the 1988 New Year dawned with Prime Minister Lange scuttling Roger Douglas' flat tax scheme, their good-natured rivalry descended into a death struggle. It was absolutely bizarre watching first Burgess and then one of Lange's press team trail around the Gallery, each scorning the other's political master, then shoring up their boss's public position with gossipy titbits and the occasional leaked document.

So I can take little credit in retrospect. Labour's press handlers were savaging each other — National had none. That left a pretty vacant field in which yours truly could manage, shape and generally extol the image of his new partner.

By now I had come to the conclusion that newspapers and magazines were grossly overrated as a communicative force and that the key would be to get Winston on television as often as possible. Radio was good but a very distant second choice. If a story led the television news bulletins then morning metropolitan dailies had no option but to follow, and provincial dailies trailed their big city cousins like pilot fish.

We developed a simple political mantra — 'If it's not on TV then it didn't happen' — and even set twice-a-week targets, based on the age-old principle that out-of-sight was out-of-sympathy. The public came to enjoy watching Winston with their dinner, and Winston came to enjoy entertaining them. A good day could be measured by a crisp 30 seconds on the tube — what happened in the debating chamber became irrelevant. While the Opposition 'strategists' prepared their dreadfully earnest questions of the day and twittered between themselves over the speaking order for the next mind-numbing array of parliamentary debates, Winston was playing to the medium of the moment.

Of course the thing about television is that the medium is both invasive and pervasive. Watching the six o'clock news bulletin removes the self-filtering process that one brings to reading a newspaper or skimming a magazine. The reader chooses what print articles to read — the viewer has no such ability.

Once the viewer had made the decision to watch the televised events of a particular day they were at the mercy of the news programmer. That willing suspension of individual judgement was our greatest political ally.

This information monopoly was further exaggerated by the overwhelming dominance of TVNZ's evening news bulletin on Channel One. I kept a careful eye on the weekly television ratings to work out the best days of the week for viewership, which is why Winston rarely launched any initiative on a Friday or Saturday. Those evenings rated by far the lowest — Sundays and Mondays produced boom audiences by comparison.

Similarly, the advent of TV3 was ignored. The new channel was a bad joke — Equiticorp with pictures — and its news ratings were inconsequential. Interestingly the same imbalance applies to this day. No, it had to be Television One News at six or the 'Holmes' magazine follow-up at six thirty — that was our target, that was our audience. We became a sort of political butcher's shop. TVNZ's young Gallery tyro, Chris Ryan, would pop in during the morning and ask, 'What have you got for me today?' and we might almost reply, 'Ooh, ahh, Mr Ryan — a nice tenderloin of an employment scandal would be right proper for your tea tonight.'

Radio news was a useful second prize but only if the audience was achieved during the popular breakfast sessions; again, it was the State-funded Radio New Zealand network that assumed paramountcy because of its national coverage and the depth of its news team.

The conventional parliamentary wisdom was that there existed a strict hierarchy of Gallery talent, mostly based on seniority, that should be kept sweet at all costs. Winston already had well-established drinking, partying and card-playing links to many of these blokes in the Gallery — IRN's Barry Soper, TVNZ and then TV3 political reporter Bill Ralston, RNZ's political editor, Richard Griffin. He had his dislikes too — TVNZ's political editor, Richard Harman, had obviously crossed swords with him at some point and seemed to hover in a Winstonian purgatory. But it was my view that most of the above were so senior that they were being courted by all sides with roughly equal enthusiasm. About that time National Radio had a political commentary session on a Friday morning and it was a well-rehearsed Opposition ploy to phone Richard Griffin either early that morning or the night before and digress on the important issues from National's perspective. Sure enough, Griffin would repeat these concepts as if they were his own so I assumed he had a possible partiality towards the Opposition. What I failed to realise was that he was just lazy.

It was a bold call but I decided that it would be more profitable to bypass the more senior Gallery hacks in favour of the younger, less experienced, ambitious types who possessed an equivalent desire to produce scoops for their employers. Better still their relative youth might induce them to pursue the story on their own initiative — thus giving further legs to any Peters initiative. Winston was sceptical that favouring youth and inexperience in the press corps would work but happy to experiment.

It was thus my responsibility to get to know the more junior members of the Press Gallery and sell them first Winston and second his message. Virtually every media hit over the next two years came from those contacts. They were as hungry and silly as me — we understood each other perfectly.

Of course, politics is not just about contacts. It is all about maximising opportunity. And in terms of this country's political and social development Winston Peters just happened to be the right person in the right place at the right time. Thankfully, we both had enough acumen to appreciate this fortunate juxtaposition of the stars. Fate was on our side — only later would egocentricity crowd out this good fortune.

I had deciphered a few of the subterranean shifts in the public mood during my political exile to Hawke's Bay — an uneasiness about the Treaty of Waitangi and Maori activists; a more nagging insecurity about one's own job, personal safety, the reliability of certain professions and public institutions. The rapidity of economic and social change had created casualties, sure, but it was more than that. It was a feeling that you might just be next. Similarly, public respect for politicians and the political process had plumbed ever murkier depths, with a similar lack of respect now staining the professions and commercial community as accountants, lawyers and bankers proved themselves anything but prudent and anything but reliable. The sharemarket collapse had been like a confidence dam bursting.

And yet there was no party, no individual, not even any profiled lobby group that articulated these feelings of dislocation, of unease, of insecurity. Such anxieties had strayed well beyond the traditional poor — they were now fiercely nipping at the heels of the middle class.

As both the Opposition's employment and Maori affairs spokesman Winston had been gifted the two key political issues of the late 1980s — burgeoning unemployment, with its insidious antisocial effects, and race relations. Winston had the profile, the portfolios and the presentation skills to offer both an alternative vision and a set of policies to embrace this new reality. Ironically we were both well equipped to gauge the public mood. As relative loners and outsiders our psychological antennae empathised immediately with this growing public perception that they too were being squeezed to the margins and ignored. If misery loves company then Winston could offer the best piss-up in town.

FIRST STRIKES

The first two issues that heralded a revitalised and refocused Winston Peters followed personal dabblings during my abortive Hawke's Bay campaign — the Department of Labour's ACCESS training scheme and the Department of Maori Affairs' MANA and MACCESS programmes. All three proved absolute shockers in terms of quality, accountability and end results.

ACCESS delivered three- to six-month training schemes for unemployed people who lacked the ability or inclination for a tertiary education. In other words, people with a fine sense of discretion. They were contracted to a diverse range of private training providers, most of whom were unable to gain employment in any of these same tertiary institutions, so as to learn new skills that might equip them for 'productive employment'. There was obviously unproductive employment but no one was too keen to sponsor a course for prospective local-body politicians. The basic problem would have been obvious to anyone except the pea-brained bureaucrats who dreamed up this idea: those lacking skills or qualifications needed a damned sight longer than thirteen weeks to become social workers, New Age therapists or Amway salespeople — the only jobs available for the new millennium.

The real jobs created were for those who set themselves up as training providers — scarcely more able than their prospective clients but possessing a rudimentary business cunning and an instinctive appreciation that an ACCESS contract was more lucrative than a welfare cheque. The really smart providers established Life Skills courses, realising that no formal education or qualification was required to teach their clients about Life, the Universe and Everything. Thus there could be no embarrassing moments if the Labour Department auditors ever caught up with them.

The accountability for over $100 million of taxpayer funds worked on a simple climate of trust. Departmental officers trusted that the money was well spent with the touching faith of a Lourdes devotee. Attempts at local discipline could produce the most unpleasant of interactions — the local Hawke's Bay committee chairman received a number of abusive late-night telephone calls and even a death threat from a now prominent member of the strictly accountable Association of Consumers and Taxpayers (ACT) after his shonky module was declined. It mattered not. The recalcitrant stumped off to the Maori version of ACCESS — cleverly titled MACCESS — and got his contract anyway.

To this day I am convinced that both ACCESS and its indigenous cousin were a clever Treasury plot. These training schemes cost much less than the community employment PEP work programmes introduced by Muldoon's administration, and by shunting them off to private agencies the State could even eschew day-to-day responsibility. Masterful. It was mean and cheap — but clever. Treasury all over, really. No wonder they employed the same techniques for the health reforms.

By mixing the various official information requests with parliamentary questions and a few judicious off-the-record conversations with disgruntled Labour Department staff, we discovered that fewer than one in five ACCESS trainees actually ended up with a job. I then compared these statistics with the job prospects of an individual registered as jobless with the Department of Labour but not in receipt of ACCESS training.

Surprise, surprise. The comparison suggested that an average unemployed person had a better chance of getting a job by *not* going on an ACCESS scheme. The research completed, the results summarised and the media readied, Winston was then unleashed. Fortunately he appeared to be better briefed than his counterpart, Employment Minister Phil Goff, and easily generated the necessary heat for Press Gallery attention.

This was the kind of department that every MP wants to be against — a fat, bloated Spanish treasure ship lurching its way to nowhere. Winston was the British privateer swinging his cutlass and watching the bodies fall. He loved it — you could see the Errol Flynn exhilaration in his eyes and as each ministerial defence was trotted out another raft of leaked reports and accusations would return a fresh, withering salvo.

For all my research and analysis it still required an effective presenter to sell these mini-scandals to the public with the same successful sincerity that sells Natural Glow. Winston pioneered advertorial television — each measured appearance generated the kind of political sales that the maker of the Ab-Shaper would kill for. He possessed a simply stunning natural talent as a television communicator — New Zealand's first retail politician.

Peters approached the camera in the same way that his Maori ancestors might have regarded early pioneer photographers — as if it was about to steal his soul. He therefore perfected a unique method of preparing himself — a ritual that included going to the mirror, repeatedly combing his hair, straightening his tie, checking his front teeth, pulling down his jacket (an affectation later adopted by the entire *Star Trek Generations* crew) and then fretting about the most trivial item on his desk. This ritual was always exact and it was always the same. And then no matter what his previous mood — happy, tired, angry or just plain diffident — Winston flicked himself on; his eyes would deepen, the tone of his voice would drop an octave, and a dark, double-breasted statesman would miraculously appear, oozing respectability from every pore.

Winston understood the demands and delusions of television brilliantly. He had instinctively created a new persona, a self-image that displayed sincerity, acumen, gravitas — all the things that politicians lack. In that regard he was entirely different from other MPs, who thought that a sincere television demeanour was best achieved by speaking in a polite manner and grinning like an idiot at the interviewer. Not Winston. He knew that a 23-inch screen demanded more, that his performance would be judged against those of the preceding soap stars and later dramatic actors — and he was determined to lose nothing by comparison. Mind you, up against *The Young Doctors* maybe it was not such an effort.

The MANA and MACCESS investigations were proving no less fruitful. In some ways they were even more startling, because the subjects grazed like Wild West buffalos on the prairie plainly unaware of human existence and the Sharp rifle. You could shoot one beast without alerting the others and Winston's barrel ran hot.

Like all roads to Hell the MANA programme was paved with good intentions. The spirit of the Maori cultural and language renaissance of the early eighties was not matched by a corresponding lift in Maori education or employment. Far from it. As State behemoths like NZ Rail, the Post Office and the various departments of Works, Lands and Forests were first corporatised and then dismembered, it was the Maori labourer who was the first in the gun. Similarly, as the agrarian sector went through its alarming slump and stock numbers dramatically declined, it was the Maori freezing worker who was made redundant. Maori jobless rates soared in much greater proportions than the national average.

To replace such manual work, the Labour Government offered a Maori business scheme, MANA, which offered low-interest or no-interest seeding grants, MACCESS training schemes, or the dole. Treasury later convinced an incoming National Government to replace these three options with just the one — a welfare cheque. Their logic remains chilling. It was (fiscally) cheaper to write these people off with a weekly dole payment than create complicated and integrated education/training/community work programmes. Forget the woeful social consequences — Treasury were only ever interested in looking at the yearly balance sheet.

Unwittingly both Winston and I ended up doing Treasury's job. By destroying the public credibility of both MANA and MACCESS we gave the policy bureaucrats every reason they ever needed to chop such schemes. And, similarly unwittingly, both Koro Wetere and his department seemed hellbent on giving us as much ammunition as we would ever need. No wonder Roger Douglas had such a soft spot for his Maori affairs colleague.

Now any sensible bureaucrat would have learned their lesson after the first few embarrassments. Not chief executive Tamati Reedy, not the Department of Maori Affairs. In the end I surmised that we were dealing with someone who was either braindead or was being ruthlessly set up by his underlings. I never did figure out which.

The Press Gallery came to love our new sport and we ensured that they always had ringside seats and a complimentary glass of bubbly for each confrontation. It was the kind of choreographed cruelty so beloved of the Spanish bullfighting fraternity, Winston assuming both the protagonists' roles — first the prodding picador, then the haughty caped matador delivering the coup de grâce to the confused and clumsy beast. Meanwhile I had the dual roles of valet swordbearer and orange-seller during the intermission.

There were some classic skewers. One involved taxpayer funds going to a non-existent MACCESS committee in the Manawatu area. The committee had been appointed by the minister all right but had never met, never been allocated any government funds and never made any decisions with regard to local Maori training providers. Despite that a particular Palmerston North provider associated with Professor Ngatata Love had been granted over a million dollars worth of projects and was just starting on its second million. So who granted the approvals, we asked?

Incredibly both Wetere and Reedy asserted that every project in the Manawatu area had been analysed, approved and funded by this same totally inactive MACCESS committee. We knew that to be untrue — their entire membership were sitting in Winston's room pouring out their hearts about decisions being made in their name without their consent.

The trap was then laid. Could the minister tell us on which dates this MACCESS committee met to approve these training projects? About that stage — and way too late — the danger signals started ringing, with Winston and the media feasting themselves on yet more startling evidence of ministerial and departmental incompetence, or worse — a total lack of accountability in the handling of public monies.

There were renewed calls for resignations. One Sunday newspaper splashed 'Tut tut, Tamati' across its front page banner and accused the chief executive of directly misleading Parliament. Incredibly, Reedy kept his job. We were later informed that the Prime Minister's department began to take a vivid interest in all press releases emanating from the minister's office after this episode, causing the Lange/Wetere relationship to sour further.

For all our petty trip-ups and triumphs, so lovingly recorded by a

Press Gallery eager for the same petty sensations, it was becoming obvious to both Winston and me that an ingrained racism pervaded the country's public service. Both the government and the State Services Commission had suspended normal judgement when it came to things Maori, second best being not only acceptable but all that could be expected. Maori programmes were obviously regarded as kids' stuff and the usual rules of accountability could not be applied. In private, then in more measured public response, Winston railed at the double standards as an insult to both the taxpayer and Maoridom.

Another blatant MACCESS rip-off rammed this double standard home. It concerned a fledgling strawberry farm near Hastings and a trainee Pakeha housewife supposedly enrolled to learn pre-apprenticeship building skills. The trainee had spent most of her module picking strawberries for the training provider — a Mr Wi Huata — the husband of former Maori radical and now ACT MP Donna Awatere. It transpired that the Huatas had been provided with an inexpensive and government-subsidised labour force under the guise of the MACCESS training scheme, which, I am sure, was the kind of commercial fillip that every fledgling market gardener must dream about. Winston's *Colombo*-type ambush of Dr Reedy on this issue tore away the remaining vestiges of professional reputation within the department.

The strawberry farm affair was pure theatre, played out during the annual round of Maori Affairs Estimates. The Gallery had been alerted to the prospect of 'further damaging revelations', which was their equivalent of being promised live sex. Winston had begun his questioning with a series of accusations about the lamentable state of all the various programmes administered by the department, accusing Reedy of presiding over a realm of self-defeating, shonky and nepotistic schemes that advanced Maoridom not one inch. Reedy's denials were dutifully placed on the record.

Peters tabled the affidavit of the Hastings strawberry trainee, claiming that she had been used as cheap labour on a MACCESS scheme. Reedy took on the requisite air of concern — yes, he would investigate this; that kind of thing should not be tolerated, Mr Peters — rapidly disassociating himself and his department from the shady training provider. Winston egged him on.

'So you don't know of this MACCESS project, Mr Reedy?'

'No, no. Never heard of it.' Reedy shook his head emphatically.

Peters leaned across the committee table. 'And I suppose you don't know anything about this strawberry farm either then, Mr Reedy?'

'Absolutely not. Never heard of it.' And he crossed his arms with an air of finality.

At which point Peters pushed a newspaper clipping across the committee table and down toward the Secretary.

'Then perhaps you could explain this...'

The television cameras zoomed in on the clipping, Reedy's gathering motion, then panned to the poor man's face. The clipping was a large photograph published in the Hastings *Herald-Tribune* two months previously, recording the official opening of a Maori horticultural initiative — a photograph that contained three individuals: the proprietor, Wi Huata, his wife, Donna Awatere, and a third man in their midst greedily devouring a large, ripe, succulent strawberry. Tamati Reedy.

Reedy's face dissolved as if immersed in hydrochloric acid. Peters leaned back in triumph; the rest of the committee's Maori MPs smirked in approval. The attendant press hacks openly laughed in appreciation as they dashed for the door to file the story of this latest gross denouement.

Despite all the proven inefficiency, incompetence and incommodious behaviour of both the minister and his department, Winston struggled to gain any respect within either his Caucus or the House for his crusade on accountability. MPs on both sides of the House continued to shrug their shoulders with the same 'So what? It's Maori' attitude, with Peters' political victories seen as substandard because the target was so easy. One MP observed to me, 'It's easy to score tries against Buller. What would Winston be like against Canterbury?'

Winston boiled over this lack of Caucus recognition and in one late-night chain-smoking frenzy poured out his frustrations. For all his endeavours, his steady rise in the popularity polls, his standing within the wider party, his repeated embarrassment of the government, Peters could gain no respect from his colleagues. This rankled deeply. He had done his job and more but still he was treated as a secondary player in the Opposition's strategems. And then a decision:

'One more Maori affairs scandal, Laws, and then we'll branch out. Make it a good one.'

It was not in my power to conjure wrongdoing or political embarrassment from thin air. By now Winston was indeed spreading his wings beyond mere sensation to the more pressing issues of public pronouncement and policy. My role was evolving at a frightening speed from investigative researcher to speechwriter and policy analyst. I was in a bind — there were no more titbits or titillations in my files. But then a lucky break.

An internal review of the Department of Maori Affairs housing portfolio in Auckland had been dropped off at Winston's office by one of his many departmental snouts. It told the depressing but familiar tale of mismanagement, inappropriate expenditure, inadequate controls and the general running down of the department's multi-million-dollar housing stock. In itself it was a one-story wonder, yet more confirmation of the department's wanton management of public monies.

I convinced Winston to hold off breaking this story because a whisper had found its way to me that if any government department received an Official Information Act request signed by either Winston or me it was to be referred to deputy Prime Minister Geoffrey Palmer's office. This office was to oversee the response and excise any material that might prove damaging if publicly released with the usual Winstonian twist. I wanted to test the veracity of this rumour so I placed an official request for this same Maori Affairs housing audit under the Act.

Within days Wetere's office had answered our request, thus proving the rumour to be wrong — at least in Koro's case. But the housing report delivered to us had been so heavily excised that only the occasional word had survived a whirlwind of dark ink; whole pages were literally blacked out, others were missing in their entirety.

At that point we called in our favoured TVNZ co-conspirator, Chris Ryan, and provided him with both the doctored report and the uncensored, clean original. A good story about hundreds of millions of dollars' worth of housing stock in decline had just become a great story about government censorship. We then kept the issue bubbling along by making grand and official complaints to both the Chief Ombudsman and the Auditor-General over the alleged irregularities and illegalities — all lovingly recorded and televised with Winston in his best righteous indignation mode and Wetere refusing comment.

The Auckland housing cover-up and the Hastings strawberry affair were Winston's last dabblings in the miasma of the Maori Affairs Department — a midden of incompetence proven ad nauseam. But they had recreated the reputation of Winston Peters — no longer an ill-disciplined back-bench cowboy but an avenging Opposition frontbencher who chose his targets and hit them with unerring accuracy. He had also been elevated in the public mind to the Opposition's most effective MP bar none by harrying the Labour government to distraction.

Now, reputation reshaped, it was time for more ambitious projects, for a wider field of activity. There could be no doubting that Peters was a destructive force, but could he also construct and create?

'We need policy, Laws. We need an alternative vision!' Peters would exclaim as he leaned back in his leather chair, yet another cigarette twirling through his fingers. I was unsure if this was the royal 'we' or the partnership 'we', but whatever the interpretation it was clear that policy-making had just been added to my list of duties. I watched all thought of weekend relaxation dim and then softly extinguish — there was only going to be one water carrier in this relationship.

And I would not have had it any other way.

CHAPTER 4

WINSTON

BANGING THE DRUM

Winston and I have always disagreed on one outstanding matter and despite the passage of many years it has become impossible for us to find consensus. He insists that his star had risen to two per cent in the 'preferred Prime Minister' rankings before I came to work for him; with equal certainty I maintain it was one per cent. Whatever — even before I was assigned to be Peters' researcher there were a small number of misguided souls who saw Winston as their political Messiah and suspended rational judgement long enough to publicly assert this choice. This group also claimed alien abductee status and swore they had met Elvis on the mothership.

I had developed a peculiar fascination for public opinion polls during that fateful dabble with failure in Hawke's Bay. Each month TVNZ would telecast their strange amalgam of scientific research and chicken entrails to provide a snapshot of the country's political mood. An immigrant German market researcher by the name of Paul Heylen had obviously worked some kind of contra deal with TVNZ News and claimed naming rights to these fuzzy photographs of the body politic. Like most out-of-focus efforts they were subject to innumerable interpretations and in the hands of a skilful strategist could be used to advance any number of pet hypotheses. Usually, though, the reverse occurred — the results were used to kill ideas (and potential leaders) rather than promote them. Jim McLay was one such victim. 'Mr Three Per Cent' developed a weakling persona courtesy of Heylen and had the mortification of watching this polling image transformed into political reality.

TVNZ did their best to refine such ephemera by treating their viewers as unthinking morons. One of their Gallery staffers explained to me that the evening news was presented on the basis that the average viewer had the intellectual ability of an eleven-year-old child.

Nothing should ever be too complex, too long or too boring — which certainly put Bill Birch at an immediate disadvantage. Given that the average eleven-year-old is being ruthlessly stalked by the messy process of puberty then I cannot say that I was much comforted by this information. On the other hand, it provided Winston with an automatic advantage. His attention span exactly matched that of his audience so they understood each other's needs perfectly. Television and Winston were made for each other.

Of course TVNZ could not trust its viewers with any of the 'real' polling results. Far too indecisive and far too boring. Television needed monthly winners and losers, so they engineered the results to that end and still do. This could produce quite warped results and frequently did. But the reality needed to be made entertaining. The on-air reporter could then excitedly prattle on about National 'jumping three points in this poll' as if forcefully kicked in the scrotum when, in reality, the party remained fixed on the same level of real support as the previous month.

This shorthand deception was achieved by removing the decisively indecisive respondents from the final results and thus inflating popular support for the respective parties. It became my responsibility in the research unit to calculate the 'real' results from the various polling agencies and distribute them to the Opposition members. The differences between 'real' results and those broadcast were often significant — particularly when around 30 per cent of respondents described themselves as unsure.

But this was all a sideshow to my real aim: getting Winston listed in the 'preferred Prime Minister' section with those polling agencies who prompted their respondents with leading choices. There was no real resistance, although one polling company initially refused on the basis that Peters was 'not a serious candidate', an argument that fell rather flat when I pointed out that Gary Knapp and Bruce Beetham were still listed on their prompt sheet.

Winston's steady climb up these informal leadership rankings became the clearest indication yet that our campaign had plugged directly into the consciousness (or unconsciousness) of middle New Zealand. It was more of a void really — the Labour Party was flushing itself down the toilet and Jim Bolger was still struggling to come to grips with a multi-syllabic vocabulary, so Peters' public utterances met no really credible competition.

Our various mini-scandals had attracted enough salacious media coverage to guarantee public awareness, and Peters' physical appearance and television image amplified the attraction. He was good-looking, well groomed, serious — the exact antithesis of David Lange really — and there was a hint of the civilised warrior about his demeanour. The camera loved him, he loved it, and with careful coaching the sound bites rolled off one after the other. no one could bumper-sticker an issue better than Winston — I might have created, borrowed or stolen them but Winston could intone each with a gravitas that seemed to come direct from Mt Sinai.

The marketing and promotional campaign had worked better than I could ever have imagined and quicker than I had dared to hope. The messenger was now a political and public celebrity. Phase One had been completed. It was now time to deliver the message.

THE MESSAGE

There is a wonderful tale of a speech-writer who has carried his political master for many a day and has now finally reached the end of his tether with the egocentric, selfish and patronising conduct of his boss. He is required to write an incredibly important address for the ungrateful miscreant and determines upon revenge. The speech is a stunner — it flows with metaphor, irony and imagery, and the audience are enthralled by the power and poetry of this address until, finally, the politician winds up this spellbinding oration with the climactic promise of how 'I intend to introduce the most innovative and radical policy programme ever devised in this nation's history...' and turns the page.

On the next page, the aide has scribbled, 'Right, you bastard, now you're on your own!'

There would not have been a week when I did not harbour similarly treasonous thoughts. Very early on in the piece Winston automatically assumed that mystical elves and sprites produced press releases, policy papers, speeches and newspaper articles and that they worked at night with but one collective thought, which was to please him. This is not to suggest that Winston would simply click his fingers and policy would magically appear. With few exceptions policy was formulated in brief discussions between us as we agreed on the broad parameters and the general theme to be advanced. It was then my job to fill in the detail, which Winston considered the easy part — like painting by numbers. In contrast I soon discovered that the devil lay in the detail — shoddy research here, an imprecise interpretation there, and suddenly the whole thesis has been publicly ridiculed and voided. I wanted no repeats of the Casey fiasco. My professional credibility was on the line too.

The other problem was that Winston's legendary impatience imposed often suffocating deadlines. After agreeing on a particular concept he would then demand the finished product in a speech to be delivered the next day. And I would stupidly comply — working all night in the research offices and thus messing it up for myself entirely. Do it once and Winston considered it routine. Elves existed after all. But a sleepless Michael was a lesser evil than a wounded Winston.

Our attention turned first to the most pressing issue, rising unemployment, and the construction of appropriate policy responses. Labour's 'structural change' had pillaged traditional industries, and casualties mounted with every passing day. Unskilled jobs were being atomised as freezing works, clothing factories and manufacturing businesses were swept away by the tide of deregulation and tariff reform. The public sector was not immune. No longer was a government job a job for life, as tens of thousands of ex-railway workers, Post Office staff and Works labourers could testify. The traditional security of the public service had evaporated as new profit-driven hybrids took shape — consultancies, short-term contracts, casual labour — and the first in the gun were always those on the lower rungs.

But the clever caught on quick. The redundant tea lady returned as a private caterer and made a killing. Meek and mild middle managers metamorphosed into avaricious consultants with the meter running. And overnight the sense of serving the public became meaner — patients became clients, employees became human stock capital, and the Inland Revenue Department even demanded a stamp on your tax return. The place had gone to the dogs — the dogs of an unrestrained, unprincipled capitalism that worshipped the excesses of the market.

In the traditional rural industries similar shake-outs were occurring, with SMPs removed, mutant inflation rates, interest charges of 20 per cent and more, and declining meat and wool prices. Pastoral farming ceased to be a business, it became an act of religious faith. Well, more of a cult really. As whacko as WACO and the Solar Temple. One half-expected the two-tooths to drag themselves over to the nearest drinking trough and drown themselves. A tsunami-like change rolled over provincial New Zealand and offered just two choices. Lie back and think of England — or just lie back. Labour and its Treasury Iago consciously parked tens of thousands of New Zealanders on the sidelines hoping like hell they might have the gumption to emigrate or, at the very least, keep the noise down.

For some inexplicable reason I felt a particular attraction to the employment portfolio. At first I assumed it to be some kind of harmless infatuation. The monthly Labour Department releases always ended up on my desk 24 hours before the media embargo was lifted — a sort of jobless 'First Copy' — and I would prepare the executive summaries, correlate the new numbers for each region, compare them with the previous month and year, draw diagrams of long-term jobless as a proportion of total numbers, and generally reconstruct the figures to create the most dramatic effect. After this careful massage Winston would release his own more detailed version of the original releases and the Press Gallery loved him for it. It saved them having to place the new numbers in context and gave them a hook for a headline — 'Long-term jobless numbers worst in 50 years' — that sort of thing. In return they felt duty-bound to report Winston's stern reaction.

But it was all too easy kicking sand in the faces of political weaklings. Caucus was demanding that each of its spokespeople deliver policy drafts for both public release and party discussion, and with his usual prosaic communication skills Peters commanded that the elves comply.

With structural unemployment now bedevilling the developed world, abandoned pilot schemes littering the recent past, and not the first clue as to Caucus thinking on the issue, it had suddenly become my task to find some kind of miracle cure. Or at least a political panacea that could pass as a cure under the inspection of an election campaign. There was no hurry, Winston assured me, it was not needed until the next Caucus.

'But that's only three days away,' I protested.

'Yeah, plenty of time,' and he sauntered off to his next media interview.

I devised a plausible if simple plan, as befits a simple researcher. Abolish the dole after three months and replace it with a living allowance of the same financial sum. Then assess each unemployed person and discover their current level of education, skills, motivation and work readiness. Develop a specific plan of action for each of these people within a government-sponsored continuum of remedial education/formal training/on-the-job training/work experience/community work.

The aim was to ensure that each level 'staircased' to the next, so the individual jobless person could enter at the particular level that matched their assessment. Some might need to be taught to read and write before anything else, others might have sufficient skills to perform community work until an unsubsidised job opportunity arose. The normal welfare entitlements of the individual would continue but failure to enrol in any of the modules or to turn up at the allotted time for interviews, training or the like would result in deductions against that payment. The stick would be applied as liberally as the carrot, provided the State discharged its obligations to provide a professional service. The draft policy advocated an entire climate change with regard to the unemployment benefit, whereby people no longer received payment to do nothing but used that payment as a way to keep motivated and prepare for new job opportunities. If there were none, well, that was when the compulsory community work option slotted in.

This policy draft had one great virtue. From a New Zealand political perspective it was new. Politicians are like magpies — they love to collect shiny new things that glint in the sunlight — and Winston was no exception. With nary a backward glance he promoted the draft both within the party and to the public at large, eventually gaining Caucus acceptance and an election-year promise of an additional $200 million per annum for the community work component. It was all too simple.

But that is the gift of opposition. No one scrutinises your policy in great depth and any holes in the detail are easily papered over with headline-grabbing one-liners. 'No work, no dole' received a surprising level of public support and particularly appealed to those taxpayers who considered the unemployed to be a bunch of malingering bludgers. On the other hand the unemployed were pacified by the slightly contradictory one-liner 'Blame the system, not the victim' and the offer of additional State assistance to find a job. On this issue Winston united both conservative and liberal viewpoints for the first (and last) time and his Gallery credibility rose as a consequence. He might still be a cowboy but he was now a clever cowboy.

The only real problem with Winston's plan was that significant resources were needed to establish such a programme. Not a problem.

The beauty of opposition is that you can always spend money that does not exist. And National had a magical pre-election Visa card with no predefined credit limits.

But the employment draft had a more personal effect. It bound me to Winston ever tighter. A frontbencher was turning my policy concepts into political reality, and nothing is so intoxicating or dangerous for a back-room boffin. Being taken seriously is always the first step down the slippery slope to ruin.

MAORI ISSUES

The National Party and the Maori people are mutually exclusive beings. Since the formation of the former in 1936 this has been an immutable fact. Polite people will explain this irresistible antagonism as a result of Ratana's political alliance with the Labour movement but that is not true. Ratana never did influence all Maori voters, and whatever influence he did have was killed stone dead by Maori urbanisation in the 1960s. One of the great modern political fictions is that the small, run-down spiritual centre of Ratana, just outside Wanganui, has any influence other than a ceremonial one. And even that is somewhat tainted by the questionable musical tastes of the Ratana brass band and its love affair with the colour purple.

No, the truth is that Maori have always considered the Nats to be anal retentive types and National's collective membership have always considered that their party's philosophy of thrift, hard work and enterprise did not quite fit the Polynesian ethic. Those Maori members who did stray within the National tent could be divided into the confused and the opportunistic, with a good smattering of the latter. Perhaps the best example of this was Graham (later Sir Graham) Latimer from Northland, who carefully engineered himself into the vice-presidency of the party and enjoyed warm and secure friendships with both Muldoon and Bolger. He expertly manoeuvred himself around the dangerous shoals of the capital to secure considerable advantage for both his pet projects and himself, and despite a later criminal conviction for taxation offences retained his knighthood and much of his lustre within the party at large. He would become one of Winston's greatest opponents.

Maori delegates at party conferences were instantly recognisable. They were always overdressed (even for the National Party) and tended to exhibit the same kind of wild-eyed, quizzical expressions that one might expect from isolated pockets of Liverpool supporters seated in the midst of a Manchester United crowd. This was hardly surprising. Pakeha conference delegates either insulted their culture or patronised it. 'Why can't they speak bloody English?' was a frequent response if a stray karakia or waiata ever intruded upon conference proceedings.

Winston had joined the party in the early 1970s and been National's candidate for Northern Maori in the National landslide of 1975. He would remember the wonderful hospitality paid to him during that candidature, which was made more remarkable by the fact that he could neither speak nor understand the language. His wife, Louise, later told me that this failed northern expedition taught her that the Maori people have a thousand ways of saying 'No' while treating you as their favourite cousin. Whatever Winston's experience during that election it convinced him well and truly that there was no point in flogging himself for no return. Three years later he would contest the general constituency seat of Hunua and triumph over both National Party head office interference and Labour Party trickery. He never forgot that he was booed into the Chamber by the Labour MPs after winning the Hunua petition in the High Court. That legal experience would later assist Roger McClay and Wyatt Creech to win their Taupo and Wairarapa electorates in the same manner.

Winston was profoundly European in his background, education and social outlook, and there was scarcely a hint of anything else in his public or private behaviour. Even in later decades, and especially during the 1996 election campaign, his unease with lengthy Maori greetings and speeches was palpable, and he would publicly complain at a church service performed in Maori during Waitangi Day celebrations. What incredible irony then that his own creation should become the modern vehicle for Maori political aspirations.

Despite his unfamiliarity with things Maori, there was no shortage of National Party activists who dismissed the possibility of Peters ever leading their party precisely because of his part-Maori lineage. A subterranean smear began to circulate that Winston would 'go native' if ever given any position of authority. As a divisional councillor I would regularly come up against party activists who openly professed that Peters 'will revert to type, you know'. He would always be suspect in some quarters of the National Party solely because of the colour of his skin. I daresay that is still the case today.

Emotionally, this was a tricky time for Winston. On the one hand his repeated attacks on the quality and accountability of Maori programmes were condemned as 'shitting on his own people'. On the other, he was acutely aware that his motivation was being questioned within his own party, at least partly because of his Maori lineage. No matter how popular he might become with the public at large there would still be those that he would never convince, and they lived at polar extremes of the spectrum — Maori activists and intractable Pakeha racists.

I was similarly appalled to note that there were those Nats who wished to sabotage our working relationship by twisting their own version of the race card. Winston informed me that he had been warned off my research because of my alleged 'white supremacist views'. When I enquired from which direction this bullshit was being thrown Peters made it quite plain that 'the third floor' was the principal source — the Leader's quarters.

We both detected a faint whiff of panic underlying these insidious attacks. Anyhow, it was all too late to have any damaging impact — we now knew each other too well and whatever strengths or weaknesses either of us possessed (and they were legion) racial intolerance was not among them. Still, I had been warned. We were treading on dangerous ground and various slithering creatures were being stirred up in the undergrowth.

Our more immediate and public critics were those who accused Winston of 'Maori bashing' for personal and political advantage. Far more than any shady Maori entrepreneur or training provider who made light with taxpayers' money, Winston came to loathe do-gooder liberals and central policy-makers who shrugged their shoulders at the inefficiency, incompetence and plain corruption within Maori policy programmes. Very early on he identified such misguided tolerance as the real enemy and it was my job to invent a catch-all phrase to capture Peters' snarling contempt — 'sickly, white liberal' became the put-down of the year.

TREATY TROUBLES

From our first discussions Winston's strongest emphasis was on 'a new interpretation' of the Treaty of Waitangi. He saw this ancient document as a snare to the modern progress of Maori — a 'security blanket' that confined rather than exalted Maori aspirations. Rather than arming young Maori with the skills and education necessary for economic security and stability, the Treaty had become a false talis-man, its non-observance by the State a lazy excuse for failure.

None of these ideas were remotely mine. I had never considered the Treaty as anything more than an excuse for a day's holiday — Maori activists tended to amuse me. In contrast Winston could inflame himself in an instant, instinctively rejecting anything that smacked of self-determination, tino rangatiratanga or any other phrase that hinted at apartheid. Of course it was my responsibility to encapsulate and distil these sentiments for public attention, but on this issue more than any other Winston possessed a clear vision of the future.

From the first, Winston demanded the tools to deliver a vastly improved standard of Maori educational attainment. Instantly he encountered virulent criticism from academics, liberals and activists alike that the New Zealand education system was inherently biased against Maori. This was a 'Western' education system that incor-porated 'European concepts', it failed to accept Maori cultural mores, the language of instruction was English and thus possessed an impenetrable alien ambience. It was no wonder that Maori children failed in such record numbers at external examinations — no surprise, surely, that fewer than half of all Maori students stayed at school beyond the fifth form.

Winston exploded. Not only were he and his family living proof that children of Maori descent could and did succeed, but what of the gifted Maori leaders of yesteryear — Ngata, Buck, Pomare, Carroll — and were there not countless modern examples — Peter Sharples, Ranginui Walker, Timoti Karetu ...

'These, Laws, these,' — and he contemptuously tossed the newspaper articles across the desk at me — 'these are the sickest, the whitest and most stupid liberals I have ever encountered. Prepare a defence. No! Prepare an attack.'

I remember the scene and every word of this encounter vividly, as if endlessly replayed on video. It was the kind of passionate outburst that I wished his Caucus colleagues could have witnessed personally, if only to convince them that the man did have a soul, that he was sincere in his passion to raise Maori expectations — that this was not all some grand display of cynical self-promotion.

But I was still young and naive. It mattered not that Winston believed. Nor did it matter if he was right, wrong or just plain lucky. His popularity made him a threat to both the government and to his Caucus colleagues. The destructive vanity of all politicians is that they never admit the competition might be onto something for fear of being shown up. Thus Winston would continue to bang his drum in splendid isolation — and so stake out this new territory uncontested.

Meanwhile, I performed as bidden — digging out all the School Certificate marks for various ethnic groups for the past three years, and preparing numerous articles and speeches responding to the liberal criticism. If the New Zealand education system was so biased in favour of Pakeha children then how was it that Asian children repeatedly topped the academic polls? Even recently immigrant Asian children outperformed their European peers and they certainly had a wholly different cultural heritage and background. You could not get more alien than Kampuchea, or Hong Kong, or South Korea.

Fortunately the Ministry of Education had commissioned some excellent research for that rather shambolic beast, the Royal Commission on Social Policy (a weedy creation notable for excreting solid blocks of undigested information then collapsing from the exertion). This research included studies of the reasons for Maori educational success and failure and identified a cultural impediment all right — a Maori one. Whereas academic achievement is, inherently, a personal success, it was found that teenage Maori peer pressure demanded a more homogeneous approach. In other words, to stand out through one's examination successes was considered most uncool. Peer group pressure was exerted to 'dumb down' the bright kids.

Winston ended up one step away from saying that Maori cultural mores were part of the problem, not part of the solution. Although he never directly made this association both his critics and his conservative supporters did. They saw the political and social implications of Winston's speeches, if from entirely different vantage points — and between them they gave Peters the kind of press most politicians would die for.

Almost overnight — and it was that quick — Winston Peters was the name on everyone's lips. By the middle of the year his TVNZ/ Heylen ratings had gone from one per cent (or two per cent if you listen to Win) to four, to eight and then to sixteen per cent. He had leapfrogged Bolger and was stalking Prime Minister Lange as the 'preferred Prime Minister', and as each poll came out the media focused more and more on what Winston was saying. From that point on, perhaps mid-1988, we never had to work the Press Gallery again; they came to us. But it was all far too quick; our policy had not yet reached embryo stage, it was barely a foetus, and now the media were insistent, demanding, even pleading for the Winstonian blueprint that would cure the very ills that he himself was exposing.

For the first time we were under real pressure to deliver not just the headline but the content as well.

We considered the solution lay in embracing the best of both Maori and Western worlds and moulding them together into a practical whole. Fortunately there were examples of such melding, and the Catholic Maori girls' boarding school of St Joseph's (Hato Hohepa) in Greenmeadows, Napier, provided us with a tangible example. The school was led by an outstanding principal in Georgina Kingi — one of this country's few real living treasures. She and her staff had taken children from relatively poor family backgrounds and armed them with a vibrant Maori culture, yes, but also a strong emphasis on academic attainment. Unlike the Maori boys' boarding schools which overdosed on the worst excesses of the macho myth and possessed appalling academic standards, St Joseph's had achieved the right mix of discipline, culture, academic excellence and pride.

Education was the key. No great insight there — but an education that started with the Maori parent and within the adult community and was supported by unflinching discipline and quality standards. Winston was also prepared to make a direct linkage between welfare benefits and early childhood development to achieve these aims. For example, he had no difficulty in linking the payment of the Domestic Purposes Benefit to mandatory children's health check-ups and enrolment in preschool educational programmes. To those white liberals and civil libertarians who protested at such allegedly draconian ways Winston would reply with withering accuracy that the State had tried their ways and look at the mess.

Winston's rise in both profile and support was complemented by another phenomenon of the times — the similar rise of the Maori protest movement and a new breed of upfront, unattractive activist who mistook insolence for intelligence. The blinding contrast between the groomed, conservative Peters and the unkempt, unpresentable, radical fringe of the Maori protest movement provided Winston with a considerable natural advantage.

Labour's breathtaking Maori policy, with its emphasis on settling Treaty claims dating back to 1840, devolving government programmes to tribal agencies and recognising Maori as an official language of New Zealand, was brave and bold stuff. There was just one problem — it scared the living crap out of middle New Zealand. A brilliant

Tom Scott cartoon summed up the prevailing mood. A Pakeha couple are driving through road works in grim weather and have just passed the ubiquitous Maori 'Stop/Go' signaller. The man turns to his wife and comments, 'Race relations have gone to hell ... they all used to wave at you in the past.'

But the thin line between a bemused Pakeha agnosticism and outright anger was soon crossed. The new breed of Maori activist — direct, impassioned, a hint of violence in their language and demeanour — had scared 'Mother of Three' and Labour was perceived to be pandering to their demands. Winston's unequivocal and public opposition to the activist agenda, and the personification of that agenda by the notorious Harawira clan, tapped directly into such latent fears.

I must confess that I never took these overweight activists too seriously. Their appalling dress sense, wraparound sunglasses and stolen Afro-American imagery transformed them into poor Billy T. James caricatures, and Winston would freely opine that New Zealanders really had no idea how lucky they were. There were no visionaries, evil prophets, suicide bombers or terrorists among this motley lot — just a bunch of bedraggled renegades addicted equally to the evil weed and Kentucky Fried. No Basque bombers, no IRA kneecappers, no Baader-Meinhof gangsters, no Red Army mercenaries — not even a prospective Martin Luther King or Bishop Tutu civil disobedience disciple. The worst actions of these so-called dangerous radicals involved throwing a wet T-shirt at the Queen, strewing disused refrigerators across state highways and hacking down a lop-sided tree before the tussock moth got it. But Pakeha New Zealand still jumped at these shapeless shadows. They had watched *Utu* once too often.

As the Opposition's Maori affairs spokesman Winston repeatedly attacked these messy few, each denunciation drawing sackfuls of adoring correspondence. It was the easiest support any MP was ever gifted — a baying crowd that agreed with you before you had uttered a single word. After one outburst from Titewhai Harawira, a woman who appeared to have stumbled straight on to the national stage from Macbeth's blasted heath, we laughed that perhaps the woman was more cunning than she was given credit for. Surely, we surmised, this was her contribution towards creating the first Maori Prime Minister, even if it did involve ritual media humiliation via this same leader. The misreported 'kill a Pakeha' comments of Hana Jackson and Titewhai's reference to 'necklacing' opponents delivered legions of white fans to the urbane, educated Maori leader, who urged his people to put aside past trifles and concentrate on earning their stake in the new reality.

However, despite all the ham acting and hyperbolic rhetoric we were still confronted with a major policy problem: the Treaty of Waitangi.

It was not something that could be lightly brushed aside in the modern setting now that it had been given legal credence by both Parliament and the courts. My proffered solution was to dump the thing and start again. Unlike the American Constitution and its associated Bill of Rights there was nothing in this tatty, rat-nibbled document that allowed for modern progress. After all the Treaty was pretty explicit in 1840 — Maori iwi and hapu would retain undisturbed possession of their 'Lands, Estates, Forests and Fisheries' unless they were willingly sold in a fair sale.

The Maori translation had provided a more encompassing definition of such possessions by defining them all as 'taonga', which included the lands, estates, forests and fisheries and a lot more besides — in essence, anything a Maori claimant might consider to be one of their 'treasures'. As a piece of nineteenth-century colonial trickery the Treaty was on a par with various other agreements with indigenous people in the Empire. But who could possibly have believed that such an ill-defined and expedient document would be used as a quasi-Bill of Rights for an independent nation 150 years later? What country could be that silly?

Of course, Article Two of the Treaty had its balancing outriders, but these largely signalled the rights and responsibilities of the British government and Queen Victoria. Any sane reading of the Treaty (indeed even any legal reading, a distinctly different proposition) must reach the inevitable conclusion that special rights had indeed been granted to the Maori people in perpetuity and woe betide any future generation and/or government that might tamper with them. Of course they did tamper — well, not so much tamper as commit grand larceny — and the Treaty ceased to exist to all practical effect.

But the moment the Treaty was given legal sanction, either by its own statute or in other legislation (e.g. the State Owned Enterprises Act 1986), then it was all over. It was just a case of waiting for the various courts of the land to uphold the common-sense reading of the rights forfeited by the Crown in 1840 and then enforce them.

Winston could not accept such a modern legal interpretation of the Treaty, nor could he accept that the Treaty of Waitangi should be junked. Yes, he believed that the Treaty was an impediment to the future development of the country and in particular to its race relations, and he delivered impassioned speeches to that effect. But his innate conservatism was offended by the idea of scrapping or even amending anything that old.

It was the concept of tradition that wedded Winston to the Treaty, not the concept of Maori people enjoying indigenous rights. He genuinely loved tradition with all its pomp and circumstance, whereas I could not abide the stuff. For those who suggested that I had an untoward influence over the man, both the Treaty issue and a similar royalist/republican split in our constitutional loyalties stand as sharp contradictory evidence.

In private conversations Winston would admit the virtue in my argument, but his solution would be much more subtle than the 'Let's start all over again' refrain of his researcher.

'Concentrate on Article Three, Laws,' he would instruct. 'Article Three is the solution.'

Well, I had no idea what this meant. Yoda had been more descriptive. But in later conversations I discovered that Winston had an idea of making Maori 'full citizens' by raising their level of education, employment, business opportunity and health to the same standards as Pakeha New Zealanders'. It seemed that once these standards were attained then the need for the Treaty would steadily evaporate, rendered superfluous by the new reality. No amount of 'You're joking, Win' or Russian eye-rolling had any effect on this singular conviction.

'No-one gives up advantage, Win,' I would argue. 'Why would Maori people give up their additional rights just because their kids are getting the same grades as the Pakeha kids in School Certificate?' But my protests were airily waved away — Winston had made up his mind and 500,000 volts of plasma energy would not have persuaded him otherwise.

Winston insisted that our first draft of National's 1990 Maori Affairs policy include the statement that the Treaty of Waitangi was New Zealand's founding document — which was a constitutional nonsense, of course, but no one actually tripped us up on this rather glaring error. However, the thrust of the draft policy was to fulfil Article Three of the Treaty — raising Maori standards and accountability — and Winston would later adapt these ideas to produce 'Ka Awatea'.

This is not to suggest that Winston saw no merit in learning the Maori language or in the development of the Maori culture. Far from it. He saw both as positive developments in the sense that they provided a kind of discipline and structure to an otherwise disorganised social environment. But he was equally adamant that learning te reo should not be a substitute for learning the ways of Western academia and technology. Over and over again he would repeat the critical need for young Maori children to compete against young Americans, young Australians, young Japanese — and beat them. A good Maori vocabulary and a certificate in bone carving was not going to achieve that end, hence his fierce criticism of any non-skills focus in the MACCESS training programmes.

On the issue of settling outstanding Maori land claims back to 1840 Winston was much less enthusiastic. The impetus for accepting that development came more from Remuera MP Doug Graham and Leader Jim Bolger. Again Winston saw such claims as slightly irrelevant. His concerns were for the generations of today and tomorrow; the Maori sense of the present being part of a continuum between yesterday and tomorrow left him stone cold. And yet he loved tradition. It was a personal dichotomy that I could not grasp.

On one thing this edgy Pakeha researcher and his conservative Maori master were in absolute agreement. The powers of the Waitangi Tribunal would require severe pruning. In fact their recommendatory powers needed to be excised completely. What madness within Labour's ranks had inspired them to endow the Tribunal with these powers was beyond us to comprehend. In later years Mike Moore would tell me that he argued at great length with then deputy Prime Minister and Minister of Justice Geoffrey Palmer that the Tribunal should be given no powers other than to research the claims and establish their veracity. But Palmer was a jurist, not a politician. He instinctively trusted lawyers more than he trusted politicians (the kind of character flaw for which there can be no forgiveness) and thus the Tribunal retained its quasi-judicial powers.

On these issues Winston spoke at great length and with significant fervour, his speeches and articles drawing substantial support from media commentators and editorial writers alike. Our central theme was that the Waitangi Tribunal would actually create a fresh round of Maori grievances. If the Tribunal assessed the merits of a land claim, found the case proven, and recommended a five hundred million dollar settlement — but left it to the Crown and the claimant tribe to work out the final details — then it was like allowing a poker player to take a loaded gun to the table.

If $500 million is an independent assessment of proper justice, and the Crown settles with the claimant at, say, $200 million because of pressing economic conditions, then justice has not been achieved. It is $300 million short and a fresh grievance has been created for a new generation of Maori claimants.

We worked on a series of speeches and newspaper articles to high-light the dangers of both the Treaty and the Tribunal — dangers made even more explicit when an activist Court of Appeal ruled in favour of the New Zealand Maori Council (chaired by Graham Latimer) with regard to the interpretation of the State Owned Enterprises Act (1986). Having made the horrendous mistake of insisting that the new corporate bodies were subject to the principles of the Treaty of Waitangi, the Crown now watched the Court interpret their obligations. The Treaty suddenly assumed both a legal interpretation and a political reality. It was obvious that the government had not intended this outcome; rather, that there would be some ritual head-nodding to the concept of the Treaty and that would be it — the kind of empty gesture that Parliament specialises in.

But this time they had stuffed it up good and proper.

The Treaty was alive. And short of a messy and very public execution it was going to stay that way. The immediate winners in this situation were the various tribal claimants and Winston Peters. As popular unease shuddered through the community our tiny partnership felt the aftershocks. Our task now was to distil that anxiety and articulate it.

SURFING THE WAVES

Winston may have had a clear vision as to the future of the Maori people, and a vague idea of the place of the Treaty in New Zealand life, but outside those issues his political consciousness was virgin territory. The employment and race relations issues had certainly raised his public profile but the constant demand from the press was for something new. Something exciting. Something sexy.

It is yet another curse of this demon profession. After you perform one trick, and perform it well, the public want more. Oh, so you can stand on one hand — what else? Personally I blame the media for this insatiable public appetite for new sensations. Headlines sell, so the modern politician needs an inexhaustible supply of headline grabbers to satiate this demand. And there are only so many radical outrages that one can condemn and only a finite number of taxpayer rip-offs to highlight.

If I was being fair, I would have to concede that this was partly our own fault. Winston had come to relish this new drug of public approbation, with all its beguiling tendrils — the fawning maître d' at the restaurant, the back-slapping and supportive handshakes at airports, the packed provincial halls, the standing ovations. In short, Winston liked being liked — an entirely human reaction. But being adored was even better. Winston had crossed over the line from being a minor public celebrity to being a leader of popular emotion and there were no complaints — especially not from me.

Various newspapers and magazines began to publish articles on the 'young researcher who is behind Winston Peters' stunning rise to power' — rather forgetting that public opinion polls and political power are two wholly different propositions. I was amazed one night to return home and watch TVNZ's 'Fourth Estate' programme devote an entire programme to the 'young image-maker' who had foxed a supine news media into elevating Peters from backbencher to political phenomenon.

This was all very flattering and, yes, I was flattered, but it was also starting to get out of hand. I was being credited with Machiavellian stratagems and political planning way beyond my ken, and even the vaguest hint of an Opposition success in the House was being wrongly assigned to my scorecard. Of course, being a fledgling strategist I remained totally silent. To disclaim responsibility might have eroded some very useful myths and, in politics, a reputation as a classy intriguer was not necessarily a bad thing. A perverse truth.

But that reputation would be worth nothing and Peters' star would have no further burnish if we could not set the political agenda and thence continue to dominate media attention. The two were completely interconnected. No issue — no media. No media — no public.

'We need an issue, Laws,' would become Winston's favourite observation/command for the next eight years. And lo, I would journey to that dark place of my imagination and find one. Trawling the farther reaches of one's own consciousness is always an exercise in terror — one never knows what lives at such depths.

Fortunately, there were some ideas that came to mind instantly and were already being wheeled through the streets. They just needed a quick detour. But others required identification and then retrieval, and they could often surprise. An inner loathing for the political system itself was one that became apparent after much soul-searching, and would eventually have the widest repercussions for all concerned.

There was something else, which Winston instinctively understood and I later rationalised. Popularity provided Peters with a kind of influence. I say 'a kind of' because it was not real power; it was not a raw, visceral force nor a clinical potency, but it was a perception that Peters could change things. When you are riding high in the polls and every newspaper, magazine and television documentary wants to include a piece on the new Maori wonderboy, then you can be considered to be an influential personality.

Such a perception is not confined to the public at large. It affects party activists, colleagues, the Press Gallery and all the other feral life forms that inhabit Parliament. And sometimes that perception alone, that chimera of strength, can be enough to make others react and make decisions in response.

It was time to test the strength of this illusion.

DANCING WITH NUKES

In the weeks leading up to the 1987 general election, Labour's dynamic yuppie advertising agency, Colenso, had constructed a series of fearsome images designed to scare potential doubters away from any electoral dabble with the Opposition. By far the most graphic of these images was that of a toxic mushroom cloud erupting and expanding to fill the entire television screen. The smart advertising types at Colenso had brilliantly captured the potential menace: a vote for National would be a vote for nukes, Dr Strangelove and the malevolent stupidity of the Cold War.

But it was much more than that. A vote for National would not only be a vote against the new anti-nuclear legislation but also a vote against New Zealand's struggling sense of nationhood and identity. Prime Minister Lange had reserved his most devastating Oxford Union rhetoric to ridicule the Nats for 'snuggling up to the bomb', an image that stuck fast to the electoral consciousness. The bullying antics of our ex-ANZUS partners and the salacious aftermath of the *Rainbow Warrior* sinking all combined to provide a wonderful distraction for the duration of the entire election campaign. Labour played the no-nukes card to ease the troubled consciences of urban liberals and female voters who had begun to fret over the macho breast-beating antics of Douglas, Prebble and the other New Right brethren. One wonders, in retrospect, if the then Prime Minister did not similarly distract himself as a therapeutic remedy for the weekly policy massacres in Cabinet.

Anyway, who cares what the motivations were. The ruse worked, which is all the justification you ever need in politics.

National's so-called strategists were completely outflanked. They clung to the pre-'84 verbiage about how ANZUS protected New Zealand from 'potential aggressors' and how nuclear ship visits were an integral part of our mutual defence obligations. This was, of course, all pure, unmitigated, breathtaking bullshit. The United States only rallied to their allies' causes when it suited US interests to do so. If New Zealand got involved in any scrap then Uncle Sam would apply the test of self-interest well before the innocuous protocols of the ANZUS Treaty. Given the test of Indonesian insurgency in the 1960s, for example, the US had shrunk from commitment.

Such details mattered not to the National Caucus. The Americans were our friends and if committing a few divisions to Vietnam or some US-sponsored peacekeeping operation was the price of that friendship then so be it. Jim Bolger's strong conservative views on ANZUS were reinforced by his militarist chief of staff, Rob Eaddy, and defence spokesman and new deputy, Don McKinnon. Deputy Don was not passionate about many things so it was a rare privilege to watch him work up a political sweat over things ANZUS. Rare and incongruous — like a sloth in heat.

Desperate for a division line between Labour's reformist economic policies and National's private enterprise sensibilities, the Opposition eagerly seized upon the ANZUS breach as a clear rallying point for supporters. Which was a bit like campaigning in central Otago and siding with the rabbits.

It was obvious that New Zealand's anti-nuclear stance was as much about self-identity as it was abhorrence over weapons of mass destruction. So when particularly dumb Pentagon officials admitted that New Zealand was part of their Neanderthaloid nuclear 'shell game' with the evil Soviet Empire my reaction was much the same as everyone else's — go home Yank. I admit the immediate prospect of the Auckland isthmus being atomised in some thermonuclear Superpower game had an initial appeal but when one considered the likely effect on the All Blacks' forward pack then I drew the line. No — it was too high a price to pay.

Plainly it was time for National to catch up with the public mood, although with Bolger, McKinnon and Eaddy in the ascendant this was one train they seemed bound to miss. Even the rough experience of losing the '87 campaign and a long list of defeated candidates could not alter their convictions. 'There are some principles that cannot be compromised,' the Leader would heroically assert, thus setting himself up for an even greater fall.

I was determined that Winston should not suffer the same fate of political irrelevance. I was equally determined to find out just how successfully he could convert popular appeal into real, visceral, political grunt. Again there was a marriage of minds and egos — Winston wanted to know too. Which probably made him susceptible to my advice that he should take the leading role in maturing the National Party past its pro-nukes phase. Winston had been a strong proponent of ANZUS but he understood one great truth about New Zealand politics: Americans cannot vote.

To his credit Winston tried to convince his Caucus colleagues before taking the debate into the public arena. But his efforts were batted away as an irritant and Winston was provided with a salutary reminder that senior National MPs, including the Leader, still refused to take him seriously. His pride was bruised after one particular Caucus encounter and I knew enough about Win to realise that any assault on his vaulting pride was like chopping up his favourite pets and feeding him puppy pie. There would be, in the immortal words of RoboCop, 'trouble'.

'Laws,' he barked through the usual acrid haze (I speculated that if I wore a name tag with 'Michael' written in large capital letters I might, one day, persuade him that my parents had given me a Christian name), 'I want a speech.'

What he really wanted, of course, was a political war, but a speech would do fine for now — a speech heralding war.

As speeches go, particularly as Winstonian speeches go, I thought the end result a rather tame affair. A simple message was promoted: 'Time has marched on ... the people have spoken ... the National Party should democratically accept the new consensus ...' There were the usual arguments as to why the 'neither confirm nor deny' policy of the US military was unacceptable, including one recycled from former Nat radical Marilyn Waring, who argued that such a policy contravened Sir Keith Holyoake's promise never to base nuclear weapons in this country. Plainly if the Yanks were visiting and bringing

119

their weaponry with them that amounted to a siting of nuclear arms, however temporary. Quite a nifty line that, and it was suitably plagiarised and made to appear a Winston original.

Winston duly delivered his address and was not disappointed by the reaction. Peters had not just farted in church, he had abluted in the confessional — this was the full performance. National's post-war holy of holies, that blessed trinity of all things traditional, American and in uniform, had been brutally assaulted from within.

Bolger was upset. No, he was more than that. He appeared to me to be at the very edge of his self-control and I had the misfortune to encounter this rage directly. I had popped into the research offices early on a Saturday morning to retrieve some papers for a weekend assignment and as I strolled nonchalantly down the third-floor corridor Bolger met me at the double doors leading down to the unit. He had the morning's *Dominion* in his hand and wore a thunderous look that I had only ever seen once before, and that had been on my father after I had just pranged the car. My jaunty greeting of 'Hi, Mr Bolger' only served to further colour the Leader's already florid expression.

'In my office — now!'

It was more a snarl than a command. I felt my intestines prise themselves loose from the stomach wall and my bowels ready themselves for evacuation. They say that certain oriental monks can contract their testicles into their body and out of harm's way if under attack. Well, my testicles deserted me without the faintest demur and it took days before they found their way home again. Plainly, I was in donkey-deep doo-doos.

Bolger led me into his private quarters in the Leader's suite and thrust the newspaper at my chest. 'Did you write this?' he demanded.

At such times I must admit to a wholly inappropriate and surreal sense of occasion. My consciousness disassociates itself from its immediate surroundings in the same manner as those who recount near-death experiences. This feeling of isolation is then exemplified by some disconnected neuron that takes over my power of speech and blabs the very words most calculated to offend the enraged individual before me. Not content with near death, the all-powerful id demands to be put out of its misery.

'Not all of it, Mr Bolger — the quotation was Voltaire's.'

This smart-aleck reply intensified the atmosphere. For the next five minutes I was angrily accused of sabotaging Caucus policy, sabotaging the National Party, sabotaging the Leader's authority, sabotaging the Western alliance — I gave up comprehending at that point.

Realising that today was likely to be my last as an Opposition researcher I protested strongly. This was Winston's speech, I argued, — not mine. He wanted those things said, those issues raised — I was merely the speechwriter carrying out instructions as required by my work contract. The Leader's gripe should be with his independent-minded frontbencher, not me.

Bolger was having none of it. 'These are your ideas, your thoughts,' he spat back. 'Winston is not capable of thinking like this.' And in that one sentence Jim Bolger displayed all his dislike, all his displeasure and all his contempt for the Tauranga MP. To the Leader, Winston was just a showy, insubstantial vessel, a cypher whose every word and action was scripted by another. I suppose I could have chosen to be flattered but in that situation such a reaction would have been tantamount to resignation. Besides, it was not true.

I strongly asserted that Winston's anti-nuclear views were sincerely held and that he had instructed me to formulate them into a speech. What was I to do — refuse? Bolger started to lose his way a little at this point and advanced the argument that I 'should have known better' than to accede to drafting such a speech — a potentially mutinous action for any lowly researcher.

Eventually Bolger talked himself out and I was released after a tense hour of argument. But the whole issue had now crystallised the internal difficulties within the Opposition. Bolger was edgy and apprehensive at Peters' sudden rise in both public popularity and credibility and, instead of giving him credit for opening up another front on the Labour Government, he was looking for someone to blame. Given that Winston was perceived as some kind of lobby lightweight incapable of either original thought or sophisticated political planning, then, according to Bolger, I must be the responsible party. Ipso facto, I was the threat and not Peters.

Fortunately, I continued to enjoy warm relations with Bill Birch and Bolger staffers Eaddy and Eagleson, so that opposing viewpoints as to my worth were advanced to the Leader. But all equally dismissed my protestations that Winston was his own man — a common sentiment in the Opposition lobbies. In so doing they underestimated the durability and reserves of political cunning that welled within Winston.

Despite the reaction of the leadership and some of his more senior

Caucus colleagues Winston continued to run the anti-nuclear theme in public and at party gatherings. His speeches even earned him a month-long US State Department-sponsored 'study trip' to the States and briefings from Pentagon and State Department officials — ostensibly to 'inform' Winston all the better on US–NZ relationships.

It was all rather a waste of US taxpayers' money. no one is as passionate about their new faith as a convert, as any good Catholic will tell you (or any reformed smoker for that matter) and Winston was most definitely a convert. Given that he was out of the country for a month it was my responsibility to continue stoking the media fires, and thus a series of press releases, pronouncements and speeches haunted the Gallery from half a world away. Well, my office actually, but who was to know?

One evening, though, Winston telephoned me to say that his hosts appeared to have arranged a meeting with the outgoing US President, Ronald Reagan. I was staggered. All top-level diplomatic relations with the States had been frozen in the wake of the ANZUS row but here was a leading New Zealand Opposition MP (and a professed anti-nuclear one at that!) about to meet with the self-styled 'leader of the free world'. What a coup!

It was my job to get the Press Gallery excited at the prospect of such a meeting. Excited — hell, this was the political equivalent of a naked lap-dancer at a stag party. There was no effort required. The media response was feverish. Unfortunately (or fortunately as it turned out) Winston proved impossible to contact in the States for three entire days. My immediate response to this isolation was that, plainly, the great coup had not occurred. If it had then Winston would have found a way to contact me even if by relay carrier pigeon. By now both the US Embassy in Wellington and my office were being flooded with calls desperately seeking confirmation and details. The Embassy's chargé d'affaires, Al la Porta, phoned me to try and verify the media reports and expressed his understandable unease that such a meeting should occur without the Embassy's knowledge. Al was a very pleasant man and I had no wish to compound his delicate position nor add further to the speculation. I frankly told him that the whole story was likely to be utter bullshit — just Winston being mischievous.

My candour was met with reciprocal consideration. The US Embassy replied to media enquiries by suggesting that it was entirely plausible for Peters to meet Reagan simply by being at, say, a Republican party fund raiser, and to shake his hand and exchange pleasantries as part of the event. But no official or private meeting would be held. Thankfully, this explanation and Winston's non-availability to the hungry Gallery steered most reporters away. Expectations had been deflated, but once Winston emerged from his self-imposed isolation he flatly refused to confirm or deny the story. The irony was lost on no one and the Leader's office had great sport with me, openly wondering who Winston might not be meeting tomorrow — the UN Secretary-General, Mikhail Gorbachev, Nelson Mandela? Win's audacious attempt at world peace had deflated to a whimper.

Fortunately the media found a new sensation but I was reminded yet again of my partner's proclivity to talk up a story before it was even alive. A talent for exaggeration is always useful in politics but only if there is a text to gild. In this case the fact that Reagan and Peters were on the same continent seemed the only spark of reality to the story.

It mattered not. Winston's push for National to re-examine its nuclear policy built up significant pressure and expectation on both the Caucus and its leader. A group calling itself 'Nuclear Free Nationals' actively promoted a changed policy and there was support for a reappraisal within the strong Auckland and Wellington divisions of the party. Even within Caucus mutterings had begun that the nuclear issue represented an impediment to power that National did not need. The party had just required that first push and Winston had delivered it by appealing to a higher authority — the public. Maybe this popularity thing would work after all.

THE REAL REVOLUTION

One side effect of working in Parliament was that I lost all respect — and I mean all respect — for the political profession. I soon discovered that this was not a unique emotion, but one shared with secretaries, Hansard reporters, messengers, security guards, committee clerks — the works. The closer you got to the centre of political power the more nauseating the stench. It was as if the inner heart had died and was decomposing while the zombie body stumbled on.

Having witnessed at first hand the petty egos, the refined vanities, the hypocrisy between public utterance and private action, the game-playing, the myriad personality conflicts that passed themselves off as policy disputes, I had come to loathe the process itself. The very fact that I had proved so good at manipulating the various triggers and sussed the system so completely only increased my disrespect. There were no miracles here, no wholesome messages that triumphed in their own right — just an unremitting contest for advantage, some kind of leverage to advance the personal agenda.

An MP's inner motivation might well be good, altruistic, kindly or any other word that signified beneficence. However, the means to convert the vision into practical reality required a wholly different set of principles and values. You had to do bad to do good. Never tell the entire truth. Never admit to human weakness or frailty. Never work with your political opposites to achieve common ends.

As for the public — well, they were only to be listened to if they agreed with you. Otherwise you praised your own prejudice as 'real leadership', the kind that refused to 'pander to the mob'. Democracy was only a good thing if it advanced the agenda.

At the time I considered that the core of this disease was the two-party political system. (I later discovered this was only a small part of the problem.) The party system had been used as an insidious device to separate New Zealand MPs into two rival and feuding camps. The Westminster style of government may have been transported to New Zealand as part of the colonial legacy but unlike British class snobbery and Old World sectarian stupidities this malaise had survived the journey. Dammit.

The Hawke's Bay experience (why is it that you always learn more when you lose than when you win?) taught me that the wider public had already made their judgement about the moral probity of politicians and their so-called profession. This nasty tendency for people to check their watches after shaking your hand troubled me. So too did the guffaws if you ever asked an audience to trust you. No, politicians had a reputation little removed from neocosmic ooze and it was a rap thoroughly deserved.

So why work within a profession that I so thoroughly despised? Oh, that is easy to answer. To change it. Change? No, too small a word. Completely remake. Rebuild from the foundations up. I was a radical from the first instant. Of course I was not the only one. The problem, though, was that all the other radicals in the National Party — Richardson, Upton, Luxton, Williamson, secretary-general Max Bradford — were disciples of the New Right school. They did not trust the State either (although for slightly different reasons) so their solution was to privatise it and let even more corrupt business cabals run the show. To me that was from-the-frying-pan-into-the-fire stuff — at least with the State you could exercise a modicum of control. With the multinational commercial covens there was no show of exercising democratic influence. Such restraint was as passé as flares and platform shoes.

I confessed to such radicalism early on in my relationship with Winston. Emboldened by his indifference I then preached long and hard that the political process had ossified while personal, economic and societal development had evolved and modernised. We were trying to solve late-twentieth-century problems with a nineteenth-century political system.

Despite his conservative views and great passion for all things traditional and constitutional Winston accepted the premise that was being promoted. It was not a Damascene conversion and in later years I was forced to wonder if it was anything more than a symbolic immersion, but Winston was prepared to let some of the water splash over him. He promised to 'give it a try' although I noted the same distinct lack of enthusiasm that met my suggestion he be nicer to Ruth Richardson as he might need her one day.

Winston's agreement to at least dabble with different policy ideas was not matched by a similar reaction to my advice on Richardson. This was jettisoned to the distant reaches of the galaxy — there was some advice that proved just too radical, too out-there. Being nice to Richardson was such a case.

His immediate reaction to the new political reform agenda was, 'One speech, Laws. I'll give it one speech' — a concession to his underling for being a good boy. One speech on the general issue of political reform it would be — a testing of the public waters. But I knew one speech would be enough. And so it proved to be.

My initial thesis was that if people neither trusted nor respected politicians the public themselves could not be blamed for their chronic lack of faith. Even this observation proved unsettling in some quarters. There was no shortage of MPs who blamed both the media and public ignorance for their plight. Could they not see that what was being done was for their own good? No? Then they were a bunch of ungrateful miscreants.

I advanced to Winston a general series of policy steps that might help regain the fragile public confidence. What was required, I argued, was an entirely new political process that empowered (the 'in' word of the 1980s) the people and provided them with a tangible input into the decision-making process.

Of course, this was all very well in theory and you would be hard pressed to find an average audience likely to disagree. Such sentiments, after all, simply confirmed their own good judgement. Those bastards in Wellington were a shifty lot. Peters' first attempt at articulating the public distaste for politicians could not fail. I knew, but Winston needed to have it proven. A standing ovation, huge media attention and sackloads of supportive mail did the trick.

I had been right. It took only the one speech to persuade Winston. From then on the issue of political reform would become Winston's personal brand — more powerful than race relations, employment scandals and the anti-nuke crusade rolled into one.

And there was something else. It suited his personality — that touch of the loner taking on the establishment on behalf of the small man. We were both loners, if for different reasons. And we were both champions of the underdog — it was our natural instinct. In this issue more than any other we invested our emotions. It was our crusade. Us against the political establishment. And we gloried in those odds.

It was now my job to ensure that Winston could present a series of positive policy alternatives to the status quo. Of a raft of initiatives offered to Winston he rejected just one — a parliamentary Upper Chamber or Senate. I agreed with his judgement but smiled at the motivation. This was Jim Bolger's personal hobby horse.

Winston became the first (and only) frontbencher from either National or Labour to champion proportional representation. He matched this vanguard stance with a personal agenda that included binding citizens-initiated referenda, the abolition of the parliamentary 'conscience' vote, a truly independent select committee process, a reduction in the number of MPs, and even a Bill of Rights to satisfy the jurists. He was the right salesman with the right pitch at the right time.

For the next year Winston's jihad against the political status quo launched a thousand editorial pages. Just when the public had totally lost faith in its politicians it discovered a politician-hero who railed against the process and promised a better tomorrow. I crafted the speeches in best southern-Baptist style — show the people the pits of Hell and then offer a redemptive Heaven. Winston delivered them with that strange mixture of passion and polish that was uniquely his. He was now a true populist — he had the charisma, he had the message and now he had the public.

It is my firm belief that Winston Peters can rightly claim to be the father of MMP, the mixed member proportional electoral system that had its birth at the 1993 general election. His public utterances and the attendant popular support convinced both Jim Bolger and the National Caucus that Peters had discovered an issue that would allow the party the constitutional high ground at the next general election.

Labour's refusal to hold a referendum in the wake of the 1988 report by the Royal Commission on Electoral Reform was not just the breaking of a prime-ministerial election promise — it was also politically dumb. It provided National with a much-needed stick to beat the Government with and allowed Jim Bolger to present his party as one that trusted (or at least professed to trust) the will of the people.

Wayne Eagleson had been instructed to research the Leader's pet Senate project and despite the total lack of any Caucus or public support for the idea it delivered an opportunity to Winston to advance his own reformist agenda. We were smart enough not to decry Bolger's Upper House — at least in public. This might prove the Trojan horse for the Winstonian suggestions. And so it proved.

The National Caucus was not required to choose between competing options. Rather it was required to promote a referendum on all the various issues — a binding referendum. It was a promise that caused much grief in the upper echelons of the party. They had no intention of promoting proportional representation or the hybrid variant of MMP suggested by the Royal Commission. But Jim Bolger could not have his Senate concept without Winston Peters' wider agenda somehow being included. Caucus decided on an unspoken compromise. It would endorse both personal agendas but leave the final choice to the public. The older hands breathed easy. The public were not complete morons, they reasoned. They would never vote for MMP. The rest, as they say, is history.

Peters was ecstatic. He had grafted his agenda onto Bolger's and used the latter as his stalking horse. The strong public support had convinced Caucus that electoral and parliamentary reform was an election issue after all and now a specific policy and series of promises had been delivered.

I was ecstatic for an entirely different reason.

I reckoned that MMP would win easily. The referendum would turn into a confidence vote on the political process in general and on politicians in particular. There was no way the status quo could hold on. This would be the end of the two-party domination of Parliament. And that in itself would create vast vistas of opportunity.

The dam had been breached.

My parents, Helen and Keith, around the time of their marriage in 1956. Dad, an unabashed romantic; Mum, pretty and assertive.

Top right: The Dettol kids at Harper Street — from left, me (aged 9), sisters Susan (5) and Diane (7).

Already looking over my shoulder – the infant Michael.

Schoolboy rebel complete with gravity-defying Afro (back row, second left) in Wanganui Boys' successful if thoroughly disorganised First XI of 1974. Just turning up to the photographer's studio proved an adventure; at least two of my team mates were lost to Wanganui's wilderness.

One of the first BNZ Festival Debates in Dunedin. Deputy Prime Minister Jim McLay in the chair; MPs Trevor de Cleene (speaking), Norm Jones and Michael Cullen proved irresistible entertainment.

The only picture in
existence that has me on
the same side as Ruth
Richardson. In a Young
Nationals 'fun' debate
with team mates
Richardson and
Rangiora MP Jim
Gerard in 1984 and,
ironically, accusing the
opposition of deviant
practices.

Karen and I celebrating
election to Parliament
from Hawke's Bay in
1990 — and like most
New Zealanders
completely oblivious to
Treasury's takeover of
the Hammer Horror
studios.H.B. Herald
Tribune

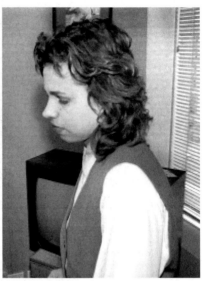

Sarah Neems: her intense relationship with Winston attracted vicious gossip, but without her, New Zealand First would have been a hole in the ground. Evening Post

Three days before the 1990 general election, Winston Peters campaigns in Hawke's Bay for his former researcher — a twin threat to National's veneer of unity. The Daily Telegraph

Below: *The first of the famous/notorious Super Surtax avoidance seminars of 1991. Thousands would attend and propel me into direct confrontation with my Cabinet and Caucus colleagues. Great fun, though.* H.B. Herald Tribune

Chapter 5

PRIDE

THE BOLGER SUMMONS

Any pretence at retaining political anonymity had now been well and truly blown and I was not entirely displeased with this new state of affairs. Being mistaken for the intelligent influence behind the Peters visage had its own intoxicating allure. All power, no responsibility; it was just like being in Treasury.

In addition, it presupposed that Winston was now acting in a strategic fashion and with some rational forethought. That marked a considerable shift in Press Gallery perception from the days when Winston would ride into town, shoot up the sheriff and then wallow in the horse trough. No more yahoo cowboy.

Certainly no one in National's Caucus credited Peters' stunning rise in popularity to the man himself. Oh, he had impressed them all right, but as a party animal with a good suntan and a natty array of multicoloured neckwear. Collectively the Caucus surmised that either something or someone had taken control of the Peters persona. There just had to be another reason for Winston's new image — it was either the Moonies or something even more sinister. Rightly or wrongly, Caucus and the party executive decided that Korean mind-snatchers were not the culprits. They pointed their fingers closer to home.

As I have explained, this was both a flattering and a dangerous perception. However, it was not sufficiently flattering to compensate for all the obvious perils. For a start, the dubious mana of being Peters' water-carrier barely spread beyond the insular environs of the Press Gallery and its chattering Wellington associates. Such inner notoriety could never protect any staffer, no matter how artful, from a presumptive strike from a nervous Leader's office. If the Leader became unduly anxious (and Bolger's staff repeatedly exclaimed that it was difficult to define where one anxiety attack ended and the next started) then I might well prove the lightning rod to expunge such welling unease.

And I was far from earthed — one properly directed Bolger bolt and I would be unemployed crispbread.

Of course, there was a solution. It had been half-heartedly proffered to Bolger some six months earlier, before the unfortunate appointment of Hazel Whiteoak.

Put Laws on the Leader's staff.

This radical concept was actively promoted by both Bill Birch and Rob Eaddy as a neat way to nab my alleged communicative and research skills while nicely skewering any Peters leadership pretensions. Their hardest job was to persuade Bolger, although the monthly poll reminders began to work their own insidious magic.

I was summoned to the Leader's office and the concept was put to me directly. I would be attached to the Leader's office as a researcher on 'special projects'. It soon became apparent that 'special projects' consisted entirely of finding any issue or incident that might revive Bolger's flagging public profile.

The offer left me feeling both uncomfortable and strangely disloyal. I was enjoying my work with Winston, the profile was humming, my frontier policy concepts were being domesticated by Peters' public charm and we had developed a firm friendship. But Bolger's offer smacked of Mediterranean climes. To decline outright would be dangerous.

Somehow, and trading on the Leader's distinct unease, I brokered a compromise. I could work for both men. I would continue to develop employment and Maori affairs issues with Winston but create controversy in fresh fields for Jim Bolger. At first, the suggestion was dismissed, especially by Birch. He knew a crock when he saw one — all those years promoting Think Big I guess.

But the idea suited Bolger. It allowed him to keep a close eye on my Peters activities while I searched out any latent issues that might be used to improve his own public image. On the other hand, he could bat aside any internal Caucus or party quibbles about a notorious radical being attached to his personal staff. Officially I would remain a member of the research unit. It was a deal that suited both Bolger and me. Unlike Eaddy or Eagleson, there was never any personal rapport between us. This would be a strictly professional relationship based entirely on mutual disregard.

There was just one problem. Having been escorted into the inner sanctum I was now expected to perform. Like right now. Instantly. 'Luigi's ferret', as the *NBR*'s Fran O'Sullivan characterised me, was put to work hunting rabbits for a new and impatient master.

Fortunately, I had two things going for me. First, there were still a number of half-formed leads in my bottom drawer that I had intended to develop at a later stage for Winston, and second, attention to any issue, no matter how small, would represent an improvement in Bolger's profile.

The first cause célèbre was an abandoned chemical site at Mapua, near Nelson. Toxic waste was leaching into the neighbouring waterway and I sold the lack of central government action as an opportunity for Bolger to act against type and demonstrate a concern for environmental issues. One of the chemicals left decaying on-site was the banned pesticide DDT, which prompted the Leader to reminisce fondly about how he had spread the stuff on his own farmland, by hand, to eradicate grass grub. I bit my lip. It explained a lot.

Anyway, both Bolger and his staff were delighted with the sympathetic media coverage and the rare appearance of their man on the evening's television news. This arrangement might work after all. Winston was less effusive. In fact, he positively scowled at the incident. 'What's your next trick, Laws?' he rumbled. 'World peace?'

I suddenly realised my predicament. Any story I might research and market for Bolger would draw Winston's ire and he would demand an explanation as to why 'his' researcher had not prepared the story for his personal consumption. Conversely, any issue developed for Peters outside the strict parameters of either employment policy or race relations would incur Bolger's ire. There were also accessibility issues involved. I had been working 50 hours a week for Winston — drafting press releases, speeches and policy papers, researching various stories and mini-scandals, selling the boss to the doubting Gallery.

Now I was being required to service Bolger's staff as well and write the occasional media release and speech. But Winston's demands would not correspondingly decline. To compensate I moved from a 50-hour week to an 80-hour, seven-day-a-week routine. It mattered not. I was still getting squeezed in the middle by the personal antipathy between the two men, leader and pretender.

The tension in their respective offices was so raw that you instinctively looked for the body. The very mention of the other's name would cause sinews to stiffen, jaws to snap rigid and eyes to narrow. Words of derision were superfluous for these two men loathed each other with a physical intensity not immediately appreciated outside, say, Northern Ireland or the West Bank of the River Jordan. It is perhaps the most enduring miracle of the MMP electoral system that these two would one day lie down beside each other.

I was now in a unique and schizophrenic situation — a foot (and a hemisphere of the brain) quite literally in both political camps. But it was also emotionally exhausting. Making sure that personal quips and comments from the one about the other were never repeated; trying neither to defend nor criticise either man; doing my level best to play the straight game. It was an impossible task and one that could never suit my personality. Playing the dumb technocrat was not my style. I determined on a course of benign intervention — I would play Kissinger and broker first an understanding of each other and then a peace. After all, I reasoned, they were not entirely dissimilar individuals. Conservative. Private. Driven. Petty.

Ah, the naivete, conceit and arrogance of youth.

For this purely personal stratagem was based on two wholly erroneous conclusions. One, that Bolger would accept the need to accommodate and promote his most popular front-bench MP, and two, that Peters would be content to succeed to the deputy leadership and there bide his time until Bolger's eventual retirement or resignation. Both paths of logic slammed into a brick wall of remarkable and reflected personal detestation.

Bolger had become jealous of Peters' public profile and popularity — Peters envious of Bolger's position and prominence. Mindful, no doubt, of his own gutting exploits as a deputy leader, Bolger had no wish to let Peters have even the merest whiff of power. And Peters regarded the deputy leadership as a worthless bauble — a nothing substitute for the real prize. My plans would always founder against these jagged rocks of irreconcilable animus and ambition.

There was one thing, however, on which the two men agreed — the other was the most shallow, venal, self-seeking opportunist each had ever encountered. Who knows — they might both have been right. Anyway, at least I would try to broker détente, although it must have become obvious what I was about. Don McKinnon started giving me the most peculiar looks.

THE GANG OF TWENTY

During this time the capital's morning newspaper, the suitably anaemic *Dominion*, had been running a series of investigative pieces on contributory mortgage companies. Unfortunately the prose style of their business reporter, David Hellaby, incorporated quasi-legal and commercial jargon that made comprehension nigh impossible. Nigerian insurance scams had less complex contracts.

So I passed over these turgid pieces and their equally opaque headlines on my way to the funnies and the sports news. Plainly I was not alone. Hellaby's articles received scant attention from other media outlets and none whatsoever from the Press Gallery or the Opposition. Which, in retrospect, was a rather categoric failure of the political process. For these arcane descriptions of shady dealings on the financial community's fringes contained the pungent whiff of unstable nitroglycerine.

Apparently, three contributory mortgage companies — Registered Securities Limited, Landbase and Advisorcorp — had all (independently as it transpired) been involved in misrepresenting a variety of commercial and residential properties to potential investors. In turn these companies had attracted investment income from primarily retired persons attracted by the better-than-average interest rate returns. These investments were then channelled to various speculative enterprises with all the reckless derring-do of a pyramid selling scheme.

In hindsight it is hard to escape the conclusion that greed motivated all the players in this sad little drama — from the company managers and fraudulent valuers to the individual investors. The first rule of investment — security — was blithely ignored. Mind you, with most of the country's trading banks similarly motivated by a kind of collective casino craziness few fingers were pointed. It was not the financial sector's finest hour.

At the same time as Hellaby was doing his stuff in the *Dominion* another journalist, this time from Napier, Claire Johnstone, was researching the strange commercial dealings of the doyen of the Hawke's Bay community, Sir Peter Tait — the former Napier mayor and National MP. I had been granted an audience with the elderly Tait during the 1987 election campaign and foolishly believed that his grace might extend to a sizeable boost to my local campaign funds. No such luck. Instead I received an hour-long lecture on his peculiar brand of Christian morality (a strict Calvinist ideology with a free-market twist. Why is it that fundamentalists proclaim the virtue of profit over social responsibility?) and was then given a book by former Nixon associate and Watergate jailbird Chuck Colson. Colson got religion in prison — a peculiar brand of redemptive religion that reeked of intellectual syphilis — and unfortunately decided to share it on his release. And still no donation to my campaign funds!

Claire advised me that her editor was spiking reporters' stories on an investigation into Tait and his finance company, Alexander Nominees. Alexander Nominees was part of the Advisorcorp fraternity so the coincidence pricked my interest. But as a typical lazy researcher I shied away from following up that particular lead. It smelt of hard work. Like the parliamentary Press Gallery, I preferred the easy headline.

And so it may have remained if David Hellaby had not contacted me directly. He was upset that his investigative pieces had died in the *Dominion* without the merest flicker of public or political interest. Was I interested in the real story? The prospect of live sex always stiffens my sinews — this was the political equivalent. A meeting was immediately arranged.

Hellaby and his paper's desire to go national dampened any personal unease they might have felt about dabbling in the occult arts of, literally, backstairs politics. That the *Dominion* was aware of Hellaby's startling offer I was in no doubt. Its chief reporter, Fred Tullett, confirmed to me that the newspaper's interests were in escalating Hellaby's research beyond the capital's morning daily. And so a new and strange conspiracy was entered into between the supposedly independent Fourth Estate and an Opposition researcher. Not for the first time, nor for the last.

Thus was recounted to me a devious if human tale of fraud, deception and personal avarice — with a classy stinger in the tail. By its very ineptness the Commercial Affairs division of the Justice Department had been sucked into the vortex that spun around this drama's principal characters. They knew there was a problem but in their best bureaucratic style they were not prepared either to admit its scope or investigate its consequences.

An investigative accountant (a term I have yet to fully comprehend) within Justice had been making his own independent enquiries. Keith Petersen had a reputation for both hyperbole and earnest endeavour, which, in Wellington's civil service community, was a most unusual combination. He was also a flamboyant and dramatic individual — God knows what he was doing in the Commercial Affairs division. Anyway, he had compiled a suitably melodramatic list and called it the Gang of Twenty — a list of companies and individuals involved in the contributory mortgage business whose commercial behaviour reeked of impropriety. Many of those on his list were involved in the same scams detailed publicly by Hellaby and privately by Claire Johnstone. Naturally Hellaby and Petersen had found each other. Both men were conspiracy theorists at heart and, dammit, they had stumbled on to one. Forget live sex — they had found the real thing.

But Petersen's further investigations were blocked by his superiors; Hellaby's by Press Gallery and public indifference. My job was to provide them with the parliamentary (and hence public) profile that their joint endeavours had thus far been denied. I had been sought out by Hellaby because he assumed that I would, in turn, feed the story to Winston Peters. Normally I would have — but these were not normal circumstances.

Here was a superb chance to deliver juicy prime-time television coverage to the Leader. It was a fateful decision for which I am not sure Winston ever really forgave me. Certainly for the next nine years it would be a bone that was dug up repeatedly in the wee hours of many a tipsy evening. 'Laws,' Winston would smoulder, 'I could have made that Gang of Twenty burn.' For once he was absolutely right.

Against his better judgement Bolger had bought a stunt dog, a mixture of retriever and bloodhound, and he wanted proof of its performance. So too did Bill Birch, who had taken the gamble of advocating my alleged skills to his leader. It was time for the stunt dog to perform. Sitting up to beg was a trick all Bolger's staff performed. They wanted something more, and I was equally determined that the Gang of Twenty would be that something.

The problem with any complex scandal is that the facts must be masticated and half-digested before they can be regurgitated for public consumption. That is not entirely the public's fault — it is just that such news must be filtered through semi-illiterate news editors who would prefer pictures of burning ambulances and speeding houses. So if the supposedly smarter Press Gallery found Hellaby's prose unintelligible then whoa. We needed to break this complex story down into bite-sized meaty chunks. Even then it was too complex for some in the Gallery. The electronic media, in particular, complained that the story was 'too hard' for them, as anything multisyllabic would always be.

My aim then was to directly connect the commercial shenanigans of these contributory companies to the inaction of deputy Prime Minister and Justice Minister Geoffrey Palmer. Palmer had the pre-parliamentary reputation of having been a red-hot academic, with his warning tract *Unbridled Power?* becoming a how-to guide on abusing the public trust. For all his glowing university credentials Palmer's trusting acceptance of his department's defensive denials marked him as a piss-poor judge of character. It is a modern mystery of politics. Why do MPs distrust bureaucrats when they are in Opposition yet suddenly believe them when they are in Government? There is no sane answer to that riddle.

Palmer was placed in an invidious position — he could either admit that the mortgage companies were under investigation, possibly panicking existing and potential investors and thereby potentially collapsing the companies, or he could assert his confidence in them and deny all knowledge of wrongdoing. For some reason the Justice bureaucrats convinced Palmer to take the latter course of action. Worse. They managed to convince him that he should utter such statements of confidence to Parliament. This then would be the *pièce de résistance*: Palmer trapped into a comprehensive commercial guarantee. From that moment on the end result was inevitable. The pack of cards was already collapsing as Palmer gave his increasingly shrill assurances.

A few weeks later virtually all the named contributory mortgage companies — first RSL, then Landbase, then Advisorcorp — went belly-up. Palmer's hollow assurances shattered, along with his squeaky-clean reputation. Worse, he had allowed a supposed simpleton who had left school at an early age to best him.

It should have been a complete victory — the kind of victory that demanded Palmer's resignation as the minister responsible. Thousands of investors had lost tens of millions of dollars. Some elderly folk had flushed away their complete life savings. There were stress heart attacks and the occasional tragic suicide. Even as the companies fell over, some of their principals were still urging the public to invest their savings. Palmer's parliamentary assurance was given at the exact time that the companies were collapsing — who knows how many people invested or reinvested on the basis of the minister's public assurances?

But Bolger momentarily lost the plot. Totally. At a time when Winston would have been in for the political kill two minor events threw the Leader and severely blunted the Opposition's parliamentary attack.

The first concerned Sir Peter Tait and Advisorcorp. Claire Johnstone and her *Daily Telegraph* associates had probed a number of investment options being offered by Advisorcorp through Tait's Napier offices. They involved mainly disused dairy factories that had been grossly overvalued, with investors being offered the opportunity to develop the derelict sites into sound commercial entities. It was nifty fraud, complete with shonky valuations and glossy bullshit brochures. Home runs do not come any cleaner in politics and Bolger outlined the scam in a media conference.

Within hours Advisorcorp's principals had sicked their legal pit-bulls onto Bolger for alleged defamation — a fairly normal defensive technique. In a blind panic, Bolger summoned his own lawyer and a hasty meeting was arranged in the Leader's suite. The lawyer's advice was typical — publicly apologise now and potentially save thousands of dollars in legal fees. So-so legal advice; appalling political counsel. I was suitably scandalised.

'Apologise? We have these people dead in the water,' I remonstrated. 'Everything you have said is documented — every statement, every sentence, every fact.' By now my voice was approaching the pitch of the Vienna Boys' Choir on Ecstasy at the Hero parade, my face flushing through several shades of puce. It mattered not; Bolger was adamant. Lawyers cost money — he should cut his losses.

The public apology to Advisorcorp and to Tait derailed the whole thrust of Bolger's crusade. Far from having Palmer backing ever closer to the precipice we now faced the unedifying spectacle of Bolger back-pedalling at an equal rate.

To make matters worse Palmer's parliamentary chiding of the Opposition leader for his lack of responsibility and his unfortunate lack of any functioning cranial neurons drew the most puerile and injudicious of reactions. Bolger hurled the nearest object across the floor of the House in Palmer's direction. A blue plastic biro. If Ruth Richardson had been close then dwarf-throwing might have become fashionable long before its time.

Over the next few months the principals of many of these contributory companies were charged, found guilty and imprisoned. Sir Peter Tait escaped prosecution by pleading that he was unaware of the actions of his business associates, although his public reputation in Hawke's Bay had been destroyed. Unbelievably he still kept donating sizeable sums to the Hawke's Bay National Party and even contributed to my 1990 campaign coffers. Classic proof, I guess, that he truly was unaware of his surroundings in his later years.

But for the rest of the Gang of Twenty fraternity the end results proved less than overwhelming. Hellaby was the only real winner. We had taken his story and given him nationwide publicity, with the *Dominion* editorial staff actively collaborating in embarrassing both Palmer and the Labour Government. Hellaby himself received recognition by being designated Journalist of the Year — an award granted by his peers but earned courtesy of having his claims amplified by the political process rather than by the Gallery. Poetic.

Jim Bolger was not displeased either. Despite his self-inflicted silliness he had garnered the publicity he so desperately sought as well as a measure of Caucus credit for pursuing Geoffrey Palmer and finally bringing the man down. On the other hand, while the deputy Prime Minister's reputation had received a severe dent he, poor man, then succeeded to Labour's shattered leadership. Which proved two things. One, that public stuff-ups are not necessarily fatal. Two, that Palmer was not such a brilliant individual after all.

And then, just as quickly as it had appeared, the Gang of Twenty blip disappeared off the political radar screen. As the contributory mortgage companies collapsed, one after the other, legal and court actions followed. It all got very messy and very complex and neither politicians nor the Press Gallery could be bothered sifting through the wreckage. There were easier headlines to harvest elsewhere. The Labour Party was imploding, and right under the Gallery's noses. Now that was sexy.

TESTING THE EDGE

During the Gang of Twenty affair I was verbally assaulted by one of the Opposition's leading frontbenchers for 'setting Jim up'. This bizarre accusation was levelled by the excitable Tarawera MP, Ian McLean, whose bushy whiskers and nervous manner suggested a possum on acid. McLean was the kind of individual that Prozac is just made for.

According to McLean's rant, my pursuit of the Gang of Twenty principals had besmirched the reputation of decent and honourable businessmen and had led Jim Bolger directly into disrepute. I was clearly a Peters fifth columnist, undermining the leadership from within. After the affair was over McLean did have the decency to apologise for this outburst and admit he may have been mistaken.

Nevertheless, for me the incident highlighted the fact that I would always be regarded as the Svengali behind Peters' public rise — again emphasising Caucus' lack of respect for Winston's intellect and judgement. McLean went so far as to suggest that Peters was essentially a pre-programmed hologram — a kind of political zombie brought to evil life by a youthful Frankenstein. I realised the utter impossibility of Winston ever leading National's Caucus. They did not just dislike him — they despised him. And alas, unknown to Winston, they still do.

In part their perception was correct. Winston was not a beastly swot, he did saunter through the daily chores of Caucus committees and he was a party animal in entertainment terms only. He also brazenly thumbed his nose at the long-established and hallowed National Party dictum that 'an ounce of loyalty is worth a ton of cleverness'. What most Nats did not appreciate was that the astute Keith Holyoake had coined this phrase to give most of his Caucus something to aspire to. He knew damned well that cleverness was beyond the reach of most of them.

By this time Winston had also employed a new executive secretary, a young and attractive arts graduate of Canadian extraction, Sarah Neems. Sarah was smart, ambitious and politically aware — qualities not usually associated with parliamentary secretaries of the time. In fact, she was the first of a new breed — a secretary who typed and also provided political advice. Or, in the case of this Canadian dasher, a secretary who proffered counsel and also attempted to type. Over the years Sarah would become Winston's closest confidante — closer than me; closer than his university rugby mates; closer than his Salamanca Road political colleagues Philip Burdon, Paul East and Don McKinnon. Sure, the tongues wagged. This was closeness of the horizontal variety, whispered the gossips.

Soon such gossip had been escalated into fact and then into living legend. Sarah had dedicated herself to Winston from the first. Maybe dedication and hero worship would be enough. Maybe not. I was never prurient enough to pry. Sorry.

Normally such relationships matter not in Parliament. As both a staffer and later as an MP I became acutely aware that some Members regarded consensual relationships with executive secretaries as one of the perks of the job. Even those who did not display such outmoded attitudes entered into affairs with other parliamentary staff — researchers, Hansard secretaries, select committee clerks and even security guards. It always seemed more of an occupational hazard among National MPs than their Labour counterparts.

There was even a delightful suggestion that such incidents in the past had influenced current hiring policy for Members' secretaries. In an attempt to curb wayward randiness the appointment of attractive secretaries was actively discouraged. Temptation was not to be resisted — it was to be completely denied. Sarah's appointment — a young, pretty, ash-blonde graduate with a strange accent — 'Well, we all know what that's about, don't we?'

But Peters' alleged relationship with Neems was actively promoted within National circles as a knee-capping technique. Whether it was true or not was irrelevant. In fact, I observed not the slightest hint of proof. It was still a useful slur with which to denigrate Peters' character, often used by the same MPs who bonked their own staff, or at least attempted to do so. It was just another way to dispense Caucus' collective jealousy.

THE NATIVES GET RESTLESS

Despite the improvement in Bolger's public standing after the Gang of Twenty affair, the effects proved to be temporary. With the resignation of Hazel Whiteoak, Bolger had appointed ex-*Listener* editor and television journalist David Beatson to the vital role of chief press secretary. Beatson was an elder Gallery statesman, although he too found difficulties in communicating the Bolgerian spin to the younger members of the Fourth Estate. I daresay his vocabulary scared them for a start.

Beatson was stolid rather than brilliant, an educated and considered individual who never seemed entirely at ease with the daily slap-and-tickle required in dealing with the Gallery. He immediately distrusted my motives, which made our relationship both fractious and frustrating, although one could hardly blame him. From the first instant he would have been bombarded with party and Caucus propaganda, making him wary of both Peters and me. Difficult to establish any kind of working relationship under those conditions.

Of course, my manifest personal failings did not improve things. I took Beatson's appointment as a challenge. Here was a much-vaunted and saluted media high-flier, a true pro. It was the old hired gun against the young pretender.

Despite the significant resources of the Leader's office the public contest would prove an unequal one. Bolger's image as a pedestrian, rustic plodder was well established. Short of a brain transplant, a year's elocution lessons and a personal trainer he would always be at a media

disadvantage against the glamorous, dapper and handsome populist. Only plain old-fashioned power could tip the balance Bolger's way. Either that or a mistake (and a big one) by Winston. In the event the two combined — but I rush ahead.

By now Winston was on the receiving end of probing missions from many other National MPs. Despite his much quoted (and much disbelieved) statement that he was 'happy just to be the Member for Tauranga' his colleagues wanted to ingratiate themselves in case Tauranga became too small. The first stirrings of an anti-Bolger plot were similarly occurring.

Incredibly (and I mean incredibly), Winston assumed that his media profile and undoubted political popularity would deliver him the National Party leadership. There would be no messy coups, no back-room planning, no fateful stratagems. In Winston's mind the National Caucus would finally recognise the inevitable. The political Messiah was in their midst and the light of revelation would soon cast its brilliance upon their stuffed-up and envious consciousness. I sometimes wondered if Winston did not consider that his fellow MPs would only come to their senses once they had recovered from his blinding brilliance — it was just a matter of time.

Anyway, it became the subject of increasingly terse debate between

Winston and me which would be replayed over and over again. Even
Sarah, who was increasingly taken into Winston's confidence,
attempted to convince him of the fanciful nature of such thinking.
To no avail. The Caucus would wake up sooner or later — reasoning
that rendered both Sarah and me wholly impotent, reduced to mutual
shoulder shrugging, eyebrow raising and deep sighs. Even had I drip-
drip-dripped for a thousand years there would have been no effect on
this adamantine state of mind. Winston would not lobby for himself,
formally or informally. 'Laws,' — he would puff out his chest in his
best Mussolini style as if to mask the fragility of the argument —
'they will come to me. They will have to.'

It was not as if Winston did not have his personal lobbyists. His
close friend Philip Burdon paraded him around any number of
commercial acquaintances. Something of a mistake really. Winston
had neither head nor heart for economic policy nor the minutiae of
fiscal policy and its arid derivatives, a fact that was often made
apparent, although never fatally. Winston was a fine proponent of
the art of bluff. He could be so obtuse that one was given to wonder if
the questioner had been intellectually deficient in framing the enquiry
in the first place.

By now Winston had spread his political wings far beyond issues
of race and employment. His special joy was in twitting finance
spokesperson Ruth Richardson, which had the effect of really souring
my relationship with my former mentor. Ruth now reviled me as if I
had indecently assaulted her favourite pet.

'How are you enjoying yourself with that nasty little populist?' she
would enquire through clenched teeth. It soon got so bad that we
took to ignoring each other in the parliamentary corridor. Of course
it took more effort (and acting ability) to suddenly be consumed with
that speck of lint on one's shoulder, but it was preferable to even the
most minute of pleasantries.

For his part, Winston considered Ruth's monetarist focus to be
vaguely immoral. Of course he had no idea why he thought such
thoughts, he just instinctively rejected Ruth's 'more market' philosophy as wrong. It was my job to explain why. Fortunately I shared
Winston's viewpoint.

The market is a wonderful place if you harbour the initiative, the
skills and the contacts to exist within it. In this brave new world the
most vocal proponents of the market invariably happen to be the
best-armed. It is the human condition to prefer games that you know

you will win. As a general rule the 'players' are white, Western and well educated (the new tyranny of the three Ws), hail from stable, middle-class backgrounds, and have frightening levels of self-confidence. They are the commercial equivalent of being fit, fast, strong and Polynesian in the rugby world. A no-contest.

The real problem with the Rogernomics revolution though was that it atomised the last vestiges of a social conscience. Zealots who attacked the welfare state for its inefficiency and torpor misunderstood its *raison d'être*. The welfare state was society's way of caring for its sick, poor, weak and vulnerable precisely because individual compassion and charity were just too difficult. You had to institutionalise such concepts because they would not happen otherwise.

Altruism may be a human virtue but it is in precious short supply. If the State does not perform these caring tasks then the lesson of history (and human experience — not the same thing) is that the sick, the poor, the weak and the vulnerable will be driven to the wall. Forgive my cynicism but the same kind of people who tend to argue for tax cuts are precisely those who intend to spend them on themselves — the welfare state was created to ensure that the wealthy and the moderately comfortable could not thus evade their compassionate responsibilities.

And since we pretend to be a civilised society (despite massive empirical evidence to the contrary) the welfare state was our way of making up for the general paucity of individual altruism. Basically we are just bloody lazy. A dollop of tax dollars looks after education, health, welfare needs, the elderly — taxpayers are only too pleased to part with a portion of their income so that someone else can address infrastructural social problems that they would rather ignore. Unlike some, I saw no difficulty with the arrangement. It had the virtue of practicality.

Rogernomics changed all that. It inherently assumed that the weak and the vulnerable were just panhandling panty-wasters, that the poor were poor by dint of their own individual indolence. Forget the socioeconomic, the ethnic, the cultural divides and barriers; the Right assumed that the underachievers in their midst underachieved simply because they wanted to. Being poor was a lifestyle choice.

Now that David Lange had paused for his 'cup of tea' — an act of retrospective caution that contributed to the subsequent meltdown of Labour's Cabinet — the National Opposition saw their chance to not so much regain as requisition the radical garb of the Right.

143

National's criticisms of Labour's economic policies began to change. Instead of branding the Government 'heartless' and 'doctrinaire', the Opposition now chided it for its inability to 'manage change' and for 'not going far enough'. Labour market deregulation, reform of the waterfront, education vouchers and 'work for the dole' schemes became the next obvious policy steps. Richardson carefully positioned National as the only party with the balls to deliver.

In terms of 'Where to from here?', the National Caucus had split into two evenly matched camps. Richardson, Upton, Luxton, Williamson, Shipley and McCully wanted National to embrace Rogernomics with a twist. The conservatives — Muldoon, Birch, Burdon, Venn Young and Peters — argued that New Zealand was undergoing 'reform fatigue'. It was time to consolidate rather than go forward. At the same time as the Caucus Right were preaching further privatisation and self-reliance, the conservatives were protesting against Post Office closures and promising to abolish the super-annuation surtax.

The problem with the Caucus conservatives was that they lacked either strategy or unity in their policy approaches. Muldoon's support was a double-edged sword; Burdon and Birch were clearly motivated by the personal desire to trip Richardson's ambitions; Peters was never going to form an alliance with anyone unless he was placed at its forefront. And yet, ironically, the Caucus conservatives probably outnumbered the market liberals. They just lacked discipline, an intelligent strategy and teamwork. Fatal stuff, really.

This was never better demonstrated than with the epic Caucus battle over the National Party's position on the Reserve Bank Act. New Finance Minister David Caygill had continued with the Douglas/Treasury agenda by creating an independent Reserve Bank that would have one singular goal — the control of inflation — specifically, the pursuit of an inflation target somewhere between zero and two per cent.

It is difficult to appreciate but the idea of providing the central bank with such independence, and such an obsessive focus, horrified most policy conservatives. Certainly a large number of the National Caucus were scandalised. Tinkering with the economy was a time-honoured political tradition; take away that power and you may as well hand the economy directly over to the Japs, the Swiss or the Americans. Again, Sir Robert Muldoon led the charge, and he was far from impotent in his effect on his wavering Caucus colleagues.

Both Bolger and Birch still regarded the old boar as having enough intellectual gas in the tank to be genuinely scary, while younger members had learned to smile wanly in the cowardly hope that the great man would not be suddenly distracted and verbally dismember them.

According to Winston, the Caucus decision to accept Labour's Reserve Bank Act without amendment was as close as twelve votes to eleven, with a number of conservative MPs absent from the key meeting. And so the National Party bought into Rogernomics, four years after its effective launch and despite Caucus misgivings and grassroots party disfavour.

But that was National's dilemma in opposition. It could not work out if it should pass Labour on the right or the left. There was so little room remaining on the political Right that a step into relative oblivion presented a clear and present danger. Instinctively, intuitively, Bolger decided that the National Party must reject the fashionable dogma of the market — that social responsibility was as much an imperative for government as economic liberalism.

To Bolger's credit, he openly discussed such concepts with his staff. As the token quasi-socialist I was able to offer an alternative viewpoint and I found myself agreeably surprised that Bolger would genuinely acknowledge issues of socioeconomic disadvantage.

But the National Party still had no coherent or consistent philosophy or message. It could not. The personalities and their disparate policies were too diverse. When Bolger talked of leading a broad-church National Party he actually presided over a party that contained elements of both fundamental evangelism and devil worship. In the late 1980s the National Party surely was the most Catholic of persuasions.

A DOOR OPENS . . .

Winston's addiction to the media spotlight began to demand greater and greater doses, and by now I had exhausted the gamut of petty scandals, departmental peccadillos and bureaucratic hiccups that might create a sympathetic headline or two.

I was like a drug seller who had run out of the hard stuff. Between writing speeches, cajoling various media hacks and ferreting out the occasional 'leak' I had no time for tracking down the real nuggets. That required extensive and exhaustive investigation and research.

And for what? Thirty seconds on TV's six o'clock news and a couple of embarrassing questions in the House. This was not my idea of making a difference.

By now I had become both overly and overtly cynical about the entire political process. Politics really had degenerated into just another game, Parliament merely the playing ground. The Westminster parliamentary system, as interpreted in its antipodean setting, had evolved into a tribal battleground where no prisoners were taken and where truth had long since been put out of its misery. Even within the various parties there had evolved factionalised and bitter camps motivated as much by spite and personal aggrandisement as by any philosophical principle.

And the so-called Fourth Estate, my once professed vocational yearning, had been exposed as a bunch of grasping and often biased nonentities searching for the instant fix of a sensational story. If it was not sensational then a careful pruning of the facts could always render it as such.

Yet still that wicked allure of power — or rather the proximity of power — wove its sickly magic. I was as much of a political junkie as everyone else. As much wedded to creating those same headlines that other parts of my consciousness actively despised. As much a peddler of dubious persuasion as all the other politicians and press secretaries and party strategists. I was still hooked. Maybe more so now than ever before. The vortex of the parliamentary environment made any thought of escape both remote and futile.

And then came a new challenge. In a move that stunned the country, and especially his Labour colleagues, David Lange upped and resigned as Prime Minister. At the time it seemed an act of exhaustion; in retrospect it now reads as a failure of imagination rather than will.

Lange had presided over an economic and social revolution that he now considered himself powerless to halt as it ripped the lungs out of every Kiwi virtue he held dear. Like all such revolutions of spirit this one had begun to devour its creators. Labour's Left had been siphoned off by the rebellious Jim Anderton; Labour's Right had marshalled itself into the Backbone Club. From thence they were to form the polar extremes of the post-MMP parliamentary environment — the Alliance and ACT parties. All that destructive/constructive energy had its internal emotional consequences.

David Lange was also presumably smart enough to foresee his own spectacular demise had he stayed. The collapse of the sharemarket in October 1987 had a lasting impact on the economy as jobless numbers continued to scale ever new heights, and the public had become hostile to having their concerns dismissed with irreverent Lange aphorism. After five years of often bellicose foreign policy, if beguiling domestic policy, David Lange had the last laugh. He left his warring Caucus colleagues to fend for themselves and the public to find a new parliamentary whipping boy.

Initially, the elevation of Geoffrey Palmer to the premier spot seemed to work. The new Prime Minister was the exact antithesis of his unpopular predecessor. Palmer had qualities Lange would never possess — he was sober and solemn, thorough and thin. Yeah, but extraordinarily boring. The more you saw of Palmer the less you wanted to see.

However, the new Labour leader was gifted a brief honeymoon with the Press Gallery and consequently with public perception. Political polling provided ample proof that the leadership change had gone down a treat. For the first time in eighteen months Labour fashioned a narrow lead with the pollsters and Palmer accelerated out of nowhere to become the pollsters' 'preferred Prime Minister'.

The entire National Opposition were plunged into Stygian gloom. Well, almost the entire Opposition. Winston and I found it almost impossible to contain our delight. There could be no more 'sleep-walking to victory', as Winston had undiplomatically described National's performance to date. Caucus would have to face the very real possibility that Labour might just hang on in 1990 — and that realisation would lead them to one critical consideration. The leadership.

By mid-September 1989 even Bolger's staffers were talking of 'when' their boss might be replaced and I relayed this titbit to Winston with relish. Now was the time for Winston to be talking to his colleagues. Now was the time for a few quiet drinks and even quieter talk. Now was the time for Roger McClay and Philip Burdon to be preparing lobby lists.

Certainly the Ruth Richardson bloc in Caucus were not inactive. Richardson's chief cheerleader at the time was East Coast Bays MP Murray McCully and he had begun to sound Winston out on the latent possibilities contained in the latest polls. Neither man was entirely comfortable in the other's presence. They both knew that there were vast chasms of comprehension between the economic philosophies represented by Richardson and Peters. But at least McCully understood that only the combination of a Peters/Richardson challenge could unseat Bolger.

Despite this it became my view that McCully was playing a double game. It suited Richardson to have Bolger and Peters publicly playing each other off, and soon Winston independently discerned that McCully's interest was double-edged. Ruth might be interested in a coup if Winston accepted the No. 2 slot. On the only occasion that Peters and I openly discussed the McCully overtures Winston ended the chat with a snort of derision at this prospect.

Given this strategic stalemate, and with Peters convinced that his Caucus colleagues must finally 'see sense' and draft him for the leadership, there could be only one winner. Bolger might well have been boring, unimaginative, petty and pedantic, but he had the one great advantage all National Party leaders understand. Incumbency. In this case, incumbency matched with a Caucus that possessed neither the planning skills nor the unity to mount a serious challenge.

Certainly there were those Richardson supporters in Caucus who regarded each bravura public performance from Winston as a direct attack on both Bolger and themselves. After one Caucus meeting new Ashburton tyro MP Jenny Shipley stormed into the research unit offices and fiercely denounced my alleged meddling.

'We will make the Leader, Michael,' she asserted with that peculiar blend of hooded malice and cultured charm that is uniquely Jenny's. 'Not you.'

I stammered a vague protest but Shipley would hear none of it. She had made up her mind, and I soon learned that Jenny's mind possessed an unshakeable quick-dry conviction. The rotten seed of ambition planted within Winston's cranium had not been scattered there by genetic accident or self-revelation.

'Winston would not break wind without you scripting it,' she heatedly declaimed, and with that the same torrent that had brought her to me rushed her away.

Shipley's outburst troubled me. Apart from the disquieting experience of having Jenny's vast bulk verbally detonate at such close proximity the whole incident demonstrated, yet again, that Caucus forces who disliked Bolger reviled Peters to an even greater degree. Winston would never lead these people. They neither liked nor trusted nor respected him. To his Caucus colleagues Peters showed up both their own failure to properly connect with the public mood and their own selfish antipathy to the message that he was delivering.

For at the heart of Winston's message was the basic populist theme that the institution of government is inherently untrustworthy. And those National MPs who currently rested in Opposition coveted that institution for themselves. They did not want it reformed, they liked it just the way it was thank you very much. It just needed new tenants — them.

. . . AND CLOSES

Such nuances were lost on Winston. He was having too good a time riding the popular currents and dismissed Caucus sensitivities with almost regal disdain.

'They'll come around, Laws,' he would soothe me. 'They have no option,' and he would point to the latest public opinion polls. Maybe his confidence had a basis in fact but I doubted it. Jealousy will always justify its negativism. But then a glimmer...

A month after the *New Zealand Herald* poll had shown Prime Minister Geoffrey Palmer elevated to the 'preferred leader' position, another poll, this time the influential TVNZ/Heylen snapshot, provided even grimmer news for the Leader's office.

Sure, National maintained a slight five-point margin over Labour in party support, but Bolger had slipped down to just six per cent in the 'preferred Prime Minister' slot. Palmer's honeymoon continued with a remarkable ranking of 31 per cent, while Winston's steady nineteen per cent shamed Bolger's feeble listing.

Renewed gloom descended on the Opposition — except in a certain ground-floor office where the Member for Tauranga was merrily batting away media speculation by joyfully proclaiming that he was 'just happy to be the Member for Tauranga'. The mischievous grin that accompanied these words made this the most public private joke in the country.

A day later Peters landed another telling blow on the Labour Government by stitching up the new deputy Prime Minister, Helen Clark, for political interference in the awarding of a half-million-dollar advertising contract to former Labour staffer and prime ministerial press secretary Ross Vintiner. The so-called DDB Needham affair provided yet more favourable media coverage — further proof, if it was required, that Winston was the most effective and destructive force the Opposition possessed.

Conversely, it also provided his colleagues with yet another reason to dislike him. Envy surfaced again. With each issue, each new political hit, each new media fête Peters unwittingly walked further and further away from the Caucus leadership he so coveted.

You can be too successful in this business; perhaps that was Winston's true crime in the eyes of his colleagues. He showed them up for the rank amateurs they were and they loathed him for it. They expected the man to play 'the team game', to be mediocre and mealy-mouthed just like them. Jim Bolger was thus their natural leader; neither Peters nor Richardson could truly empathise with Caucus' collective or individual insecurities. Neither Opposition star would stand a chance. They were the talented, non-conformist outsiders and, after the last nasty experience with Muldoon, talented outsiders were to be instinctively distrusted.

These were my thoughts at the time although Winston continued to consider them overly pessimistic. Caucus would come round. Just you wait and see, Laws. My reaction was to engage in yet more Russian eye-rolling. A rhino gun would not have damaged his unwavering faith in his colleagues' ability to finally see political sense and recognise the latent leader in their midst. Yeah, right. If Peters refused to privately canvass for Caucus support to raise the leadership issue then he must do so publicly. It was my rather prescient view (I claim it on the rare occasions that I am right) that Labour and Palmer could not hold their honeymoon together until the next election. Too much hate, too much history, and too much humbug. Besides, the economy was in the toilet.

Winston decided to use a speech to the Auckland Chamber of Commerce to slyly criticise Bolger's leadership abilities, without ever openly admitting to such a thing. It was my job to write an address that included such denigration within Winston's very public crusade for political reform.

My first draft was presented to Peters and rejected as 'too tame'. Winston wanted an alternative Opposition front bench promoted, and it was my task to submerge this sabotage within the much higher principles of democratic transparency. The end result was sufficiently combustible to satisfy Winston's curious demand — he wanted smoke but no conflagration.

As it was the speech inflamed the media and immolated any remaining Caucus tolerance. Winston exposed not so much a raw nerve in the Leader's office as a quivering mass of interconnected synapses all primed to explode. The introductory remarks were fairly standard: Labour were the meanest bunch of misbegotten simians ever let loose from captivity — standard deprecatory fare. Not content with this gratuitous roll through the proverbial cowpat, however, Winston's speech then zoomed into the stratosphere of high principle.

'The enormous gulf in New Zealand politics relates to leadership and power-sharing. Put simply — the public do not trust the politicians... This should not come as a surprise to those involved in the political process. As a profession, no other grouping has so abused and misused power...'

To buttress this viewpoint I had included in the speech a recent public opinion poll that had found only four per cent of New Zealanders fully trusted their political representatives. Pretty disturbing evidence of the level of mental derangement in the wider community — I excused that four per cent as recent escapees from Lake Alice. Interestingly, the same survey taken in 1975 had found a remarkable 38 per cent of the population professing faith in their politicians — the stunning subsequent decline was a rather sad commentary upon both Sir Robert Muldoon and the fourth Labour Government. But then the bite.

'New Zealanders are searching for effective political leadership. The polls suggest that has not been found... In the National Party, we must accept our share of responsibility. The New Zealand people want to be rid of Labour. They want a reason to vote National. Too many of them feel that reason is lacking. That means that my party must get hungrier, leaner, more innovative, more daring and strong enough to say to the public what our working alternatives are...'

So far, so good.

I had written into the speech some Winstonian self-criticism so that he might justify this wider criticism to his Caucus. This was tippy-toeing to the edge stuff — in the next paragraph Winston gladly stepped over and into the void.

'We have yet to provide the political leadership that the electorate craves of us. There are signs that we are progressing ... certainly the talent exists in the Caucus and the Party...'

And then he named his rival front bench — seven MPs who might expect to share the Opposition front bench with their self-anointed leader. This so-called 'vital team' was more remarkable for its absentees — Leader Jim Bolger, the *éminence grise* Bill Birch, deputy Don McKinnon, frontbenchers Doug Graham and John Falloon. Peters' speech clearly identified, by omission, those senior MPs content to 'sleepwalk to victory' and, in contrast, those 'earnest, innovative and competent' MPs that the public 'craved'.

Of course, it was just like Winston to publicly announce this alternative front bench without discussing it or lobbying the intended recipients of such illusory largesse. Bolger was infuriated. If Bolger alone had been infuriated then the issue may have met with the usual carpet-storming activities in the Leader's suite. But both McKinnon and Birch understood that the threat was just a little more immediate than that. Peters was signalling their demise as well.

Within seconds of the speech's embargo being lifted Bill Birch had rushed into my office demanding to see a copy. He was not happy, his thick eyebrows now mingling in a black frown, his exasperation as palpable as his perspiration. It was one of those moments when you fear that your bowels have become independently mutinous.

As a copy of Peters' speech was ripped from my grasp a departing Birch tartly promised, 'You have worked your last day here.' I was still young, stupid and naive enough to believe that research staff could not be fired for the peccadillos of their masters. Besides, Winston would protect me. As it transpired Winston could not even protect himself.

The Richardson camp saw their opportunity to kneecap their chief leadership rival and took it. Dark mutterings about a leadership coup began to publicly surface all right, but a leadership coup led by the Selwyn MP. Excitable new Pakuranga MP Maurice Williamson publicly floated the idea of a Richardson challenge, which prompted deputy Don to issue an ultimatum to any plotters: 'Put up or shut up.'

Through all the intense media speculation Winston still refused to countenance either an overt challenge or a covert arrangement with the Richardson camp. Despite party president John Collinge publicly supporting the tenor of Peters' comments (a move that almost drove Bolger to despair — from that moment on New Zealand would always be too small for both Jim Bolger and John Collinge; the president would later receive his luxury exile to London) Winston could not marshal the Caucus support for a real challenge.

One evening we idly discussed possible Caucus supporters and came up well short. Wyatt Creech (who owed his Wairarapa seat to Peters' efforts with the electoral petition), Bay of Islands MP John Carter (reviled by Bolger for using his position as electorate chairman to roll incumbent duffer Neil Austin for the party's 1987 selection), good friend and fellow electoral petitioner Roger McClay, Waitotara veteran Venn Young, fellow Bay of Plenty MP Robert Anderson, Philip Burdon and the dissident remnants of the Muldoon era, Merv Wellington and Sir Robert himself.

Nine MPs including Winston. And hardly the cutting edge of innovation.

The only leadership coup that could work was a joint ticket of Peters and Richardson but such an arrangement would always founder on personal and philosophical grounds. Besides, they would never be able to agree on who should be number one and who should be the deputy. One thing was for sure. The winner would not want to turn their back for an instant.

Richardson's camp was perhaps slightly more numerous but it had a similarly intractable problem. Ruth. The stumpy, stony-faced Selwyn battler may have been a wonderfully warm individual on the inside but that was not her public visage.

We summed up Richardson's possible Caucus support: Simon Upton, Maurice Williamson, Murray McCully, Jenny Shipley, John Luxton, Denis Marshall, Ian McLean, Doug Graham; with Ruth that also equalled nine. As with any such list Rangiora MP Jim Gerard appeared as a 'maybe' in both camps. The logic was ineluctable. Only a united Peters/Richardson challenge could succeed. And Hell would freeze over on the same day. Bolger's leadership was impregnable. Ruth was the first to appreciate such indubitable logic.

When Jim Bolger finally did take decisive disciplinary action it proved both unexpected and unprecedented. Egged on by Birch and McKinnon the Leader asserted his authority for the very first time since the shadow Cabinet reshuffle that had followed the '87 election.

As was my habit I had arrived at the research unit around ten and there, awaiting my arrival, was Winston, engulfed as always in the trademark cigarette haze. I frowned. It was Thursday. Caucus day. Winston should either be involved in an animated plea of self-justification or dozing — these were the two most common variables that governed his Caucus activities. Instead he was in my office, and he had ominously closed the door as I sat down.

'I've been sacked,' he stated stiffly with a mixture of shock and dangerous resignation. This was no time to gulp with amazement. Clearly the man was in my office for some kind of political or emotional succour, although within moments that defiant brand anger — later to become a Winstonian trademark — was bubbling its way to the surface and dashing away his initial deflation.

As Winston told it, Bolger had struck with unexpected swiftness. Caucus had barely breathed when the Leader announced that, 'for disciplinary reasons', Winston was to be removed from the Opposition front bench and stripped of his shadow employment portfolio. Presumably this was to cut off both his public access to the political issue of the day and his private access to yours truly as the unit's employment researcher. Outspoken Whangarei MP John Banks had been gifted that dream opposition portfolio.

Winston had stormed from the Caucus on receiving this news and thence made his way to my garret office. Apparently Bolger had trailed after him for some way, insisting on getting an answer to whether Peters would now also be quitting the equally high profile Maori affairs portfolio. It was clearly Peters' intention to do so.

Fortunately wiser counsel (even if it was only my own) prevailed. For the next few minutes I argued strongly that quitting Maori affairs would give Bolger a complete victory, and that by retaining the role he could still comment on just about everything ('Maoris are unemployed, aren't they? ... they buy houses ... send their kids to school ... serve in our armed forces ...' etc.) while keeping our partnership alive.

His mood soon swung from depressed to jubilant. He would show them ... my God, 'they' had made a mistake when they had crossed him ... the public wouldn't stand for it ... 'Just like MacArthur, Laws ... I'll be back.' And with that he commanded me to draft a suitably defiant press release before preening and readying himself for the media onslaught.

I did as bidden but more immediate and disturbing undercurrents were beginning to surface. Birch's promise of great personal harm was reinforced by a sympathetic Philip Burdon and also by John Banks. Both informed me that the Leader wanted the evil succubus gone as well; Burdon went so far as to describe Bolger's antipathy towards me as 'paranoic'. This truly was bowel-loosening time. Both Eaddy and Eagleson, with whom I still enjoyed friendly relations, made a special point of warning me about the imminence of Caucus knives. Other researchers reported similar sharpenings.

Despite these manoeuvrings I retained my position, John Banks' private entreaties complementing the difficulties of ending the employment contract of a researcher obeying an MP's instructions even if with overzealous endeavour. Whew.

A new partnership with Banks began to blossom and within days he was demonstrating to good effect the fact that the feisty Opposition stance on unemployment would not alter one little bit. Similarly, my relationship with Peters simply carried on — Winston found that being Opposition spokesperson on Maori affairs gave him the liberty to extend his political commentary even further than before.

When one querulous MP tackled Peters over his continued outspokenness, and demanded to know what gave him the right to dabble in others' portfolios, Peters mischievously replied, 'The Treaty of Waitangi'.

TOO CLEVER BY HALF

I have said it before but it is worth repeating. You can be too smart in this game. Not only is cleverness much distrusted in politics (hence Sir Keith Holyoake's dictum) but it makes one overconfident. Careless. Reckless even. Having survived the Peters demotion, and some very nasty collective Caucus indignation for doing so, I breathed my relief too easily. And too audibly. It is one thing to dance on the edge but you do not waltz there too long.

The occasion was the arrival in this country of the new United States ambassador, Mrs Della Newman. Newman had no greater qualification for the job than that she had sold real estate in California. Oh, and she had also donated handy sums of cash to the Republican Party and just happened to be 'an old friend' of President George Bush. One did not like to enquire beyond that.

She was a thoroughly inoffensive individual who displayed stoic resolve at the deeply embarrassing antics of her husband, a man who believed that every moment of her time in this country required his photographic accompaniment. So the various antics of male New Zealand politicians would not try her patience. Which was just as well.

The relationship between the United States administration and the Labour Government was still in a process of deep cryogeny so the normal process of diplomatic communication was understandably fraught. Top-level meetings between the US ambassador and the Prime Minister had been frozen by the ANZUS impasse, the Yanks working on the rather strange theory that not allowing New Zealand to shelter behind either their nuclear umbrella or their *noblesse oblige* would soon bring the country to its senses.

It thus became a matter of some political pride for the National Opposition to enjoy friendly relations with the United States, especially as this feat was beyond the current Labour administration. National MPs still drooled and dribbled uncontrollably when in the same room as any American official — even a real-estate salesperson. To that end a meeting had been arranged between the Leader of the Opposition and the new ambassador, and was to be heralded a political coup. Jim Bolger, international statesman. That sort of thing.

Unfortunately this simpering embrace was sabotaged by Winston, who was to lunch with Mrs Newman at a private function organised by a financial company. I was bidden to alert the media as a demonstration of Winston thumbing his nose at his recent demotion, and for being the first Opposition MP to shake her hand. Incredibly the Press Gallery considered this meeting to be of some diplomatic and political consequence, especially as Winston's anti-nuclear line was at direct variance with current official National Party policy.

Rather than sell the meeting as childish brinkmanship I decided to advise the Gallery that this lunch would allow Winston to explain to the new ambassador the strength of public feeling against the visits of United States nuclear warships. In other words I would cloak Winston's intent with noble sentiment.

No such luck. TVNZ ran the story as a classic piece of Winstonian teasing, complete with a rather arid commentary on how yours truly had alerted the Gallery to this formerly private luncheon meeting. I watched the television news in complete horror. Messing around with Jim Bolger was one thing. But messing around with Bolger's beloved ANZUS was quite another. This was one step too far.

So there I sat in my Wellington flat and watched all and any political dreams — Winston's elevation to the leadership; being an influential ministerial aide; even having a cosy consultancy post-election — evaporate. I could survive the scripting of an incendiary Winstonian speech; I could not survive the direct mocking of Bolger's pretensions at diplomacy. The next morning Jim Bolger would have me dismissed and there would be no rescue from any quarter. Winston had been unable to save himself, the Leader's staff knew I had crossed a line, and John Banks could never exert that much influence.

And then an idea occurred to me — one so ironic that I openly laughed at its cheek. I would escape my likely Caucus persecutors by the one move they would least expect. I would become one of them.

– Chapter 6 –

ABYSS

DEJA VU

This audacious plan to cheat the abyss was by no means flawless. There were three fairly significant obstacles in the way of personal salvation — namely, finding a friendly electorate, getting the party's nomination and then winning the election itself. Hawke's Bay was the obvious choice of electorate but I had burned my bridges there earlier by repeatedly confirming that I would not be contesting the 1990 nomination. Besides, the wounds of past defeat were too fresh and the emotional scars a little deeper than I cared to admit.

And yet — where else? The prospect of the Manawatu nomination temporarily tempted until I learned that the son of the former and highly respected National deputy prime minister, Duncan McIntyre, had already declared his candidacy. Hamish McIntyre had it all — he was a farmer, a medical practitioner and the son of one of the party's modern legends. I would not have a show. My vision of McIntyre was of a stuffy rustic patrician — much in the mould of his predecessor, Michael Cox — but this perception would later be well and truly shattered.

I was stuffed — there were no other options. I guess this was one of those situations that Treasury considered when they invented the TINA (There Is No Alternative) scenario. Tomorrow I must find a secure bolthole to protect me from the wrath of the Leader and that meant Hawke's Bay or nowhere. Now if only a sense of collective amnesia could overwhelm the party's electorate committee and take with it all memories of my previous and excessive immaturity.

So on the same evening that TVNZ News so blithely flushed my research career down the toilet I made the fateful decision to again seek a parliamentary career. I could not think of a lesser motivation to seek public office — a combination of a betrayed 'off the record' comment and the wrath of Jim Bolger. Within the hour I

157

had contacted my previous campaign secretary, Anne Averill, informed her of my momentous decision, and was begging for help. This entreaty was greeted with an unsettling silence and then the kind of gurgling noises one might associate with catatonic shock. Not a good start, Michael.

But my personal adage that if you want something done properly give it to a woman to do proved right yet again. Anne recovered sufficiently to inform me that nominations closed at 5pm the next day and that the best and brightest of the possible nominees, young Hastings farmer and electorate treasurer Lawrence Yule, had decided his young family came before the pursuit of any silliness in Wellington. Finally, Fate had decided to even the odds. Now to break the news to everyone else — gently.

I had hoped to skulk from the unit with a few muffled goodbyes and at least a hint of foolish dignity. No such luck. Rob Eaddy tracked me down and informed me that the Leader had some unfinished business to attend to that involved my presence and would I mind popping in after I had cleared my desk? Well, yes, actually. The request escalated to a command.

The atmosphere in the Leader's office was every bit as intense and unnerving as I had feared — it was one of those rare occasions when the actual experience matched the awful anticipation. As I was ushered into the room Bolger glanced up from behind his desk and openly scowled with displeasure. I stammered an insincere greeting but to no effect.

'I think it would be very unwise for you to seek the Hawke's Bay nomination,' he intoned imperiously. I assumed that the proper response to this indirect command was to tug my forelock in reverential respect and profusely thank the great man for his wise counsel.

'Thank you for your advice Mr Bolger,' I replied. 'I shall certainly consider it.'

Bolger steepled his hands, reattached the disapproving stare and settled further back in his chair. My attempt at deflection was clearly not going to work.

'It would be most unwise for you to seek any nomination at this time' — stressing the word 'most' as if it had been graven on stone tablets and handed down from on high. Of course this quasi-command rather begged the question as to whether there could ever be a 'right time'. But my many months of working on the periphery of Peters' insouciance had not been for nought. The last thing the Leader needed now was a very public and damaging row over my departure and I pressed this illusory advantage.

'I'll do a deal with you, Mr Bolger. I'll go quietly and never darken your doorstep again. You leave me alone to contest the Hawke's Bay nomination in a fair fight. No interference from the top.'

The head office intelligence at this time was always late and invariably wrong. It continued to posit Lawrence Yule as the most likely nominee, with divisional women's section chair Joyce Gibson also a likely contender. Already I was hearing whispers that I was unlikely to win reselection anyway. I can only suppose that such erroneous information had found its way into Bolger's enclave.

'It would be most improper of me to influence a nomination,' Bolger sourly noted. Yeah, but that would not stop him, I surmised. This observation would be as close as I would get to any post-resignation 'arrangement'. Thankfully Rob Eaddy still had a vestige of affection for his fellow Otago history colleague and diplomatic media releases were now framed and distributed.

Michael Laws had resigned from the National Research Unit and the Leader had accepted his resignation. It required a companion release of my own to explain that the resignation was in order to seek the party's Hawke's Bay nomination, and I was duly staggered to note that most of the Press Gallery actually accepted this explanation.

However, it did not take long for my tacit arrangement with Bolger to be breached. A leak from the Leader's office characterised my resignation as the political equivalent of being prodded to walk the plank. Well, I could survive Bolger's covert hostility; overt opposition would have been an entirely different issue. Fortunately, the Hawke's Bay electorate still had a fond regard for Winston Peters, and my close association with the popular Tauranga MP would even the odds. Or so I reckoned. I was wrong.

Within 24 hours of the news breaking an anonymous group calling itself Hawke's Bay First had publicly declared its vehement opposition to my candidacy. If I were selected as candidate they warned of mass resignations from the local membership, the selection of an alternative National candidate and the ultimate indignity of a re-elected Bill Sutton. Michael Laws was not wanted in Hawke's Bay — he was an unstable, immoral radical. Marilyn Waring with a perm. And then the most cruel gibe of all — perhaps, they suggested, Mr Laws' personal characteristics might be more attuned to a Wellington electorate.

The severity of this personal attack stunned me but I was even more concerned that the local Hawke's Bay media seemed to be treating this vindictive vendetta as valid criticism. I could handle local crazies being crazy but not if the newspapers began to accord them a respectful hearing. In its turn this prompted the Hawke's Bay First grouping to ever more outrageous actions and accusations, and a blizzard of similarly anonymous anti-Laws correspondence showered the Letters to the Editor page. If I were selected as National's candidate then all manner of pestilence would descend upon the Bay — damaging spring hailstorms, the provincial rugby team relegated to the Second Division, and unnatural midnight ceremonies in local graveyards. Hmmm, they might have had something there after all.

Fortunately though, the voting delegates refused to be blackmailed into blackballing any nominee and party gossip soon identified the culprits as the faction of former members who had supported Kevin Rose three years earlier. In addition the distinct Hastings versus Hawke's Bay hostility within party circles was considered to be playing its corrosive part. But there were other troubles.

Despite the Leader's implied assurance of non-intervention it was painfully obvious that Bolger did want to send a very direct message to National Party voting delegates just in case they went completely mad and selected me. A few days before the crucial selection contest Bolger made an impassioned public plea for electorates to select more women candidates for the coming election. It escaped no one's attention that my most serious rival was now Napier schoolteacher Joyce Gibson. Senior divisional party figures then began telephoning wavering delegates to warn them of the possible consequences of selecting the renegade researcher. One branch chairman accepted this message with such enthusiasm that he began warning his branch's voting delegates that 'Jim Bolger would never visit Hawke's Bay if Michael Laws was selected'. This prospect had the galvanising effect of immediately converting two doubters to my camp. 'Were there any other politicians he could stop?' one old dear enquired.

The word may have been out but National Party delegates have always possessed one admirable characteristic that served to infuriate party bosses — a defiant independence that, in this case, combined with a fine sense of the ridiculous. Both conspired to deliver me the verdict, again, on the first ballot. This time, though, the achievement was lessened by the paucity of competition. Only the hierarchy's favoured Joyce Gibson and a jovial Maori freezing worker with dreadlocks, Larry Jessup, who also happened to be a financial member of the Labour Party, provided any competition. At least our selection speeches provided some entertainment, with Joyce tartly urging delegates not to select me; Larry jokingly urging delegates to select him so that he could afford a haircut and a decent suit; and me arrogantly suggesting that it was time to 'send some magic to Wellington'. One delegate later remarked on my singular generosity in wanting to make Larry the MP and had cast her selection ballot accordingly.

I did not think much of it at the time but the paucity of nominee talent was not confined to Hawke's Bay. If anything the intervening three years had lessened further the interest of quality individuals in a professional political career. Similar contests in marginal seats were producing just a handful of nominees and there were dark mutterings about the quality of many of the selected candidates. The Leader's office had already begun to worry about the possible size of National's 1990 majority — it had the potential to escort half of Lake Alice onto the back benches.

The selection evening itself was a muted affair compared to the tempestuous excitement of three years earlier. A television crew hovered around all evening and then vanished in an instant. I was later informed that they had been present on the off chance I might lose and their interest had evaporated the moment the announcement had been made. Charming.

But while the delegates may have approved of my re-entry into national politics they seemed a distinct minority the next day. The Hawke's Bay First madness resurfaced and redoubled its efforts to discredit me. Despite promising to reveal a vast array of Hawke's Bay identities in opposition to my candidacy, these remained firmly in the shadows. I remonstrated with the local newspapers about the credibility of an organisation that refused to identify its spokesman or its supporters but to little effect — political controversy, even if manufactured, made a welcome change from the normal provincial pap of cats in trees, stolen bicycles and Mrs Adams' prize-winning plum jam.

Such editorial indifference was, thankfully, not universally shared by the news staff. A local journalist gave me a copy of the group's most recent press statement, which contained a dire warning to all female reporters about my likely amoral and amorous modus operandi. Apparently at the last election the conniving Casanova Laws had seduced a lovelorn local reporter with the direct aim of gaining favourable news coverage, promised to marry her, rendered the poor girl pregnant then dumped the pathetic creature after the election, thus callously ruining her career, reputation and life all in one fell swoop. A moral lesson had been imparted.

The press release might have been anonymous but the fax cover sheet foolishly identified a Hastings insurance agent, John McCormick, as its author — Rose's 1987 campaign manager. A quick lawyer's letter and a threatened suit for defamation and Hawke's Bay First dissolved overnight. But the intrigue did not end there. After being served with the defamation papers McCormick was observed driving directly to the residence of National's Hastings candidate, Jeff Whittaker. I would have to watch my back.

The next ten months dragged interminably. I asked Neil Kirton to head my campaign team, and with Anne Averill, Lawrence Yule and Yvonne Guerin prominent, the team proceeded to keep me out of as much trouble as electric cattle prods would allow. We all knew that National would win the 1990 election and that the Hawke's Bay electorate would be one of the first seats to fall. The conclusion was so inevitable that the incumbent, Bill Sutton, even quit the race. Not officially, of course. He just refused to expend time, energy or mental effort on even the semblance of campaigning. Such pessimism was justified — every internal party or news media poll on the Hawke's Bay electorate provided National with a massive lead.

The following months at least afforded me the opportunity to get to know my prospective constituents and to conduct the most ingratiating of relationships with my long-suffering bank manager. Despite promises from Winston that private finance had been arranged to ensure my continued production of speeches, press releases and newspaper articles on his behalf, such patronage ended after the first payment.

Oh, and one other thing. I got married.

There are two sides to that particular story. Mine — and just about everyone else's. My story is that back at a National Party conference in 1987 secretary-general Max Bradford's personal assistant, Karen Miller, threw herself at me in a frenzy of lustful enthusiasm. Being an infinitely polite and obliging chap I considered it rude to reject such wanton advances.

Strangely enough Karen has no such recollection. She had briefly noticed me at the conference and been instantly interested when party president Neville Young warned her off. 'He's trouble that one' — or words to that effect. There is a certain type of woman who regards such danger signals as faintly alluring and I can only suppose that Karen was one of them. Like most irresponsible and emotionally immature males desperate to avoid commitment, I was determined not to enter into any stable relationship; or at least, no one was too keen on starting any such relationship with me — Karen included.

We stuttered along as friends and flatmates for the next couple of years until it became obvious that I was expecting to be elected a provincial Member of Parliament and needed to demonstrate some solidity. It remains one of Karen's and my most intense quandaries as to how that realisation led to our marriage in July 1990.

Friends and relatives gave us a matter of weeks, a couple of months at most. We were such total opposites — Karen was sensible, self-disciplined and serene. I was a complete emotional yobbo. But Karen had also refined tolerance to an art form and I suppose I represented the most testing challenge to one of her disposition. It may also have been that it was the United Nations Year for the Emotionally Bewildered and Karen therefore adopted me as her charity case. Whatever the motivation we were married at All Saint's in Taradale in the same church as my parents and my grandparents.

I remember very little about the day itself as I had risen from my sick bed after being confined there by a virulent strain of influenza that saw me delirious with fever and pumped with all manner of medicinal drugs and self-pity. So I was present at the ceremony and post-wedding function although not fully conscious — a defence I have tried with Karen from time to time to absolutely no effect. Thus I failed to appreciate Winston's witty performance as Master of Ceremonies at the reception, and the obvious irony of having Winston tease Rob Eaddy and Wayne Eagleson, who were also present, about finally having the opportunity to 'listen to a real speech'. Mention was also made of my wonderful sense of timing — not only getting married when my consciousness was visiting Pluto but also on the same weekend that the local media had decided to go on strike after promising stellar coverage of the event.

But my wedding had more sinister and long-reaching consequences for Winston. As a personal favour he was to meet with prominent businessman and Brierley executive Selwyn Cushing at Cushing's Hastings home on the Sunday morning after the wedding.

A couple of months earlier Anne Averill and I had met with the multi-millionaire to seek his financial support for our local campaign. Anne had teed up the appointment in her role as the campaign's canvassing co-ordinator — she was directly responsible for raising over $60,000 during this time, a good part of which was siphoned off to Wellington to support the useless party bureaucracy at divisional and national headquarters. Cushing was a millionaire with National Party sensibilities — ergo, he might be able to donate some of his Brierley's largesse to the local pretender's campaign.

Selwyn was both welcoming and convivial on that occasion and the three of us shared a bottle of the local vintage and generally chatted about the coming election, National's prospects in the Hawke's Bay region and Cushing's various directorships. He was aware of my close association with Winston and expressed an interest in having a similarly informal discussion with the man, while admitting to considerable sympathy for Peters' general policy pronouncements. Both Anne and I received the clear impression that in return for Cushing's possible financial favours we were expected to give the most favourable consideration to this request.

Subsequently the meeting was arranged for the morning after the wedding and instructions provided to Winston as to how to reach Cushing's residence, which Winston proceeded to lose and thus arrived late. As I was allegedly on my honeymoon (which consisted of me being ill in Taupo for a week and then Karen succumbing to the same virus in Rotorua — the marriage could have been annulled on the grounds of non-consummation) I did not immediately follow up on the canvassing success or otherwise of this Cushing visit. But when Winston and his wife, Louise, popped into our Taupo motel unit the next evening on their way back to Tauranga and deposited our suitcases (some idiotic wedding guests — friends of Karen's I hasten to add — had decided it would be hilarious to remove all our clothes from the trunk of Karen's car), Winston informed me that Cushing had been most generous with offers of personal financial support. Great, I thought. Maybe now I can get paid.

I later relayed this conversation to Anne, hoping that such enthusiasm from a millionaire might spill over into our campaign coffers as well. Some weeks before, Cushing had duly provided a personal cheque for $1000 to the Hawke's Bay campaign and a similar sum to Jeff Whittaker's Hastings team, but this was certainly less than the generosity I had in mind. We were later informed by the party's divisional staff that Cushing's principal donation had been relayed to

National Party headquarters in Wellington and that the sum had been in the region of six figures. The same indiscreet party official noted that Cushing had also been the party's largest individual donor in the previous election — brave stuff from a Brierley company director whose company profited so handsomely from Labour's economic and financial reforms.

Yet Cushing struck me as a capitalist with an old-fashioned paternal conscience who seemed genuinely repelled by the excesses of an unfettered market. They did not seem the personal characteristics of an alleged bagman for the right-wing Business Roundtable, who might allegedly attempt to bribe Peters into political silence.

The Cushing affair was to have the most enormous personal, political and financial costs for Winston, and I can but guess at the exact nature of that post-wedding meeting. Certainly Winston mentioned that money had been discussed but in such general terms that I interpreted his remarks to mean Cushing had offered to finance Peters' election campaign in Tauranga.

Equally, Selwyn Cushing's later public account of the circumstances leading to this fateful meeting did not square with either Anne's or my recollection of the facts. It was Cushing who eagerly pushed for a meeting with National's stellar attraction; neither Anne nor I possessed sufficient influence or personal standing to make Cushing give up a relaxing Sunday morning to meet Winston.

Then again the whole matter may have been a genuine misunderstanding. Cushing talks as if his mouth is filled with stale cake — a sort of mournful mumble. According to the various accounts of our wedding guests, Winston had clearly enjoyed a 'big night out'. The combination of these circumstances could easily have produced any number of disquieting mutual impressions.

Meanwhile, waiting for the election proved an interminable exercise, and I entertained myself by creating as much local media mischief as possible to try and build my profile up before the fateful day. I need not have bothered — no one seemed even vaguely interested in the antics of any of the political candidates and Bill Sutton refused to rise to my almost daily baiting.

The public opinion polls continued to plot the downward progress of Geoffrey Palmer's popularity and with it Labour's last hope of pre-election rescue. The public mood then turned very nasty after TVNZ's 'Frontline' current affairs team produced a damning documentary on Labour's big-business links and their personal financing of leading

Cabinet ministers. The programme was artlessly and deliberately provocative and I was not in the least surprised that it provoked a swarm of defamation suits from outraged Labour principals. Certainly I had met the team producing this polemic some six weeks previously and agreed to be interviewed, I thought, on the untoward influence of the Business Roundtable in the policy development of both major parties.

I confirmed that Ruth Richardson's economic advisers were paid with private business monies and that private funders had financed the launch of National's 'Economic Vision' — these facts were matters of public knowledge. Did I feel that the Business Roundtable was essentially purchasing sympathetic policy via these donations? I honestly replied that this was unlikely. Ruth Richardson's zealotry did not require payment — she would promote the excesses of the far right for free! At that stage the filming came to an angry and abrupt halt and the female interviewer accused me of being 'gutless' — surely I must suspect that the Business Roundtable had a corrupt influence over the National Party; why would I not 'go on the record' and denounce such calumny?

Well, because I had no proof to that effect, I answered. In a flash the interview team scrambled from my Taradale flat in blatant disgust that I had not provided them with either the evidence or an accusation to fit their predetermined partiality. I breathed a sigh of relief when not one syllable of the interview was eventually telecast. But I had lost my last remaining traces of faith in the impartiality of the news media.

HAWKE'S BAY FIRST

My ponderous 1990 campaign stumbled on, punctuated only by the occasional dose of local media coverage and insistent demands from my bank manager to lose first my Autoaccess card, then my credit card, and finally my cheque book. Labour were a cruel bunch — they seemed intent on stretching out both their misery and my bank balance until the last possible moment.

But at least I had the time and the space to get to know the various and differing aspects of my constituency again and develop further some of the concepts I had only begun to explore within Winston's populist crusade. My premier interest related to the issue of democratic representation. If/when elected, what was my proper role?

Fortunately, as it transpired, I had already developed some preliminary ideas on the topic. During the preselection meetings with party members and delegates, and later at sparsely attended joint candidate forums, I pledged my prime loyalty to my future constituents. My constitutional responsibility was to advocate the interests of Hawke's Bay in Wellington, rather than act as Wellington's apologist in Hawke's Bay. In turn, Bill Sutton publicly rubbished me. Just you wait until you get to Wellington — you will be mewing like the rest of them, he warned.

Sutton's scepticism was shared by those party loyalists in the electorate organisation who had no intention of promoting a candidate with such an individual interpretation of party service. More senior electorate personnel soothed such disquiet by noting that I was still given to youthful idealism and a couple of months at Caucus boot camp would soon have me marching in step. They were grievously mistaken. I meant to execute every single promise I had ever made.

Now that I had been forced to seek a parliamentary career I had no intention of just journeying to the capital to eat my lunch. Neither did I have any vaulting ministerial ambitions, an admission which scandalised my campaign team. No, they thought, Michael must be feigning rare modesty. But I knew that harbouring such hopes would prove to be an exercise in futility. Talent did not elevate one to a National Cabinet — sucking up to the leader did. On that basis it was beyond the realms of the most psychotic delusion to even consider such elevation under Bolger. And the man looked to be headed for an election win of tsunami proportions. I could forget any political promotion as long as Jim Bolger commanded the most minute influence in party circles. By that reasoning I should be safe some time in the middle of the twenty-first century.

I then committed the most mischievous of logo larceny and stole the Hawke's Bay First motto from my previous detractors for distribution on all personal election propaganda. Foolishly just about everyone — and I include the local party organisation, the party in general, the media and my political opponents — thought I was kidding. They should have known better.

I had the rare opportunity of bringing my thoughts directly to the attention of the Leader when he made his one and only promotional trip to the Hawke's Bay electorate — a mistake he was determined never to repeat. Bolger was making one of his interminable provincial tours, also trying to fill in the time before the commencement of the campaign proper, and it just happened to be Hawke's Bay's turn. Despite considerable advance publicity only a smattering of locals actually turned up for his evening address. There was something good on the telly that night, we explained to Bolger's disappointed entourage — yeah, like the test pattern.

Anyway, it was my responsibility to make suitably soothing introductory remarks to the Great Man's visionary lecture and I used the opportunity to speak on the need for a properly representative democracy that was properly accountable for its actions. If that included, say, one's local MP voting against their own party then so be it.

It was a short speech but it irritated Bolger enough for him to tartly exclaim that crossing the floor would mean voting with Labour and he was sure local voters did not predict that outcome when selecting their local candidate. My soft interjection to the contrary did little to restore his humour. The next day the local papers recorded that National's local candidate had pledged himself to become 'Hawke's Bay's hired gun' if elected, which prompted a flood of deprecating calls from local farmers inviting me to start with the rabbits in their back block.

My next brush with the Leader was no less ill favoured. During the campaign proper Jim Bolger was holding a lunch-time rally in Hastings and my presence was required to show the full slate of National candidates in the region. In the days prior to Bolger's visit there had been something of a public contretemps within the Caucus over the Reserve Bank Act and the zero to two per cent inflation target. Some enterprising journalist had done a quick whip-round of party candidates to get their views and hopefully gather enough dissenting opinions for a good story on intraparty division. I had not disappointed such expectations and professed the inflation target to be wholly inappropriate given international trading circumstances and the comparative rates of New Zealand's major competitors and partners. Would I cross the floor over such an issue? Without hesitation I replied in the affirmative. It seemed such a useless exercise to pronounce certainty and then refuse to contemplate the means by which to express it.

My dutiful attendance at the Hastings rally was followed by Bolger's visit to a local cut-flower business, where, in a private moment, the Leader's new minder and press strategist, Michael Wall, dressed me down amongst the carnations. It was a surreal scene — in the middle of a large commercial glasshouse, surrounded by multicoloured blooms and a gaggle of bored journos, the overwhelming perfumes invading the senses, being angrily abused by a self-opinionated, malevolent leprechaun. What is it about short men and anger? Or are they just perpetually angry because of God's callous indifference?

Anyway, I was not in the least perturbed. In a month's time I would be in the Caucus and Wall would not and then we would see who had the most influence over monetary policy. So there. Such naive stupidity — I should have known better. The answer would of course be that neither of us would have the slightest influence.

The rest of my Hawke's Bay campaign primarily consisted of the most predatory of promise-keeping — there was not an electoral itch unscratched, and where no itch existed they were tickled and then scratched just for luck. This was made possible by a comprehensive range of party policies that seemed to leave no stone unturned, no question unanswered and no one safe even in the privacy of their privy. National was going to do everything — we would provide jobs for the jobless; homes to the homeless; deliver three per cent economic growth, single-digit interest rates and the lowest rate of inflation in the OECD; abolish Labour's hated superannuation surtax; cut hospital waiting lists; resolve racial tension — the list was endless. In Hawke's Bay we were attempting to target specific policies for specific voting groups, but we just gave up in the end. Neil Kirton suggested we just put out a single household flier: 'Vote National and win Lotto.'

But I was becomingly naggingly suspicious about both the reliability and the affordability of some of these more extreme campaign promises, and started shelving and then burning the mass of campaign literature directed to our campaign team by party headquarters. I was going to win anyhow — what was the point in escalating expectation beyond possible delivery?

Then, finally, the momentous day. Despite the inevitability of the result and Labour's last fevered gamble of passing the poisoned chalice to Mike Moore, I was still as nervous as a schoolboy virgin at a hookers' ball. Mad doubts surfaced. What if the polls were wrong? What if the Moore leadership had worked? What if the punters had not believed us?

Around 7.30pm on a warm, calm Saturday spring evening the first booth results trickled and then came tumbling in. Surrounded by Karen and my parents and the inner core of my campaign team I watched this country's worst-ever political massacre unfold on the television screen as marginal seats fell, then safe Labour seats and finally impossible constituencies like West Coast and Wanganui; eight Cabinet ministers lost their livelihoods, plus the Speaker. National had a 37-seat majority. But the evening's largest cheer came when New Labour's Jim Anderton comfortably acquired Labour's impregnable Sydenham electorate. This was no mere massacre — it seemed a calculated act of political genocide. Among all this spectacular hubbub the election of a new National MP in Hawke's Bay mattered not — except to us. The final majority of 2895 votes propelled our celebrations into overdrive.

It was time to party.

EXHILARATION

There is an exhilaration that comes with election to Parliament that cannot easily be described. I have no doubt that it varies from individual to individual but for me it approximated the sensations associated with having good sex, winning the Ranfurly Shield and a sneezing fit all at the same time. This unstable ecstasy was like a devout Catholic exhibitionist being discovered in flagrante delicto by a troop of nuns.

The morning after the election I woke early and dashed out of bed and down to the gate to retrieve the Sunday newspaper — just to confirm that I had been elected. Oh, I had been elected all right, for there was a large and unnaturally prominent photograph of me on page two, surrounded by a cautionary story of how the new Prime Minister had just inherited, courtesy of the electors, a barrel full of back-bench monkeys. Yours truly was portrayed as the number one orang-utan, my combative comments on Reserve Bank monetary policy receiving rebellious recognition.

The rest of the day was spent in recovery mode — fielding congratulatory calls from party workers and family friends and generally recovering from the overdose of excitement and alcohol the previous night. A plethora of inquisitive media calls began to interrupt and then dominate the warm afterglow as insistent Press Gallery reporters started demanding ever more complex answers to their ever more vapid questions. By afternoon the telephone was not just off the hook — it had been unplugged from the wall socket and stored away in the hot-water cupboard.

Perhaps that was the most immediate transition required of me. I was now public property; the personal privacy I had taken for granted had been stripped away in an instant. It was the small, almost petty things that reinforced this loss — the avalanche of telephone calls, the greeting of recognition as you picked up the milk from the dairy, the stranger who would suddenly interrupt a private conversation, the furtive glances and whispered comments as you passed people in the street.

In a day I had been elevated from relative anonymity to one of Hawke's Bay's leading public citizens, and although that progress certainly gratified the ego it also atomised my domestic surroundings. Mayors and business leaders who had kept a cool distance from me as a candidate now gushed civility and cooperation. A heady mix of instant status and local influence rushed through my little world.

Ah, but how much more intoxicating to be fêted by the national media. TVNZ enquired as to my likely availability for 'a personality piece' on any dreams or ambitions that I might care to share with the rest of New Zealand now that I had won a seat in Parliament. It would be run as a companion piece to an item on defeated Hastings MP and Cabinet minister David Butcher, and his reactions to being expelled from that same institution. Would I be interested? Hell, I would pay them to broadcast it. But it was not just the gratification of ego that prompted enthusiastic assent. This would be my very public upraised finger to all those narrow-minded and nasty Nats who had wanted me excommunicated, expelled or otherwise exiled from the party over the past seven years — nyaah, nyaah, nyaah — a very mature response.

By Monday the exhilaration and enthusiasm were beginning to wane as the awful reality of my new job began to crystallise. I knew enough about the parliamentary environment to have a rough appreciation of my duties at that end but I did not have the first clue as to what a Member of Parliament did in their elected constituency. I had become the democratic representative of 33,000 people. What on earth did that mean?

Fortunately my predecessor had struggled with this same problem for the previous six years so public expectations of their new MP were severely limited by their experience of the old one. Bill Sutton had still not conceded or congratulated me and when his constituent files were finally turned over they consisted of one piece of paper relating to an outstanding adoption case. I was going to have to design a constituency service from the ground up and the lack of assistance from both the National Caucus and the Parliamentary Services Commission stupefied me. Their collective advice seemed to consist of just the one word: 'No!'

Again I turned to Anne Averill. She had carried the electorate and my campaign for the past twelve months; could she perform another minor miracle? And like most former school dental nurses (a distinct breed of New Zealand women — my wife Karen trained as one as well) she had both the no-nonsense attitude and the adaptive abilities to fashion both a professional and a user-friendly service. When she finally relented and agreed to accept employment as my senior electorate agent I knew that my administrative back would always be covered in the Bay. That reassurance would turn out to be critical because I was soon in trouble.

Strangely enough my first post-election contretemps with the Prime Minister had nothing to do with monetary policy, the inflation target, Winston Peters or my rumoured permanent posting to Scott Base. Prior to the election two outgoing MPs, Roger Douglas and Ian McLean, had denounced the scale of members' salaries and allowances and posited that their relativity with other professional groupings contributed to the paucity of political talent. Their argument was best summarised by the popular parliamentary aphorism, 'If you pay peanuts then you'll only get monkeys' — a saying that had no doubt been stolen from one of those specious American business management manuals; the kind that posit there is only one God and He is Greed.

Putting to one side the thought that such critical self-analysis seemed remarkably apposite with regard to both gentlemen, I had rejected this assumption that good men and true were repelled from public service simply because it did not, literally, pay. I possessed sufficient socialist sensibilities (and still do) to believe that those who make a vocational choice based solely upon income are not the kind of people you want in that vocation anyway. Particularly with regard to the supposed pinnacle of public service. Besides, the salary of a back-bench MP on election in 1990 was more than useful at $63,500 a year, and then there were the tax-free allowances, including an expenses allowance ($6150 pa), an electorate allowance ($11,700 pa) and a Wellington accommodation allowance (another $12,400 pa), all in addition to a $52-a-day meals allowance for every day spent on parliamentary business. Over a year that all added up to quite a tidy sum — in comparable gross terms it equated to a $110,000-plus yearly salary. From my relative penury it seemed, and was, a princely sum. If one added the generous parliamentary superannuation scheme; the free business-class domestic air travel for Karen and myself; the free telephone and toll calls; then a host of attendant business-related freebies like free postage, a free electorate office, an executive secretary in Parliament and another back in Hawke's Bay then hey, remuneration was not an issue.

Besides, the salary had never been my motivation. I would have done it for $20,000 a year and a lap in the Beehive swimming pool. My bank manager would not have. The first congratulatory call I received at the start of the next working week was from a very relieved loans manager, who had been looking at my $25,000 unsecured debt and sweating over the consequences of a nasty election surprise.

HAMMER HORROR

It was with such thoughts of debt, personal finances and spared bank officials that I greeted the news of a gazetted four-per-cent salary increase by the Higher Salaries Commission. This unusual grouping of judicial bureaucrats had deliberated upon the representations of various self-interested, public, professional groupings and set a supposedly equitable scale of salaries and expenses until the next selfish entreaty. MPs were to get a four-per-cent salary rise and a similar amount added to their tax-free salaries and allowances.

A local news reporter, no doubt jealously comparing their own weekly income with my projected largesse, enquired as to whether I would be remaining true to my pre-election commentary on parliamentary salaries. Of course, I replied. I would be refusing this and any other salary increase over the next three years until I saw a similar rise in the level of income of my Hawke's Bay constituents. Times were tough, I added, and MPs had a moral obligation to share the public's pain and sacrifice during these unsettled years of economic restructuring. This reply was soon published throughout the rest of the media and gained surprising coverage. I had assumed, wrongly as it transpired, that most other MPs would be voicing similar thoughts. But no. I had farted in church — again.

I had just completed an interview with the 'Holmes' television crew when Karen informed me that Rob Eaddy was on the phone — the Prime Minister wanted a word. I assumed that this would be a word of congratulation upon winning the Hawke's Bay seat and a general 'welcome to the team' homily. Eaddy's cool tone suggested a different reason.

'The Prime Minister wants to talk to you,' Rob noted stiffly, and with all our usual small talk about wives, weather and other wonders of Nature suspended, my call was transferred direct to Jim Bolger.

'Your comments on MPs' salaries,' Bolger began. 'They are most unhelpful.' By now I was holding the telephone at a distance and wondering if either Telecom was garbling the impulses or I was not the victim of an elaborate prank. How on earth could the Prime Minister possibly be upset about a nothing comment to a nothing provincial newspaper about a nothing issue — surely there had to be more pressing national and international concerns to occupy his time. As I have explained before, my natural tendency, when confronted with such excessive idiocy, is not to remain silent. I know I should, but I just cannot do it. That microchip in my brain is missing, or malfunctioning, or something. Don't blame me — blame God.

'You're joking,' I informed Bolger. This erroneous observation changed Bolger's mood from disapproving to downright dangerous.

'I'm warning you now,' he growled menacingly. 'I will not tolerate any of your nonsense. You carry on like this and you won't be here for long.' And with that cheery thought the telephone call was ended. So it was true. A new diplomatic posting to Antarctica was in the offing.

Directly after this prime ministerial shot across the bows came another telephone call, this time from a journalist in the Press Gallery seeking elaboration on my earlier NZPA comments. Elaborate? Hell, I was now in the mood to give a 60-minute sermon and this time I had every intention of marketing my personal stance as a precedent for all other MPs. Such a principled stand would demonstrate to the public at large that its representatives were prepared to put the nation's interests before their own — a symbolic display of political leadership for the troubled times ahead.

Unbeknown to me the times were a good deal more troubled than I could ever have imagined. Wayne Eagleson was later to tell me that the post-party Te Kuiti hangovers were brutally reinforced by the almost instant appearance of funereal black crows from the Treasury with a dark and foreboding tale of a major blowout in the 1990/91 Budget, hundreds of millions of dollars of unbudgeted pre-election expenditure and an attendant plunge in growth projections. The talk was not so much of slow down but of crisis, with mooted Budget deficits of $4-billion-plus, a stagnant economy, worsening terms of trade and rising unemployment. This appalling news was amplified by the disastrous state of the Bank of New Zealand, which was reputedly close to collapse. All this information had been deliberately withheld from public view by the outgoing Labour Government, a fact that seems no less shocking eight years later. It is little wonder that Ruth Richardson regarded the Fiscal Responsibility Act as her most enduring legacy.

There was a fascinating postscript to this incident. Despite his running National's election campaign and being one of Bolger's closest confidants, Treasury insisted that Eagleson be excluded from these crisis Treasury briefings. Incredibly, Bolger complied — a portent of Treasury's likely influence on the Prime Minister elect.

Even had the nation's financial accounts been in pristine order Richardson had already expressed her concern over National's pre-election attempts to bribe every sector of society. In a supposedly confidential memo she alerted Bolger, Birch and others in the National Caucus to the fact that the National Party was promising spending that could not possibly be afforded — all this long before the fateful Treasury mission. A billion-dollar gap existed between projected expenditure and government revenue, but Bolger dismissed this prophetic warning with his usual indifference to anything emanating from Ruth Richardson.

Besides, there were no real worries. An incoming National Government would be able to finance all its campaign promises out of increased economic growth (courtesy of the mere fact of National's being elected) and anyway, not all the promises need be honoured in the first year. There were three full years in any electoral cycle and it made pragmatic political sense to hold back some of the goodies until the final year.

Plainly Richardson was far from convinced that the 'Don't worry — be happy' lunacy of the time was a sufficiently compelling reason to abandon her qualms. Mysteriously her confidential memo found its way to the media, where it caused only a minor public kerfuffle. Labour's ongoing immolatory efforts were being rewarded, with Geoffrey Palmer's corpse now being tossed upon the funeral pyre. no one seemed much interested in a comparatively drab policy duel in the Opposition — the conflagration was elsewhere.

Certainly Treasury's post-election Hammer Horror had the desired effect. Bolger's much-hyped 'decent society' disappeared in an instant;

henceforth it was derogatively titled the 'descent society'. Sorry, the Cabinet began bleating, we wanted to be decent but we just could not afford it. Only incoming Police Minister John Banks refused to be stampeded. He had promised 900 extra police and by heavens he intended to deliver. Had it not been for Banks' peculiar mixture of bloody-minded obstinacy and moral principle that promise too would have been jettisoned into deep space.

The appointment of Bolger's first Cabinet reflected the man's ultra-cautious nature. Richardson's pre-election pressure had successfully combined with big-business lobbying to win her the top finance slot; there was no way the new Prime Minister could risk alienating the commercial sector so early in the piece. Birch would have to be content, at least for now, with the labour and state services portfolios, although he maintained a higher Cabinet ranking than Richardson and retained his intense desire to usurp her role. For Richardson's Canterbury nemesis, Philip Burdon, there would only be the booby prize of commerce.

The portfolios relating to social policy were no less predictable. Perhaps the only surprise was that Simon Upton had been entrusted with Health, for which deputy Don McKinnon had assumed responsibility in opposition. But Don was no dummy. The comparative political luxury of foreign affairs was a much preferable alternative to the chaos that was health. On the other hand, Simon greeted the whole haphazard mess as a splendid academic challenge and quickly decided on a marvellously theoretical and theatrical restructuring of the entire sector. Initially this task attracted Upton's usual zealous enthusiasm but his unpreparedness for the vicious and venal currents that whirled and swirled under the surface — the professional jealousies, the selfish personal agendas, the irreconcilable dichotomy between the public and the private — soon evaporated such goodwill. Sometimes imperfection is better than well-intentioned alternatives — this would prove to be one of those instances.

Meanwhile Rakaia MP Jenny Shipley had assumed the diverse and gargantuan social welfare portfolio, Maurice McTigue was appointed to the troubled graveyard of employment, and Lockwood Smith predictably scared the bejesus out of the liberal lobbyists by assuming the education portfolio. My relationship with each of these three ministers would prove particularly difficult — and the clashes would not be long in coming.

But the biggest surprise was not so much an appointment as an absence. Muldoon's continued haunting of the back bench was to be expected — for Rob it would be finance or nothing, and nothing it was. But East Coast Bays' bright young star, Murray McCully, was conspicuously missing from the swearing-in ceremony at Government House, and a variety of speculative gossip proffered an impressive array of reasons. However, Bolger's hesitation was based on an ongoing Serious Fraud Office investigation into one of McCully's communications companies for alleged insider trading, and only when McCully was cleared of any criminal misconduct in mid-1991 was he added to the Prime Minister's Cabinet. Tuku Morgan had his precedent.

But that decision was still in the future. For the moment Cabinet was being well and truly spooked with Treasury's tale of woe and soon it would be Cabinet's turn to spook Caucus.

Indeed, the first hint of wide-scale reneging on the election manifesto indeed came at my very first Caucus meeting. It was an excited affair — 67 MPs bumping into each other amid boisterous if insincere mutual congratulations; TV cameras and press photographers pressing their lenses among the throng as if this moment begged immortal capture; the grizzled veteran, Sir Robert Muldoon, artlessly demanding the name of the new MP who had just sat down beside him; Bolger at top table acting out his best Irish bonhomie for public show. Then, after the press had been shooed from the Caucus Room and the heavy doors closed to foreign intervention, the mood perceptibly altered. The ready smiles of the senior MPs vanished, the excited laughter trailed away and the new Prime Minister gravely nodded toward a copy of the party's election manifesto carelessly askew on the table in front of him.

'We're going to have some trouble with that...,' and the words reverberated in my nodding consciousness. Uh-oh. I exchanged glances and raised eyebrows with Winston. This was not a good start.

And so followed the dark and sombre tale of overheated Treasury projections and overextended government coffers. The economy was stuffed, the Bank of New Zealand was stuffed, the government's finances were stuffed — and in that singular moment so too were the political careers of a good proportion of these brand-new shiny back-bench MPs.

Jim Bolger had argued during the campaign that this would be the last chance that any government would have to win back the trust of the New Zealand people; that the last Labour Government had so severely eroded Parliament's credibility by practising the exact opposite of their preaching that National must arrest this dangerous trend or be equally vilified — and who knows where such widespread disenchantment with both major party forces might then lead? The quickest route to political oblivion is simple — you stoke up public disenchantment, market your party as the political saviour, then dash all hope on election. The incoming National Government managed that remarkable sequence of events in just one month. Winston Peters, who observed these events at even closer proximity, would be condemned to repeat this folly six years later, but this time there would be no looming fiscal crisis to blame.

Certainly the tale spun to the Government Caucus evoked images straight out of Spiritus Mundi. Between them Bolger and Richardson suggested a scenario that could see the Weimar Republic reborn in southern climes and, just like gullible boy scouts around the nightly campfire, our expressions conveyed horrified belief. If Treasury's aim was to spook the incoming government then it had succeeded beyond its wildest imaginings. Bereft of independent economic advice, or even a range of considered policy alternatives, Richardson boldly charted a course to the right. Treasury had thoughtfully provided the compass, the map and a packed lunch and Ruth had been good enough to purchase some sturdy walking boots. As the only navigator who could understand Treasury babble, Richardson, with her incisive decision-making, would prove irresistible to Cabinet, given no other option than to fall in line, and where Cabinet went the Caucus was sure to follow.

Prior to the election, the Prime Minister had promised 'one hundred days of action'. But this was action of the headless chicken variety — plans were hastily drawn up to slash government spending regardless of the impact, a gaunt and gaudy Employment Contracts Bill was introduced, capital expenditure plans were cancelled, further state assets readied for sale, state sector wages frozen. In such a hair-shirt environment the Prime Minister had instructed me to pull my head in over refusing a four-per-cent salary increase! What surreal arena had I entered?

Certainly the first couple of Caucuses proved to be more personally fractious than I had expected. My suggestion that the Government Caucus show some moral leadership in dealing with these fiscal troubles and refuse the Higher Salaries Commission's increase went down like a cup of cold sick. I was not only attacked by new MPs like Ian Peters (who used the bizarre argument that it had cost him plenty to stand for Parliament so why should he not receive extra remuneration) but by old stagers like Muldoon, who accused me of adopting such a populist theme purely for personal political advantage. When Muldoon's ironic comments provoked a deafening chorus of 'hear hears', I received my first real inkling that Caucus' collective consciousness was not just different from mine — it emanated from another planet. After one of these meetings the door to my parliamentary office was forcibly kicked by an outraged passer-by, and as I dashed out to engage the culprit I saw the Amazonian Lyttelton MP, Gail McIntosh, sauntering away surrounded by other giggling Members.

I was back at boarding school.

LAMBS TO THE SLAUGHTER

The Caucus intake of 1990 was an unusual mixture of youth, middle-aged conservatism and balmy eccentricity but it shared one enduring characteristic. Everyone seemed to possess the highest possible opinion of their own individual brilliance. I suppose such implausible self-confidence had enabled most of them to be elected in the first place, but most were not content with that step. Each seemed to possess the singular fantasy that it was onwards and upwards from here. I doubted if any of my new colleagues had arrived here by accident or as part of their personal Plan B — that seemed to be a uniquely personal experience.

The intake certainly had no shortage of vaulting personal ambition. I will be polite and suggest that there was a minor skills mismatch between that collective confidence and the relative abilities on offer, but it would also be fair to note that many saw their election to Parliament as a logical consequence of their previously successful careers. Provincial businessmen like Jeff Whittaker (Hastings), Grant Thomas (Hamilton West) and John Armstrong (New Plymouth); middling lawyers Hamish Hancock (Horowhenua) and Alec Neill (Waitaki); ex-rugby stars Graham Thorne (Onehunga) and Tony Steel (Hamilton East), who had carved out successful post-All Black careers but now wanted a fresh challenge; local-body honchos Trevor Rogers (Howick), Wayne Kimber (Gisborne) and Margaret Moir (West Coast), who now desired the larger stage — if there was one characteristic that this solid slab of Caucus conservatism shared then it was an unyielding belief in the virtue of the team, even if it was wrong and even if you were not in it. Oh, and one other characteristic — the above crew all lost their seats on election night 1993. They would prove to be Cabinet's idea of sacrifice — a sacrifice that saw the backbenchers lose their credibility and their constituencies but the ministers safe in their solid blue enclaves.

Then there were the overtly ambitious types — Max Bradford (Tarawera), having the last laugh on former party president Neville Young; the bratpack of Roger Sowry (Kapiti), Tony Ryall (Eastern Bay of Plenty), Nick Smith (Tasman) and Bill English (Wallace), who had risen through the ranks of the Young Nationals organisation — all twenty of them; Joy McLachlan (Western Hutt), who had worked as John Banks' parliamentary secretary and been near-blinded by the revelation that talent was not the ultimate prerequisite for a political career; international businessmen Bruce Cliffe (North Shore) and John Robertson (Papakura), who, having been gifted a safe National seat for the rest of their natural born days, would both go mad and decamp for the greener grass of the United Party (at least, one presumes that is what they were smoking before making this bizarre decision). As a whole, this grouping of MPs were smarter, smoother and smugger than the rest of the 1990 intake, knowing that time would ultimately deliver to them the baubles of higher office.

There were three other distinct and restless back-bench entities — the white dwarf Muldoon and disappointed second-termers Rob Munro (Invercargill) and Jim Gerard (Rangiora), who all believed that the Prime Minister had made a ghastly mistake in leaving them out of his first Cabinet and that, sooner or later, sanity would prevail; the bovver boys Peter Hilt (Glenfield) and Ian Revell (Birkenhead), without whose verbal abuse no Caucus could possibly be complete; and then, finally, the lonely rebels, Hamish McIntyre (Manawatu), Gilbert Myles (Roskill), Cam Campion (Wanganui) and Peter McCardle (Heretaunga), who would instinctively fight National's repeated lurchings to the right but ultimately be destroyed or detrited by constant Caucus hammerings.

Oh, and then there was me — totally cognisant of my absolute impotence as a government backbencher and enviously watching my former research colleagues garner the plum advisory jobs in various ministers' offices: Wayne Eagleson to coordinate the research unit itself and attend the daily House strategy meetings; Lindsay Scott to John Banks' office; Mary Brown to Jenny Shipley's; John Benn to Philip Burdon's; and Paul Sherriff to Maurice McTigue's. Each would have infinitely more influence over government policy than I would, without the public scrutiny or hassle. Yep, being an MP was most definitely Plan B.

Jim Bolger knew that much of his immediate attention would be focused on the twin evils of a befuddled BNZ and a rampant Richardson, but he still had the dilemma of what to do with the back bench other than vivisection. The polar trek across Antarctica was an attractive option but, dammit, some of them might survive. The other alternative was to load each of the backbenchers with titular responsibilities that allowed them to feel important without actually giving them any real responsibilities — a sort of poor man's Board of Trustees.

Because I had drafted the party's pre-election employment policy I was appointed chairman of the Government Caucus Employment Committee, which at least had the virtue of sounding impressive. As well I was placed on the education and science and Maori affairs select committees under the respective chairs of Tony Steel and Joy McLachlan. McLachlan later 'retired' from this onerous task and was replaced by Ian Peters because (a) she was a woman (and some tribal protocol had a problem with any woman in authority — very enlightened) and (b) she was Pakeha. In contrast Ian Peters was clearly masculine and his Mediterranean looks at least suggested a Maori heritage. With regard to Maori affairs I thus learned my most valuable lesson — form overrules substance every day of the week.

TREASURY'S CHRISTMAS CHEER

Treasury had thoughtfully provided the Bolger Cabinet with its suggested plan for escaping the same economic crap it had previously helped create. This was contained in its tamely titled 'Briefing to the Incoming Government 1990', a smorgasbord of both logical and loony policy prescriptions that Richardson would religiously apply over the next three years with a zealotry that would have made Margaret Thatcher blush.

In fact, Ruth was not beyond plagiarism of any sort and recycled Thatcher's clever utterance 'The lady's not for turning' for local consumption. Richardson obviously had eclectic tastes, as she showed by later liberating Saddam Hussein's tragic observation in describing her 1991 economic opus as 'the mother of all Budgets'. It said a lot about Ruth that she would draw on the combined inspiration of Treasury, Thatcher and a mad Iraqi despot during her first six months as the Minister of Finance. But as David Lange had forewarned, those who live by the quip die by the quip, and Richardson's peculiar brand of castor oil and self-flagellation would cleverly be branded 'Ruthanasia', as any number of government backbenchers were about to discover.

Treasury's redemptive prescription included the rapid balancing of the Budget, the slashing of social spending, deregulating the labour market and generally reducing the size of the State so that it might pass through the measure at a piano-smashing contest. However, it was Ruth's genius that such dismemberment should commence immediately and so was framed the notorious Christmas package of December 1990 — a Yuletide gift to welfare beneficiaries that transformed Scrooge into a gentle philanthropist.

The December 19 economic package that Richardson presented to Caucus and the country was shrewdly timed. The nation's thoughts were on Christmas, the Gallery's thoughts were on surviving last night's bender and most MPs' thoughts were on catching up on months of lost sleep.

Perhaps Cabinet assumed that this slumber was already under way because the Executive began as they intended to carry on and treated their back bench with disdainful contempt. Caucus were deliberately excluded from the deliberation process and only informed of the December economic package in a misleading presentation precisely half an hour before its public release. Again the calamitous state of the nation's accounts was dramatically emphasised, but then came the shocking detail of how the Bank of New Zealand was to be baled out of its former gambling losses. Beside me sat the new associate Finance Minister, Doug Kidd, and as Richardson hastily sketched out plans to reduce government expenditure a nasty thought flashed through my synapses.

'My God,' I turned to Kidd. 'We're not cutting benefits are we?'

Kidd smiled at me as an indulgent adult might regard a slow, plodding primary schoolchild.

'No, no, no,' he soothed. 'We're restructuring them.'

A good number of my colleagues, including me, did not have the slightest inkling as to the scale and magnitude of these welfare cuts until we read of them in the next morning's newspapers. A combination of ministerial obfuscation and Treasury jargon hid the true extent of the December package until experienced Gallery journalists like the *New Zealand Herald*'s Simon Collins interpreted the small print and its implications.

But Kidd was not the only minister to withhold the true extent of the welfare cuts. That very morning a solo parent from Flaxmere had telephoned and fearfully recounted a rumour circulating her suburb that the government was about to slash her benefit. I assumed this worried enquiry was idle child-centre gossip but, just to be safe, my office contacted Minister Shipley's private secretary to confirm the government's intention to honour its pre-election commitments.

On the same day that welfare benefit cuts were publicly announced, the office of the Minister of Social Welfare confidently advised both me and my electorate agent that my constituent had absolutely no cause for concern. In turn, we relieved the anxiety of this tearful domestic purposes beneficiary and a number of other constituents who had obviously listened to the same rumour.

Later that evening I would remonstrate personally with Shipley at being deliberately lied to by a senior policy officer who had known the score when they had provided the assurance.

Shipley dismissed my protest with imperious disdain. Her private secretary had made exactly the right call — Caucus MPs were not entitled to such information. I had no right to know that Freddy

Kruger had been let loose in Social Welfare.

My response was neither wonderfully witty nor derisively precise. As Shipley turned on her heels my mouth opened and closed, and then opened and closed again, but no noise escaped. It was now crystal clear that this Cabinet considered its backbenchers irrelevant lobby fodder — mere drones of party dictate. We were not to be involved, informed or trusted with any policy formulation prior to its public release, and my very being recoiled at this grim realisation.

I had not cheated the abyss after all.

– CHAPTER 7 –

REBEL

HAWKE'S BAY

I would like to be able to say at this juncture that I had a vision, a plan, even a rudimentary stratagem about what to do next. I would like to say that — but it would not be true. My primary objective was simple. Having been elected an MP I wished to be re-elected. All my actions over the next three years would accumulate merit or demerit points toward that objective.

It was thus with considerable amazement that I encountered a whole swag of new MPs who considered the 1993 election to be so far away as to be rendered inconsequential. This unhealthy indifference pervaded our Caucus until about nine months out from the next election, when the most curious and contradictory mixture of resignation and panic ripped its way through the marginal seat holders.

The Cabinet had no such qualms. Back-bench casualties were collateral damage; it saved on getting to know their names. We were now in the Great War against inflation, interest rates and unbalanced budgets and it was only to be expected that insanely enthusiastic first-termers should scramble over the top, wade through the mud and barbed wire and then be shot to bits by enemy machine guns. I noticed that it was always those MPs in the safest seats who preached such Kitchener 'human wave' tactics.

This noxious whiff of party jingoism pervaded each and every Caucus meeting for much of the next three years. My most common Caucus thought during this entire period simply consisted of one three-word phrase endlessly repeated: 'Are they mad?'

After the December 1990 package I had also come to understand something else — just a little quicker than most of my other back-bench colleagues. Cabinet was going it alone. To be precise, Ruth and Treasury were going it alone and in the absence of alternative transport the rest of Cabinet had hitched themselves along for the ride.

My firm impression of Jim Bolger was that, devoid as he was of any personal vision or philosophy, much of his energy and enthusiasm would be satiated on election night. He was a National Prime Minister after all — what else was there to do? Over time that impression would receive wider and wider confirmation. The man did not have a clue what he wanted except for one thing. He wanted to be Prime Minister.

Usually this is enough — unless you have a Roger Douglas or a Ruth Richardson in prospect. Then you have just two choices — hang on tight or scram. Both Lange and Bolger made the same foolish mistake of opting for the ride but leaving the control panel on the ground.

To Richardson's eternal credit, she never saw power itself as the final destination. Would that she had — I would have slept much better. Bolger's political vanity had gifted to Ruth the plotting of government direction. And it would be the Ruth/Treasury path or stagnation. The Leader knew enough about practical politics to comprehend that stagnation signalled decay and decay suggested demise. By the time the poor man had worked out that he had actually stepped on board a Treasury bullet train which had been deliberately stripped of its brakes it was all too late. The political damage had been well and truly done.

But that was all in the future and given that no one was inviting me to the Monday Cabinet meetings I determined that the government's inevitable unpopularity should not be mine. Yes, it was that selfish. No altruism, no particular insight — I would become a constituent MP and a damned good one because that would be the only way I was going to survive the electoral carnage three years hence.

What I was wholly unprepared for was the implications of this simple expediency. I would be propelled, literally, into the lives of thousands of ordinary folk who would seek out my assistance with varying degrees of desperation and disintegration. And each one of these constituent encounters would affect me in ways that I could never have contemplated. In short, my constituents civilised me; their experiences and troubles affected and shaped my perceptions; my efforts on their behalf chipped away at 33 years of affected and refined cynicism.

In short, Hawke's Bay made me human. This is not to suggest — as my political enemies have over many, many years — that I was born of either primeval ooze or some dark incubus. But it is the sad nature

of the late twentieth century that we prize cynicism over sentimentality, worldliness over wonder, and the material over the mature,
and I was not immune from such humbug. This insensibility had been
further amplified by an academic training and five years within the
precincts of Parliament. It is a wonder there was any sympathetic
DNA left to clone.

In those first few months I encountered constituents facing bank-
ruptcy, criminal proceedings, eviction, incestuous family predations,
unemployment, incompetent surgeons, departmental neglect and even
death. The range and intensity of the issues and problems took away
my reserve and, with it, any sense of splendid isolation. I discovered
a childhood facility within me to empathise, and gradually each vestige
of my asinine youth was stripped away. This was serious stuff.

These people had come to me as their last chance. It became our
office credo — we were 'the court of last resort' and if we failed them
their next step would be debt, disgrace or despair. Perhaps it was their
pathetic trust that I could leaven their plight, perhaps it was the sense
of hopeless challenge, perhaps it was my innate and instinctive support
for the underdog; whatever the emotional catalyst within me I became
a constituency MP possessed.

Moments of almost aching awareness were lightened by a steady
supply of utter nutters — individuals who had been deemed way too
weird for assistance by other MPs or community agencies. Within
weeks I had been accosted by an array of conspiracy theorists, elderly
eccentrics and religious millenarians who came alternately to warn
and lecture me about the evils and perils lurking in their fantasies.

My two favourites were an elderly hobo who would ride his
dilapidated bicycle into the office and demand that I find him a
woman, a house and a piece of land in roughly that order. We reasoned
with him that we might find the last two, but the first would prove
tricky. No problem, was the reply, he would be happy with just one of
my young staff for a few weeks. I bet.

Then there was the lovely young lady who believed that I had
sicked the SIS onto her for not voting National at the last election.
She was also something of a Catholic zealot and had confessed this
great sin to the Pope and he had forgiven her — so why hadn't I? I
immediately picked up the telephone and ordered 'Brigadier Smith'
to cease his 24-hour surveillance or I would expose his penchant for
latex underwear. This conversation instantly reassured her, although
she returned a week later to lay an official complaint about the UFOs

landing in her back garden. Something about interfering with the carrots.

The news soon spread that my constituency office provided an excellent service and that the women in my office were friendly (if unavailable for marriage) and made great cups of tea. By now I had employed a part-time agent, Kathy Leach, and a succession of office assistants; Kathy funded by Parliamentary Services to complement Anne, and the assistants by my various rortings of whatever employment schemes the local Employment Service was offering. For some perverse reason it had been decreed that Taskforce Green and similar work experience schemes were not available to MPs or electorate offices so I created an endless array of community and charitable groups, made myself the chairman of each, and then employed these community workers through that facility. It was a win-win situation for everyone — the worker gained invaluable experience and a glowing reference from an MP; my office expanded its range of constituency services; and the taxpayer's investment was returned when the worker found employment.

Of the seven or eight young women who worked in my office over the next five years, mostly as office assistants, all found a job upon the scheme's conclusion, and I recruited my parliamentary executive secretary, Louise Sampson, direct from such a programme. I had no hesitation in breaking the rules if it produced such positive outcomes, even if various ministers and MPs tut-tutted at such a flagrant abuse of the system. Tough.

It is true when MPs say that their most rewarding work is that which they perform on behalf of their individual constituents. But it was much more than that for me. I was being educated on an almost daily basis about the trials and tribulations of human existence — experiences that my family background and academic ability had thankfully spared me. I put all my efforts and enthusiasm into my constituency service, knowing that each hour spent in Wellington would be a negative and soulless experience but that I could do some tangible good at home. I became part social worker, part advocate, part sympathiser and part confidant, and came to regard the electorate as nothing less than a secular parish. When I described this concept to a fundamentalist religious gathering in my electorate, noting that I was 'a secular steward' and my audience were the ecclesiastical equivalent, there were unsteady murmurings.

'No, Mr Laws,' one of them contradicted me. 'In our profession we have to tell the truth.' And sat down again with an air of righteous vindication.

Too quick my tongue.

'So, why do you preach the Creation myth and the Virgin birth then?' I ribbed him. I think right there and then I lost the right-wing Christian vote. I might be turning human but divinity was still a distant planet.

Ironically, my greatest supporters in Hawke's Bay would be the National Party, or at least the local party organisation. Fortunately, my campaign team of Neil Kirton, Anne Averill and Lawrence Yule had assumed the major roles within the executive's ranks and they recruited like-minded individuals in Alan Baldock, Brian Woodhouse and Tania Wright, each of whom would assist in repelling the repeated efforts of both the divisional hierarchy and disaffected dissenters to impose order and discipline on their rogue MP. Every political move I was to make over the next five years drew the public support of my party executive even if they were privately outraged. But we shared a common view that a Member of Parliament had a primary responsibility to their constituents and that this loyalty preceded obedience to the party. Frankly I think the executive also enjoyed the vicarious notoriety and the succession of television camera crews and current affairs personalities who found their way to Hawke's Bay.

The first three years in Hawke's Bay became a blizzard of activity. I immediately summoned a meeting of the region's opinion and business leaders for a hastily convened Hawke's Bay Summit so that I might divine the kind of representative leadership this community expected of me. It was a public relations success but little else. Hawke's Bay had the same irreconcilable political divisions as everywhere else in New Zealand and the same debate over whether a government should spend more or tax less. The summit reached a general concensus that a decent government does both — great.

In addition I was introduced to the ceaseless, petty civil war that raged between the Napier and Hastings communities — or rather raged between the civic leaders and newspapers of these proximate provincial cities. As my electorate straddled both cities and parochial sensibilities I resolved to stay out of local-body affairs — an eminently sensible decision which I would later disregard to my cost.

A newly elected MP has an immediate choice — whether they want to be a reactive or a proactive MP. A reactive MP will wait for local problems to find him, which has the virtue of being safe. Some reactive MPs also interpret their task as assuming the role of the government's chief apologist in their region, an exceedingly onerous task during this first year of office. It was the worst of all possible worlds really although those MPs who mixed the two, like Nick Smith and Joy McLachlan, would prove that local effort can eventually outweigh party political distaste.

In contrast I determined to be a creative MP who identified community needs and set out to meet them. This involved more toe-crunching than I originally envisaged because each civic or community leader had their own prescribed patch and resented any intrusion no matter how genuine. But I had not become an MP by being careful (far from it) and thus plunged into any number of local endeavours.

By the end of my first term I had recreated the Bank of New Zealand Festival Debate in Hastings as a moneymaker for local charities; established and chaired community work trusts in both Flaxmere and Napier; founded a boarding scholarship for the local St Joseph's Maori Girls' College; conned the BNZ into supporting a tertiary 'summer scholarship' for the Christmas holidays; organised a series of rugby dinners to raise funds for the impoverished Hawke's Bay rugby team; become the chief advocate for a new high school in Flaxmere; and generally involved myself in a considerable array of community projects that might announce my presence as a hard-working local MP who was making a positive difference.

Of course it was a deliberate personal strategy and, of course, there were considerable political and personal advantages to be gained. But the strangest of transitions was taking place within me. I was becoming trapped by my own expedient altruism. Having refused the first parliamentary pay increase I was obliged to refuse all consequent Commission awards; having gone the extra mile in a high-profile constituency case I was obliged to go the extra mile for all constituency concerns; having creatively assisted one spectrum of the community I was now obliged to assist all with equal endeavour.

Little by little, case by case, issue by issue I developed a constituency consciousness and the guidelines — political, administrative, ethical — for each of my subsequent actions. I was not just becoming human, I was becoming a compassionate human, and I guess the stark contrast between that Michael Laws and his somewhat dissolute and licentious prototype was all too much for some. I could understand the accusations of play-acting or grandstanding from my political enemies. It was as if Michael Laws had got religion, and no one was buying that concept for an instant.

Except me.

And there was something else. I was becoming a socialist. My God, Barrie Leay had been right all along.

And now the personal challenge was more than just to be a decent human being and a caring MP — I wanted to prove that I truly was Hawke's Bay's Member of Parliament, that my constituents had a personal stake in my life and I in theirs, that a real political partnership had been formed and, best of all, that this partnership could survive the vicissitudes of an unpopular National Government.

This unusual blend of genuine altruism and political strategy would deliver me an increased electoral majority in 1993, despite adverse boundary changes and a swing against National of over eleven per cent in the provincial cities.

It would also make me question the fundamental philosophy of the National Party. For I had come to believe that the self-help and private enterprise features of the party failed the real test — that the path to reward and riches was largely predetermined by family background, socioeconomic status and culture in roughly that order. And unless the inequalities were remedied then the race would not be won by the fastest and the best, but by those who got the 50-metre head start.

But of all the wondrous mysteries that I would encounter in Hawke's Bay the most inexplicable would be the hissing hatred of my neighbouring National MP, Hastings' Jeff Whittaker.

Countless party workers and constituents would suggest that this passionate dislike was based on jealousy although, attractive as this proposition was to my ego, it seriously underestimated Jeff's particular talents and achievements. He was a successful pharmacist and owned the most popular gardening centre in the region, his business skills reputedly making him a millionaire; he had married a charming and capable woman and had charming, capable children; he was a notable equestrian and yachtsman; and he had reached the highest hillock of local body service as the Mayor of Havelock North before its amalgamation with Hastings City. Frankly, I even thought he was better looking than me. Lord knows, he had no reason to be jealous.

But for the next three years my most virulent local opposition would come not from the Labour Party nor the Alliance nor the fathers of past girlfriends but from Whittaker. Everything I supported, Jeff

opposed. Everything I opposed, Jeff supported. We were feral doppel-
gängers and the entire region soon became acutely aware that an
Appalachian hillbilly feud had been successfully transplanted to their
backyard.

Whittaker and I had shared a common pre-election view on economic direction — namely, that Rogernomics had gone too far and
that the 'more market' philosophy of the right was morally bankrupt.
However, within months Jeff had become Richardson's primary
apologist in Hawke's Bay, a backward flip that not only astounded
the locals but led to the resignation of his electorate chairman and
earned him the bitter enmity of many previous supporters.

Jeff and I would clash on just about every political issue of
consequence: the welfare benefit cuts, the superannuation surtax,
privatisation, Winston Peters, electoral reform — even on whether
or not my Flaxmere constituents should have their own high school.
You name the issue — our names were the first to appear on the
opposing lists. It even reached the stage where he publicly threatened
to sue me for defamation in the aftermath of Caucus' later decision to
expel Winston Peters.

In just about every public discussion I was confident that Whittaker's attack only harmed his credibility and buttressed mine, for
Jeff had the most peculiar penchant for always choosing the most
indefensible and unpopular of political options. But Jeff was to have
the last laugh, and in such an audacious manner that I could only
shake my head and admire the trumping.

Towards the end of my first parliamentary term I received an
amorous letter from a woman in Auckland who thanked me for a
shared night of sensual abandon and enquired as to my availability
for the next wanton session. This struck me as a little odd because I
did not recall this chance encounter, at which I had apparently been
alternately charming, polite and extraordinarily sexy. I might be able
to muster the first attributes on a good day but even with the wind
behind me and a good cosmetic surgeon I would never manage the
last. Fortunately my correspondent had thoughtfully included a
photograph of the two of us dancing at a private party, with swirling
schoolgirl kisses drawn on the back. One look at the photograph
reassured me that the woman was most definitely not in my fond
embrace. That honour belonged to Jeff. I can only surmise that he
had found it convenient to describe himself to this dotty woman as
yours truly — possibly in the vain hope that my name might repel

her, or that at least he would enjoy the encounter without consequence. I should have been livid; instead I smiled at Whittaker's cheek and wondered what other Auckland matrons I would be wooing in absentia.

THE REBELS

Within weeks of that first fateful post-election Caucus it had become apparent that some of the back-bench lemmings would independently choose their own cliff. They were branded 'the rebels', and were a rag-tag assortment of MPs with varying degrees of initiative and IQ but sharing an adamantine opposition to the Richardson/Treasury line.

The motivations, acumen and intensity of each rebel MP were so diffuse that it would be wrong to characterise this internal opposition as either homogeneous or homologous. Over time we would socialise with each other (if only because no one else would drink with us) but there was never any stratagem or consolidated lobby — we were far too ill-disciplined and individualistic to allow even the most haphazard organisation.

The first inkling of trouble had come, as explained, in the variety of candidates' reactions to the Reserve Bank Act and its obsessive focus on an inflation target of zero to two per cent. A good number of the new intake had expressed unease but doubters were soon pacified by blarney briefings from the new Finance Minister and the projection of the TINA scenario. It is my firm belief that in encountering economic and Treasury jargon for the first time (and finding it near incomprehensible) most MPs meekly assented rather than be thought thick. When the full extent of the BNZ bale-out and the fiscal blow-out became apparent even those few remaining querulous back-benchers embraced this alien creed in the absence of any constructive or immediate policy alternative — well, everyone except the true mavericks.

Initially Sir Robert Muldoon was regarded as the leading dissenter but his objections exhibited a nostalgic pining for the good old days of Think Big, wage/price freezes and baiting Brian Edwards. His public and Caucus forays had a touch of the ageing great-uncle about them, complete with ramblings about some mythical golden age and the dreadful manners of modern teenagers. I soon felt pangs of sympathy for the old tusker because it was clear that younger Cabinet ministers were sneeringly intolerant of this former great and began treating him as if he were in the first stages of senile dementia. Disillusioned and acutely aware of his diminished Caucus status, Muldoon resigned from Parliament at the end of 1991 and died shortly thereafter.

Our last conversation came just three days before his death, when he asked me to host his radio talkback show one Sunday afternoon because, I assumed, of some temporary illness. We chatted for a few moments and somehow his role as the narrator in the weird and wacky *Rocky Horror Show* came up. Despite this association with ghouls and alien transvestites nothing, he chuckled, could have prepared him for Ruth Richardson as Minister of Finance.

The other leading pre-election dissenter had been Winston Peters, but he was now Maori Affairs Minister and rapidly fading from public view. By the middle of that first year his 'preferred Prime Minister' rating had plummeted as he sought to produce the policy framework that would lead the Maori people into the promised land of economic and educational parity with their Pakeha cousins. Winston and I would joke during this period that attaining parity with Pakeha was setting one's sights way too low. Thus it was that two of the expected leading rebels had been effectively neutralised — Muldoon by age and Peters by the zombie doctrine of Cabinet collectivism.

Neither man would vote against any of the government's legislative programme in 1991 — neither the welfare benefit cuts nor the superannuation surtax nor the health reforms — and I lost a good deal of respect for both men as a consequence. Sometimes it is just not good enough to shout; the body must go on the line.

It was left, then, to a smattering of innocuous first-term back-benchers to lead the real charge — one that would make the Light Brigade's effort look professional by comparison. At least in the former bungle the victims reached the Russian guns — our loose grouping would be devastated even before standing in the stirrups.

Whatever the subsequent events, whatever their respective fortunes and fates, whatever the media or public impression of these individuals, I came to both like and respect those MPs who made up the rebel enclave in National's midst. For they all possessed one rare quality — the courage not just to voice their concerns but to match their words with actions. Their final actions might have been foolish and feeble but they at least made the effort, shaming those of their smarter and smoother colleagues who shared their concerns but found it easier to acquiesce.

The two most 'out there' rebels were Myles and McIntyre — two men who did not possess even a peripheral understanding of the relationship between action and consequence. The world of politics may have been an arid desert for these two but they would launch their journeys without water, sun block or even a sensible hat. They would become the term's tragic triers, but they gained my affection for even trying in the first place.

Hamish McIntyre was a gentle, naive, Christian soul who regarded his word as his bond and his campaign promises as symbols of personal integrity. It was unanimously agreed that Hamish was too good and too sensitive for politics — a vulnerable and emotional individual totally unsuited to the wiles and witchery of Wellington. Each manifesto backdown or equivocation would provoke zealous and sincere indignation, and his boyish tantrums in Caucus became a talking point among his colleagues.

'McIntyre is cracking up,' would run the Government gossip, but it was not so much that Hamish was unstable as absolutely mortified that no one would take any of his views or comments seriously. Clearly he had not learned the golden rule that backbenchers should be like well-behaved children — seen but not heard.

Roskill MP Gilbert Myles was a different character entirely. He would lovingly exaggerate every conspiracy theory within his grab-space and believe them all with the fervour of a religious convert. But the same sincere and sympathetic heart that beat in Hamish was matched within Gilbert's frame, and he willingly spent thousands of his own dollars in tending to the needs of his poorer constituents. His heart was in the right place — it was just that his head was in the toilet.

Whereas Hamish loathed the media spotlight Gilbert was excessively flattered by its attention, but he lacked the ability to take the vital intermediate step between half-formed cranial blancmange and coherent verbal utterance. On numerous occasions he wandered into my room sighing over his latest media misfortune and resolving never again to be so silly. Then he would walk out, spot a roving microphone and plunge down a fresh crevasse. But I could not help liking the man — his inordinate generosity was matched by enough self-deprecating humour to forgive him all manner of foolishness.

Gilbert's lack of political diplomacy reached its spectacular zenith when, after marching down Queen Street at the head of an anti-benefit-cuts march, he accused various Cabinet ministers of 'sleeping in satin sheets while the poor starve' — an observation that particularly riled both the Prime Minister and Social Welfare Minister Jenny Shipley, who would spend a fruitless hour at one Caucus retreat bellowing for proof. Short of personally exploring their bedrooms this would always prove an impossible quest.

For their efforts both men were subjected to increasingly vile and violent verbal batterings, the like of which I had not witnessed since the adolescent cruelty of boarding school. In Caucus after Caucus they would be singled out for special criticism and ridicule, with ministers and backbenchers taking turns to pursue their favourite bloodsport. Invariably the two ex-coppers, Hilt and Revell, would lead the charge but they had no shortage of support from a host of other backbenchers who demanded cowed submission. The attacks were so personal and persistent that I cringed at the spectacle — they were repulsive and gratuitous gangbangs, gross behaviour over which Bolger presided with a malignant indifference.

Certainly both men felt the verbal and social torment of their peers keenly and it affected them in different ways. Hamish would flash into face-reddening rages in an instant; Gilbert would confide that his vodka supplies were taking an undue hammering. But the Caucus wolves could smell the palpable weakening of spirit and redoubled their efforts — even the most petty of transgressions now provoked frenzied assault. I was to experience similar beat-ups but none quite so malevolent, for my attackers knew that I had a quick tongue and a strong appetite for vengeful retorts. But McIntyre and Myles were softer targets, and of this the bullies were acutely aware. It would all become too much — soon, both men would break. The Labour Party might have its Rule 242 with its demand for collective loyalty or expulsion, but National had the more effective weapon of social ostracism.

Joining Myles, McIntyre and me in the 'Noes' lobby against the welfare benefit cuts would be a fourth MP — Heretaunga's Peter McCardle. Peter was another of life's gentle souls, a devout Catholic and an even more devout family man whose life centred around his adored wife and two young children.

As a former Employment Service manager, Peter had entered Parliament to pursue one objective and one objective only — a reordering of the State's resources for the express purpose of outlawing unemployment. As chairman of the Caucus employment committee I had a great deal of sympathy for his radical initiatives although I was realistic enough to confine such ideas to persons who had been unemployed for longer than six months.

Together we worked on replacing the dole with a variety of remedial education, training and community work options that could be structured to meet the individual's needs. We greedily eyed the promised pre-election funding of an extra $200 million for Taskforce Green, but this pledge also received the customary Treasury tampering, torture and then turfing.

In the absence of any positive policy alternatives we both viewed the benefit cuts as little more than punitive sanctions and wanted no part of them. In the end it would be just the four of us who would outrage our colleagues and editorial writers everywhere by rejecting the cuts and voting with the Labour enemy — a move that drew hoots of derision from Jenny Shipley and countless threats from a wide variety of Caucus MPs that our political careers were finished. I had the express satisfaction of watching most of these taunters lose their seats at the next election.

Although McCardle joined us in 'crossing the floor' over the benefit cuts he was conspicuous by his absence when it came to opposing the superannuation surtax as outlined in Ruth Richardson's 1991 'mother of all Budgets'. He would later confess that he had been sufficiently cowed by the Caucus reaction to his earlier defiance that he did not wish to further compromise his chance at getting the grand McCardle Employment Vision implemented by Cabinet. It was my assessment that New Zealand would win a cricket series before that particular miracle would occur.

No, the fourth anti-surtax rebel would be Wanganui's Cam Campion — a gruff, rough, tough Wanganui farmer who possessed the most rudimentary academic skills but made up for his lack of formal learning and social graces with a steady diet of funny, crude, and rustic one-liners. 'Cam the Man', as he styled himself, had the kind of restless vigour that forced the invention of animal tranquillisers — there was not a waking moment when he would not be devising some new entrepreneurial venture. The standing joke on our parliamentary floor was that fax machines had been created by God so that the most distant African state or the most ignorant eastern European commune would not perish without first being informed of Cam's fabled farm by-products.

Cam was loathed by a good portion of Wanganui's genteel National Party set for being too obvious, too overweight and too bloody basic.

His wife, Margaret, was the undoubted brains in the relationship but Cam's winning gall proved irresistible in securing both the party's nomination and the Wanganui seat for the first time since 1969. Parliament itself was just a little too quick and Byzantine for any of Cam's attributes to be made obvious — most of Caucus dismissed him as an amiable buffoon, but that was to seriously misread the man, as later events would show.

THE SUPER WAR

I once heard Ruth Richardson describe the superannuation debate as the only one in which politicians sought to bribe the public with not just their own money but the unearned income of their children and grandchildren as well. As a leading member of the National Party Ruth would have known — she had observed such sophistic solicitations at close quarters.

Of all the enduring policy scraps in opposition the most intense had always been over the affordability of state pensions. The debate divided on roughly generational grounds, the older Venn Young arguing for the status quo and the younger Jenny Shipley stressing that demographic changes would, one day, bankrupt the nation. To be honest I did not have a clue which one was right; in fact, I secretly suspected they were both wrong.

Anyway National had gone to the 1990 general election with some very explicit promises to the over-60s and the almost-60s — namely, inflation-indexing of the Guaranteed Retirement Income (GRI); the gradual increase in entitlement from 60 to 65 years of age; the abolition of Labour's hated income-tested surcharge; and the really big one — the changing of the name. GRI sounded like an electrical appliance store — National Superannuation was much better, as it might remind all the venal, elderly punters just which party had given them the best deal.

Poor Jim Bolger was mercilessly hounded on the 1990 trail by the two modern devils of campaigning — a bored press corps and yapping Grey Power mercenaries. These aggressive supplicants finally cracked Bolger by forcing him to sanctify his party's election promises on superannuation — they would be more than just election promises, they would be the sacred symbols of National's and Jim Bolger's political credibility. At that point, any self-respecting retiree should have headed for the hills. Instead, foolishly, they believed, but then a good number of them also thought Elvis was alive and living in a Golden Bay resthome.

Superannuation was National's big bang for the 1990 election — the one policy promise that possessed the blessed trinity of embarrassing Labour, offering a huge sector of voters a direct inducement, and righting a 'moral wrong' so that we could hint that even God was on our side. That is one of the great things about opposition — the angels are easier to find.

These pre-election promises were repeated, repeatedly, by the new Prime Minister and even contained within Her Majesty's Speech from the Throne which opened the 1991 parliamentary session. This was despite Treasury's gloomy post-election briefings, the BNZ fiasco and the Christmas welfare cuts. There you go — even the Queen lied.

Fortunately (and you would have had to be braindead not to recognise the signals) it became clear to this new backbencher that the super campaign promises were striking some very nasty turbulence during the Budget bilaterals of early 1991. A John Banks outburst in Caucus may have been the first visible sign, although there was already back-bench gossip about worsening Treasury projections and the need for heroic, even quixotic, attempts at parliamentary parsimony.

Police Minister John Banks had two great hates — anything remotely liberal and 'rat swallowing'. Breaking solemn manifesto promises was very definitely a major case of rodent consumption, and breaking super promises represented the cordon bleu of this culinary practice. It was one of Caucus' magical moments when Banks let rip in one pre-Budget Caucus about the nature of Ruth Richardson's Iraqi budget and provided a fascinating insight into the ministerial tension and trade-offs during this secretive planning process.

By May 1991 Cabinet had decided that Caucus should be entrusted with some information on planned GRI changes, although on a strictly need-to-know basis. Cuts to the standard rate of GRI were floated, and received the kind of jolt one might receive from a 100,000-volt electric fence. This was 'over my dead body' stuff and a surprising number of even moderate backbenchers seemed prepared to lie down in front of the Treasury steamroller. I found it all rather ironic — these were the same backbenchers who justified draconian benefit cuts.

Fortunately this was soon placed in perspective for me.

'Yes, Laws,' said one impatient rural backbencher. 'But superannuitants vote for us. Solo mums don't.'

Instantly I realised the proper policy position. We should income-test all non-National voters. Now I understood what 'targeting' meant.

It was then that the happy juxtaposition of my 'direct democracy' ideals and straight-out bum-watching coincided. If my party was going to commit the eighth Deadly Sin then my local constituency ground should be properly prepared. There is nothing quite so nasty as a sudden bump (especially for people of a sensitive age) and I wanted my Hawke's Bay superannuitants to at least see the bus coming.

To that end I organised a postal Superannuation Referendum and used a very clever computer programme that informed me of all those in my electorate over 55 years of age. Then I wrote to each, outlined the general economic situation, informed them of my decision to forego the recent parliamentary pay increase and asked a few leading questions as to their preferences on the future of GRI and their preferred contribution to the present economic crisis.

I would be the only MP to engage in such a calculated exercise, but I blessed the heavens that I performed this first attempt at 'direct democracy'. It would rescue me from all manner of lobby group and party political accusations while providing a clear mandate. It also did something else — it kept me honest, providing the kind of external discipline I would need once the Caucus pressure was exerted. Now I was safe from Grey Power, the Government and the Opposition because I knew something they did not: I knew what my constituents thought and wanted.

Rather than stifle my future actions, the polling results actually liberated them. The results showed that 68 per cent would accept a GRI freeze as their contribution to the forecast tough times; two-thirds supported raising the age of eligibility to 65 years; a good majority supported my personal concept that GRI should have a 50-per-cent universal component and a 50-per-cent means-tested component. However, any suggested cut to the basic GRI rate received an overwhelming thumbs down.

Meanwhile Richardson was drafting the back bench into her personal A and B teams. The A team were privy to sensitive Budget information and seemed pathetically grateful to have been admitted to the outer portals of the Treasury holy of holies. The B team were told nothing — they could not be trusted. There was also a C team — those who could not be trusted even with no information — but I detected no special Richardson stratagem for Ross Meurant. Surprisingly, I was still A-team material and Ruth personally invited me to pre-Budget briefing and bickies in her Beehive office.

Instinctively I rejected this offer. Not only did I feel uneasy that Caucus were not receiving the briefing as a group (and thus the message could and would be altered depending on the audience) but I also knew that the briefings would compromise my future actions. And I would require both sword hands to be free.

The great joke about the 1991 'mother of all Budgets' was that even the Caucus 'trusties' were double-crossed. Their briefings made no mention of the final draconian surtax that was to be visited upon the elderly. But despite being deliberately misinformed and misled they still accorded Richardson a standing ovation and trooped and trilled through the 'Ayes' lobby like giggling schoolgirls. It would not be until they had read the newspaper analyses and returned home to their constituencies that they would realise something had gone dreadfully wrong. By then it would be way too late.

My personal stock with my colleagues plummeted even lower when news of my absence from the subsequent urgency sitting of the House raced through the back benches. Cabinet had decided that 'extraordinary urgency' would be required to pass a whole series of legislative measures contained within the Budget and had unilaterally decreed a kind of martial law. Government MPs could not leave the building; the House would be sitting past midnight and all through the wee hours to administratively digest the Richardson diet. The

Whips sold this nonsense as both necessary and a wonderful way to build back-bench morale — we could toast marshmallows together and tell ghost stories around the camp fire. I made a mental note to stop drinking from the parliamentary water supply.

Thus I called a taxi, went home to my Wellington flat and went to sleep. They could play their silly games without me. The next day the Prime Minister admonished me in the lobbies for my combined lack of stamina, teamwork and generosity of spirit, with a heaving, grunting mass of red-eyed, dishevelled Government MPs egging him on. When I remonstrated that passing legislation at three in the morning on Tokelauan stamp duties did not seem a particularly intelligent way to transact democratic business Bolger batted away my protests.

'There are things you just have to do in this place,' he thoughtfully, if forcibly, justified himself. Clearly doing ridiculously stupid things at ridiculously stupid hours was just one of those 'things'. I felt much better for the explanation.

But the Budget itself was just the preliminary skirmish in my jihad against the surtax. Sure I had voted against the measure but so what? The Government's huge majority could easily absorb the pinprick dissent of yours truly and three others. Even those who had most thundered against GRI changes in the lead-up to the Budget — Muldoon and Hobson MP Ross Meurant — had refused to cross the floor and instead abstained. The whole idea of picking a fight and then not turning up struck me as particularly pointless.

The usual political avenues of resistance had been well and truly closed. I thus determined to frustrate the intent of this iniquitous legislation by devising various legal and financial stratagems that might evade the surtax altogether. In concert with a lawyer, a banker, an accountant and an insurance broker I fashioned a series of plans and financial products that would allow retirees or near-retirees to restructure their existing income and asset bases to avoid the Department of Social Welfare's definitions of both. It proved breathtakingly simple and involved an amalgam of devices including family trusts, Bonus Bonds, capital investments and the like. The idea was to present the options, explain a little about each of them and then allow the individual to choose the range of products and/or devices that best suited their personal circumstances.

These instructive seminars were just too successful. I had originally planned to run two or three within my electorate and expected a hundred or so people to come to each. In the end I was required to run six of them and over four thousand people were estimated to have attended, with elderly folk spilling out of almost every venue. Incredibly, people actually drove to them from places as far afield as Wanganui, the Wairarapa and Gisborne. And the national media flocked as well, finally comprehending that one troublesome back-bench MP could actually frustrate a government's will if he was prepared to match its rhetoric with intelligent action. I had become Grey Power's favourite grandchild.

Perhaps the most eager attendees at the early superannuation seminars were anonymous representatives of the Department of Social Welfare. They were easy to spot — about twenty years younger than the rest of the audience in their sensible suits and skirts, still wearing their ultra-cool hairstyles of the 1970s, and scribbling away in their notebooks. But the best indicator was that they would pointedly refuse to applaud any comment made by me or the panel members. In the end I began to identify them and sportively suggest they go and clamp the audience's cars now. In turn, the gathering would glower at these minor bureaucrats and openly wonder if they were the devil spawn of ex-SS concentration camp guards.

Meanwhile, I revelled in being the star am-dram turn. I was becoming Gilbert's Sullivan.

But I had made a mistake. By publicly revealing every device and manoeuvre to circumvent the Social Security Act's definition of 'assessable income' I had kindly identified each DSW loophole that needed plugging. Sure enough, officials soon drafted a catch-all declaration of asset and income that each retiree would need to complete and sign before receiving their national super. Faced with such a trumping I did the only thing possible — I introduced Adolf Hitler and Nazi Germany to the debate.

Adolf has been a great political demon for many a year but his resurrection at this moment in the superannuation war was critical. TV3 took the credit for the leaked draft declaration but contrived to get an 'Oh my god!' reaction from yours truly for that night's news bulletin. The *New Zealand Herald* led its front page with 'Laws warns of Gestapo tactics', and just about every voter who had lived through the Second World War nodded their head in vigorous assent.

Suddenly every ex-Desert Rat was being quoted as saying that they had not fought Rommel at El Alamein to let his bastard brethren rob them of their home and savings. Virtually every Government MP's office was besieged with a constant river of hostile telephone calls that began with a story on the Depression, wound their way through the Second World War, then compared these traumatic experiences with the slick, self-satisfied and supercilious lifestyles of modern politicians and bureaucrats.

It had its effect. So too did the public opinion polls of the time, which showed National as low as sixteen per cent — the kind of polling figure that makes safe Cabinet ministers start thinking about updating their résumés. Prime Minister Bolger's popularity was facing similar knocks, which caused me to blurt out about the Leader's 'credibility problem' — I sure had caught Gilbert's disease and received a right royal shafting from the Caucus as a consequence.

It mattered not. Cabinet was in full-scale policy retreat and abandoned first the draft DSW forms and then the dreaded surtax itself. In a humiliating U-turn the Government was required to repeal its own Budget legislation and return more or less to the pre-Budget surcharge.

But retirees and near-retirees had absorbed the lesson and super surcharge avoidance schemes proliferated. The middle class also discovered family trusts — a useful device for evading not just the surcharge but also other asset-testing regimes that might affect their later life. In that respect they were simply taking advantage of the same structures so beloved of so many wealthy Cabinet ministers.

This little war had been fought and won. Realising his predicament Bolger began talking about the need to take politics out of superannuation, having ridden it so hard for the past five years. Unbelievably, Labour's Mike Moore consented to do so and the Superannuation Accord of 1993 was born — which just goes to prove that sometimes politicians do recognise deep doggy-doos when they see it and that just shoving your opponent's face in the smelly mess does not remove the stench from your own garments.

Having said that, Moore did not let the occasion pass without a spectacular demonstration of the metaphor. After evoking images of raped and burned Bosnian refugees Moore then progressed to goat molestation. Mercifully the press conference moved on before he was asked to react to something really important.

But that was in the future. For now I had earned the everlasting enmity of Jenny Shipley and in a perverse kind of way I relished the notoriety. I could handle the hostility; it was always indifference I found impossible to accept.

'TELLING THE TRUTH'

During the super surtax fiasco of 1991 I had unwittingly opened a second front on government policy — in this case a quasi-Russian front against the inaccurately named Employment Minister, Maurice McTigue.

I had first met McTigue when I was involved with Young Nats and we had both attended a highfalutin South Island Policy Conference in Oamaru presided over by Sue Wood and Barrie Leay. I was too naive and dim at the time to appreciate that these seminars were primarily intended to project the egos of Wood and Leay, for it was Caucus that made policy and this task was (and would be) jealously guarded from pesky party interference. Maurice was present as one of Canterbury/Westland's senior representatives and the rumour was that great things were expected of this Timaru farmer. My only impression was that he hogged the buffet table and seemed inordinately conservative, not realising that both these attributes were clear marks of a stellar destiny.

Elected in the Timaru by-election of 1985, McTigue soon distinguished himself as a good Catholic mate of Jim Bolger and exhibited the same solid and stolid characteristics — ideal requirements for a Cabinet slot, and McTigue was not disappointed. The appointment struck me as a little odd because Maurice possessed all the dynamism of road kill, and employment was one portfolio area where National had promised stupendous action — indeed, the halving of unemployment in three years and a brand-spanking-new $200-million Taskforce Green community-work programme for all long-term jobless.

Within weeks Maurice had been captured by the officials, although which ones I was never quite sure — Labour Department, Treasury or Prime Minister's Department — with none wanting to implement National's pre-election employment policy. Too expensive, too hard and too innovative — it was cheaper to keep all the unemployed at home on the dole and hope to God they could not afford to travel to the more salubrious parts of town.

As you can imagine, I was mortified that McTigue had abandoned the manifesto, and as chairman of the Caucus Employment Committee I attempted to draw these policy and ministerial inadequacies to my colleagues' attention. It soon became clear, however, that Maurice had the solid support of both Bolger and Richardson — Bolger because McTigue was snotting his least favourite backbencher, and

Richardson because McTigue was not spending any money.

The great employment solution proffered by this brilliant trium-virate was that in a deregulated labour market (courtesy of the new Employment Contracts Act) wages would drop and thus the unemployed could 'price themselves onto the market'. In other words, the great scheme was to drag everyone else's income down to welfare benefit levels or lower and then let this new begging class knife themselves in the race to a succession of pitifully remunerated employment opportunities. Brilliant!

I had a better idea. Form government-funded partnerships with local councils and communities and create local jobs for local people. If that meant three years on a low-paid community work scheme then so be it. At least productive work would be done, the individual would retain and build their work habits and skills, and taxpayers would see a direct return on their investment. The incentive to move from a community work scheme would always be there because the committee's plan was to pay the minimum wage plus any necessary family supplements. In essence it was a refined 'work for the dole' or 'workfare' scheme.

McTigue hated it. Too expensive, too cumbersome and too much bloody work. Our relationship raced downhill from there on, to the point where he threatened to have me prosecuted for innocently assisting some Hawke's Bay squash-growers with their migrant labour difficulties.

Finally McTigue confronted me in Caucus and demanded my resignation as the committee's chairman. Apparently I had deeply offended him and lost his 'trust' (a miracle; I didn't realise I'd ever had it) by confirming to a journalist that National could not possibly reach its pre-election target of halving unemployment within three years. In fact, I was being diplomatic — I actually considered that by that stage we might just double it.

Anyway, my comment outraged McTigue, who was planning to let the country in on this state secret but at a time of his choosing and under careful media management. Only the truly mentally im-poverished would have regarded the facts as in any doubt, but then the NZ Employment Service was chock full of such types and they had Maurice's ear, eyes and a good part of his stomach securely attached to their advice.

I refused to resign. 'What for?' became my most common utterance for the next 24 hours until the Prime Minister stepped in, told the

Press Gallery I had been sacked and they, in turn, kindly informed me. The next morning the *Dominion* banner headline proclaimed 'Laws sacked for telling the truth' — which proved suitably ironic on any number of counts.

The Government's immediate problem, apart from justifying my sacking, was to find an innocuous, pliable and slothful replacement who could match McTigue's pulse rate and IQ level. Not an easy match — you could search the mortuaries for weeks and still not find a suitable candidate.

This reverse talent search clearly excluded the only other employment policy devotee, Peter McCardle, and instead the phlegmatic Wayne Kimber was appointed — a man who used to boast that he hardly ever distributed a press release for fear that it might be reported. In retrospect a brilliant strategy.

Fortunately, the Prime Minister recognised the wider problem in the portfolio and replaced McTigue with his old mate Bill Birch. We were now out of 'park' mode and stuttering along in first gear, but any forward momentum was to be welcomed. Meanwhile Maurice would further hone his peculiar talent for inertia and be run down by a slow-moving combie van called Jim Sutton in the next general election. From thence he was posted to Canada, where, one presumes, his true talent for consuming finger food drew appreciative gasps from the diplomatic corps.

LIBERAL MIDWIFE

In the much later and interminable discussions that I would share with Mike Moore, as we plotted and schemed to create a new political force for the 1996 general election, there would be one constant recrimination I could not avoid. I had gifted 'the best bloody name in New Zealand politics' to the Myles/McIntyre wackiness. No matter how many times I sought to explain to Mike that they had actually liberated the name from the conservative regime across the Tasman, it was one of those issues for which I would be eternally condemned in the former Labour Prime Minister's eyes.

Following the 1991 Budget both Hamish McIntyre and Gilbert Myles had decided that for their own political and emotional sanity they must depart the National Caucus. There was no shortage of MPs holding the door open for them and queues formed to pack their bags and give them their lunch money.

Gilbert had come to me in the days leading up to their fateful announcement and explained that Hamish was intent upon resignation and that he had no option but to follow. Numerous MPs, Winston Peters included, attempted to talk both men out of taking such a precipitate step. We were selfishly aware that removing Caucus' twin lightning rods would be to our personal disadvantage, while also offering the plaintive if slightly pathetic logic that they could achieve more within the system than outside it. A complete lie, of course, but generations have been similarly conned. Hamish, in particular, was smart enough to see that crock.

And so Hamish and Gilbert performed their dual Captain Oates act, although with not a smidgen of the same nobility; indeed, they had not even prepared their home electorates or party workers for such an announcement.

There is an old adage in the political game: 'Always prepare the ground.' Never plant anything unless the soil is receptive. Confidential briefings of your party workers are essential — you will need their public support when the time comes. But such details escaped the duo's feverish rush into the void and Gilbert even committed the cardinal sin of informing a 'Holmes' television crew before advising his electorate executive.

I was still friendly with both men — you do not abandon a friendship simply because someone's political acumen has never struggled out of the Petri dish. Under the guise of a reunion of the 'floor-crossing four' Cam Campion and I met with the two runaways in an Auckland 'family' restaurant and discussed their next move.

Both Gilbert and Hamish understood that their life spans as independent MPs would be limited, and that a new political party with two MPs would actually become the third largest parliamentary grouping, eclipsing Jim Anderton's solo effort for New Labour. Both Cam and I enquired as to what this new party might stand for, then instantly recognised that that was why we had been invited — to provide further political ballast, a philosophy, the guiding principles and a good measure of the policies. Everything really.

And so that night we scrabbled to provide some semblance of literary credibility, and a logo, to their combined imaginings, using the traditional tools of paper napkins, place mats and beer coasters. Cam provided the logo; I provided the Liberals name (harking back to Seddon and Ward rather than across the Tasman to Peacock and Howard) and the 'New Zealand First' subheading, and we all generally contributed to the party's public principles.

It was generally agreed that Gilbert and Hamish would be preparing the vessel for the arrival of a full sailing crew and a high-profile captain — Winston Peters was identified as the most likely master, although Gilbert had some fantasy about me should the Tauranga MP slip on the gangplank. I did not have the heart to tell either of my former colleagues that any ship prepared by them would be holed below the waterline even before its launching.

One of my old university debating mates, Malcolm Wright, assumed the presidency of the Liberals and generally sought to bring some organisational order to the chaos that accompanied the Myles/McIntyre pairing. Initially the Liberals attracted some very able talent, including a couple of National Party divisional councillors and Winston Peters' older sister, but they would eventually be undone by first joining Jim Anderton's protean Alliance and then dithering over whether or not to join Winston's extension of his ego. It was entirely apposite that Hamish would stay with the Alliance and Gilbert decamp to New Zealand First, thus destroying any remaining hope of parliamentary influence.

Toward the end of 1993 Gilbert wandered gloomily into my office, sat down and buried his head in his hands.

'I've been a fool,' he intoned. 'I've totally destroyed my credibility.' I tried to make suitably soothing and placatory noises but to no effect. Gilbert had promiscuously bounded from National to Independent to Liberal to Alliance to New Zealand First in one parliamentary term and the rest of the country now tut-tutted at such excessive licentiousness. Then he lifted his head and grinned.

'Yeah, but at least I don't have to go to your Caucus every week,' and with that cheery backhander Gilbert was off.

The man had a point.

GOING . . .

In retrospect it seems difficult to comprehend that all these various strands — my superannuation war with Shipley; the Caucus Committee sacking; the resignation of Myles and McIntyre; the Budget U-turns; the commencement of the health reforms; the passage of the Employment Contracts Act; National's plummeting poll ratings; and significant party dissension over the direction of economic policy — occurred concurrently rather than consecutively. 1991 was quite clearly National's annus horribilis.

I guess that is why Jim Bolger decided to go for broke. If you are going to empty the septic tank you might as well empty it all. That meant getting rid of his major Cabinet irritant, Winston Peters.

In all my post-election chats with Winston it was clear that he regarded his portfolio and Cabinet rankings as little less than political slurs. Sure, he was interested in improving the general lot of the Maori people, but there was a hint of the ghetto about the appointment. His resentment was vividly expressed at the executive's swearing-in at Government House. The trademark grin was gone and he affected a manic, distracted air as if remembering that he had left the gas on back at the flat.

Nevertheless Winston's great virtue was that he knew he was no rocket scientist, and any politician who is aware of their frailties (à la Bill Birch) cannot be wholly disregarded. He gathered a group of competent officials and individuals about him, held the occasional policy retreat, and produced 'Ka Awatea' — a blueprint for Maori development. That he created this document outside the normal policy-clobbering machine of Cabinet committees and interdepartmental haggling added to its lustre.

Predictably Winston launched 'Ka Awatea' as a personal triumph, and just to make sure everyone regarded it as such he bypassed the normal Cabinet imprimatur. This was the political equivalent of trying to collect the money before passing 'Go' and the document would eventually languish in limbo.

Meanwhile Winston was being entreated by various MPs to launch the centrist fight against the Treasury policies of Richardson and the rest of Cabinet. Over innumerable tumblers of whisky a variety of back-bench MPs would seek his leadership and direction, even to the extent of launching a breakaway party.

But my colleagues underestimated Winston's psychological, even primal, attachment to the National Party. The same bond of filial loyalty that Peters had displayed in opposition remained within him in government. He was not so much loyal to its Cabinet, Caucus or membership as to its history and traditions; as if the National Party was some holy temple and it was just awaiting his arrival to drive out the merchants and the moneylenders. I was later to witness the same kind of atavistic attachment from another populist leader in Mike Moore. Both Moore and Peters shared the same characteristic — their ambition resembled a helium weather balloon but their sentimentality was the tethering rope. In the end the gas escaped before the rope wore out.

However, in Caucus and around the Cabinet table Winston's lack of an economic or policy alternative had become obvious. Prior to his sacking from the Cabinet Winston played little constructive part within Caucus and it soon became clear that he lacked the academic rigour and skills to challenge the prevailing orthodoxy. Even his querulous public speeches lacked a ready alternative, and in politics you must always offer Plan B if you are intent on publicly trashing Plan A — or at least pretend to have Plan B in your back pocket.

Peters' isolation from his ministerial colleagues was no secret but he had also made an implacable enemy of the party's Maori vice-president, Sir Graham Latimer. The reasons for this personal feud were never made entirely clear to me; I gained the distinct impression that Latimer did not like being upstaged as the party's premier Maori member. Certainly Peters was initially respectful of the northern knight — so much so that he required me to discontinue an Opposition investigation into some dodgy MACCESS and MANA programmes in the Far North when the trail began leading to Latimer.

The relationship between Latimer and the Prime Minister was warm and friendly, and Winston would mutter uneasily at the backstairs access that Sir Graham enjoyed to Bolger's private quarters. This became important when Peters' policy initiatives became frustrated, and the two would clash seriously over the sale of the Quality Inns hotel chain to a shadowy Maori–Hawaiian consortium. Peters wanted an inquiry into the sale and the source of the buyers' monies; Bolger blocked all such probing. A little over a week later the Prime Minister reshuffled his Cabinet and Winston's name did not appear.

From then on Peters assumed the role of leading Caucus rebel, and all fellow dissidents looked to Winston to provide them with a degree of tactical leadership. The resignation of Myles and McIntyre and the retirement of Muldoon might have stripped this grouping of three potential recruits but there were still enough back-bench MPs professing apprehension at the Reserve Bank's sadistic flogging of the economy to provide prospective acolytes.

Sadly, Winston fluffed his only real attempt at providing an alternative economic vision by serving up a mishmash of tried and failed quasi-Keynesian policies which included further and massive public borrowing, favourable tax breaks to companies, and rewarding workers with productivity bonuses. Yet one should not judge him too harshly — all manner of economists, business leaders and political commentators were equally critical of the Government's economic direction without providing a balanced, sensible or even coherent alternative. I was not immune.

Though on some issues I was dead right.

Treasury were a hypocritical and callous bunch who could not have forecast the conclusion to a Mills and Boon novel. At the same time as they were pushing for expenditure cuts and yet more social slashing they gifted themselves a backdated salary increase and spent hundreds of thousands of dollars refurbishing their chief executive's quarters.

As for Don Brash and the Reserve Bank — these people had the kind of obsessive relationship with inflation that one usually only experiences with Madame Lash at the misleadingly named Velvet Touch parlour. The aim was to ease the economy down to two per cent inflation by the end of 1993: Brash and his subordinates nose-dived the CPI down to one per cent two years earlier and needlessly junked 20,000 jobs at point of impact.

My solutions were wishy-washy — slow down the pace of reform to let the stragglers catch up, and enter into an Asian-style partnership with the export sector. I always envisaged an activist state role, and used Japan's Ministry of International Trade and Industry (MITI) as a prime example of a government preaching free trade but practising the opposite. Such eastern pragmatism seemed entirely preferable to New Zealand's naked sporting in the marketplace.

Anyway, now that Winston had been liberated from his Cabinet duties he felt more and more free to challenge Government policy, and the monthly rises in his polling fortunes suggested that he was onto a good thing. However, there were some fairly direct costs.

For a start both Winston and I were being hammered virtually every week in Caucus by our outraged colleagues, who seemed to think that freedom of speech was a glorious concept until practised by someone holding a differing view from theirs. Then it was transformed into treason. These attacks became ever more personal and hysterical until at the Picton Caucus retreat of early 1992 the Prime Minister was good enough to invite both of us to quit Caucus now and swim home. It was a most unsettling experience to have the Prime Minister, his senior Cabinet ministers, and a roomful of enraged back-bench MPs tell you directly, forcibly and with the kind of passion

best reserved for South African rugby referees, that you were 'a traitor', 'a treacherous dog' and, worst of all, 'a Muldoonist'.

I should have developed a complex about it but once again my boarding-school training proved invaluable. I could always handle the verbal bullying at Caucus retreats — it was the deathly cocktail functions with the snobby spouses that really turned my stomach.

During that particularly bitter attack I had been scribbling wildly, jotting down the names of each speaker and their remarks so that I might answer each one when my turn came to speak. Occasionally a stinging remark would make me glance up and catch the expression of the accuser, but during much of this time my head was down and my pen was flying across the paper. I had no shortage of material. Beside me Winston was taking an amazing interest in the morning's newspaper, particularly the classified advertisements.

Behind me a backbencher hissed to his neighbour: 'Look at those bastards — Peters is studying the races and Laws is writing home!' I think it was the feigned boredom that upset them most of all.

Peters' response to this hostile torment was classic Winston. As Caucus broke for the usual afternoon social events, this one a trip on a small ferry for the MPs and their spouses, Peters hired a very large and very fast launch complete with local skipper and fishing tackle. As the Caucus ferry slowly made its way down the Sounds, Peters took over control of the launch and zoomed past the startled gathering with a cheery wave, accelerating with just enough effect to rush the wash against the slower vessel. One of our fishing companions, Brian Neeson, had scampered below when he realised Winston's intentions but I destroyed his anonymity by pointing to the launch floor and shouting to the bemused onlookers, 'Brian's here too!' He never forgave me.

Our irresponsible band of rebellious fishers comprised just the hardy few prepared to tolerate Caucus scorn — Winston, Neeson, Cam Campion, Winston's older brother Ian, Ross Meurant and me. It was not a meeting of the brains' trust.

It would not be long after this that Winston would enter his 'conspiracy stage' of political existence. If I closed my eyes I could swear I was listening to Gilbert's older brother. I guess the difference was that Winston could generate enough verbal smoke to suggest fire, and even if the flames were not immediately visible it mattered not. For Winston had picked his targets well and tapped into a deep core of middle-Kiwi resentment.

I have a theory about the New Zealand character. We are instinctively intolerant of commercial success. The egalitarian nature of our heritage is only part of the answer. The other lies in our good old-fashioned envy of any bastard who is doing better than us. I am sure the social historians would say such sentiments are a natural evolution of our immigrant past as the British poor sought to escape the economic caste system of northern climes. But for some dark reason New Zealanders have adopted egalitarianism as a quasi-religion and we allow few exceptions.

If you have to be rich (and we'd prefer you not to be) then don't flaunt it — that is the Kiwi motto. The sharemarket crash of 1987 and the nose dive of the yuppies actually cheered most New Zealanders more than we care to admit. 'The smart buggers got their just desserts' was the common sneer.

I digress because it partially, but only partially, explains the enormous public support that Peters won when he took on the big boys in the commercial sector — the Fays, the Richwhites, the Congreves, the Brierleys of this world. It took a rare combination of courage and lunacy to launch Peters' parliamentary attacks upon the Bank of New Zealand, the taxation rorts of livestock and film partnerships, and later against those companies contained in the Winebox series of commercial transactions.

Courage because Peters did expose an altogether unpleasant underbelly within New Zealand business. Lunacy because he did not do the job properly. Indeed he fell back into his old cowboy ways, although this time he would be riding into town atop a Sherman tank. Same result though — the whole town would be shot to bits and this time innocent townfolk with it.

Peters' calls for an inquiry into the Bank of New Zealand and the conditions leading to its post-election bale-out were wholly justified. Although he personalised the target in Sir Michael Fay the general concerns had legitimacy. At an early Caucus both Max Bradford and I would push for just such an inquiry, for the solid political reason of finding villains that we could later blame for the spending cuts. We needed a few gypsies to round up and exile from the town limits if the crops were going to fail.

The strongest opponent of such an inquiry was Finance Minister Ruth Richardson. An inquiry would be 'bad for business confidence', she suggested, but with a startling lack of evidence or conviction. A few evenings later I would see her dining in Bellamy's with David Richwhite and the association troubled me — if Richardson and Bolger were to be believed then this man and his fellow BNZ directors had set up the fiscal conditions for the welfare benefit cuts. Only later did I fully comprehend that the cuts would have occurred anyway, crisis or no crisis.

But I guess the clearest evidence that Winston had returned to his old ways was the return of the dreaded 'one step too far'. In this case it would be a television interview with an Australian current affairs show in which Peters alleged that a leading Business Roundtable member had attempted to buy his political silence. The charge of bribery crackled through the parliamentary air like a lightning strike on a hot, humid summer's day.

You could smell the sizzle.

GOING . . .

Everyone makes mistakes. It is the human condition. We are born, genetically predisposed if you like, to cock up.

Personally I find this an endearing characteristic of the human race because it provides the more insecure of us with the opportunity to revel in the misfortunes of those bigger, better and brighter than ourselves. US President Ford prat-falling down aeroplane steps, President Bush regurgitating his sushi, or Prime Minister Jim Bolger hoiking up the same sushi in trying to pronounce the word 'confidence' — these are the kind of human errors we like to witness in the most mighty and powerful. It is comforting to know that we are not the only twits inhabiting the planet and, more importantly, it is comforting to know that twits like us can aspire to the highest political office.

However, there is one exception to this general rule: when your hero of the moment slips on his tongue, launches himself into the air and lands head first in the largest cow pat available — all accomplished, I might add, at the exact instant that you are publicly extolling their virtues. So it was with Winston.

Peters had his former ministerial colleagues on the ropes over the Bank of New Zealand, the convoluted role of Fay Richwhite and the bank's shady captive insurance scheme. Every parliamentary sitting day that he made a new allegation or tabled a new document the public cheered him on. He had reassumed the role of the people's champion — this time the lone battler against the alley-cat morals of Big Business — and the Caucus rebels revelled in Cabinet's discomfort.

But the charge of corruption would be that one bridge too far. When I looked at the 'Four Corners' interview I immediately felt uneasy. I knew Winston enough to read his body language and this time, too late, he realised that the interviewer's questions had led him off the tarseal and onto a metal road. Typically Winston refused to touch the brakes now that he was on such an unsteady surface — instead his foot plunged down the accelerator pedal.

Under enormous political, media and commercial pressure Winston then made his next mistake. He decided to outline the details of the bribery attempt. And because bad news always comes in threes he then decided to name the one person least likely to satisfy the standard curriculum vitae of a Big Business fixer.

I was in Auckland at the time attending one of the interminable meetings of Parliament's education select committee — the kind of committee that makes you suddenly realise that the general sector is a cesspool of relative envies. Winston's brother, Ian, was with me and we had excitedly tuned into Parliament on an ageing transistor because today was the promised day. Today was the day when Winston would reveal the name and the circumstances of his attempted nobbling.

When the name came I recoiled as if the radio had turned to

muck. Selwyn Cushing? Not in a million years.

I remembered Cushing's speech to launch Whittaker's Hastings campaign and his introduction of the 'misery index' — this man was no fan of Rogernomics or its later derivatives. In addition, I knew Cushing was not a member of the Business Roundtable, that he had privately expressed misgivings to both Anne and me about that organisation's objectives, and that Winston did not visit him in February 1990 as claimed but in the aftermath of my wedding celebrations — five months later. I groaned at Ian — 'He's got the wrong man' — and then shrugged.

That would be one campaign donation I could not rely upon for the next election.

GONE

There is a popular mythology that the Cushing condemnation was the last straw leading to Peters' expulsion from the National Caucus. Certainly the upper echelons of the party were scandalised by his naming, with the Prime Minister moved to offer his public support and sympathy. I always wondered if Cushing's later elevation to the chair of Electricorp and the board of the New Zealand Symphony Orchestra were not some kind of embarrassed attempt by the Nats to apologise for one of their own's excesses.

The immediate aftermath of the Cushing naming was condemnation from virtually all the country's leading newspapers, the Prime Minister, the commercial sector and even the Labour Opposition. The Press Gallery instantly disbelieved Winston and began dredging up former failed claims relating to Russian submarines and sunken Russian cruise liners. But then the most curious happenstance — the power of telegenics entered the equation.

Naturally the media were keen to focus on the accused. When Peters named his man most New Zealanders' natural reaction was 'Who the hell is Selwyn Cushing?' and television crews beat a path, literally, to his door. In return Selwyn blinked at the television lights and peered through the flashlights, resembling a very old bloodhound rising from a deep sleep. Cushing has one of those epic lived-in faces although sometimes you could swear that half of Bangladesh has lived there too. His drawling, nasal voice complemented the image of a world-weary soul who had seen it all and done it all — a sort of antipodean precursor to the X-Files' cigarette man.

Beside him Winston's good looks and magnetic empathy with the small screen made for an odious comparison. Whatever the evidence, tens of thousands of viewers made instant judgements of the two men and they were not favourable to Cushing. So Win made a mistake with the date, they rationalised. But that Cushing — he looks shifty. It was the only time in my life when I have ever felt truly sorry for any Brierley director.

Caucus' displeasure with Peters had now flickered well through all the degrees of Celsius and could be measured on the Kelvin scale. Winston's allegation of Big Business being able effectively to buy Government policy was taken as a direct slur on all Government MPs. In one classic Caucus moment John Banks stood before Winston and glared at him.

'You make me feel dirty, Mr Peters,' Banks barked in that curious clipped voice that hovers between extreme self-control and extreme lung-ripping menace. 'When I walk down the streets of Whangarei people don't know if I'm a politician or a crook.' Sotto voce I un- graciously mumbled, 'Probably both,' which earned me the hard stares of the MPs around me. Banks' troubled childhood was well known and understood — he wore his personal integrity stitched in rhinestones across his breast.

Winston's response was typically irreverent. He picked up the morning's newspaper, opened it with a flourish, and then affected the same unwholesome attention to the classified advertisements that I had witnessed at Picton.

But none of these events prompted that final decline. And as is usual with such traumatic events it was something relatively incon- sequential in public terms that finally goaded Caucus into flinty resolve. Treaty Negotiations Minister Doug Graham had just signed the Sealord Maori fisheries deal and was determined to explain its significance and impact to the House.

However, his initial attempts to do so were frustrated by Winston continuing to take a series of pointless points of order and thus run the clock down past the 10.30pm House rising time. In Winston's defence it was a retributive step for the same tactics earlier being employed against himself by Government MPs as he sought to detail a fresh batch of alleged financial calumnies.

As the House rose to an uproar from his colleagues a satisfied Winston marched from the debating chamber to the parliamentary elevators. But as he entered one of the crowded lifts the entire occupying group scrambled out in hostile disapproval. Even breathing the same air as the Tauranga rebel had become repulsive.

It was all over fairly quickly. When the National Caucus acts it acts with haste and efficiency, as both Jim McLay and his successor would testify. There was a half-hearted Caucus debate at which I played the Jeremiah and warned of political hail, fire and brimstone should Peters be expelled, but to no effect. The final vote to expel him was overwhelming — 50 votes to twelve, with even the majority of the dissenters professing disapproval. Christine Fletcher rose and told Winston directly that if he drank less he could contribute more — as if suggesting that Winston's rebellion was fuelled by other than political motivations.

At that Peters folded up his newspaper, arranged his papers and calmly walked from the Caucus room. Much against Caucus' expectations he would return — but next time as the deputy Prime Minister, and as their political saviour.

As the Caucus broke up and I made for my office a voice to my right broke in on my sadness.

'You're next.'

I turned to catch the determined glare of Jenny Shipley and the equal hostility of a group of surrounding colleagues. Shipley repeated her threat, this time a little louder in case I had not heard, and the surrounding heads nodded their approval.

Now I was the lone rebel. There were no more wagons to circle, no others left to take the blows. Myles, McIntyre, Muldoon and now Peters — yeah, I was next.

It was just a question of when.

– CHAPTER 8 –

LIMBO

DIVORCE

I was, in fact, not next. That dubious honour would belong to Cam Campion.

Cam had made the fatal error of not protecting his constituency in the intervening period, nor had he dealt properly with those disaffected with the original selection. This is a lesson all new MPs must learn about their local party executives — keep them sweet, but make sure you kneecap the nasties. Poor Cam did neither. In addition he faced a venomous local media who hovered between disgust and disdain in their rejection of Cam's less than subtle PR skills. With Cam Campion it was not just some of politics' dark arts that escaped him but the whole infernal box.

I had some sympathy for his plight, and not just because he was a mate. For Wanganui was the kind of place where faction fighting and the ritual disembowelling of its National candidates was considered an acceptable blood sport — although these same dumped candidates then refused to expire quietly and hovered around like poltergeists in a crystal factory. Wanganui prides itself upon both its river and its sewage outlet (thoughtfully contained at the same site) and possesses an eclectic array of ambiguous eccentrics. Any place that produces both Ken Mair and Mayor Chas Poynter clearly has a toxic waste dump somewhere near the town water supply. So toffee-nosed nobs cannibalising their own was just part of the general madness. Cam should have remembered that — after all, it was how he got to be an MP in the first place.

If you are going to be a winning rebel then you need a loyal executive, a favourable press and tangible signs of your local steward-ship. Cam had none of these things. Instead the party locals chose a former Dunedin North candidate, Gail Donoghue, as their 1993 election candidate — a sort of middle-aged Chloe of Wainuiomata but without the brains. But her main claim to fame was that she was not Cam — and that counted for a great deal with the party's selection committee.

Campion's travails in this antipodean Bermuda Triangle were the least of my immediate concerns. My constituency was secure — it was the full-frontal attacks from Caucus that were becoming progressively debilitating. Bolger always delayed these verbal onslaughts until near the end of a Caucus so that I might be left to stew in my own apprehension for the preceding three hours — a more exquisite torture than the experience itself. As Caucus chairman he had the unusual right of ordering the Caucus agenda upon personal whim — a powerful Leader's privilege. Often controversial items would be shuffled down the agenda until there was barely time left to introduce them let alone discuss their merits. I am sure that a Laws beat-up session was seen as a valuable time-management tool just in case anything really serious should occupy Caucus' consideration.

Such intense little psycho-dramas were hardly leavened by the alternative of my colleagues' shunning silence. It got to the point where I would sit alone in the crowded Caucus like an evil-smelling European on a peak-hour Japanese bullet train. Any contact might contaminate — or at the very least be viewed by other Caucus members as fraternisation with the enemy. One of the traditions of the National Caucus is that you retain the same seat at every meeting after a mad dash for position at the start of the parliamentary term. I ended up seated directly in line with the Prime Minister's gaze, with Gilbert Myles to my left and Cam across the narrow aisle to my right. As the rebel ranks thinned and then evaporated I became stranded in a not-so-splendid wasteland. Even the nearby Brian Neeson and Nick Smith migrated to new seats rather than be positioned in the same row. And yet I could never resist the challenge of confrontation — Caucus was just another version of boarding school and I was determined never to bow before the bullies again.

Oh that my protagonists had similar feelings! No such luck. With the Peters expulsion, the political suicides of Myles and McIntyre, and Campion's clubbing, I was now the last remaining dissident and the sole target. Sadly, my appalling sense of timing provided my protagonists with no shortage of excuses to attack — if I made any incendiary public remarks it always seemed to be on the Wednesday before a Caucus Thursday. It was almost Freudian. Ross Meurant once commented that he had noted my difficulties and learned from them.

If ever he strayed into a controversial area he tried to do it on a Thursday afternoon or a Friday because it would be a full week before the next Caucus and I was bound to put my foot in it before then.

'Y'know, I always thought you were bright, Laws,' he would smile, then shaking his head he would wander away.

But Meurant also had the ability to irritate his Caucus colleagues, sometimes to the point of spectacular outburst, by taking copious notes at each of our Thursday meetings — an act that seemed to petrify the other MPs. The minutes of each Caucus meeting were taken down by one of the MPs then typed up by the Whips. However, no MP was allowed to view these minutes except in person in the Whip's Office, and so order was kept. Meurant's personal minute-taking appeared to threaten this order — if he ever published the unedited highlights he would have a genuine best seller. Or perhaps no one would really believe that Government Caucus meetings were so preoccupied with the banal and the bizarre. It was just like a war — 90 per cent boredom, ten per cent sheer terror.

Another source of nervousness was the fashionable belief that the supposed rebels and dissidents always leaked Caucus' hush-hush discussions to the media. It took me a few months to work out that it was in fact various Cabinet ministers who were the finest proponents of the strategic leak, but by blaming the rebels they had an ideal excuse to further restrict the ministerial information flow to the back bench. It was all quite clever really. Of course, this strategy was fully exposed when Caucus secrets were betrayed even though neither I nor the other suspects were present at the fateful meetings. It mattered not — a lie told often enough is always believed if it is told about someone universally disliked.

Meanwhile Winston Peters was proving at least one of my earlier predictions true. He would not be going quietly. It was the kind of prediction on which the TAB would refuse to quote odds.

For some reason, despite demonstrable and repeated rejections, Winston refused to be spurned. He would leave the National Party when he was good and ready and he was definitely not good and neither was he ready. When it became apparent that the party's executive would formalise the Caucus dust-off by vetoing his nomination for the Tauranga candidacy Peters acted instinctively. He took the matter to the High Court without regard to the expense but with the kind of obsession rarely witnessed outside the Hollywood stalker fraternity.

Of course there was an explanation for this seemingly irrational behaviour. Winston really did not want to go. The emotional and political ties were just too intense for him to accept the divorce.

Certainly I was far from convinced that Winston had emotionally (let alone politically) accepted the bust-up. Just after his expulsion from the National Caucus, and with his consequent popularity reaching into the polling stratosphere, I approached him with the suggestion of leading a breakaway party into the next election. Other National MPs held similar views and persuasive conversations were attempted. We were reasonably confident that Winston could garner seven or eight MPs for a 'New National'-type party that might tap into disaffected National supporters but also cross over and gain support from potential Labour voters. A huge credibility gap had opened up in New Zealand politics, with both major parties not just disliked but distrusted and even despised. Winston could fill that void.

This was the moment all right — it just needed the right man.

These entreaties took place over August/September 1992 and there would hardly be a parliamentary day go past that I would not urge Winston to make a clean break, make the commitment and mark out a new political future. MPs suggested for this breakaway included the two Liberals, Campion, Neeson, Ian Peters, McCardle and me, and I reasoned that three or four others might be tempted once the framework had been completed.

Far from encouraging the concept, Winston refused even to be flattered by the suggestion. Maybe it was the quality of the talent he had to work with; maybe, but when the stock Winstonian denials were trotted out — 'Now is not the time … I'm not going to lose this High Court action … I'll be back … the membership won't stand for it' — then I became reluctantly convinced that Winston was existing in some parallel universe — one in which the *Titanic* still plied the trans-Atlantic route.

Naturally I considered my own rationale on the timing to be flawless — this was the perfect time to capitalise on Peters' popularity, and we would need to give the new party time to establish itself, allow the defecting MPs to prepare their local ground for the next year's general election, and construct a solid parliamentary base that might eclipse the struggling Opposition parties as National's major electoral competitor. In addition, we would need a good twelve months to set in place the financial and administrative structures required to support a nationwide campaign. This was the moment. Any later would be too late — the window of opportunity would be closed tight.

But we could not do it without Winston. And Winston was obviously not coming. It was a classic opportunity lost. A severely unpopular government, the Labour Party in disarray and the country's most popular MP leading the populist charge — but Winston's will failed him and I bitterly regretted that failure. It was the final proof that I must chart a course separate from my old boss. The man did not just lack the will — he lacked the imagination.

So it was that a number of potential defectors also determined that their political longevity was best achieved within National's camp. When Winston finally decided to launch his ego in May 1993 it would be way too late — we had already made our personal commitments and plotted our own selfish election plans. In the end the only MP who would join Winston would be Gilbert Myles — his last stop after the grand political party tour.

And there was something else. Winston had proven to me that he lacked the greatest attribute of leadership. Vision. Of all my regrets that realisation would prove the most discomforting, for it would mean that all our work together in opposition had not grafted within my Tauranga friend. The headlines and popularity had been the puffery; but there was no point in having power unless there was an overarching vision that might be attempted. I had failed to instil that vision in Winston — even to provoke its gestation.

I arrived at a horrid conclusion. Maybe Winston Peters and Jim Bolger were not so different after all.

'SORRY . . . WHO CARES?'

In early 1991 moon-faced US chargé d'affaires Al la Porta offered me one of his Embassy's prized month-long study tours of his modern Roman Empire and I was packed before the conversation had even concluded. I had never been to the United States but possessed all the usual Hollywood misconceptions about the place.

Ostensibly the purpose of the study tour was to examine the plight of the underclass in that great nation and view innovative policy programmes aimed at eradicating their misery. It was my firm view at the time (reinforced every instant since) that the 'more market' ideology would similarly create a dispossessed class in New Zealand and it would be the purpose of a caring government to construct the pathways out. Yes, I was an optimist.

The Super Surtax rebels of 1991: Cam Campion, Gilbert Myles, me, Hamish McIntyre. Whatever their faults the rebels possessed the courage to confront the Richardson/Treasury 'mother of all Budgets'.

Good works. The Flaxmere rugby club extensions built by my Hawke's Bay Community Work Trust. Next to me is Trust director and All Black Norm Hewitt, with Peter McCardle MP appreciating the fruits of our joint vision.

Another Hawke's Bay venture — organising the 1992 Trustbank rugby dinner series. A convivial top table of Norm Hewitt, Stu Wilson, Australian rugby coach Bob Dwyer and Karen.

To be honest, my Maraenui rugby opponents were tougher than National's Caucus — minutes after this shot I was nursing cracked ribs. So much for the macho experiment.

After twenty years of lobbying, celebrating a new high school for Flaxmere with the local community's 'action committee'. But the struggle would not yet be over. The Daily Telegraph

Australian World Cup captain Nick Farr-Jones shares an evening with my Flaxmere fifth grade rugby team mates. He would return the Flaxmere presentation jersey with the signatures of all his World Cup players attached.

Election night 1993. Balance of power — and don't I know it!

Key supporters in the Hawke's Bay: electorate chairman Lawrence Yule, publicity co-ordinator Sally Kershaw and campaign chairman Neil Kirton. North and South

Cocking a snook at party rivalries — the post-1993 'Hawke's Bay Lobby'. Napier MP Geoff Braybrooke, me, Hastings MP Rick Barker.

It was a depressing month. The inescapable lesson is that the United States is being corroded from within. The interlinked perils of welfare dependency, racial dislocation, drugs and crime are just the symptoms. Worse, much worse, is the lack of public or political will to address such beasts. Oh, the US middle class wants social stability and cohesion all right, but not if they have to pay for it. At that point the poor are regarded as undeserving and ungrateful. And I have encountered the same perverted rationale in too many informal gatherings in this country to feel any smugness about our own social future.

The lack of regard and compassion for those born into poverty, parental neglect and urban decay is the great Western disease. Its modern description is class insensitivity. It has a less sociological predecessor. Greed. As far as I was able to discern the Americans have elevated two qualities above all else — illusion and self-delusion. Nothing will stop their social rust — there is insufficient strength of national character to deny such excesses. If the United States represents the best and worst of human aspiration then it is a depressing talisman. The worst will win.

But it was while I was in the United States that Winston exacted the most bizarre of personal revenges.

Winston has always believed that any personal stumble or hiccup is the fault of a third party. If you want to work with or for him then this is the first lesson: Winston is never wrong. Never. So the continued if good-natured ribbing from a variety of his acquaintances over his meeting of minds with Alzheimers victim Ronald Reagan had festered a sense of grievance. After three years of late night badinage Peters had settled on a culprit to blame for this minor embarrassment. Me.

On telephoning my electorate office one American evening, I was congratulated by Kathy on my recent audience with President George Bush, and she went on to express her amazement that an obscure first-term backbencher could be entertained in the Oval Office during the ANZUS freeze. My initial thought was that Kathy was either too near an ammonia gas leak or had made the fatal error of combining strong prescription medication with a lunch-time chardonnay. Kathy obviously detected my puzzlement because she proceeded to read out a prominent newspaper report concerning my White House rendez-vous with the most powerful man in the world. Apparently I had used this audience to lobby the President on having 'World Superstars of Wrestling' returned to TVNZ's late-night programming slot, the show having being canned in my home country by overzealous do-gooders because of a spate of crippling bodyslams in school playgrounds.

That sections of the New Zealand media took the story seriously gave me a wonderful insight into the Fourth Estate's gullibility. But Winston would never let me forget this public spoofing, nor that revenge is a dish best served cold. In this case under layers of perma-frost.

Despite his reluctance to lead our group of Caucus dissidents to the Promised Land, or even to a fishing weekend in Taupo, I was selfishly pleased that Peters had elevated his scrap with the party to the High Court. For it was the intention of the national executive to require electoral nominees to sign a new 'loyalty pledge' — a virtual restraint-of-trade contract that effectively barred losing candidates from standing as independent candidates or assisting the campaigns of other than the selected nominee. I foresaw a personal risk should my Hawke's Bay nomination be similarly vetoed by the hierarchy in that I would be legally barred from contesting the seat as an independent.

I was far from convinced that cool heads would prevail in Wellington. Nasty rumours began circulating about a hit list of undesirables and my name was reputed to be at the very top and underlined for emphasis. So I crossed out the pledge from my nomination form and returned it to party headquarters with fingers crossed. I was not the only National back-bench MP to do so, which suggested that my paranoia was in good company. Thankfully, Peters' High Court action cleared that obstacle, with Justice Fisher ruling that the pledge could not be enforced and thus was legally null and void.

Winston then decided to regather his Tauranga mandate now that the relationship between him and the National Party had been deemed irreconcilable. We chatted briefly about this decision because it did not seem to make political or financial sense — the New Zealand public well understood the breach and with the general election but six months away it all seemed an unconscionable waste of energy and money. Far better to utilise the time to plan a new party, I urged.

But obstinacy is a prized Peters trait. That and excessive secrecy. He had no intention of allowing his former colleagues to taunt him over a perceived lack of representative authority and wanted to draw a sharp and public distinction between himself and other defectors.

He would enter Parliament in his own right and under his own steam. Besides, he winked, it would not do his profile any harm at all.

So it was that Winston threw a by-election to which no one else came. Well, that is not entirely true. A very odd assortment of weirdos and wannabes entered the Tauranga race but the major parties declined the inevitable humiliation. Despite such inactivity about half the Tauranga electors actually voted and Peters was duly returned with what was then the largest majority in electoral history — something over 11,000 votes. Urged to 'Show them what you think' about the state of New Zealand politics, Peters' expulsion and the performance of the New Zealand cricket team, Tauranga had done just that.

I had driven to Tauranga to personally support Winston on his by-election night and was joined by his brother, Ian, and Gilbert Myles as a surrogate Greek chorus should we be required. But it was a long drive from Napier, a stiflingly hot autumn day, the hospitality was lavish and I had skipped tea ... Can you see where this is heading? Truth be told I also have a very low tolerance for alcohol (a virtue while at university because I could get pissed for next to nothing; a liability thenceforth) and the consequences were utterly predictable.

As the results were read out and Winston and his wife, Louise, showered with applause, confetti and adoring adulation on their arrival (and that was just my effort) I was most definitely Excitable Cheerleader Number One. Even Gilbert, not known for his public tact, suggested that I might like to 'steady on', although somehow I interpreted this as advice to 'party on down' like a spastic crayfish on acid and whoop ever more exuberantly at anything that looked remotely like an excuse.

It was while I was in this alcohol-induced fudge that a particularly cruel television journalist thrust a microphone under my drooling moosh and directed that the full glare of the lights be cast upon me. This had the galvanising effect of rerouting all my functioning brain cells through the 'Who gives a shit?' decoder and I duly obliged my inquisitor with a series of garbled and injudicious ramblings about the future of the National Party, Jim Bolger's leadership skills and the reporter's inviting cleavage. Winston was most displeased — not so much over the aforesaid criticisms or even my lack of social couth, but because I was unwittingly distracting from the main event. Him.

I should get blotto more often. That evening I predicted the future perfectly. Winston would form his own party, I opined; MMP was

going to succeed the status quo as the new electoral system, and
Winston's new party would then hold the balance of power. Fortunately I can still produce the *Dominion's* front page to verify the story
— if only I had fixated on something useful like the next week's Lotto
numbers. Anyway, I was still not done.

Trailing hopelessly behind my runaway rhetoric I blundered into
the most obvious query of the lot.

'And what do you think the Prime Minister will make of your
presence in Tauranga, Mr Laws?' the reporter enquired sweetly.

'Sorry ... who cares?' I guffawed, and blundered off in search of
cool air and an even cooler ale. It had suddenly become very warm.

The next morning I awoke in my motel unit with my clothes strewn
around but thankfully no sign of anybody else's and no diced carrots.
I had survived. At least until Gilbert dashed into my unit.

'Jeez, Mike,' he enthused. 'You were in great form last night. TV
reckon you're their lead story tonight.'

I groaned. Oh my God, what on earth had I done? The last time I
had wiped out this many neurons in one hit I had woken to find a
loaded council rubbish bin in my bedroom, a duck from the botanic
gardens swimming around the bath and, much more sinister, I was
wearing undergarments that were clearly not mine. But I had been
an anonymous student then, not a high-profile rebel MP with enough

prominent enemies to staff the Red Army. As I slunk back to Hawke's Bay a multitude of fantasies erupted, virtually all related to faulty electrical equipment, power blackouts and Maori activists invading television studios.

Actually it was not too bad. When I viewed the offending portions of the broadcast I rationalised my demeanour as more pithy than pissed and the 'Sorry ... who cares?' remark had been nonchalantly tossed out rather than reinforced with the dreaded one-finger salute. Sure, I had labelled my back-bench colleagues a bunch of 'sycophantic toadies' but, hey, that was the truth. Nah, I thought. Nothing to get too worried about.

Given that my judgement was still existing in the same surreal space/time vortex as the previous evening I was unprepared then for the deluge of media calls that followed my television appearance. The telephone went back into the hall cupboard. When I turned to Karen for affirmation her admonition that I should have a meal before I go out on the town rather had the opposite effect.

Sure enough the print media enjoyed their next morning's sport. They had thoughtfully prodded a few of my Caucus enemies out of their weekend retreats and were not disappointed when a duly provoked Prime Minister and Caucus enemies Peter Hilt and Max Bradford described me as a disloyal, disreputable and disturbed individual. All claimed to be outraged and speculated that I would soon desert Caucus' ranks and join Winston in the wilderness. I gained the impression that a high degree of wish fulfilment had overridden any dispassionate analysis on their parts.

I credit current affairs personality Paul Holmes for the rescue. We had come to know each other relatively well through the charity BNZ Festival Debate series and discovered an empathy that only true stirrers could understand. My personal view of the man had altered considerably since the infamous Dennis Connor interview when Connor suddenly remembered he had left the gas on — back in San Diego. Indeed, in person I found Holmes to be mercurial but generous and a hopelessly nostalgic sentimentalist.

By now the Caucus mercury had begun to scale new and more dangerous heights as MPs egged each other on in a contest to see who could be the most outraged by my antics. The same touch of dangerous hysteria that had accompanied Peters' demise began to infect proceedings and I mentioned this anxiety to Holmes.

'Well, if I was you, I'd apologise to the PM and get it over and done with as quick as possible,' Paul advised, which I recognised as surprisingly useful counsel. 'But not until tonight,' he added mischievously, '... live on my show.'

I concurred. Holmes then chartered a flight down to Hawke's Bay, chanced a vox pop with my Taradale locals (who solidly backed me, with one old dear declaring, 'We don't like Bolger either — good on him') and allowed me to explain my Tauranga attendance as the act of any good friend. I then apologised to the PM 'for any offence taken' — a classic Clayton's apology which suggests that those offended are far too sensitive for their own good but, hey, if it makes them feel better then here is my most insincere effort.

At which point Jim Bolger lost interest and Chief Whip Jeff Grant was instead delegated the task of giving me what one newspaper described as 'a stiff dressing down'. In fact Grant laughed, told me that I had made a right prick of myself and that enduring the hangover would be punishment enough. Caucus sanctions would remain leashed — for now. Which just goes to prove that the art of the public apology is vastly underrated as a tactical political device.

And then, bless him, Jeff Whittaker went completely (politically) troppo.

Whittaker had already announced his intention not to contest the Hastings seat at the coming election. In making this decision he complained of the stress of public life and how politicians like Winston Peters had made things impossible for decent types like him. Just how was never properly explained. Whatever the rationale, Jeff made it plain that he had had enough. Which was just as well. Because so had Hastings.

So it was with a sense of mullet-like disbelief that the entire province now heard Jeff announce that he was not so tired after all. Whatever his doctor had prescribed him — vitamin B shots, a new diet or the distemper injection — had clearly worked. He was going to stand for election after all — just not in Hastings. Hawke's Bay would be the ideal constituency.

Local reporters declared themselves amazed by my casual reaction to this bombshell. Little did they realise that I was inordinately relieved. Any politician in deep doo-doos always prays for a distracting event and this attempt at provincial Restoration comedy went well beyond a slight distraction — it was the relief column at Mafeking, the charge of the US cavalry and Madonna flashing her boobs all rolled into one.

Because Whittaker would not be challenging me as the party's nominee for the Hawke's Bay seat. That contest had already been settled by my unopposed selection weeks earlier. Jeff would be standing as an independent 'true blue' candidate in Hawke's Bay, and attempting this feat while the National MP for Hastings. My embarrassing Tauranga effort had just been obliterated by the even more embarrassing news that a retiring Government back-bench MP had just gone gaga.

It took days and some fairly turgid editorial and party criticism for Jeff to be dissuaded. He was going to fix me once and for all; he was no 'sycophantic toadie'. As the *Dominion* dryly noted: '... out of loyalty [Whittaker] will be disloyal and will wear the ignominy with pride.'

At least Whittaker baulked at the precipice. Lyttelton MP Gail McIntosh had already leapt and discovered that it was a long, long, long way down. Using logic that made Cervantes' creation appear phlegmatic, McIntosh decided that she would abandon her South Island haunts and quixotically challenge the Great Windmill Winston on his own field and head-on. So underwhelmed were the National Party's locals by this ridiculous venture that even after Peters had been vetoed they instead selected cadaverous accountant John Cronin to be their champion. The poor man confronted almost immediate resignation calls from his mutinous campaign team, most notably for lacking a visible pulse rate, but he was not a boorish Amazonian from Canterbury and that was considered sufficient in itself to garner the poisoned chalice. The whole experience so addled Cronin that he would resign from National after the '93 election and form his own political party, YES — an unnatural coupling between Youth and Superannuitants, although where the E came from I was never game enough to enquire.

Meanwhile Parliament, the Press Gallery and the public now awaited Winston's next move. Predictably a good part of the Gallery read the wrong chicken entrails and predicted that Peters would retain his Tauranga seat as an independent but only form a new party should MMP be chosen as the new electoral system. It was yet another classic misreading of the Peters personality. Now that he had a measure of influence Winston had the prospect of revenge. He saw forming a new political party as having the greatest potential to hurt National in key marginal electorates, although I was never convinced by this logic. Winston's supporters actively disliked the Government — in his absence they were more likely to back Labour or Alliance candidates in their local electorates.

It remains a pet theory of mine that Winston has actually helped National secure power twice. Once in 1996, by entering into formal coalition, but previously in 1993 by distracting anti-National voters. The '93 election was so close that even a handful of distracted voters in a handful of electorates would have made the final difference.

Still Winston dithered. Although this time there would be a cost.

In early May 1993 a TVNZ/Heylen poll noted that Winston Peters was the nation's 'preferred Prime Minister' and also that a new Peters-led party would capture 31 per cent of the popular vote 'should a general election be held tomorrow'. That is the sad thing about such polls. Elections are rarely held tomorrow, as Labour's Helen Clark would regretfully discover five years later. Nevertheless the Heylen research had a Peters party just trailing Mike Moore's Labour with National languishing in third spot. The new five-party Alliance, under its New Labour leader Jim Anderton, had fallen off the pace after reaching similar heights in the polls just one year earlier.

Mind you, that is the dreadful thing about third-party voters. They are inherently promiscuous. Social Credit, Bob Jones' New Zealand Party, the Greens, the Alliance, NZ First, ACT — it is a new partner every election and to hell with what the neighbours think.

Instead of using his post-Tauranga result to immediate advantage Winston then attempted a brief courtship with the Alliance — or rather they with him. That Winston publicly hinted at the possibility of co-operation with the Alliance was a tactical mistake. In later conversations he would admit to me that the two things he most disliked about the Alliance were the separate party structures and Jim Anderton. For Winston to have been even faintly interested the Alliance would have had to sacrifice their defining characteristics. But it could never have worked. Just as nature abhors a vacuum so too is it impossible for two bodies to occupy the same space. The combination of these two would have made *The Fly* look like a nature ramble.

Liberal's president, Malcolm Wright, informed me over dinner one evening that 'mud-wrestling with the Kremlin' was not his preferred option either. Both he and his parliamentary leader, Gilbert Myles, were hoping to recruit Peters to lead their organisation despite its nominal attachment to the Alliance umbrella. However, Winston rejected both the Liberal and Alliance machines. He wanted his own vehicle. It was just that he was unsure as to its make, model or even colour — and his indecision eroded the public goodwill secured by the Nat's veto and the subsequent by-election triumph.

Contrary to speculation, Winston did not attempt to draw me into any new political party until after its announcement on a blustery July Sunday afternoon at the Alexandra Park raceway in Auckland. The whole launch was a flop — the projected 10,000-plus audience failed to materialise; the new party's principles were diffuse and contradictory; and even rally organisers like Grey Power's George Drain reserved public judgement as to their future support. Apart from the name, New Zealand First, I failed to detect a philosophy, a principle or even a defining policy that would flame the Peters personality into the kind of all-encompassing prairie populism needed to win general elections.

I had made the right choice in staying with National — Peters' lack of vision had been confirmed, although I remained vaguely disappointed at receiving this confirmation. Instead of promoting innovative and exciting methods of democratic representation Winston had instead resurrected the much-abused and now neglected National Party manifesto of the previous election as some kind of political nirvana. His answers lay in a mythical past — not in the fond embrace of any radical or alternative future. I wanted to explore the frontier — Winston was happiest in the drawing room reminiscing over the good old days.

Shortly thereafter Winston did make his one and only political approach to me in the downstairs lobby of the new Bowen House, where we encountered each other purely by chance. After the usual good-natured banter Peters motioned me aside.

'I'm not going to beg, Laws,' he began, and so formal was this opening gambit that I assumed he had mislaid his parliamentary taxi chits and wished to borrow one of mine. Then he continued, 'But I want you to join my party. We need your organisational skills.'

Up until that point a nagging disquiet had occasionally flared within my political consciousness as to whether I had indeed made the correct decision in remaining with National. The Nats were not perfect, that much was blindingly obvious, but I could see no ready alternative until the new lands of MMP had been broken in. Winston's unsteady invitation chased away such phantom anxieties. In one instant he had pinpointed the greatest weakness of his new party and I assumed that the further the distance from his Tauranga power base the greater the logistical problems were becoming.

For there was but one Winston Peters. He now had to find candidates for 96 other parliamentary seats, finance a national campaign without the benefit of state broadcasting funding (again, because he had left his party's formation too late to satisfy the legislation), draft a manifesto, and still retain a parliamentary presence with just Gilbert as back-up. It was *Mission: Impossible.* And Winston was no Tom Cruise.

My reaction to his request was more direct than either our friendship or even polite diplomacy would normally have allowed. I reminded Winston of my endless entreaties the previous year when the timing, the potential recruits and the public desire had been at its apex. Now I owed my primary loyalty to those executive members back in Hawke's Bay who had endured the party's flak, still chosen me as their candidate and were now working solidly on my behalf to ensure my re-election. In addition I noted that my primary and personal focus for the next five months would be in campaigning for the success of the new Mixed Member Proportional electoral system — and that between these twin imperatives the success or otherwise of New Zealand First was irrelevant.

Plainly my misgivings about New Zealand First's abilities were shared by the rest of the nation. Within two months the party's poll rating had dropped to just 8-per-cent support, and now languished well behind the two major parties with even the Alliance eclipsing NZ First's earlier promise. The heady heights of 30-per-cent-plus were a recent but fading memory. Yet another portent of three years hence. When the public had been ready to purchase the goods, New Zealand First had been unprepared and unwilling to sell. Rehashing stale leftovers from another party's rejected manifesto was never going to satisfy — this was not the taste experience that Winston had promised.

And so, a little sadder but none the wiser, I turned my interest back home to Hawke's Bay.

HAWKE'S BAY '93

Neil Kirton headed my campaign team for the '93 election although this task was largely confined to keeping the local party executive off my back as I adopted the most individual of election stratagems. With the tireless Anne Averill and striking PR professional Sally Kershaw prominent, my local glee club then secured the constituency against all invaders — internal or external.

I was fortunate that Labour chose a candidate who decided that I should be roundly condemned for my lack of loyalty to the National Party. Mike Moore would later tell me that my candidacy had perplexed Labour strategists in 1993 because mine was clearly the most effective of all anti-government campaigns. Thus reminding National Party voters that I was not the dinkum 'true blue' was somehow supposed to undermine my local appeal. How that realisation was to translate into votes for Labour always mystified me.

Then again, that is Labour's historic weakness. Their unthinking tribal affiliation to party partiality is both archaic and artificial. It is no longer possible to divide the country into National and Labour camps and pray that your organisation is better on the day. The old party loyalties erode with each passing election and every political event since 1975 has merely hastened that breach.

It had been my intent since being elected to Parliament to redefine the role and responsibilities of a constituent MP. Having attempted to make such a visible difference there was now little point in being modest with a general election in prospect. If that meant dressing these minor achievements in the most gaudy of neon lights then so be it. The time for subtlety was past. I wanted to sledgehammer reluctant voters into a grudging acceptance that I was not such a bad bastard after all — even if my appetite for self-promotion had occasionally strayed into the megalomaniacal.

However, my campaign strategy for the Hawke's Bay seat in 1993 was much more radical than saturating letter boxes with self-penned panegyrics. Such were mere devices of detail. My aim was to make Hawke's Bay voters choose Michael Laws as their Member of Parliament rather than select the local representative of the National Party.

But I was also a realist. I justified my continued membership of National's Caucus as sheer pragmatism. Obviously I could better represent my constituents' interests if I was a member of that group which supposedly made the policy decisions. But I knew that to be no longer true — three years of watching Cabinet and Treasury perform their animal trainer routines had disabused me of that particular delusion.

The awful truth was that I wanted to be re-elected and if donning the blue colours assisted that process then so be it. I had sufficiently evolved, or rather devolved, within this demon profession to the point where I could justify such shabby perfidy as equally beneficial for both Michael Laws and Hawke's Bay. In fact, what was the difference? All politicians may publicly disclaim indispensability but equally believe that the world would be a poorer place without their intervention or contribution. After all, it is precisely that quality of ego that propels nondescript individuals into Parliament in the first place.

I had come to regard re-election as absolutely essential if Hawke's Bay was to receive superior representation. Ipso facto, if retaining a National Party label assisted my re-election prospects then retain it I should. Dostoevsky was right, the ends do justify the means. But I did not perceive such smug conceit as either smug or conceited. That is the thing about politics. You can fake sincerity so plausibly because the first person you con is yourself.

Besides, I had achieved sufficient local success to suspend such brutal self-analysis. Consider the charity debates, the community work trusts, the scholarships, the super-improved constituency services, the unpaid court appearances on behalf of my poorer constituents, the instructive community seminars on everything from how to hide your income from the Social Welfare surtax snoopers to everything-you-needed-to-know-about-MMP-but-were afraid-someone-would-explain, topped off by the *pièce de résistance* — a new high school for the Flaxmere community. Dammit, I was good.

Sadly, even with such immense character flaws demonstrably evident this was still an accurate assessment of the comparative talent on show in the Hawke's Bay electorate in 1993. I was reminded of Yeats' 'The Second Coming' and the observation that 'the best lack all conviction while the worst are full of passionate intensity'. Those lines will stand as an epitaph for all modern politicians.

Ironically the achievement I regarded as my most complete attracted the least popular support. For twenty years the Labour haven of Flaxmere had played the honourable lobbying game and been outwitted, outgunned and outmanoeuvred by a succession of departmental bureaucrats, Hastings secondary schools and expedient politicians. Although placed at a safe distance from the rest of Hastings, the children of Flaxmere were required to cycle down the dangerous Omahu Road and play chicken with a succession of impatient motorists and heavy trucks on their way to schools nearer the city. Despite every other comparable suburb in Napier/Hastings having their own secondary school Flaxmere was denied to suit the imperial ambitions of Hastings educationalists.

I determined that darker forces were required to produce a beneficial outcome and Flaxmere's pressing need for a high school would justify all manner of subterfuge. To this day I remain unrepentant. Logic had failed and lost too often — we were dealing with unreasonable forces and only unreasonable tactics might overcome them. This included convincing Flaxmere's primary schools to take advantage of the new recapitation policy (retaining their Form One and Two pupils) so as to gut the neighbouring intermediate of a viable roll, and then convert that physical asset into the needed secondary school. Not surprisingly such plans were vigorously resisted by the intermediate, the teacher unions and an unusual array of sector representatives, but to no avail. Daily lobbying of Education Minister Lockwood Smith and his officials began to have its effects.

Fortunately there were also those in the Flaxmere community, including Hastings Labour Party doyen Mike Cullen (no relation to the current Labour deputy leader), who had some knowledge of the occult. Cullen's father had served as a Minister of Agriculture in one of Peter Fraser's ministries, while Cullen junior had challenged Sir Richard Harrison for the Hawke's Bay seat in the 1978 and 1981 general elections. Mike was an uncompromising trade union official with the requisite reputation for mayhem and mischief and I liked him immediately.

In the midst of the recapitation controversy Cullen launched an audacious hoax designed to convince gullible local media and departmental bureaucrats that Flaxmere did have other options. Prominent Japanese industrialists were prepared to finance a private high school in the suburb if the state would not come to the party and Cullen had been requested to act as their local agent. With my assistance he even managed to gain the official support of Commerce Minister Philip Burdon for this illusory venture, and in so doing opened another window to Lockwood Smith. In turn Smith recognised the general principle that schools should follow pupils and not vice versa, and with a typical disregard for the self-interested antics of the education sector gazetted a new Form One to Seven high school for Flaxmere using the intermediate as its physical base.

The minister's announcement remains my most complete moment in politics. Little did I realise that Smith would later seek to reverse this decision and I would need to revert to blackmail to secure the victory. But that is a tale that still awaits recall. For now the High School Action Committee and I revelled in our shared ecstasy — it was one hell of a night.

But would this high-profile mixture of faith and good works still save me from the predations of Bolger, Richardson, Shipley et al? It is the most frustrating experience for any back-bench MP — the clear knowledge that whatever decent efforts you might attempt at a local level your front-bench colleagues can scatter any such impressions every Monday around the Cabinet table. The backbenchers' lament: they make the decisions, you wear the consequences.

There was also another anxiety. This was an uncertainty that I shared with virtually all my parliamentary colleagues regardless of their party's leadership or popularity. How did your constituents truly perceive you? There was no shortage of individual opinions — a dilettante, an insincere populist, a surrogate social worker, an outspoken rebel, a radical reformer, even a minion of the CIA. But how did my electorate in toto really view me? Was I doing a great job or a shocking one? Did my charges even relate to my views on representation and political reform? Or was I perceived as just a noisy self-promoter with an unnatural personal grooming obsession?

To reassure myself (and my party workers) I sought the assistance of my old university debating mate and now even more exasperated Liberal Party president, Malcolm Wright. By profession Malcolm was a marketing lecturer at Massey University and he approached my request for assistance as an expedient opportunity for academic research. His eye for pedantic detail was infuriating but then Malcolm was never satisfied with a quick read of the tea leaves. Everything had to be just so. Of one thing, though, I became utterly convinced. Market research is the true voodoo science — the science being its touching embrace of mathematical probability; the voodoo being in its interpretation of the raw results.

Malcolm framed the questions, I organised the telephonists, and over two separate periods polls were completed involving over 800 Hawke's Bay constituents — surely the most extensive and detailed analysis of any individual electorate in modern political history. The results proved startling yet faintly reassuring, even if a gender analysis suggested that elderly women loved me, middle-aged men loathed me, and young women were supremely indifferent.

Fortunately my electorate organisation had conducted a similar poll on the voting intentions of Hawke's Bay constituents prior to the 1990 general election. We were thus able to measure a quite perceptible alteration in public mood in the intervening period; whereas only 11 per cent of total respondents in 1990 had determined their voting choice on the strength of the individual candidate now some 37 per cent of voters regarded that as the essential element in their final deliberations — an exponential increase.

The results were so startling that we initially disbelieved them. The entire exercise was repeated exactly one month later, again with a poll sample of over 800 completed telephone interviews. No discernible difference between the results could be detected other than Labour moving upwards against National in terms of party preference. As regards the rationale behind voter choice there could now be no doubt.

If I wanted to win well I would need to run a campaign primarily based on personal achievements, target women (who were more impressed with personality than party) and avoid Rotary Clubs, the Chambers of Commerce and any other organisation that might host disapproving businessmen. Our campaign team then made an even more far-reaching decision. We should remove the National Party logo from all personal election hoardings, newspaper advertisements and campaign literature. This was duly done to howls of outrage from executive loyalists but even greater public criticism from my Labour opponent. At that point Sally charmed all the middle-aged farmers on my executive into grudging acceptance of the marketing rationale and my long-suffering electorate chairman, Lawrence Yule, batted away the resultant media queries with diplomatic aplomb. There had been, he explained, 'a technical hitch'. Incredibly, nobody enquired as to the exact nature of this malfunction, otherwise, Lawrence laughed, 'I would have told them it was the bloody candidate.'

The rest of the local campaign was something of a doddle. If so many people were influenced by personality considerations then I had three years head start over my low-profile rivals. Mike Moore would later tell me that Labour convinced themselves they could win both the Hastings and Hawke's Bay seats and had party polling to confirm this. I was stunned because even the most incompetent agency would have picked up the general support trends in my constituency.

'Not if the results were invented,' Moore replied, and I detected in him a post-event realisation that Labour's '93 campaign had been appallingly mismanaged in any number of marginal electorates. When I put this to him Mike ran his hands over his face in that peculiar gesture of resignation I came to know so well, then forced a grin.

'Mate, it wasn't just your area. The whole campaign was a disaster. In the end we had to do it all ourselves.' I rather gained the impression that the 'we' referred to consisted of no more than Mike, his personable wife, Yvonne, and some personal staffers. Certainly I could detect neither intelligence nor intuition in any of the Opposition's local efforts and even when my campaign billboards were vandalised Labour activists were so demonstrably guilty that my campaign team cried 'Foul' to quite dramatic media effect.

The Leader's visit is always considered the essential highlight of any candidate's election programme and I anticipated that the Prime Minister's regional fillip to the Bay would prove no exception. Except for me. Even putting aside the local stratagem of muscular independence I very much doubted if it would be physically possible for either of us to verbally restrain ourselves should we be pushed together in public embrace. Take any devoted Bosnian and quarantine him with an activist Serbian and maybe, only maybe, you might get close to the mutual hostility between the Prime Minister and his rebel MP.

I contacted the party's campaign director and former research unit colleague, Wayne Eagleson, and enquired as to the Prime Minister's projected provincial itinerary. A date was provided for the Hawke's Bay region and this was duly relayed to my staff with strict instructions to uncover an alternative event. Fortunately my parliamentary assistant, Lisa, uncovered an obscure invitation to speak in the South Canterbury township of Waimate on the general issue of MMP. No particular day had been suggested. That deficiency was soon remedied and I found myself, regrettably and sadly, obliged to be elsewhere on the day the PM came to town. It was 'just one of those things' I explained to my disbelieving local media.

Now you might have thought that my Tauranga experience of six months earlier would have grafted some fairly potent lessons into the cranium. Election night — alcohol — Michael — an unstable association of event, ether and ego.

To be fair, and with a television outside broadcast crew in close proximity, I initially succeeded in retaining a coherent speech pattern. My campaign team had booked a Taradale winery for the election-night festivities but even this temptation was sidestepped. The prospect of a live interview with Ian Fraser on nationwide television demands temperance.

However, the planned interview was quickly shelved as the night's dramatic events began to unfold and I abandoned any pretence at sobriety. My constituency results were better than I had dared hope. I had not just won handsomely but increased my personal majority against massive anti-National swings in the neighbouring Napier and Hastings seats. It was time for raucous self-congratulation with the local Brookfields wine serving as the high-octane fuel. It was party time — turn up the music — remove all small children and domestic animals from the vicinity — I had won!

Then came the most curious realisation. Instead of sharing in my good fortune my guests became ever more immersed in the large television screen that we had hired for the event. National MPs were falling like ninepins, yet no consistent trend could be discerned. I had assumed from my own results that most incumbent Government members would survive. Sure the likes of Hastings, Lyttelton and Wanganui would revert to Labour, but not Hamilton, Invercargill and Waitaki.

All those optimistic pre-election newspaper predictions were being dished — this was neck-and-neck stuff with even the minor parties having their influence — the Alliance's Sandra Lee ousting Labour gargoyle Richard Prebble; New Zealand First's Tau Henare defeating the somnolent Northern Maori MP, Bruce Gregory. Each and every constituency mixed national trends with local personalities, propelling the national drama to unbearable intensity.

In my hazy state the final verdict mattered not. It scarcely interested me if Jim Bolger pipped Mike Moore or vice versa. In the past three years I had come to see the National and Labour parties as mirror images of each other, both preaching democratic principle yet usurping every associated nuance for tribal gain. The real game was power — or at least its illusion. The inherent arrogance of each group dwarfed their collective appreciation of circumstance or societal reality. I had ceased to care which party would govern for the next three years. Either way I would remain an Opposition MP.

I stumbled away from the screen and into the warm Meeanee night. On one of the most satisfying nights of my political life I had become a melancholic lush. The self-imposed limbo of the past three years would remain. Increased majority or not I would remain a parliamentary outsider preaching a message no one wanted to hear. Well, maybe not. A more portentous sea change was also under way that evening.

Then a tap on the shoulder and Sally was beside me. Ian Fraser wanted a chat after all. 'You'd better get used to the attention,' she beamed. 'It's even. You have the balance of power!'

Two minutes later, desperately searching for a vocabulary beyond grunts, and with my lips severely anaesthetised, I appeared on national television. Dredging up a fragment of a forgotten speech and trying to get my mouth to move in rough unison with my befuddled thoughts I gravely intoned to one million bemused viewers that, 'from henceforth ... if people enquire, "How says the country?" ... then let them first ask ... "How say the people of Hawke's Bay!" '

Mercifully some kind of electrical fault interrupted the interview (probably Neil Kirton pulling out the wall socket) and no further mangling of diction, metaphor or good taste could be attempted.

But in a distant Te Kuiti hall the Prime Minister's staff had taken note. As one of Jim Bolger's aides later told me, 'At that moment, we all agreed. It might just be better to lose and be done with it.'

THE REAL ELECTION

My election night celebrations were fuelled by more than just the relief of personal victory and a particularly quaffable sauvignon blanc. All right then — a few particularly quaffable vinos.

Something much more important than a general election had just taken place — the most fundamental reform of New Zealand's political structure since the signing of the Treaty of Waitangi. And, arguably, of more future relevance.

The majority of adult New Zealanders had just leapt into the unknown and selected a radically new, largely untested and much criticised electoral system despite all manner of dire warnings from senior politicians, newspaper editors and business leaders. Or maybe it was precisely because of those warnings — the unholy triumvirate of senior MPs, Big Business and the metropolitan media being enough to scare most thinking New Zealanders in the opposite direction.

I had long been an adherent of the principle of proportional representation — probably from the moment of the 1978 general election when Bruce Beetham's Social Credit Party captured 21 per cent of the popular vote but just two parliamentary seats. Any electoral system that produced such a grossly unfair outcome was plainly wrong. Nevertheless I took no active interest in the issue of electoral reform until after the Royal Commission's 1986 report.

This report and my experience as a candidate in the 1987 general election persuaded me to the view that our political system had become a discredited relic of a bygone age. The electoral system suffered the additional handicap of perpetuating the cosy two-party club of National and Labour, repelling any new groups that might dare to represent alternative viewpoints. As our society became increasingly diverse in its structure and sentiments the political system needed to reflect such diversity. Instead, political expression was effectively straitjacketed into the unnatural allotments of the dominant parties — a predominance equally maintained by the repeated gerrymandering of the electorate boundaries.

It was like going to the supermarket and having the perpetual choice of cornflakes and rice bubbles when neither satisfied and you wanted to try the toasted muesli. Breakfast analogies aside, politics had neither adapted nor modernised to meet public needs and expectations. In opposition I had alerted Winston to the populist possibilities latent within any tilt at the political system. He had proven a reluctant convert but a convert nonetheless. The hostility of the general populace to party domination of the process itself was manifested whenever Peters publicly broached the issue of reform, and such approbation was sufficient to calm his natural conservatism.

Of course once Winston had launched New Zealand First there were inherently selfish reasons to champion MMP — the new system would convert his popularity into cold, hard, parliamentary representation.

In contrast, I perceived MMP as only the first step, but a necessary one, on the long journey towards real and radical democratic reform. I understood the flaws in this pseudo-Germanic system, but it seemed to possess the virtue of breaking down the *ancien régime* and allowing some of the country's diversity true political expression. As I have already recounted, Winston's popular championing of political and electoral reform in opposition had its effect on National Party policy development, and the party's manifesto promised a referendum on electoral reform, including Jim Bolger's quixotic attempt at an Upper House. Incredibly, this was one election promise that the 1990–93 Bolger administration actually kept — possibly because Bolger deluded himself sufficiently to believe that a Senate would be a goer.

The 1992 mini-referendum on electoral reform had one major task and that was to whittle the Royal Commission's four reform options down to one singular choice. It was a Cabinet decision that wholly unimpressed me. For a start, I saw no earthly reason why the entire electoral reform debate and referendum could not be held in the intervening period and thus make a new system, if approved, available for the 1993 general election.

In addition, the method chosen to whittle the Electoral Commission's four reform options down to a manageable favourite was clearly designed to prop up the status quo first-past-the-post system. For the 1992 referendum voters were to be presented with two questions — the first posed as a choice between the status quo and reform; the second allowing the voter to determine which reform option most appealed.

It was my view that the status quo should be one of the options — effectively, the fifth choice — and that the two top rankings could then compete in the final face-off.

My wife, Karen, was a firm proponent of Ireland's Single Transferable Vote (STV) system and, in retrospect, I am not entirely convinced that my advocacy of MMP stood the test against her STV rationale. Yet again my wife's common sense would prove correct — her leading argument being that at least every MP would be elected by direct vote and have a geographical constituency to which they were responsible.

However, STV still suffered from the same difficulty as the first-past-the-post (FPP) status quo. It did not translate votes proportionately and it was that concept that saw MMP romp home in 1992 as the favoured reform option. The reaction around Parliament to this first referendum decision amazed me. MPs on both sides of the House staggered around the lobbies as if their cerebral cortex had been brutally cauterised. It had never occurred to them, for an instant, that the public would 'go stark, raving mad' and plump for the unknown. Such was the common desperation of the time. Both major parties had repeatedly demonstrated their lack of credibility and integrity, thus any alternative, no matter how malformed, was always likely to be a goer.

Perversely senior MPs on both sides of the House decided that the public needed salvation if only from themselves. Still misreading the popular mood Parliament decided to construct an unloved hybrid of the Royal Commission's report and created the worst possible form of MMP — one that involved 120 MPs; an Electoral Commission without effective teeth or sanction; closed party lists (in case the public started ranking the chosen lists against the dictates of the party bosses); and a ballot paper in reverse order to that promoted by the Commission, with the party vote first and the constituency choice second. In other words, Parliament decided to create the least attractive form of MMP to maximise its polarity at the forthcoming electoral referendum.

It almost worked.

Telecom chairman Peter Shirtcliffe ran a multi-million-dollar anti-MMP campaign that seized upon Parliament's thoughtful sabotage and concentrated on the additional 21 MPs and the lack of public accountability in the formation of the party lists. Just to show that they were not selfish Luddites in dinner suits the same group promoted parliamentary reform as a sanguine alternative. And so the Campaign for Better Government was formed — with extremely close financial and personal connections to the Business Roundtable and the soon-to-be-formed Association of Consumers and Taxpayers (ACT). In fact, where one began and the other ended proved the Rubik puzzle of the year.

I confess to becoming extremely apprehensive at the CBG crusade for it was aided and assisted by a supplicant metropolitan media (in particular, the *Dominion*) and extremely expensive, if clever, 'attack' advertisements. The only weapon at my command to resist such reactionary endeavour was a relatively high national profile, and I determined to utilise this by joining the Electoral Reform Coalition and serving as a member of its national executive committee.

The ERC was a rather curious collection of former socialists, left-wing activists and social misfits led by former state-sector trade unionist Colin Clark. It also boasted fringe Labour activists Phil Saxby and Dianne Yates plus the Alliance's Dana Glendining and a full range of pinkish lobbyists whose names I recognised from virtually every fashionable cause from environmental activism to the peace movement. I was dealing with the nerdy remnants of Woodstock, but they proved infinitely polite if rather wary of this pseudo-Tory interloper.

Without question Saxby was the strategic brain and the restless energy within the group — in fact, I doubt if the organisation could have survived without him. Phil was the political equivalent of a computer geek but possessed such a prodigious adolescent energy that I remained in awe of him at all times. Most such individuals harbour vast libraries of Internet porn, but not Phil. His very pores oozed commitment to the ERC cause — so much so that I initially suspected some hideous thyroid disease.

My association with these earnest individuals occasioned much excitement and not a little derision from various National Party colleagues, but to no avail. Under ERC auspices I undertook a national speaking tour to promote the MMP cause and participated in the odd debate against CBG spokespeople Warren Jennings and Hilary Bennett, both of whom I found to be curiously misinformed about the MMP alternative.

Despite the best efforts of the political, media and commercial status quo MMP achieved its narrow victory on election night and shot my Brookfields celebrations from self-satisfaction into ecstasy. The balance of power would be a transitory phenomenon — MMP would create a new political environment that might give proper expression to all my motivations, hopes and ideals. Or so I dreamed.

That night more than the wine intoxicated. The rules had been changed and a new frontier beckoned. Now to race the opportunity to its limits.

– Chapter 9 –
CHOICES

STRANGE TIMES

The days and weeks directly after the 1993 general election were infinitely strange — as if Bellamy's had procured their mushrooms from some wild and toxic source. Initially it was the dreadful uncertainty that was so unsettling — no clear election-night winner; the public's blind leap of faith out onto the MMP ledge; bureaucrats unsure what to do with their departmental briefing propaganda; the Press Gallery still shocked at their predictive vulnerability being so ruthlessly exposed.

I particularly enjoyed the *Dominion's* denouement. For months they had waged ceaseless war against the MMP reform option (in fact, the *Dominion* wages ceaseless war on anything without a gold Mastercard) and given great prominence to Australian political scientist Malcolm McKerras and his predictions of a comfortable National win and the defeat of electoral reform. Like most such commentators McKerras proved a lion in print and a rather shopworn, apologetic character in person — a rather apt synonym for the *Dominion's* political consciousness.

Waitaki's Alec Neill had lost his seat on election night by less than 50 votes — a reverse feat that rivalled Rob Munro's flame-and-burn effort further south in Invercargill. Both MPs had managed to immolate safe 4000-vote-plus majorities, but Neill was required to suffer the more exquisite torture of waiting for the 'specials' to be counted. Other National MPs, including Attorney-General Paul East, similarly hovered on the edge of the precipice. Caucus' pre-election decision to shut off the electoral rolls one month before the event suddenly assumed momentous importance. This move had been vociferously condemned by both the Labour and Alliance parties, principally because they were aware that it was their voters most likely to tarry on the way to re-registration.

The Nats knew this too. Hence the surprising unanimity in our Caucus at the time. We congratulated ourselves on one of those wonderful coincidences of self-interest and administrative efficiency.

Election-night standings posited National with 49 seats; Labour with 46; the Alliance and New Zealand First with two each. Should these standings remain then the combined strength of the Opposition parties would eclipse National. Such statistics raised the possibility of a fresh election. However, Alliance leader Jim Anderton, determined to appear the statesman but not above screwing his ex-Labour colleagues on the way, then pledged that his Alliance party would support National on all matters of parliamentary confidence; a gesture that outraged Labour but clearly avoided the question of whether a government could or should be formed.

With eighteen per cent of the popular vote the Alliance might have thrown its parliamentary weight behind Labour but the bloody wounds of midwifery were still too fresh. For a man who propounded the merits of proportional representation, Jim Anderton demonstrated a startling adherence to the vicissitudes of the now discredited FPP electoral system — indeed, to the extent of supporting a party with an alien philosophy solely because it had acquired more constituency seats under the old electoral regime.

Such grandstanding became rather academic when 'specials' delivered Neill from a dreaded return to Oamaru obscurity. However, Bolger's problem remained: 50 seats to the Government; 49 to the Opposition; Michael Laws still the joker in the pack and acutely aware of his transitory powers.

Of course, it would have been useful to have taken advantage of these uncertain times and played my own peculiar leverage to maximum effect. But I could not hold my nostrils long enough to indulge in such ductile diplomacy. Besides, my impetuosity would not allow it. Instead of the necessary supine simpering and flirting I ensured that the Prime Minister possessed an exact fix on my unreliability. In the new Parliament my votes would be decided upon the merit of the legislation and the interests of my constituents, I pompously declared. Without even being asked. Not my finest moment — even if it did have the effect of galvanising cartoonists everywhere.

Certainly the first Caucus after the election found itself duly provoked. Each losing or retiring MP receives a mock silver salver from the Leader, suitably inscribed and recognising their sterling service to the party. However, on this occasion the stack of trays arrayed on the top table resembled nothing so much as a swanky restaurant kitchen at washing-up time. The demise of over twenty MPs was unprecedented, and Chief Whip John Carter apologised profusely that there simply had not been sufficient time to get each tray suitably inscribed. 'Perhaps each of you could get it done when you get home,' he added helpfully.

I could just imagine some of the inscriptions: 'To Blah-Blah, for your magnificent effort in single-handedly rescuing the New Zealand economy from 1990–93 and for being an inspiration to all your parliamentary colleagues during this time. We will not see your like again.' Thank God.

Prime Minister Bolger then conveyed his thanks to each of the former MPs as they came forward in the manner of a school prizegiving, to shake hands, receive the memento and then perhaps recount some pithy anecdote. At least, that was the usual tradition. Unfortunately the procession was performed in alphabetical order and one of the first recipients was ex-New Plymouth MP John Armstrong. The pleasantries completed, Armstrong then launched into a protracted attack on me, the gist of which went something like:

'I should not be leaving this Caucus. You, Laws, should be. I did my job as a loyal National MP. I did not shit on my mates at every opportunity. Instead you, you useless bastard, sit here with an increased majority while the good, loyal, decent MPs shuffle off [sans taxi chits] into the uncomfortable uncertainty of unemployment. This is wrong. I want you to know that I and a lot of others will be keeping an eye on you...' And so on.

During this outburst, which set a precedent for a number of similar comments from the other departers, I noticed Bolger beaming with satisfaction, riding each critical syllable, nodding for dramatic effect as if Armstrong was a ventriloquist's dummy attached to Bolger's innermost thought processes. Of course, it is entirely possible that this was the case.

It crossed my mind to protest, to resist, to stand up and shout back that the true betrayal had been from Armstrong and his ilk — that if he had half the guts of the McIntyres, the Myles, and the Campions then he might still be the MP for New Plymouth and this country might not vilify its politicians as cheating, lying, toadying sycophants. In any other Caucus I would have returned the verbal fire with denunciatory interest.

Not today. This was part of the grief process that accompanied personal loss. I might be the target for their anger but I could ride it; when the Caucus door closed I would be remaining within. However, what I could not forgive was Bolger's gloating visage hovering over Armstrong's shoulder in a blatant display of encouragement. It was such a petty act; the playground bully egging on one of his minions. It demeaned the man; it demeaned the office. The Prime Minister's fatal flaw — he stooped to conquer.

On the other hand, Bolger's rare combination of Irish cunning and pragmatic vision was seldom matched. If there was one gift that Bolger had acquired in his decades of political experience it was in knowing the exact price at which a fellow politician could be bought. It might be his only true skill but it would be enough to save the National Party — and more than once.

He was aware of exactly what one senior Labour MP wanted — nay, coveted. Under the grandiloquent guise of learning his MMP lessons, the Prime Minister offered Eastern Maori MP Peter Tapsell a hint of parliamentary immortality: the Speaker's chair, with an automatic knighthood, of course. It was an audacious offer but the Nats had picked their target well even if it meant defrocking and sidelining their own Robin Gray to the spectacularly superfluous sinecure of Minister of State.

Mike Moore later told me that he tried to convince Peter Tapsell to refuse this Greek offering but felt himself hamstrung by both the perceived mana the position would bring Tapsell 'and his people' (whoever they were), and a vague belief that perhaps Tapsell's appointment would signal a kinder, gentler Parliament. If so, then he was grievously mistaken. On both counts. Tapsell's honour counted for nought against the New Zealand First Maori tide of three years hence, and the House itself proved no less combative nor combustible for its pipe-smoking Anglophile chairman.

Peter Tapsell was a gracious fellow with a quicker wit than his critics allowed, even if he did tend to favour the frontbenchers with his rulings and archaically insist on suit jackets being worn in the debating chamber at all times. At least this direction had the advantage of disproving one of Tapsell's pet theories, which were occasionally dredged up from the dim reaches of Victorian British protocol for public amusement; namely, that formal dress produces gentlemanly manners and courteous behaviour.

Bolger's audacious tactic had delivered him, and the Government, the great gift of time. Time in which MMP might further prise apart the fragile loyalties of members to their parties, yours truly included. Labour's internal tensions were palpable and every week would produce a new House rumour on the imminent meltdown of its parliamentary team. Even so, with Tapsell in the chair the House could still be split 49:49 should some rebellious Nat decide to push the frontier and cross the floor — a tremor of nervous expectation still shuddered through the Government Caucus. Tapsell had declared his intention to progress all legislation in the event of a tied vote, bar for the final third reading.

Which was quite useful really. Because it allowed Tasman MP Nick Smith and me to press-gang the rest of our reluctant colleagues into establishing minimum youth wages, a fight we had categorically lost the previous year. There was no less opposition within Government ranks this time — especially with Treasury, the Cabinet and just about every business lobby lining up against us. But we had two precious parliamentary votes and both the confidence and the conscience to use them. Bolger bowed to the inevitable and mandated the change — a move that conflagrated Max Bradford and other right-wing colleagues into vigorous and public denunciation. With smug self-satisfaction Nick and I enjoyed our rare routing of the ministers and their bureaucrats and hoped that it might prove a portent of greater back-bench influence.

Fat chance. The National back bench remained a seething and contradictory mess of personal ambition, vanity and diffuse political belief. In addition, Bolger had expanded his post-election Cabinet to ensure that the combination of his ministers, under-secretaries and Whips outnumbered the remaining Caucus MPs. Somehow Hobson MP Ross Meurant had actually inveigled an Agriculture Under-Secretary's job out of the Prime Minister — further proof, if required, that Bolger was prepared to use the taxpayers' largesse to ensure relative governmental unity. And, I had to grudgingly admit, perhaps that Ross Meurant was not as dumb as I had believed.

Meurant would later rather contradict this temporary verdict by getting involved in a quite bizarre combination of incidents including the second-hand weapons trade, a shady Russian bank and the formation of his own party. Nevertheless he was an intriguing if odd individual, who preferred his own company and judgement. His fledgling Right of Centre (ROC) party reflected this peculiar mix of bristling virility and insensible determination by recruiting virtually every National Party rural activist with an IQ of under three figures, to be followed by the eventual recruitment of former used-car dealer Howick MP Trevor Rogers. In that sense Meurant did the Nats a favour.

Meurant has a unique footnote in this country's modern history — for creating his own political party only to have it reject him. Having departed ROC (which whimpered its way into oblivion with Rogers at the helm despite a name change to Conservative) Meurant became something of a wandering Jew, with virtually every new party (including ACT and New Zealand First) rejecting his overtures. Towards the end of 1996 Meurant approached me for a research job within New Zealand First; I simply did not have the heart to decline and instead referred him to the never-never land of Winston's decision-making. Who knows — his mummified remains may still be hovering somewhere in Peters' outer offices.

Certainly Jim Bolger was not in the least concerned that his Caucus might fragment with the advent of MMP. In fact, he positively encouraged the process in the safe and sure knowledge that the departers would vote for his administration on all matters of confidence and Budget supply. They had no option. Should they prove quarrelsome Bolger could always use them as an excuse for a snap election — at which point these supposedly independent-minded fellows would cease to be.

In short, they would not be very different from his neglected back bench — powerless, able to be whipped when necessary, and pathetically grateful for any crumb of consideration that might fall their way.

The Prime Minister was again demonstrating a practical awareness of the new MMP environment, an awareness that seemed beyond the hierarchy of the Labour Opposition or even the rest of his own party. The former were engaged in yet another of their internecine battles as Mike Moore was stripped of the leadership in a bitter post-election dispute with his former deputy, Helen Clark. Dismayed by his aberrant performance on election night and by Moore's often erratic policy detours on the campaign trail itself, Labour's academics took charge of the Caucus machine. But it was a victory that had a cost.

The Maori MPs were sufficiently discomforted to extend this new grievance to their voting supporters, and thus lose every Maori constituency seat three years hence. Moore himself corroded the party from within with withering attacks on the party's liberals, mocking their 'politically correct' agendas and labelling them the new 'cling-ons'. These internal struggles distracted the Opposition sufficiently to allow Bolger to effectively set the pre-MMP political climate. In addition, Moore was able to destabilise the new Labour leadership by continually hinting at the formation of his own enterprise.

Certainly there were ructions within National's own ranks over the PM's bold Catholic entreaty to his back bench to 'go forth and propagate'. Presidential hopeful, party treasurer and Manawatu Light Brigade survivor Michael Cox chastised Jim Bolger for his 'stupidity', while another former MP and presidential aspirant, Wellington lawyer Geoff Thompson, also expressed public unease. Wiser heads in Caucus rolled their eyes at the prospect of either man taking control of the party's administration, and there was talk in Bellamy's that commu-nications tyro and Customs Minister Murray McCully might be nominated for the chief organisational role. Wiser heads prevailed and it was Thompson who would later ride Michelle Boag's strategic skills to the top job. But by now total control of the party machine had passed to the ninth floor of the Beehive. The party would only be useful again at the next election, when leaflets required delivering, party subscriptions needed gathering, and throngs of cheering supporters were necessary at the Leader's rallies.

It mattered not. In 1994 there were a host of new parties being formed: Roger Douglas' right-wing Association of Consumers and Taxpayers (ACT); Graeme Lee's United Progressives (later changing their name to the Christian Democrats after realising that they were neither united nor progressive); Ross Meurant's primeval ROC grouping; and Peter Dunne's Future, a name he chose in the desperate hope that he might actually have one. It was Bolger's view that each and every one of these groups should be courted, although some with more enthusiasm than others. The motto was simple: you never know when you might need them.

Indeed Bolger truly tested the outer reaches of this logic by even suggesting, in early 1995, 'a grand alliance' with the Labour Party. Predictably, Helen Clark and her Caucus rejected the idea of such a rabid coupling but it did illustrate just how far the Prime Minister was prepared to go to retain the Treasury benches. Such promiscuous flirting was clearly portentous of future events.

It also demonstrated something else, at least to me. There really was no great difference between the inner cores of either the National or Labour Caucuses. The reaction against Muldoon and the pursuit of monetarist policies had scrambled the political landscape. Bolger was right. There was a common thread to both parties — not so much the symbiosis of Tweedledum and Tweedledee but rather an incipient cloning of thought. The state sector was the cohesive glue, having been successfully colonised by Treasury's policy pioneers and suitably tamed for fertile advancement.

Ironically, the greatest consternation in National ranks in reaction to the new parties related to its clear sibling — ACT. Within Caucus most moderates secretly prayed that executive right-wingers like John Luxton and Maurice Williamson would sign up and depart, and perhaps even take Jenny Shipley with them. No such luck. None of the trio was dumb enough to cast aside their ministerial powers and privileges for a pillion punt with the remnants of Lange's last Cabinet. Thus my last hopes that the National Party might steer a centrist course were finally quashed. Time to plan an alternative future.

ACT worried National strategists because it had the ability to touch the selfish excesses of its own supporters. It was no accident that ACT registered its strongest support in the genteel climes of Remuera, Kelburn and Havelock North. These people regarded a social conscience as some form of transmittable disease. National had been their home — now Roger Douglas promised them a new one although with no insistence that they revoke the former. ACT could be the time-share apartment in Taupo. To counter this attempt at duality, National instituted a new party rule; it was deemed unconstitutional for a National Party member to hold financial membership in another party political grouping.

The National Party might define itself as a Centre-Right grouping but the emphasis would remain on the right of this equation. The centre was only to be used at times that required studied pragmatism. Now was deemed one of those times. So much so that Finance Minister Ruth Richardson was dropped by the Prime Minister to make way for that arch-pragmatist Bill Birch. Or so the pundits speculated. It had always been my view that Birch was just a policy cypher, prey to whichever advisers dominated his flow of information. So it proved. Treasury had tamed Birch within weeks and he was soon advancing their agenda, if without Richardson's appalling clichés. Despite that many Caucus and party activists longed for the greener grass now being munched upon by Douglas, Prebble and all the other furry rodents of the far Right.

Fortunately not all my spoiling powers had dissipated.

There was still sufficient nervousness within Government circles, and particularly within the Prime Minister's office, for renegade backbenchers to exert a good measure of influence. These were the days before the formation of the United Party — a move that would draw Dunne and two other Labour MPs into National's ample bosom. I cursed United at the time. Their mad scramble for the middle would thwart the effect of any further rebellious raids and allow the Cabinet to retreat to their usual high-handed arrogance in dealing with the Caucus back bench. But that trek into oblivion by the seven dwarfs was still gestating. For the present I possessed a singular influence.

Just as well. For some reason beyond my immediate comprehension Education Minister Lockwood Smith had decided to bow to a curious combination of bureaucratic and personal prejudice and cap the new Flaxmere College at Form Four. 'My' Flaxmere College. I had come to regard the high school as a personal creation, while the Flaxmere community itself retained a limpet-like attachment to my sentiments despite voting Labour in '93.

Apparently Smith regarded 'middle schools' as his next, new, brave experiment and, given the school's growing pains, determined that an ideal opportunity had been presented to launch this concept. Such rationale flew in the face of every argument used previously by Smith in gazetting the high school, but with Lockwood one was never entirely sure which exact neurons were functioning on any particular day.

Instead of blue-faced rage I attempted a combination of sweet reason and grovelling ingratiation. To absolutely no effect. Smith's mind was set: Flaxmere was to become a middle school — the high school 'experiment' was over. Within days his ministry officials had marshalled sufficient misleading information to justify this idiotic stance and I was now left with just one weapon at my disposal.

Blackmail.

I sought a meeting with the Prime Minister, announced my imminent departure from the National Party, and advised both Bolger and Senior Whip John Carter that I would be voting with the Opposition on all matters of confidence and supply should the new Flaxmere high school be decapitated.

'You've betrayed me!' I exclaimed. 'Now I'm going to betray you' — or words to that effect. There must have been something in my eyes. The next day an infuriated Lockwood Smith marched up to me in the debating chamber, thrust a ministerial media statement into my chest and angrily lambasted me for my 'totally unprincipled tactics'.

The news release informed me that, officially, the minister had reconsidered the issue after the impassioned representations of the local community and various Hastings lobbies. Flaxmere College would retain its Form One to Seven status. Unofficially, Smith had received the word from the PM's office to stop farting around. My only regret was that I could not claim any public credit for fear of exposing the deceit, blackmail and general lack of good faith in my manoeuvrings. But a deal was a deal. And sometimes one must do evil to achieve good.

In that one moment I had become entirely corrupted by the political process. I perceived the right result, the just result, to be a secondary school for the Flaxmere community. But all attempts at intelligent and principled debate had failed. Easily, too easily, I had slipped into the murkier depths of realpolitik and rationalised that the final result merited its application; the end did justify the means. I was now as much a part of the problem as everyone else. Not a flicker of personal concern registered. All my public platitudes about honesty and accountability had been seared away by a mixture of self-interest and sentimentality.

I would like to be able to record honestly that this was the first evidence of my corruption — and that at least my motivation had been good. Maybe there is a modicum of truth to such an observation, but in fact I had already compromised myself a month or so earlier. And my motivation then had been far from ideal.

At the start of the 1994 parliamentary year Dunedin West MP Clive Matthewson had promoted a private member's bill that would disestablish asset-testing of elderly people in residential care. This was in reaction to Social Welfare Minister Jenny Shipley's introduction of a new means-testing regime that sought to treat public and private geriatric institutions with like regard. The logic was irrefutable: once the State provided full-time care for an elderly person then it expected some contribution from the estate of that individual. It was the details of that contribution that created the public dissension.

I had expressed myself in opposition to Shipley's new policy. It was as much an instinctive as an intellectual reaction; anything that Shipley promoted aroused special concern. Jenny had a way of coating the worst medicine with the most luxurious chocolate flavour — my experience with the welfare benefit cuts and the superannuation surtax

suggested that there was always some great evil at hand when Jenny smiled sweetly and addressed you by your first name. This was one of those times.

My opposition to the new asset-testing regime garnered considerable populist support, particularly from Grey Power, Age Concern and other such lobby groups. But I soon found myself in an invidious middle ground. I saw no great need to endorse Shipley's change of the status quo but the lobby groups were arguing for the total cessation of asset-testing. I had stranded myself in no-man's-land and Matthewson's bill exposed my position. During the crucial Caucus meeting I expressed my opposition to Shipley's scheme but not my intention to do anything other than register a protest. It was normal at such times to indicate to the Prime Minister and your Caucus colleagues if crossing the floor was the likely conclusion to such disagreement. I failed to do so.

However, the public and lobby pressure on me continued to grow and I reasoned that supporting Matthewson's bill through its first reading would be no bad thing. The issue could then be aired in the Social Services Select Committee without necessarily altering Government policy. I duly informed the Government Whips of this decision, at which point all hell broke loose. My vote would be sufficient to allow the Labour bill past its first reading and I was duly summoned to the Prime Minister's office.

And there occurred one of the more surreal encounters of my parliamentary life. The Prime Minister gestured me to the nearby settee, which indicated something of the nature of a fireside chat. Dressings-down, in my experience, were much more formal. Bolger would sit behind his grand desk in the manner of a headmaster dealing with a recalcitrant pupil. Plainly that tactic had failed often enough with yours truly to suggest a gentler course. Or so I believed.

We were then joined by deputy Prime Minister Don McKinnon, disturbed from one of his somnolent excesses no doubt, and in the kind of grizzly mood that would normally suggest a mixture of gout, migraine and hangover. For the next twenty minutes McKinnon subjected me to every vulgar insult known to the vernacular, and a few more besides. Bolger relaxed beside him as I was informed that I was 'a fucking wanker', 'an absolute dickhead' and 'a treacherous bastard', and those were just the dispassionate observations. Initially I was perplexed until Bolger cut in at an opportune moment with suitably soothing arguments suggesting that I might reconsider the issue. Then McKinnon would start again.

This good cop/bad cop routine lasted an interminably long time. By now I was sufficiently emboldened to return each McKinnon vulgarity with interest and finally Senior Whip John Carter was required to verbally separate us. I looked squarely at Bolger, cognisant of my impending Flaxmere high school difficulty, and suggested that one consideration was worth another. I agreed to vote with the Government.

Thankfully, Labour possessed their own whipping difficulties when the private member's bill was finally introduced. Two of their backbenchers, Jack Elder and Damian O'Connor from memory, had either confused the voting hour or gone on an extended jog, or both. Whatever, my vote proved not to be crucial. But I was now faced with a vociferous group of elderly activists who screamed for my head. And they were perfectly entitled to it.

At such times most politicians find there is sufficient sophistry available to disguise the real issue. I proved no different and publicly defended my position by claiming that Labour's bill 'went too far'. The abolition of all asset-testing was not an option. Incredibly, most of the media bought this self-serving bullshit and I even earned a few supportive editorials. Which just goes to prove that you can fool some of the people all of the time.

But the whole incident left a nasty taste in my mouth. The

intimidatory tactics of the leadership I could bear; my own U-turn I could not. I had wilfully misled the public about the real reasons behind the backdown — namely, that there was a local issue I deemed more important. Time to return the halo.

A NEW FRIEND

Despite almost wresting the Treasury benches from a previously dominant National administration, Mike Moore was speedily jettisoned by his recriminatory Labour Caucus and propelled into a strange twilight zone — the exclusive preserve of all dumped leaders. Most expire there; others linger exhibiting various degrees of malevolence. Those who do survive hover in anxious limbo, either willing an opportunity to once more seize the tiller or praying for their successor to really stuff it up. Either way it is an idle existence.

Moore's demise had been predicted by Labour insiders and the not-so-spectral David Lange well before the 1993 election. Put simply, he did not fit. The party had begun to perceive itself as a political vanguard for 'social democracy' although no one truly understood what the term actually meant. A social democrat was apparently someone with common compassion but uncommon ambition. In short, social democrats were the kind of urban liberals who accepted the necessity for cheap imports but still placed a touching hand of sympathy on the back of the New Zealand factory worker as they escorted him to the dole queue.

'Social democrat' became the umbrella phrase that captured all those who tacitly accepted the free market while remaining wary of its consequences. Rather than trouble themselves with the task of constructing a fairer economic model that might require a dollop of self-sacrifice on their part, social democrats diverted their energy into all the trendy 'isms' of the age. Feminism. Anti-sexism. Anti-racism. Environmentalism. Narcissism.

They were passionate about improving the standard of the country's public education system and health care because these were good things to care about. However, they were equally convinced that there should be no further tax increases to accommodate their convictions, in the knowledge that the middle-class voter held the key to electoral success. Thus a good social democrat might bemoan the state of the environment but still purchase a belching diesel Japanese import. They accepted that hypocrisy was simply part of the human condition;

people felt comfortable when their own flaws were explained away as the fault of either governmental incompetence or rapacious media tycoons. So it was that fashionable causes replaced political philosophy — Princess Di the obvious patron saint.

Mike Moore was not a social democrat. He was an old-fashioned, working-class, conservative Labourite who had educated himself by extensive and eclectic reading expeditions and generally regarded most of his university-trained Caucus colleagues as smug, self-satisfied skimmers. Despite his boundless bonhomie and often bizarre enthusiasm Moore no longer 'belonged' within the neo-liberal, politically correct conglomerate of wankers, wannabes and wanglers that comprised a good part of Labour's modern membership. Helen Clark was far more their cappuccino.

It had been quietly suggested that Moore was 'a flake', meaning that he was either emotionally or intellectually unstable or both. Our Caucus acquired this epithet from Moore's own parliamentary colleagues and were provided with enough slightly exaggerated tales to keep dinner guests entertained for hours. One particular campaign titbit would assume legendary status.

Determined to show his party's opposition to hospital part-charges, Moore had procured a sledgehammer and brandished it at a parliamentary press conference to dramatic effect. He then excitedly invited those present to join him in 'smashing the cash registers' at nearby hospitals, but instead was confronted by the sight of even his own aides slinking from the room in red-faced embarrassment. There was sufficient truth in this apocryphal tale to allow Government press secretaries to gloat and guffaw over the incident for weeks.

And yet this was also the man who so very nearly pulled off the most stunning of election upsets. A 37-seat National majority had been virtually extinguished in three years. Certainly Moore's battling campaign style papered over any number of deficiencies and disunities within Labour's ranks, although Lange's talk of new taxes and new leaders did its damage. The curse of the ex-leader had struck again.

One of Moore's favoured after-dinner stories was that on losing Labour's leadership he slept like a baby — waking every two hours and then bawling his eyes out. The sad thing is that I suspect the story was absolutely true. He had no children; the Labour Party was his surrogate charge — his entire emotional energy had been projected into that cause. Losing the leadership was like being banished from the family hearthside.

At the time my own view of Mike Moore was little different from that of my Caucus colleagues. He seemed to possess an unnatural propensity to repeatedly alter his thought patterns during the same sentence — one was never quite sure whether Mike was bored with the sentence and had plunged off into a new idea or whether he was just mouthing random streams of consciousness. To this day I remain perplexed about that issue.

However, I did appreciate that Mike Moore's empathy with the working man and the working woman in New Zealand society was unforced and genuine. Despite all his best efforts at self-education, or perhaps in spite of them, Moore was at his political best when allowing his natural visceral instincts their full rein. It was when he tried to rationalise or intellectualise that process that the problems began.

But my personal appreciation of Moore had been marred by a particularly vicious dispute we had shared in the lead-up to the '93 election. During the Whittaker controversy Moore had publicly denounced me as the most dishonourable MP in Parliament — the Alan B'Stard of the debating chamber. Quite what had prompted this attack puzzled me. It is not uncommon for opposing parties to seize upon any dissension among their opponents as proof of their general unfitness to govern (or even direct traffic) but Moore's virulence surprised me. Whittaker was the 'principled and faithful Tory' while Laws would 'do anything ... say anything ... to anybody' to be re-elected. In short, I was an egregious egotist — and that was on a good day.

I do not think Moore ever totally altered that assessment in all our dealings over the next two years. However, he did profess sincere respect for my allegedly superior skills as a deft practitioner of politics' darker arts. With Mike I was never quite able to take on human form in his consciousness; I would always be a barely domesticated succubus. He seemed to genuinely like me for all my perceived vices, and nothing I could do, say or otherwise emote would shake his adamantine conviction that I was somehow irrevocably devout but fatally debauched in the same moment.

In the early months of 1994 the political media were agog with the latent possibilities and perambulations of MMP. Given my championing of the new electoral system and my outspoken opposition to the status quo I was in regular demand as a commentator and *agent provocateur* on all manner of television and talkback radio shows. One such occasion was a TVNZ 'Fraser' current affairs programme in

NEW PARTY... WHAT NEW PARTY?

WE'RE AIMING A LITTLE HIGHER THAN THAT

which both Mike Moore and I lined up for studio interviews on the immediate future of parliamentary politics and the possible formation of a new 'centre' party.

At the time it was my considered judgement that a properly constituted centre party could garner between six and eight per cent of the 1996 election list vote and so hold the balance of power in any future Parliament. The most obvious precedent was the Free Democrats in the Bundestag, who had been in every West German government coalition since the Second World War.

Similarly, I argued, a vacuum had become clearly apparent in the New Zealand political scene with National defining itself as a Centre-Right party, Labour characterising itself as Centre-Left, and the ACT and Alliance parties content to position themselves further to the Right and Left respectively. To the inevitable query as to where New Zealand First placed themselves on this Lawsian political spectrum I facetiously replied that that entirely depended on Winston's mood of the day. Stalinist on foreign investment; radical on political accountability; schizophrenic on most social issues.

That particular evening, interviewer Ian Fraser had tried to suggest that any new centre grouping must inevitably involve both Mike Moore and me. Still chastened at his dumping, Moore refused to pooh-pooh the concept.

FRASER: Is a centre party likely to be a natural ally of Labour or of National?

MOORE: Well it depends ... I think it's got enough legs to be the dominant party by the way ... but say it wasn't the dominant party. It would be saying to Labour: 'Listen, don't wreck the economy. Sure, have stronger minimum wages but don't have compulsory unionism.' On the other hand, it will be saying to the National Party: 'What the heavens are you doing selling those state houses?' It will be the ballast.

LAWS: This is very important. If there isn't a centre party in New Zealand politics under MMP then both Labour and National stand to be captured by extremists.

MOORE: That's right ... what I'm worried about, and Michael pointed it out, is that Labour could be put over a barrel by some of the lunatics in the Alliance, or the National Party could be put over the barrel by some of the extremists in ACT...

LAWS: That's right.

MOORE: ...and we've got Ruth [Richardson] and Roger [Douglas] on one hand, and we've got the [19]60s on the other. You need ballast. You need a centre group that can be part of that future.

After the show I suggested 'a chat' might be in order; just to mull over the possibilities, you understand. To my surprise Moore did not resile from the prospect. A thaw was clearly discernible. Next week I received a number of Caucus gibes relating to my 'love-in' with Mike Moore on the 'Fraser' show, although David Lange took the quip-of-the-week prize: 'Two Mikes do not make a sound system.'

It would be a combination of Napier MP Geoff Braybrooke and a Hastings hailstorm that would provoke our next cautious communication. Braybrooke had already pronounced himself incensed, incinerated and otherwise inconsolable at his Caucus' decision to dump Moore and wasted no opportunity to express his outrage. Braybrooke was an interesting character — a burly, tattooed, insulin-dependent, ex-London bobby who had also served as a medic in Vietnam. He harboured all the various passions and prejudices that one might associate with a conservative Catholic of British working-class origins but had also developed a few quirky beliefs of his own. One was a marked and very public abhorrence at the 'infiltration' of his party 'by butch lesbians and bloody homos' and a general opposition to anything that might be termed even vaguely permissive. He had proven an implacable opponent of homosexual law reform, was an active supporter of the anti-abortion SPUC organisation and made no bones about his views on Maori independence. Clearly, Geoff Braybrooke was no social democrat.

We had brokered a political truce very early in our political relationship after an early parliamentary incident taught us the old adage about letting sleeping dogs lie. A minor exchange in the House had attracted front-page coverage in our local press and made us both appear petty, mean-spirited and puerile. There was no way we wanted such obvious personality traits to receive extensive and self-defeating publicity so we agreed to refrain from political or personal attack upon each other. It was the Hawke's Bay political equivalent of the MAD nuclear scenario.

Braybrooke was clearly enjoying his stint as a maverick Opposition backbencher complete with a huge election majority and a secure local executive. He had organised a Mike Moore rally at the local theatre and invited me along to further provoke the interest of both the public and the national media. Certainly it suited Moore to play the spurned suitor. Further, consorting with Michael Laws would excite any number of tensions in Helen Clark's nervous offices, and causing bodily discomfort had clearly become the frisson of the moment.

My own views on the need for a new centre party were well understood so it suited Moore to let the feverish Press Gallery speculate on our new relationship. It might even suggest imminent departure from the Labour Party and its further fragmentation. When I invited him to tour a number of Hastings orchards shredded by a devastating hailstorm, the media whipped themselves into a further speculative lather. Something was up. They did not have a clue what; it was enough that warm bodies were moving and giving off infra-red signatures.

In fact, nothing was happening. Moore's public show was being matched by ceaseless private doubt, which was relayed to me at every mutual communication. Yeah, he saw the opportunity. Yeah, the Labour Party was stuffed, they could not win the next election but, jeez, he had been a Labour Prime Minister. What would all his mates in the 'cossie' clubs think, 'all those ladies with the fat arms' he had just presented with Labour long-service badges?

In late 1994 I contacted my old sparring partner Michelle Boag and began to test the ground as to how various forces within the National Party might react to a Mike Moore-led centrist conglomeration. A meeting was arranged in an Auckland hotel room, with each of us gently probing for common ground. Moore was aware of Boag's activist history and prized her political acumen; conversely, Boag understood the political advantages if a post-election arrangement could be brokered between National and Moore.

Funding was briefly discussed; Moore was given to
traditional National Party donors could be convinced to
support behind any new credible centrist grouping. I was cont
let the hotel discussions remain informal, even chatty, without any hint of commitment. If anything Michelle proved the more doubtful. Mike was impressed with Boag's ability and presence, and enquired about her interest in any new grouping. In turn Michelle proved suitably cautious. Later she would draw me aside and express her surprise that Moore was nowhere near as flaky as publicly portrayed, and undertook to brief Geoff Thompson on the meeting.

During this discussion Moore was adamant that National could not automatically assume that any new party we might form would hold National's hand either before or after the election. But if business interests required a centre party that could act as a cautionary rudder in any left-leaning coalition government then there were obvious advantages in backing him. At which point Michelle's body language conveyed a deeper scepticism.

National would want to be assured that having its financial backers supporting any new group would provide them with political advantages. At which point I diverted the conversation elsewhere. Further elaboration on that point could only show up intractable and irreconcilable objectives. But it was too late. That much had already become apparent to both Moore and Boag.

There was another difficulty. Me. National would regard any centrist group in which the demon Laws was prominent as inclined to be hostile. Mike smiled and drew on the ever-present cigarette.

'So the old is out to corrupt the new already?' he laughed.

If anything the Boag meeting deflated my optimism. It had been my intention to draw Michelle into Moore's orbit as an experienced political operator with invaluable big-business connections. The combination of a former Labour Prime Minister with a former National *éminence grise* would give a new centre party instant credibility with the political media and encourage quality recruitment on both sides of the divide. But Michelle's political ambitions appeared to have been satiated; Moore's were still hopelessly scrambled. I was getting precisely nowhere.

But just as these thoughts began to gain ground the phone calls from Moore would start up again, with invitations to dinner accompanied by reminiscent chats and much good humour. He proved both ırresistible and intelligent company — ladling out nostalgia one instant, expounding upon his latest creative endeavour the next.

Always I would bring our conversations back to the same theme. Now was the time — we were the people. Life is about seizing opportunities and we were honour bound by dint of our position, our background, our ability and our enemies to seize this one. History would not forgive us our inertia. The country wanted something fresh, invigorating, understandable. Both National and Labour parties were worn out; Jim Anderton had retired from the Alliance leadership after his double family tragedy; neither ACT nor New Zealand First had the acumen or the capacity to translate the disaffected public mood into solid political support.

Moore would then stub out another half-smoked cigarette, light a fresh one, call for another bottle of wine and talk of all the difficulties that confronted us. The right people, the right money, the right candidates, the right timing. It was all too hard. Then as he read the disappointment and resignation in my face he would fling out another lifeline, another shard of hope, another faint trace of commitment. For every step we took forward together, Mike would take three to the side and then feint in retreat. I was in the middle of a crazy dance where each new rhythm would depend on the Moore mood of the day — which might hop forward to discuss specifics of policy and personnel or career backwards in regret at past events.

What I did not realise until almost too late was that I was living through Mike Moore's grief phases — an unwitting witness to the loss of Labour's leadership.

DIRECT DEMOCRACY

In the meantime I was developing my own embryonic ideas about the type of policy any new political party would have to adopt for the 1996 general election. For years I had promoted the amorphous concept of 'direct democracy' — a catch-all phrase for any series of democratic initiatives that aimed to empower electors with greater influence in political decision-making. Citizens-initiated referenda; the 'electronic Town Hall'; a 'Citizens' Charter'; voter 'recall' of elected representatives — all were examples, if imprecise ones, of the desire to wrestle power from the party machines and the civil servants and return it to the people.

I had experimented with the general principle in my own electorate by initially polling constituents on any issue that required a parliamentary 'conscience' vote. In turn, I had cast my vote in accordance with the majority verdict — a move which provoked widespread criticism from conservative newspaper editors but attracted considerable local support. The general view of most critics was that I had been elected to exercise my judgement, even if that judgement was jaundiced, nonsensical and prejudiced. This was deemed preferable to allowing my constituents to sway my vote; after all, the public were far too ill-informed and reactive to exercise appropriate wisdom. One day in the National Caucus would soon have disabused the editors about the status quo alternative.

An MP is elected for a combination of factors but the most important consideration is always the party colours the various candidates fly on election day. However, on 'conscience' issues the party colours are withdrawn. MPs are gifted a 'free' vote — supposedly, a vote to be cast by the dictates of their own personal conscience. I regarded the whole concept as stuffy nonsense and, ultimately, anti-democratic.

As the parliamentary representative of Hawke's Bay, it was my duty to cast a conscience vote on my electors' collective behalf. My own moral and ethical beliefs were clearly subordinate to the views of those who elected me, paid my salary and expected me (at least, in theory) to represent the region's best interests in Wellington. To that end I would randomly poll my constituents to divine just where the electorate's views lay and vote accordingly. If the results were too close to call then I would finally exercise my personal judgement. But they never were — the results were always overwhelming, whether in banning discrimination against homosexuals, allowing wineries to sell their products on Sundays, or allowing tobacco advertising and sponsorship of sporting and cultural events. In each case my electorate proved surprisingly permissive and belied the conventional wisdom about provincial morality.

But if the general principle of representative democracy was valid for conscience votes then why not for other matters of political expression?

The usual reply was that I was elected on the National Party's manifesto and that this amorphous outline of policies and principles equated to the necessary political contract between the government of the day and the public. The difficulty, as the Lange administration had previously demonstrated, was that Cabinet refused to have any of their actions constrained by any such 'gentleman's agreement'. At which point back-bench MPs had only two choices — they could accept the executive diktat or resist. The former course was much easier; indeed a prerequisite for personal advancement. As my parents will attest, I was not made for the easier path.

Between 1990 and 1993 I had resolved that the party's manifesto was indeed a contract and that if its terms required amendment or alteration then the consent of the electors was required. Given that no such consent had been sought nor granted then I was honour bound, particularly if I considered the alternative Cabinet policy to be flawed, to vote against Government policy. Of course such gestures were ultimately futile. The Government could command a vast parliamentary majority and the greatest political loser, in purely selfish terms, was me. Any ministerial ambitions were categorically dashed the first instant I entered the 'Noes' lobby.

But after 1993 the situation had changed. My election majority suggested a good measure of personal support in Hawke's Bay; under the shadow of impending MMP the major parties were fragmenting and spawning new political groupings; each back-bench vote had suddenly become important because of the delicate balance in the House, and I was clearly destined for a future course wholly independent of the National Caucus. If ever the time was ripe to put my principles of 'direct democracy' into action that time was now.

The Hawke's Bay Referendum 1995 occupied a good part of my waking consciousness during the first half of that year. It was not just that the relevant questions required framing but a myriad administrative details required planning and execution. The exercise had no legal or political sanction and apart from the resource of free parliamentary mail there was no financial support that I could offer to the venture.

Of course it was not an exact science. Each household received ballot papers, background information on each of the 22 (!) questions, and Freepost envelopes. The 22 questions ranged over five main areas — issues of public morality, the tax/spending/debt repayment trade-off, state asset sales, health issues and education policy priorities. In retrospect, the sheer mass of information provided and the variety and detail of the questions themselves was far too complicated. It would have been best to stagger the referendum over a period of months and concentrate on one issue at a time, but that process would have involved luxuries of time and finances well beyond my ken.

In addition, the most accurate option of personally addressing and stamping each ballot paper similarly proved prohibitively expensive. The final results could never claim to be strictly representative of constituent opinion but they would be close enough. Even then the entire process still cost over $25,000, with a good portion coming from my own salary and a generous dollop provided by the Hawke's Bay executive of the National Party. There were no party levies provided to National headquarters that year!

Given all these general inadequacies and inefficiencies the final response rate of over 54 per cent was staggering. Comparable postal ballots for local-body elections had achieved lesser results. Given the opportunity to have a direct input into the voting decisions of their local MP, and given my commitment to be bound by the majority opinion of my constituents, the electorate had responded. It was salutary confirmation that political apathy only exists when the public are frozen out of the process.

The status quo harrumphed its displeasure. Party president Geoff Thompson suggested a cynical sabotaging of National's 1993 election policies (an accusation which stunned me because I was not aware we had any); the *New Zealand Herald* carped that I had redefined the role of an MP as that of a 'mere pollster'; and even the Alliance pronounced themselves mightily unimpressed on the fallacious grounds that the referendum would allow me to escape my pre-election promises. But this was but the prelude to the major denunciation. I was flagrantly flouting the conventional mode of parliamentary representation for populist considerations — which was a bit like accusing Christian Cullen of only playing rugby to score tries and win.

Underpinning all these criticisms was one common thread. The people could not be trusted with democracy. The 'what if?' brigade demonstrated that prejudice in brilliant fashion. From the Prime Minister to the Whips to the party activists to the talkback hosts to the Press Gallery, the 'what if?' question assumed common currency.

'What if your electors told you to gas all Jews?' 'What if your constituents voted to make all Maori second-class citizens?' Or, my personal favourite, 'What if Hawke's Bay voted to win the Ranfurly Shield?' After the requisite Russian eye-rolling I would endeavour to explain patiently that the good sense and common decency of the average New Zealander militated against the excesses described. This was never sufficient answer to stop the detractors. When I went on to explain that the New Zealand public were generally more tolerant and progressive than Parliament on social issues, and point to any number of recent public opinion polls in support of this proposition, I would then meet the real objection.

'Yes,' I recall Jim Bolger stating, 'but the public do not have enough information to make a considered decision.'

'Then provide it to them,' I would reply, only to be met with exasperated sighs and distracted gazing out of the window. Such conversations always tended to expire at about that point. There would be a display of shoulder-raising and mutterings about '...the time, the expense, the logistical difficulties, the impracticality...' and so forth. But the real reason was more sinister.

It suited the political machine — that unholy alliance of party functionaries and technocratic state officials — to keep the process exactly as it was. For it delivered to them their power, their status and their salary. To admit the public into this exclusive club — to share decision-making powers with them — was messy, inefficient and prone to sentiment. Democracy was just the shop window; if you wanted to purchase the goods that was another matter entirely.

So, yes, I was a radical from the political establishment's standpoint.

Yes, I was a revolutionary if that definition encompassed over-throwing the status quo and embracing a wholly different set of political methods and objectives. The 'political establishment' was not confined to the Cabinet, Treasury, Business Roundtable and various metropolitan leader writers. This smug oligarchy included the political parties Labour, the Alliance and ACT, who also sought power for the purpose of imposing their particular bias upon the citizenry; the public-sector bureaucrats, who enjoyed the special privilege of controlling the flow of information to their supposed political masters; the lobby groups, whose specific aims were to gain selfish privilege; the Press Gallery, who fed on the bones tossed their way by the above; and, finally, the mainstream media, who unthinkingly and unhesitatingly accepted the political status quo.

'Direct democracy' threatened each of their cosy sinecures. It not only challenged the existing hierarchies but insisted on the diminishment of vested influence. For that reason the political establishment would always oppose and ridicule the very concept of the public being intimately involved in political decision-making. Loathsome self-interest had swollen into an arrogant autocracy.

If I possessed even a modicum of honour then I must chart an independent course. I might be destined for defeat but I had no choice. Sometimes bowing to the inevitable is only a justification for personal cowardice.

DYING WITH DIGNITY

There is only one real taboo subject left in this modern world. Death.

Human society is ordered by its tacit denial. We invent new policies, new medicines, new surgical methods, even new cults to cheat Death's hand. It is the human condition to reject such finality. Even when that last breath has been purged from our physical bodies a plethora of religious faiths promise the eternal passage of the soul. Our individual essence must never be lost.

Despite all our philosophers and religious leaders, all our writers and our medical geniuses, Western society barely copes with such expiration. Having been taught to exult at our individualism there seems no point to our existence if this petty earthly interlude is snuffed out so quickly. As George Bernard Shaw noted, confronted with such dilemmas Man needed to create God even had He not existed.

Perhaps it is that colossal discomfort with our own mortality that forces us to ignore the shabby demise of so many of our relatives and friends. There is no true beauty in death; it is a cruel vandal that can maim and torture long before its final sting. The older one gets the more one is forced to confront the certainty of that dreadful void. For many there is comfort in religion and the promise of an eternal afterlife; for others there is a general acceptance of Nature's will; for others still there is an obstinate refusal to go quietly, a belief in the Dylan Thomas mantra:

> Do not go gentle into that good night,
> Old age should burn and rave at close of day;
> Rage, rage against the dying of the light.

Acceptance, resignation, refusal — it matters not. Death is universal. It shall claim us all.

This final portal is also an intensely solo journey. Each person approaches their own death in their own way, in their own idiosyncratic style. Maybe the New Age theorists are right — our death gives our life a purpose and meaning.

Even when I was young it seemed obvious that if my childhood God gave me free will and thus the ability to completely stuff it all up then He also presented me with the inherent right to order my own end. It is my life; it must also be my death. That belief has rested within me for much of my first 40 years, even if thankfully dormant.

Unlike others who espouse the voluntary euthanasia cause I can point to no specific emotional or family circumstance that demanded my interest or action. Certainly the lingering deaths of my paternal grandparents went some way towards reinforcing my innate view that death can also rob, smash and vandalise long before the final exit. Certainly the death of my beloved 'Nana' caused my grandfather to lose his will to live. He would subsequently relay to me the cruelty of an existence that delivered physical infirmity, an intense vulnerability and separation from the object of his love. My grandfather's experience was not unique; those last months and even years of existence can be the most unhappy, distressing and lonely of all. When associated with the loss of memory and body functions then each day is its own purgatory.

As both my grandfather's body and mind seeped away I was required to confront this pathetic withering. Whenever I visited him he would express regret that last night's sleep had not proved eternal. Grandpop's earthly release would only come after dementia had stolen the last remnants of his reason. It could have been worse, as evidenced by the vegetative remains of human vanity only too apparent at too many 'rest'-homes I visited as an MP.

Meanwhile two political events — one Australian, one local —

had reinforced my view on the inherent right of an individual to order their own passing. The Northern Territory Assembly had narrowly passed legislation to provide terminally ill patients with the right to end their suffering, and my Hawke's Bay Referendum had delivered a massive four-to-one ratio in favour of voluntary euthanasia. In releasing these results I publicly commented that now was an opportune time for New Zealanders to consider this specific issue of public morality.

And that was it. I thought no more about the matter and initially dismissed any idea that I should pioneer such legislation. Every fibre of my political consciousness suggested danger. The great moral debates over abortion and homosexual law reform had clearly exhausted the chief protagonists and it was an unwritten parliamentary code that conscience issues should be avoided, if only for the political plague they brought down on oneself and one's colleagues. Such advice, if timid, oozed with common sense. If I wanted a real political issue to stump the country with then I should try something else.

However, on returning to my parliamentary offices in Wellington I was greeted with an overflowing in-tray and, stacked beside it, another pile of unopened correspondence. There were literally hundreds of cards and letters from persons either dying of terminal illnesses or those who had nursed or were nursing their parents or partner or child through similar travails. But the correspondence was not just from the terminally ill and their relatives. Plaintive letters from people suffering from motor neuron diseases or confined to immobility by tetraplegia also communicated their views to me — promoting a secondary viewpoint that quality of life was just as important a consideration as the immediate prospect of death.

These individual histories and remembrances were harrowing. Before reading the letters I asked my parliamentary secretary, Louise, to sort them, and would often find her in tears as she sorted through the personal stories and arranged them for my attention. Each day the parliamentary messenger would deliver yet more missives and with them yet more depictions of personal misery. Still I resisted action.

Then one day I glanced at an incoming letter which had a large colour photograph clipped to the open envelope. The photograph showed three young boys, all of primary school age or thereabouts, squealing with delight as the garden hose was played over them on a hot summer's day. Their mother was spraying the water and laughing into the camera, her pale face offset by sparkling green eyes and a riot of auburn curls. Her name was Christine. She was dying of skin cancer and the medical prognosis suggested that she had spent her last family summer on this earth. The doctors had also warned her that this would be no pretty death — the cancer would waste and then rot her body. Christine had reached a tacit agreement with her GP that when the pain became too intense he would supply a sufficient dosage of morphine to hasten her death. But she wanted her children to remember her as she was now — not how she would inevitably become. She wanted to die in the arms of her loving husband, surrounded by her family — in dignity and at peace. Why, she asked me, could she not choose the exact time of her own death and obviate the suffering and hardship of herself and her family?

'Mr Laws,' Christine wrote, 'we dying need your assistance. I want that choice. It is my right. Please help me get it.'

Still I shunned action. Still I baulked at opening my ordered and selfish existence to the obvious discomfort and emotional trauma that must accompany such an enterprise. The Prime Minister and his bullying Caucus I could handle. They did not require me to engage my inner emotions. They had never required me to confront true suffering nor to deal with the overwhelming expectations of others. I wrestled with my weakness for days.

One evening as I sat alone at my desk, immersed in such thoughts, I was interrupted by the telephone. A voice I instantly recognised chortled greetings down the line.

'Mike, you young bugger. How are the salt mines these days?' It was my old rebel colleague Cam Campion.

I returned a similarly abusive greeting and enquired as to Cam's weight now that he had been required to quit the excesses of Bellamy's. A quieter reply this time.

'Not much chance of me putting on any weight at the moment, mate. Can't hold a thing down. I'm dying of bowel cancer.'

My reaction was the normal human response when confronted with such news — an imbalanced and awkward mixture of shock and sympathy. I stammered out my inarticulate regrets but Cam cut them short.

'Don't worry about me. I just phoned to say that you must introduce that euthanasia legislation. If you need a hand — give us a yell.'

At which point I confided to him all my fears and feelings of incompetence and inadequacy when confronting the issue. I was young and healthy — this was not my fight. I lacked political support in the House and could identify no coherent organisation outside it that might proffer the physical or financial resources to assist. I would be officially opposed by the powerful Catholic church, probably most other religious leaders and congregations as well, by the medical profession, the hospice movement and just about every National MP from the Prime Minister down. It was a hopeless cause — I could not possibly hope to win. Cam's reply was typically earthy and direct.

'Mike, there's no other bastard who will do it. It's you or no one. Put yourself in my position and see if you'd want all those pricks telling you how to die.'

We chatted some more and I sought to avoid making a decision that evening by suggesting that I could only make it work if Cam himself was to co-author the private member's bill. To my consternation Cam immediately informed me that he and his wife, Margaret, would begin on the task straightaway. 'Have a draft faxed to you by the morning...' and he rang off.

Campion was right. I had no alternative. Having raised expectations I must now deliver. And even if I did lose, so what? It would be the necessary first step. After all, Venn Young had failed to liberalise the nation's laws on homosexuality but had paved the way for Fran Wilde's later successful move. But more important than any of these things, I had an obligation, a duty. It might have been provided to me by default but it existed nonetheless. No other MP would take this journey to the frontier. It was now my responsibility.

Drafting a private member's bill was one thing. Having it selected for the House's attention was entirely another. Under the arcane system required by Parliament all private member's bills were pooled into a common ballot. Every month or so a couple would be drawn out from a total of around 40 bills — each week merely increased the competition as the number of bills in the ballot swelled. Incredibly, the Death with Dignity Bill was drawn at the very first opportunity.

The bill finally submitted to the Clerk of the House was a hybrid of legislation that had already been passed by the state legislatures of Australia's Northern Territory and Oregon in the United States. Both provided mechanisms by which terminally ill persons could access medical assistance to end their own lives. However, it was still my view that any New Zealand legislation needed to cater for those incurably ill persons whose quality of life was so impaired that each day proved a living agony. This included people suffering from

Alzheimer's disease or senile dementia who had left 'living wills', and those conscious individuals suffering from a motor neurone disease or even permanent tetraplegia. If their choice, after extensive medical and psychological counselling, was to end their suffering, then what right did society have to inhibit their choice?

From the moment I publicly released the Death with Dignity Bill until the final and conclusive vote in the House was a period of less than two months. In that time my every waking moment was taken up with advocating the bill's intent, be it on talkback radio, in public meetings, in television and radio debates, in special articles intended for the print media. By the night the actual vote was taken I had worked myself well beyond the limits of exhaustion.

But what sustained me was the constant stream of letters, faxes, telegrams and telephone calls I received as literally thousands of New Zealanders shared their pain, their grief, their sense of abject hopelessness in either waiting to die or watching their loved ones die in pain, in torment, in total indignity and despair. It was not the death that had prompted their communication; it was the manner of the dying. Always there would be the more important urgings of those who were dying, willing me to continue the fight — to continue their fight so that they were placed in control of their own passing.

During that two-month period, and despite being racked with pain and unable to eat or sleep properly, Cam proved invaluable. He probably undertook as many interviews as I did and every time he spoke gifted some of his diminishing energy. He would goad me forward to greater effort, always with that trademark gruff rural wit that had upset the more genteel in the party.

If anything my desire to continue fighting with every meagre resource I could muster was further prompted by the nature of the opposition that confronted me. A putrid mess of arrogance, ignorance and irrationality.

I could scarcely believe so much darkness could exist in the human condition — that people would simply ignore the pain, the suffering and the free will of the dying and instead impose their own cruel moral straitjacket. In every argument, every debate, every discussion I would raise the reality of the appalling circumstances that confronted the ordinary people who had communicated with me. Incredibly, such experiences were airily dismissed as 'unduly emotional'.

Worse, impractical alternatives were plied like so much snake oil. Hospices were the answer, good palliative care and pain control were available — salves that failed to recognise or comprehend the particular circumstances that confronted my correspondents. If anything such 'solutions' were a palliative for the living, a panacea that could be administered in case the empirical evidence loosened the logic of my protagonists.

'Jesus Christ!' I exploded on one radio talkback when confronted with an impersonal dismissal of the issue. 'These people are dying in agony, begging for release, and you want them to carry on their suffering to please your fucking sense of ethics!' Incredibly this outburst remained confined to that one station.

I was not so fortunate with my next faux pas. In a debate with conservative Catholic MP Bill English on TVNZ's 'Holmes' show the question arose as to the age at which an individual should be able to access my potential legislation. I confirmed that it was intended for those aged eighteen years and above but then chose to raise the issue of a young mother whose child fitted regularly and repeatedly — sometimes up to six or seven times a day. Each time the small boy suffered a seizure he suffered further brain damage and the likely outcome was a permanent vegetative state. In such cases, I opined, the parents should be provided with a similar choice to that intended for the general population.

The backlash, outrage and condemnation that followed was immediate. From Prime Minister Jim Bolger through to the Catholic church through to a host of 'pro-life' fundamentalist activists I was portrayed as a person who wished to 'cleanse' society of its elderly, its sick, its weak. My personality was instantly demonised to rival that of Nazi geneticist Dr Josef Mengele. The 'slippery slope' anti-bill argument had suddenly been delivered a potency far beyond its previous ambit. Heeding the earlier political lesson of my drunken Tauranga episode I made an immediate and televised public apology, but my careless observation would bedevil the rest of the campaign.

It mattered not in the end. The Death with Dignity debate occupied two parliamentary sitting days, having been especially extended to accommodate the sizeable number of MPs who wished to display their conscience, if for the first time. Inevitably their conscience informed them that the voting angels were on the side of the 'Noes'.

Virtually every lobby group rejected the bill. The Catholic church was the principal opponent and although I considered their views both profoundly wrong and theologically suspect I was pleasantly surprised that they were prepared to enter a genuine dialogue on the issue. I could not say the same for the fundamentalist nutters, a number of whom wrote to me (always in capital letters) saying that God had created Life and that only He had the power to take it away, and should I resist God's will with this despicable legislation then they would kill me themselves! The death threats from these so-called pro-lifers began to assume a numbing familiarity.

The New Zealand Medical Association were the really insufferable bores in the whole debate. They were opposed to voluntary euthanasia on the grounds that the medical profession had sworn a Hippocratic Oath to preserve life. They could accept 'passive' euthanasia (switching off life-support machines; withdrawing food and sustenance) but physician-assisted suicide was another matter. Letting the terminally ill end their own lives was far too radical a concept; only trained doctors should have that choice. The arrogance and ignorance of the Medical Association appalled me. I found them to be the most intellectually dishonest of all the opposition.

But those MPs who thought the political advantage lay with the lobby groups were wrong. On the same evening that Parliament voted 61 to 29 against the first reading, a TVNZ/Colmar Brunton poll established that two-thirds of New Zealanders supported voluntary euthanasia as outlined in the Death with Dignity Bill. It was one of those dreadful occasions when you just know that you are absolutely right but must watch justice defeated. As Energy Minister John Luxton surprised his ministerial colleagues and strode into the 'Ayes' lobby he drew me aside.

'Right sentiments — wrong person to promote them,' he observed. Luxton's talented young wife had only recently died of cancer and left a young family, but it still took rare political courage to stand out against the Prime Minister's feverish opposition and join the despised rebel promoting his similarly despised legislation.

That evening Cam and Margaret Campion joined Karen and me for the post-vote 'wake' in my office and pored over the voting sheets. There could be no doubt that many National MPs had taken the opportunity to cast their verdict on Michael Laws as well as the cause of voluntary euthanasia, and I loathed them for this act of moral cowardice. They had allowed their personal and petty dislikes to overwhelm any sense of democracy or compassion.

Of the seven parties represented in the House that evening, only the Labour Party provided a majority to support the bill's introduction (22–15). The National Party were resolutely hostile (six 'Ayes' against 33 'Noes), while the new, 'liberal' United Party, the Alliance (nil–2), ROC and the Christian Democrats' Graeme Lee voted as a negative bloc. New Zealand First were divided — Winston joined me in the 'Ayes' lobby alongside Mike Moore, Helen Clark, David Caygill and the independent-minded Eden Nat Christine Fletcher.

What made the defeat all the more incomprehensible to the public was that the first reading would only have allowed the bill to progress to Select Committee stage. At that point the public could have had their say, and even some opposing medical and religious groups felt uncomfortable at the public being denied this opportunity. It was, I declared, Parliament's 'night of shame'.

Two and half years later I see no reason to resile from that judgement. Parliament proved itself a gutless wonder — an institution unable to confront and debate the great moral issue of our time. They say the House is at its best when debating conscience issues. Not this time. That night Parliament proved itself wholly incapable of even the most cursory contemplation of one of the more acute dilemmas of our generation.

I should not have been surprised. Political morality is, after all, a contradiction in terms.

POSTSCRIPT

Extract from an article published in the *Sunday Star-Times*, 22 October 1995:

CAMERON JOHN CAMPION
Born Wanganui: 4 June 1943
Died 16 October 1995, aged 52 years

Cam Campion was a larger-than-life personality whose short term as the MP for Wanganui underestimated his influence.

A farmer, tourism promoter and a successful sheep studmaster before being elected to Parliament in 1990, his farming instinct and humour were always to the fore.

Cam was not a natural politician. He was far too honest and decent to enjoy the rapier assassins of Wellington. Initially, he floundered in his new environment. It was too quick, too underhand and too complex to allow his easy entry.

But his defining moment was the 1991 Budget — Ruth Richardson's 'mother of all Budgets' — that included the iniquitous superannuation surtax. In an instant he knew the policy to be wrong and a betrayal. Every principle that had ever motivated him into politics was violated.

So Cam became a 'rebel'. He crossed the floor and voted against the government. As he crossed, he caught my eye. 'I'm dog tucker now, mate.' And as far as the National Party was concerned, he was.

But it is his earthy humour that will long be remembered ... Caucus didn't have 'any problems that a good eye-dog can't sort out'; or after having crossed the floor: 'Those bloody Whips would make useless drafters — they've let all the decent buggers get away.' Of one active Cabinet Minister [Maurice Williamson]: 'If he was a horse, we'd geld him.'

His defeat as both a National Party nominee and as an independent in 1993 came as no surprise. Cam simply did not have the guile required of this artificial profession.

But in his dying and in his death, Cam achieved a nobility beyond us all.

In supporting the cause of voluntary euthanasia, Cam shrugged off the debilitating effects of his cancer to fight his last good fight. While most people retreat from the world, Cam took it on.

He confronted all those former colleagues who had mocked and scorned him and won their honest respect as a battler of brave and rare integrity. That they voted down his 'Death with Dignity Bill' did not surprise him.

Cam simply redoubled his efforts and urged myself and others to launch the new public petition that will allow all New Zealanders to have their say on this vital moral issue of our times.

Rising from his sickbed — wracked with pain and pitifully weak with the final effects of the cancer — Cam signed the petition and spoke, haltingly and compellingly, in its support. Those who witnessed that sight will never forget his grim battle to fight down the pain.

When I said goodbye to Cam he could barely reply. He closed his eyes and concentrated upon every word I spoke as if each was precious. When I had exhausted every new piece of news — from politics to rugby — he opened his eyes, took my hand and drew it slowly to him, kissed it and slowly urged: 'Don't ever give up.'

His final words to me summed up this wonderful New Zealand battler. A trier. A doer. A man of humour and honour. He represented all that is best about our country.

Michael Laws MP

– CHAPTER 10 –

FALL

DANCING WITH MIKE

Whatever squalls might have rushed through my political world, I was not the only one being deluged by the unpredictable El Niño of MMP. Jim Anderton's resignation from the leadership of the Alliance proved as resolute as a George Foreman retirement — he could not resist another foray back into the brutality. But just like Foreman the middle was flabby and the one-punch knockout had replaced skilled positioning. A querulous aspect tinged the Gallery's reporting of this Anderton two-step, while Labour MPs stooped to recounting vicious rumours about the Alliance leader's former marriage and disjointed family life.

Mind you, the Labour Party was hardly at the peak of its powers and had begun to assume the public pallor of its new leader — drab, pasty and in desperate need of a Suzanne Paul makeover. Mike Moore continued to nip at any exposed fleshy bits, whether it be railing against the tyranny of the politically correct or attacking Labour's decision to remove the New Zealand flag from their party logo. Moore was beginning to gain a measure of public revenge for past humiliations; as Jim McLay suffered Muldoon, so too was Helen Clark required to endure the slings and arrows of her spurned predecessor.

While Muldoon had rallied his Sunday Club, Moore attempted a similar insurrection with the publication of an irregular newsletter misspelled *From the Center* — a provocative attempt to steer a public middle course between 'the neurotic new left [and] the narrow self-righteous new right'. The most direct criticism was aimed at Labour's head office, who Moore not-so-privately accused of deliberately selecting candidates antipathetic to his continued leadership.

By this time Mike had penned a number of texts, each an elongated essay with a propagandist bent. In an attempt to understand the man better I had read his semi-autobiographical effort, *Hard Labour,* and

281

been struck by his statement that 'the biggest betrayal of Labour principles is to lose and not have any chance of delivering to the people who need us'. If I was ever going to persuade Moore to abandon Labour the emotional impetus would roughly equate to the energy of a NASA lift-off. Merely outlining the academic or political potentialities would never be enough; this man was rooted in a political tradition so intense that his very soul would be rent by the departure. Surely I was pushing the proverbial uphill with a sharp stick.

By the end of 1994 I had almost abandoned hope of convincing Mike to launch a new centrist party — but I had not abandoned hope entirely. Nagging 'what ifs?' ambushed my thoughts at the most inopportune times, and Mike continued to tease with talk of the kind of people, policies and money any new party must husband. Moore had a way of framing hypotheses so that they assumed a kind of virtual reality — at once clear and tantalising. I was becoming uncomfortable — my own political future required imminent attention and, without a Moore-led centre party, every road seemed to lead nowhere.

By now my relationship with National had deteriorated beyond even civil speaking terms and I no longer regularly attended the weekly Caucus. They could go and find someone else to beat up. Strangely enough this pseudo-independence gained me even better access to ministers and their advisers without the usual static interference. I was still nominally a National MP representing the Government on the education, Maori affairs and electoral law select committees, although even these duties had descended to farce.

It is the conventional wisdom that select committees are the workhorses of Parliament — a myth perpetuated by back-bench MPs to justify their salaries. Ostensibly these committees review and scrutinise all the relevant Cabinet and departmental decisions relating to their particular subject area, including policy options, intended legislation and the annual budgetary process. In reality they have deteriorated into a rubber stamp for the minister, making only inconsequential attempts to hold the portfolios to account. Most bureaucrats treat them with a knowing indifference — Iwi Transition Agency head Wira Gardiner was particularly expert at stonewalling any investigation into his department, and I found Education's Maris O'Rourke similarly adept. To be fair to the bureaucrats, they knew precisely where their real masters dwelt — either in the Beehive or at No. 1 The Terrace — and divulging embarrassing information to the select committee was just not worth the hassle.

The only conclusion that could reasonably be inferred from the entire select committee process was that it gave back-bench MPs something to do when they were in Wellington. Committee chairpersons might adopt a self-important strut, but even the doddery Higher Salaries Commission could see through that charade and refused numerous Caucus requests to provide them with increased salaries.

On the other hand, the party whips did receive a slightly increased annual emolument but they were now earning their money. The imminence of MMP had become a profoundly liberating experience for many members — the political equivalent of the pill — and the continual change in the House's seating arrangements reflected the consequent promiscuity.

Despite such wantonness the parliamentary precincts were still agog when the ill-fated group grope of the United Party received its first public outing. Four National MPs, including ACC Minister Bruce Cliffe, had deserted their comfortable homes to shack up with two leading Labour MPs and now independent hussy Peter Dunne. This new commune had decided that the brave new world of MMP demanded a centrist grouping all right, but one with no defining philosophy, policies or even broad principles. No doubt the party was registered in Liberia with its magenta flag of convenience displaying a large U — short for 'taking the uretic'.

On the credit side, Clive Matthewson was forthright in admitting that he had deliberately misled the media by publicly denying any departure from the confines of the Labour archipelago, but rationalised such deception as 'necessary'. The Press Gallery accepted this justification; I should have remembered that and advanced it myself twelve months later.

However, when United leader Matthewson then announced an informal love-in with the Bolger administration, which included placing the ubiquitous Peter Dunne in the Cabinet, the public and media censure was deafening. Another object lesson. Do not get into bed too quickly with the big boys — one's virtue is lost on the first coupling.

During these fraught times I was not the only one to attempt to seduce Mike Moore to a new centrist cause. His two remaining Caucus allies, Geoff Braybrooke and Henderson MP Jack Elder, had both committed their total support and a month's rations towards any new expedition Mike might launch, while my National colleague Peter

McCardle was independently tempting Moore with hints of the greener pastures MMP promised to provide to truly adventurous souls. A third charm offensive was also under way from some of Moore's personal friends and supporters, with former private secretary Clayton Cosgrove, local campaign organiser Tony Day and former Selwyn candidate Ron Mark prominent.

The combined exertions of all these various individuals had their cumulative effect and an initial gathering of the five interested MPs was held in the Yangtze restaurant in Wellington. It was a boisterously entertaining evening, with Moore regaling the company with tall tales and true of his political past and the company responding with confidences about the past election campaign and various Caucus happenings. By the end of the evening there was unanimous agreement that we enjoyed each other's company and owed it to our collective to explore the new party concept.

The legal and administrative requirements for setting up a new political party were relatively straightforward — a party needed to register its name with the new Electoral Commission and later provide its logo, internal constitution and the names of 500 of its financial members. The MPs' group had decided on the strictest confidentiality and approved my suggestion that all initial contact with the Commission be undertaken by a relative unknown whose name would not arouse media suspicion should any information be leaked.

The previous year Sally Kershaw had introduced me to Hastings GP Rosy Fenwicke and we had had an animated and at times acrimonious debate on the dubious ethics of the medical profession. It was about this time that I had publicly chastised Hawke's Bay specialists for effectively farming the public health system for private gain, so my stocks were not high in the general health community. Rosy impressed me as an intelligent and forthright individual — an opinion later reinforced when we appeared together in a festival debate at which she proceeded to humorously dismember my political motivations and link them to any number of personal inadequacies. I arranged for Rosy to meet with Moore and they hit it off immediately, Rosy's earthy and direct humour being matched with an endearing if incisive grasp of social dynamics.

Fenwicke's participation had a palpable influence on Moore. Between us we argued that MMP was not just an electoral system, it was a symbolic public yearning for a more radical shift in the body politic — a yearning for something modern, something relevant,

"LET'S FACE THE MUSIC AND DANCE"

something responsive. Let that be us.

One evening Mike telephoned me and suggested another Chinese meal. Again we met at the Yangtze, this time with just Jack Elder and Peter McCardle for company. Moore looked tense and ill at ease.

'I've had a long chat with Yvonne over the weekend ... and a few of my mates in Christchurch.' He leaned forward, his voice dropping to a raspy whisper. 'I'm not definitely committing myself but I'm pretty certain. Let's try it.'

Peter, Jack and I exchanged uncertain glances and then nervous smiles. This was the most positive Moore had ever been, yet this was still not a definite green light. In turn we each emphasised to Moore the depth of our personal commitment: Jack recounted how he had alienated himself from Labour's post-election Caucus with Moore's blessing; Peter reiterated that he had come to Parliament to get a better deal for the unemployed and he would never get that in National's ranks; I stated that I would stand down from the new party's list to concentrate full time on organisation and policy development. And we all pushed one common theme — Mike's leadership was critical to propel any new party over the MMP five-per-cent threshold and out of the morass of other fledglings. Without him the new party could not work.

'There will only be one window of opportunity for a centre party. This election. If you don't take it then someone else will — and they'll

285

stuff it up. You owe it to New Zealand to make MMP work,' I concluded.

As I sought to persuade Moore with this half-hearted attempt at guilty patriotism I was conscious that Winston Peters was publicly positioning New Zealand First as 'the only centre party' in New Zealand politics. New Zealand First's popular support had halved since the previous election as Peters consumed himself with the Winebox exposé and associated calumnies within the corporate sector. But he still loomed as a potential and dangerous rival for that centre ground.

I had remained on friendly terms with Winston and decided that a linkage between Moore and Peters would be my objective. The combination of the two populist leaders had obvious vote-pulling potential and I did not foresee any great difficulty in deciding the future leadership. Despite the views of the political commentators the two men enjoyed each other's company — not surprising given that they were chain-smokers, liked a drop of the hard stuff and had a great love of political tradition and historical anecdote.

But they also possessed different ambitions. Winston craved political respect; Moore desired an international role. I could be the strategic glue to bind them together.

From the vantage of 1998 the idea of Peters and Moore working in tandem might appear preposterous, but at the time the concept had advantages for all parties and I paraded the possibilities before both men. Neither was dismissive, far from it, even if there were obvious reservations. Moore believed Winston's crusade against big business would severely impede the attainment of financial backing for any pre-election alliance; Winston believed Moore's taint from the Lange/Douglas era was still discernible. But when pressed both men were intrigued by the idea of a possible partnership and accepted my self-appointed role of go-between.

In the meantime our chaotic thoughts begged for administrative order, and thus was formed 'the breakfast club' — McCardle's idea and one which satisfied his penchant for detail. In fact, Peter was a scrupulous detail man — so much so that I was never sure if his initial visions ever survived their later planning. He could become obsessed to the point where the simple preparation of a media release might take an entire day, sometimes two. I ribbed him remorselessly over his pedantry but to absolutely no effect — every word, every nuance, every grammatical detail had to be just so. Even then he would fret over the final product as if it was an immortal judge of his worth.

These were but minor faults for McCardle was a kind and sincere individual, a devout Catholic troubled by the impact that politics had had on his wife and young family but driven by a belief that he had discovered the solution to unemployment. His policy agenda including abolishing the dole, a systematic dovetailing of all job assistance, training and community work programmes, and a properly funded partnership between central government and local communities. Of course it was far too radical (and expensive) for either the Cabinet or the Treasury (even if I had written the rudiments into the party's 1990 manifesto) so McCardle was forced to languish on the back benches for the foreseeable future. He had only the one string to his bow, a political vulnerability he recognised but one which would overshadow any residual loyalty to the National Party.

Our shared desire to formalise the Yangtze commitment required subsequent meetings and allocated tasks for which Peter accepted logistical responsibility, clipboard at the ready. I offered my Khandallah home as the venue for future gatherings — a purely selfish move given my infinite loathing of early starts and the prescribed Friday morning meeting times. Inevitably I would greet my three guests in an array of nightgowns and in partial recompense prepare them a cooked breakfast and provide an endless stream of strong coffee.

The breakfast club met regularly — held together by my bacon and eggs and the promise of mushrooms. The very fact that these meetings were occurring at all made us feel that Moore's commitment was inevitable, and his good-humoured vigour reinforced this assumption. There were just the four of us — Peter, Mike, Jack Elder and me. At Moore's insistence Braybrooke was not invited to participate, ostensibly because of his fluctuating health although I gained the impression that Braybrooke's often voluble enthusiasm was perceived as something of a security risk. Nevertheless whenever I met Geoff he reiterated that 'where Mike goes, I go'.

Jack Elder was the quietest member of the breakfast club if only because he was an infinitely polite man who struggled to get a word in edgeways. He was a former school teacher with conservative social views and a clear belief that the modern Labour Party had gone to the dogs — particularly the lesbian dogs. In the wake of Moore's sacking Jack had also been sacked as the Labour Caucus secretary, and had then vigorously and publicly protested over the selection and ranking of the Labour list, in turn accusing the party of betraying its heritage. Like Peter, Jack had nowhere else to go. We were the four horsemen of the lost apocalypse.

THE DEMOCRATIC COALITION

In July 1994 both Moore and I received handwritten letters from former Socred/Democrat leader Bruce Beetham offering his 'New Zealand Centre Coalition' as the organisational base for any party we might be contemplating. Beetham's group comprised three minuscule 'parties' who had banded together for warmth — the cult Social Credit, the last fragments of the New Zealand Party (those who had escaped the National embrace and were not circulating the asteroid belt), and anti-union march organiser Tania Harris' spectral United effort, which was linked to the equally bizarre Confederation of United Tribes. It was a political knackers yard, where minor celebrities of yesteryear had been laid to rest only to resurrect themselves after the ghoulish fashion of Stephen King's *Pet Sematary*.

There were also conditions to be met before we could receive the Beetham imprimatur, including senior list rankings for the leaders of each of these cargo cults and the free passage of their collective membership into our proposed party. Mike and I chuckled at these Greek gifts and wondered at the man's cheek.

At least I thought it was cheek. But after a number of badgering telephone calls I reluctantly met the former high-flier and discovered him to be pathologically serious. I brutally informed him that his gathering had little to recommend itself to any proposed centre party but we would keep his offer in mind. In turn Beetham bristled and reminded me that he too had once been an MP and that legions of fans were but waiting for the word to relaunch the Bruce experience. The man had missed his vocation. He should have been the host of a TV shopping channel, such was the unfortunate mix of self-confidence and flawed product. But my overwhelming feeling was one of historical astonishment — that this man had once commanded 21 per cent of the popular vote in a general election. Thank God there had been no MMP in 1981.

Ironically, Beetham's scout club had flogged the most obvious name for any centre party and we were hard-pressed to come up with an alternative. Mike wanted the word 'coalition' in the title to express a general appeal to all sectors of the community; I was the leading proponent of a simple description like the 'Peoples' Party', which drew hoots from the others, who assumed various eastern European accents whenever I raised it.

'Why don't you just go the whole hog,' Moore would laugh, 'and call it the Peoples' Party of the Liberation Front of the Popular Movement?'

In the end we settled on a nondescript compromise — 'the Democratic Coalition' — and began work on the rather more critical task of sifting through our various ideas to work out a set of defined principles. On one thing we were unanimously agreed. There must be no repeat of Matthewson's messy launch of the parliamentary United Party; we must hit the ground running, with founding principles, an outline of policy initiatives, regional contact persons, an 0900 membership number — the works.

To assist us with our planning a special weekend was set aside in August 1995 and hosted by Moore and Cosgrove in Christchurch. Apart from the MPs, Rosy Fenwicke and Ron Mark were prominent and vocal contributors, and there was robust debate over policies and guiding principles, with a particularly animated discussion on no-nonsense ways in which to break the cycle of failure in lower socio-economic families. My basic argument — that it was too late for this generation and we should start intervention techniques on behalf of the next — drew surprising support, with Moore offering cautious wisdom from the sidelines. By the end of the weekend Mike had upped his level of emotional preparedness to 'around 95 per cent' — a figure that still made me nervous and reinforced my nagging scepticism.

The Christchurch meeting also settled on the 'aims and objects' of this new Democratic Coalition, with very little debate over their final form; in retrospect, because they were so bland and inoffensive. We would leave the truly wounding stuff to any election policy detail. Our resident family Catholic McCardle insisted that the number one priority of the Coalition should be to 'protect and promote the family unit', while my more anarchic emphasis on 'the rights and liberty of the individual' occupied a lesser rung, providing an inherent social contradiction.

Nevertheless the 'Aims & Objects of the New Zealand Democratic Coalition' were unanimously agreed and we pronounced ourselves pleased with their final format. For those who savour such things, the declaration read:

'To select candidates of ability and integrity for election to the New Zealand House of Representatives who accept and endorse the following principles, aims and objectives:

1. To protect and promote the family unit;
2. To respect and uphold the rights and liberty of the individual;

3. To promote equality of opportunity regardless of age, gender, ethnicity, socio-economic, cultural or religious background;
4. To provide economic and social policies that allow individuals to maximise their potential for both private and the common good;
5. To ensure the equality of all persons before the law...;
6. To protect New Zealand's territorial integrity and ensure this nation's independence in all international forums;
7. To promote co-operation and tolerance within the wider community;
8. To provide and promote an open and competitive economy that recognises and rewards enterprise and endeavour;
9. To provide policies that protect the weak and the vulnerable within our community and seek to empower those individuals to reach their potential;
10. To provide for and actively encourage the maximum possible participation in all aspects of local and central government decision-making;
11. To create an educated, enlightened, enterprising and responsible society and pursue policies to that end;
12. To provide an efficient, effective and accountable public sector that services the education, health and welfare needs of the wider community and is politically neutral and free of ideological bias;
13. To provide all members of the New Zealand Democratic Coalition with the opportunity to contribute to the organisation, policy and strategy of the Coalition.'

It had been my responsibility to draft the final words of the party's constitution so I had taken the liberty of adding a section encouraging enhanced public decision-making as an obvious introduction to 'direct democracy', while all the MPs, and especially Moore, insisted on a commitment to a truly neutral civil service. One day, I suppose, we might get one. Rosy was formally appointed the party's secretary-general and the weekend concluded with most participants confident that Moore would soon formalise his commitment and lead our band of disparate adventurers into the next election.

Moore had also arranged for one of his market research buddies to test public perceptions about the proposed party and probe the underlying popularity of leading political personalities, carefully burying such questions in a wider poll so that no direct connection would be made. The initial results confirmed that the Democratic Coalition would be a player in the election stakes; eight per cent of those polled declared blind support for a Moore-led vehicle while a further 25 per cent would 'strongly consider' voting for the Coalition, depending on its final policies. These results clearly discouraged Moore and I gained the impression that he had been expecting more favourable returns. Over and over he would mutter, 'We'd have to do a lot of work — and I mean a lot of work.'

These comments again pricked my doubts. I took it as read that any campaign by a new party would require a huge reservoir of activist energy, but Mike seemed to be hinting that his tank had definable limits.

I voiced my concerns to Elder and McCardle, who reassured me, on the basis of their private discussions with Moore, that my fears were groundless.

'He's got no option,' Peter would soothe. In fact, Moore had plenty of options — retirement from politics; being repatriated to the Labour front bench; assuming the role of Labour's pesky 'conscience' — but I understood McCardle's drift. Politically, the sanest option for Mike was to transform his current popular support into the position of post-election arbiter. A TV3/CM Research poll had even declared that Moore would be more trusted in that role than any other political figure. I continued to work for the Democratic Coalition cause and pray that sanity prevailed — the true triumph of desperate hope over considered judgement.

Meanwhile we were collectively gathering the names of 500 financial members for the purpose of legally registering the party with the Electoral Commission. McCardle, Elder and I signed up most of our electorate executives, our families, our friends and anybody else who happened to stray within the proximity of a pen, while Tony Day and Ron Mark beavered away in Christchurch. Perhaps the most productive gatherer though was Rosy Fenwicke, who amply demonstrated the desire of many previously non-political middle New Zealanders for something fresh and invigorating. By the end of 1995 over 600 signed forms rested in the bottom drawer of my parliamentary desk.

The incredible thing about this entire operation is that not one form, not one copy of the 'Aims & Objects', not one whisper found its way to the Press Gallery and thence to media purview. Amazingly, we had attained both the level of secrecy we required and the requisite information to satisfy the Electoral Commission. McCardle had overseen the drafts of various policy papers; design work on a suitable logo had been commissioned; membership criteria had been fulfilled; the party's principles had been established; key individuals had been identified and approached as regional contacts for the impending launch. The rocket was on the runway; the lift-off hour approached.

In the last week of the 1995 parliamentary session Moore again met with Elder, McCardle and me in my parliamentary office to discuss final timing. By now Mike had pronounced himself '99 per cent certain' and had outlined a mini-referendum campaign he intended to run in Christchurch in the New Year to gather local support for his departure from Labour. I had provided Moore with details of my Hawke's Bay Referendum as background to this venture, thinking that at the very least I had gained an indirect convert to the direct democracy cause.

At that meeting the launch date of the Democratic Coalition was discussed in further detail, with the first week of the 1996 parliamentary session being pencilled in as ideal. As we tore at the tabs of our beer cans and toasted each other's health an air of boyish excitement and anticipation filled the room, as if all the Christmas presents awaited unwrapping.

Such optimism received a considerable jolt when that weekend's Sunday Star-Times carried an article by respected Gallery journo Jane Clifton headlined 'Moore vows to stay in Labour'. A flood of nervous telephone calls disturbed my usual Sunday rest as McCardle, Elder and Fenwicke rang in quick succession. What the hell was going on?

In Clifton's piece Moore acknowledged significant backing from former Labour workers and businessmen — but to set up a policy ginger group within Labour. There were numerous contradictions within his quoted remarks — on the one hand, he was preparing to tell Labour Party president Michael Hirschfeld to stuff the front-bench offer; on the other he was moaning about faceless friends and businesspeople 'loading the guilt on and saying that I should do something'. From a man who privately professed to be '99 per cent certain' such public equivocations were startling to say the least.

I managed to convince Moore that allowing the impression created in the Sunday Star-Times to remain unanswered would in turn provoke follow-up stories from other media. Besides, I urged, do we really want a repeat of the Matthewson fiasco? Mike accepted this advice and drafted a personal statement for immediate release. If anything the press release discomforted me further. While acknowledging that 'an exploratory committee' had undertaken political and strategic research on his behalf Moore concluded, 'I still believe Labour is worth fighting for. If I thought the fight was impossible then the only honourable course would be to leave.'

This whole exchange proved critical in determining my own actions. I had now reached the conclusion that Moore would always hover between choices and that he possessed neither the emotional application nor the crazy energy required to leave home. He might regard himself as a political cuckold but he remained in love with his unfaithful Labour no matter what. The spirit was willing — the flesh was a craven coward.

That Sunday I demanded of myself a final assessment of the Democratic Coalition's future. Yes or no. I chose to end the charade.

For I also knew something else. Even if Moore did choose to make the break over the festive period his commitment would be like a kind of transmittable leprosy — parts of the campaign would disease and wither as Mike pitched constant battle against his own judgement. A general election campaign and a new party requires a focused fanatic — Moore could never be that individual. Unlike Anderton and Peters, he lacked the necessary desperation and the resolute independence to take that fateful leap; the self-will to breach his fears was absent.

Which was just as well because the Democratic Coalition did not deserve life. We had cobbled together a centrist Frankenstein from bits of our personalities and parts of other philosophies, with the sole purpose of holding the balance of power in the aftermath of the MMP election, to be a good steward. We were no better than the misguided opportunists who had stitched together the mutant United beast. I had become a part of the problem I had sworn to combat — no longer a solution or even its shadow. We had seduced ourselves into believing that power was an end in itself which could be justified by a few random policies and our personal disenfranchisement from the political mainstream.

I confessed as much to Karen, who listened quietly and then proffered the infinitely wise counsel that I must either strike out on my own with an honest radicalism or retire from politics altogether.

'You'll never be happy compromising your vision for others. Either put it up — put it all up for public view — or walk away. But living in your limbo, Michael, is not living at all.'

I have an infinite capacity to recall excellent counsel but an equal and infuriating capacity to ignore it. That evening I telephoned Winston Peters on his mobile.

'Win, mate,' I announced. 'I'm in.'

If Moore was not going to be MMP's midwife then that left only one other player. It might be second choice but it was the only choice left. Peters laughed down the line. 'Not a bad Christmas present, Laws,' he drawled.

Even as we spoke I began to query my decision (this Moore disease was catching). What if Mike did commit during the Christmas break? What if his Christchurch friends could break down his remaining resistance? Had I been too premature in dismissing the Coalition? That Christmas my family coped with my distracted aloofness, having learnt from bitter experience to let me wrestle with my thoughts alone. Which was just as well because I had yet to inform my Coalition partners of my imminent departure, while my commitment to New Zealand First had all the stability of a summer jelly. Such an uncertain state of mind invites disaster — stranded within a maze of competing anxieties I was bound to make the wrong decision.

But why Moore and not Peters in the first place?

Initially, that answer seemed obvious. New Zealand First had already been in existence for three years, run an election campaign, decided its philosophical framework, constructed policy, established an organisational structure and chosen its leaders. Joining a party that had been created by others and over which my influence must inherently be indirect would be a risky venture — I would be inheriting the messes and mistakes of others. In addition, I was acutely aware of Winston's foibles — his obsessive secrecy, his disinclination to search the policy frontiers, his poor grasp of detail, a general disregard for administrative efficiency. Because of his refusal to delegate respons- ibility he would always be the prey of his closest advisers — reliant on their information, perceptions and judgements. I would not be joining as a powerful staffer but as a high-profile MP with a welter of distracting responsibilities.

But there were other concerns that had presented themselves during this period — the Selwyn by-election fiasco, with volatile buffoon Tim Shadbolt drafted as the last-minute candidate; the obvious paucity of able party spokespeople; the criminal arrest of the nominated New Zealand First representative on the observers' team to monitor South Africa's first free elections; Winston's own erratic television performances; and finally, a disturbing conversation I had had with Ian Shearer, the outgoing party president. Dr Ian Shearer had been Winston's star convert for the 1993 general election, a former National Cabinet Minister relatively untainted by the Muldoon legacy. Despite his experience Shearer had fared poorly in the hotly contested Onehunga seat and in its wake assumed the key organisational role of party president. His wife, Cheryl — a loud, large woman with strong opinions that could easily stray into the dogmatic — had been appointed New Zealand First's office manager at Parliament.

I could well believe rumours that Cheryl's brusque manner had put her offside with various staffers but also sympathised with her husband's defence that she was merely trying to create order out of systemic chaos. One evening in mid-1994 I had received a call from Shearer and a request for an urgent meeting; within minutes he had bustled into my office and closed the door.

'I only have one question to ask of you, Michael.' I nodded tentative approval. 'Are you joining New Zealand First?'

Shearer obviously read the puzzlement in my expression. In the world of parliamentary politics such queries are usually framed behind hours of previous and inconsequential pleasantries and the hint of inspecific positioning. Shearer continued.

'Well, it's like this. If you are, I'll probably stay. If not then I'm off. I've had enough of their lack of professionalism — even their basic grasp of what's right and what's not.' He leaned back on the couch, his demeanour conveying a desperate dissatisfaction.

Given such a blunt enquiry I felt moved to provide an equally direct reply. By this stage the first mutual teasing with Moore had begun and the initial signs suggested promise.

'No, not in a million years,' I stated. 'I agree with you. It's a thoroughly amateurish outfit. Winston may be a great frontperson but he doesn't have a clue about handling staff or developing an organisation.' Shearer nodded his agreement, rose and shook my hand. Within days he had announced his resignation, along with that of his wife. But that was not the end of the matter.

Promising a 'swinebox' of incriminating evidence, the Shearers alleged financial impropriety within Peters' parliamentary offices and the gross misuse of parliamentary mail and travel privileges. A subsequent internal investigation failed to substantiate these claims but the whole incident left an unpleasant odour.

From what Shearer had told me the entire New Zealand First party organisation was the ectoplasm of Winston's personality, exactly mirroring all his strengths and weaknesses. Jumping into the middle of that psychic morass would be taking an imprudent risk — a far greater gamble than launching a new party under the leadership of Mike Moore. I took no satisfaction in later having such fears proven correct, for by now I had purposefully blinded myself. If I wanted a political career past 1996 then I had no other option.

My corruption was now complete. I had become as opportunistic, as expedient, as politically vain as the system I loathed and publicly condemned. This profession had subtly but inexorably exposed my own ethical inadequacies — I equated the public good with my personal good; compromised my own beliefs for the promise of post-election power and influence; and had proven unwilling to test my own beliefs in the public arena, instead choosing to hide behind the skirts of more established personalities.

My fall was complete. It was just a case of waiting to hit the ground.

INTO THE PARLOUR

On a Thursday afternoon early in the New Year of 1996, a critical meeting was held in Mike Moore's office in the plush, refurbished Parliament Buildings. There were just four participants — Moore and Elder, who had flown in specially, McCardle and me. We had all agreed that today was D-day — final decision day.

'OK, Mike. Are we on or off?' asked McCardle.

Moore's reply was depressingly familiar. More encouraging remarks mixed with more doubts. He needed more time — had to properly plan his departure.

'It's just not that simple,' he complained. I could have pre-written the script.

I interrupted. 'Listen guys — I'm afraid I can't wait any longer. I've decided to take up Winston's offer and join New Zealand First.'

A stunned silence greeted this announcement, although I thought I saw a flash of relief in Moore's eyes. Eventually, he leaned forward.

'Ah ... well, that's it then.'

I then proceeded to raise my various justifications — that my withdrawal did not mean the DC was dead; that I would covertly assist in policy and planning; that my aim was to matchmake between New Zealand First and a Moore-led party in a post-election hiatus; that we could share information and target different voting groups.

Moore saw through such apologetic scheming in an instant.

'It doesn't work without you. We need your antenna, your sense of the moment. I can't make it run without your rat cunning.'

I should have been superficially flattered but for the first time I flashed anger.

'Don't you ever blame this on me, Mike. I'm out simply because you're not in. You've left it too late and I'm not stuffing up my future for you or anyone.'

With that I made my apologies and stalked from the room. McCardle later told me that he and Elder had attempted to convince Moore that my departure counted for nought. Maybe it was even a blessing, they ventured, everyone else was still committed, the planning could continue. To no avail. This was a perfect opportunity to bail out and Moore grabbed the parachute and leapt.

I had little doubt that Elder could now be recruited to the New Zealand First camp with the Democratic Coalition dead in the Petri dish. But McCardle rejected all overtures. He would stay with National and settle for back-bench impotence, drawing my facetious response that when Peter died he would bypass purgatory having already experiencing that bodyless limbo with the Nats.

Meanwhile I had met with Winston to discuss my future role within New Zealand First and the various timing issues relating to my proposed 'defection'. From these discussions it became apparent that Winston's primary concern related to policy development within the party although he also expressed unease about the preparedness of the party organisation for the coming general election. It was agreed that my role would be to oversee the strategic direction of New Zealand First while also co-ordinating the parliamentary unit's research and press team. The election campaign preparations were the party's problem.

Now it was time to meet the prospective in-laws.

My first meeting with the inner circle of the New Zealand First organisation took place at the Northern Club in Auckland and proved welcoming, if slightly fraught, for reasons that would soon become apparent. Apart from Winston and deputy leader Tau Henare, I was introduced again to Winston's personal assistant, Sarah Neems, new party president Doug Woolerton, treasurer Kay Urlich, legal representative and close Peters confidant Brian Henry, and parliamentary staffers Terry Heffernan and Rex Widerstrom. There was also a mystery participant whose identity was considered so hush-hush that I wondered if the Second Coming was really at hand. Instead, former TVNZ journalist and *The Paradise Conspiracy* author, Ian Wishart, appeared — a sufficient reminder that the Winebox hearing was considered a critical factor in New Zealand First's strategic deliberations. Winston opened the meeting, extolled my political virtues and duly required me to articulate an outside perspective of New Zealand First — its strengths and weaknesses, its future opportunities and dangers. I attempted to give a brief overview without appearing unduly knowing (never an easy task) but perceived an underlying tension that could not solely be explained by my presence. Plainly there were personality conflicts within the room and, with one obvious exception, they did not appear to involve me.

The exception was press secretary Rex Widerstrom, who displayed the least subtle body language I had seen since my mass shunning by teenage females at school socials. It was so direct it was comical, and I was tempted to confess to Rex that, yes dammit, I had impregnated his pet rabbit just so he could legitimate his hostility. Widerstrom was a rotund, oleaginous perspirant who looked older than his 35 years, having fashioned a previous career as a reporter and provincial talkback host. It was clear that he deeply resented my intrusion into his sphere of influence, and this distaste infected all our subsequent dealings — even to the ridiculous extreme of secretly taping our earliest conversations.

It also quickly became clear that New Zealand First's parliamentary offices were a complete shambles. The lack of professionalism was obvious, with poisonous personal relationships undermining even the most mundane daily transactions. Brian Henry cautioned me against a Democrat conspiracy involving Heffernan, former leader Gary Knapp and former Alliance candidate Chris Leitch, who intended to promote Knapp and his supporters to key leadership roles within the party. The ever laconic Doug Woolerton reported similar anxieties and made it equally plain that both Widerstrom and Heffernan should be removed from Peters' personal staff. In his turn Terry Heffernan poured out a long tale of woe about his broken romance with Sarah Neems, claiming that she had ditched him en route to a holiday in the United States, while also blaming Brian Henry for fuelling Winston's inherent paranoia. Sarah, to her credit, 'thought it best' that I should be aware that Heffernan could not be trusted and considered the secretarial staff to be slack and unprofessional. She was right.

I had walked into a madhouse. No, not true. I had walked into a dysfunctional madhouse.

After this mass bleating I could only assume two things; first, I was expected to correct these abuses; and second, Winston would not. Each complainant perceived me as a potential ally for their personal agenda, an impression I relayed to Winston without receiving a flicker of reaction. His lack of interest in the parliamentary unit's staffing problems amazed me until I realised that Peters' legendary distaste for social intimacy precluded him from addressing even the most pressing of difficulties. In short, Winston found it impossible to front up to any individual and inform them that their conduct or work standards were unacceptable; rather than decisively settle any staffing difficulties his answer was to postpone any action in the vain hope that the problem might resolve itself. It never did.

Of course, there must always be an exception to prove the rule — and there was. Sarah Neems. Winston had no difficulty at all in chastising Sarah for the smallest of errors; it was as if Neems was the resident scapegoat. Yet Sarah refused to buckle or cower under his verbal attacks and would return any criticism with often conflagratory interest. It was a daily Punch and Judy Show — except that these assaults rarely bruised and were forgotten an hour later. It was the weirdest relationship I have ever observed — part fury, part respect and part affection.

Sarah's role within the office was also intangible. Her primary task was obviously to try and get some semblance of order out of the equally dysfunctional New Zealand First party machine, but she scripted speeches, drafted the occasional media release and provided sensible if unsolicited strategic advice. Winston had become Sarah's life — she devoted herself absolutely to his future. Which was just as well because apart from her mixture of Canadian charm and selfless devotion there seemed no other intelligent influence at work within the organisation.

There were two other difficulties that made themselves obvious in the first few days. The two young researchers, Deborah Morris and Amy Bardsley, lacked a strategic focus for their endeavours, while the various party spokespeople were only marginally co-ordinated, poorly briefed and wholly inadequate for the purpose of advancing election-year policy. No wonder Winston had greeted me with open arms — he needed someone, anyone, to co-ordinate his parliamentary and policy teams solely because he had neglected to manage

these tasks himself. I soon came to understand that the entire party reflected Winston's character — ad hoc, mercurial, diffuse and wholly undisciplined.

The role of deputy Tau Henare was equally ill-defined and he was clearly suspicious of my friendship with Winston and any consequent influence I might have.

Privately, Henare was grumbling that the party had sufficient strength and talent to resist the overtures of opportunistic latecomers and I felt it necessary to disabuse him of any notion that I might covet his position. However, misgivings about Tau were common within the party, with senior figures condemning his political support of the Moutoa Garden occupiers. For all that I came to like Henare — he had a healthy disrespect for parliamentary tradition offset by an impish and self-deprecatory Maori humour. A former trade union official, Henare had found his way to New Zealand First only after it became obvious that the Alliance preferred the veteran Matiu Rata as their Northern Maori candidate; thus his political views were instinctively left-wing although with insufficient conviction and research to predominate in any policy forum. Winston once observed to me that Henare was 'not a detail man', which had me arching an eyebrow and speculating as to the proximate position of that particular trait.

Terry Heffernan was a detail man. The former Democrat and New Zealand First candidate had cut his parliamentary teeth as a researcher, strategist and press secretary for the Socred/Democrat duo of Bruce Beetham and Gary Knapp. He was an intense and careful individual who seemed to gain inordinate pleasure from the circuitous minutiae of Parliament but had clearly made himself invaluable to New Zealand First with his understanding of House procedure and protocol. Unfortunately he had allowed the failed Neems romance to pollute his political judgement, while his association with the Knapp faction rang alarm bells at senior levels within the party.

It was the partnership of Heffernan and Widerstrom that had intimately assisted Peters with his populist anti-immigration crusade of early 1996, with Heffernan providing the research and Widerstrom the rhetoric. In fact, the idea had been germinated by the departing Shearers, but these earlier attempts to kick-start New Zealand First out of its polling doldrums had failed to ignite media attention despite similar emphasis on the perils of foreign ownership and a particularly ill-considered attempt at hijacking an Anzac Day commemoration the previous year.

However, the flood of Asian migrants, particularly into suburban Auckland, excited enough community resentment to resurrect these nationalist themes with the requisite anti-immigrant twist. Never underestimate the capacity of ordinary New Zealanders to be upset by poor driving habits; the new Asians with their 'ostentatious homes' and conspicuous wealth became the new social enemy of ever-envious middle New Zealand.

I have a theory about the popularity of this Peters' crusade. It was not the speeches that provoked the public support so much as the reaction of the political and media establishment. The enraged denunciations of Prime Minister Bolger and the outpouring of editorial vitriol gave Winston's utterances daily bursts of pure political oxygen. He was not only perceived to be brave to voice the petty prejudice of the ordinary citizen but also to be the unfair target of an unpopular government. This heady mixture was further rarefied by the almost daily revelations at the Winebox Inquiry, which suggested that Winston had been right all along; the corporate sector was involved in the systematic rip-off of the public purse.

Shortly before my public defection to New Zealand First the party had polled eight-per-cent support in the monthly TVNZ/Colmar Brunton opinion survey. By the next poll that support had doubled a meteoric rise that I facetiously attributed to my arrival. In turn the poll ratings served to further provoke the Prime Minister and a factory of political commentators to denounce Peters for his covert racist crusade; which ironically further profiled Winston and allowed him to draw attention to the general fear of many that New Zealanders were becoming 'serfs on our own land'.

Winston's reaction to this media attention hovered between ebullience and ecstasy.

'We're on our way, Laws — we're going back where we belong,' and the Peters grin would spread beyond his face and absorb all in the room. I congratulated myself on my sense of political timing and redoubled my efforts to win over McCardle. Another couple of convert MPs would boost the party's profile even further and bring in necessary parliamentary presence and experience. New Zealand First had relaunched itself to spectacular effect but the momentum required constant firing if the journey was to continue; the Alliance's declining stock had proved that the fall to earth could be every bit as dramatic as the original take-off.

Despite Peters' heady optimism my fears remained. The party was still in total disarray, held together only by the sheer will of Winston's public personality. My job was simple; to build up some substance that might support the current illusion of a leader and a party who appeared to know what they were doing. The parlous state of the organisation, the absence of any campaign planning, the virtual policy void, the non-selection of constituency candidates, the ordering of the party list, the obvious lack of finances... This was not mere illusion; this was magic. Somehow New Zealand First had attained a public credibility wholly unmatched by its central being — sooner or later the facade would be exposed. There would now be a desperate rush against time, the prying media and our political opposition to fill in all the gaps or face humiliating exposure.

But the humiliation, the exposure and the failure would come sooner than I could ever have imagined. The malevolent lightning would not strike the endangered New Zealand First — it would sear the earth at precisely my personal co-ordinates. I had tempted the fates for too long. Retribution was on its way.

THE ANTOINETTE BECK AFFAIR

During the interminable period of indecision that plagued the Democratic Coalition I received a flash of inspiration that was misread as illuminating insight. It was not a dissimilar experience to those intuitive sparks imparted during a particularly deep cannabis stone. At the time it is as if your mind has stumbled onto the edge of God's wisdom — when sobriety returns it quickly becomes apparent that one has been wallowing in gibberish. Coleridge may have been whacked out when writing 'The Rime of the Ancient Mariner' but I will venture vast reams of other material never survived the editor's bonfire.

Sadly, in the strange world that is politics, the equivalent of reefer madness can present itself to even the most conservative and boring of individuals. The idea of the United Party was one example of this phenomenon. My decision to enter local-body politics was another.

I had no excuse. Karen warned me that getting involved in the petty drudgery of sewers, potholes and playgrounds would distract and dull my political senses. She often reminded me of my not so private observations that those who enter local-body politics had twice the ego but only a fraction of the talent of those who entered the national scene. But I had a cunning plan.

With the MMP boundaries vaporising my Hawke's Bay seat I could ensure that I retained a constituency base by standing for the Taradale ward of the Napier City Council and so have around 20,000 people to act as my personal political barometer. In addition, I toyed with the prospect of retiring from national politics and succeeding the incumbent Alan Dick as Napier's mayor. It was only after I had been elected to the council, as the highest-polling representative, that I realised my predicament.

Any thoughts of one day standing for mayor were banished by the sheer tedium of council work, while the petty personality conflicts that masqueraded as political debate had an air of the psychotic about them. In that respect I am not entirely sure Napier's council is unique — I think local-body politics attracts the truly petty like no other profession. I had always thought the capital's public servants a shiftless lot until I was introduced to the much lesser species collectively known as local-government bureaucracy. I developed an almost instant respect for Alan Dick — that he could wade in such civic effluent and still produce a coherent city strategy was an impressive feat.

The previous council had found itself in the middle of a pseudo-philosophical dispute between allegedly imperialist and allegedly minimalist forces. The virulence of this contest had resulted in five incumbent councillors losing their seats and the mayor being narrowly returned in a three-way contest. The real problem was communication

— Dick and his supporters lacked proper media skills and thus could be easily outflanked by opposing forces. But the election had not ended the tension — two of the council's fiercest critics, millionaire debt collector John Harrison and professional pest Kerry Single, had been elected and joined resident council curmudgeon and property landlord Harry Lawson as an anti-Dick bloc. Other odd personalities had also been elected to council, and thus Karen's prescience was confirmed at every council meeting; a zombie conference would be deemed an intellectual retreat in comparison.

Within weeks a series of destructive leaks and personality disputes had undermined any attempt at group collaboration, and I was drawn into the action by the very nature of my personality and profile. I discovered that the privately owned bi-weekly newspaper, the *Hawke's Bay Sun*, had an unnatural relationship with Harrison and a similarly unnatural obsession with any titbit of minor disagreement that might stray into the council's business. The newspaper had been started up by a group of Hastings businessmen with strong National party and ACT sympathies, while the editorial emphasis of the paper favoured local ACT personalities and viewpoints.

The Antoinette Beck affair that prompted my resignation as both a city councillor and an MP seems such a piddling irrelevance in hindsight. Of course, it is always the trifling that trips in politics, if only because it is so easily translated for public attention. I had discovered this rough rule of thumb when working as a researcher for Peters in Opposition; we would often muse that the media regarded a $5000 Maori rip-off as more newsworthy and sensational than a $50-million white-collar corporate fraud. Part of the answer was that the public could identify with smaller sums of money and measure them against their weekly wage, or the price of their car or their house. But start talking seven-digit numbers and their collective eyes would glaze over. It became unreal because there was no ready reference against which to measure the defalcation. Mind you, that was only part of the answer — the rest being blatant racism.

In an attempt to improve the council's falling image I had suggested a civic working party (headed by me) to look at the ways in which boring council information could be transmitted directly to the residents without the miserly filter of local media or the malevolent interpretation of the critics. As part of the working party's duties it was decided to conduct a poll of Napier residents to attain a better understanding of public concerns. One of the seventeen questions

measured people's awareness of councillors in their respective wards
— earlier indications had suggested an astonishing level of ignorance.
Such a query was an invitation to disaster given the pettiness of some
of the councillors and, sure enough, Harrison and Single soon began
fussing and fulminating over the results. In general awareness was
uniformly poor, with less than half of my own ward residents able to
identify me as their council representative. But the point had been
proven — a recognition gulf separated the average councillor from
the average resident, which rather dented one's vanity.

A similar gulf also separated some councillors from polling reality;
I should have provided them with a dictionary so they could understand the difference between 'awareness' and 'popularity', although
with Harrison, Single et al. a negative Pavlovian response had long
greeted anything I was involved in. For some reason they intensely
disliked, indeed, even hated me — a reaction made even more
remarkable considering I had never once dated any of their daughters.

Despite the working party commissioning the poll there was
insufficient money in the council budget to pay a professional polling
company to undertake the exercise. Quotes started at around $14,000
and soared above the $20,000 mark, with the chief executive making
the task even harder by deciding that neither council staff nor premises
should be used to reduce the costs. As a consequence I called in a
whole series of personal favours to have the thing completed in the
quickest possible time for the least amount of money. My electorate
office was to be used as the polling base; I asked Tania Wright to
recruit and supervise the necessary telephonists; I requisitioned Karen's
part-company Piece of New Zealand to handle the necessary PAYE
paperwork; I asked my parliamentary secretary, Louise, if she would
mind doing some extra typing; and I sought out my former research
colleague, Paul Sherriff, to complete a cursory analysis of the initial
raw results. In the end the whole exercise cost just over $2000, with
the five telephonists, Tania and Paul being scantily remunerated for
their time and effort.

Then all hell broke loose.

The whole polling saga occupied around six weeks and provoked
the most lurid, vicious and hysterical reaction I have ever experienced
or witnessed. It was as if my every personal and political enemy had
decided this was their one and only opportunity to get their own
back for past grievances, real or imagined. There was no shortage of
these individuals — the Prime Minister, National Caucus MPs, the

fledgling ACT madness, my city council opponents, various media hacks, even an old girlfriend — all were involved at one stage or another in seeking to publicly and privately denigrate my actions in connection with this minor poll.

And under that pressure I made the greatest mistake of all — I loaded the shotgun, cocked the trigger, gave them the weapon and defied them to shoot. At the end of it all both my career and my public reputation were smattered in great bloody chunks all over the wall. But that would not be the worst of it.

No, the greatest heartache was that my actions harmed my wife, my family and my friends. I did not give two stuffs for the blathering judgements of either media or politicians; I had never considered their views particularly important and I was not about to start now. But my stupidity and my mistakes had affected those I most loved and cared about. Watching Karen sob in frustration and disappointment at my actions destroyed every last vestige of arrogance and hubris in my frame; I felt guilty then — I feel guilty now. I will be making it up to her and to the rest of my family for every day of my life.

It is possible now to rationalise what I did and why I did it. It does not make it right but it makes it at least comprehensible. But I do not want to play the self-justification game. Having deluded myself these past 40 years that I could make the world a better place and materially improve the prospects of others I would be a greater fool to allow myself to be diverted from confronting the truth of my own weakness. That other politicians and parties might share my flaws is no defence.

The details of this so-called scandal are relatively inconsequential. Because of a number of logistical delays the polling reports were prepared in an inordinate hurry and within such feverish circumstances that a minor late-night prank was played — the reports were signed off 'Antoinette Beck' instead of under Paul Sherriff's name. As far as Paul and Louise were concerned the report was intended merely as a private commentary on the polling results — neither of them had any idea I would release the reports to the local media. Neither the phantom Antoinette nor the reports themselves created the initial media furore in Hawke's Bay — that was occasioned by a half-witted local newspaper and the spurious claims of Harrison and Single.

In brief, the charge was that I had lined my family's pocket by having the poll conducted by Piece of New Zealand. Such claims were fatuous nonsense — PNZ was brought in only to sort out the IRD details; there had been no profit to either company or individuals; and I had never been a director of PNZ or its public relations predecessor, Harlequin. These denials counted for nought with the Hastings-based *Herald-Tribune* and the politically inclined *Hawke's Bay Sun*, whose editorials hinted at impropriety, nepotism and the taint of corruption. I was outraged if unsurprised.

The *Herald-Tribune* had already betrayed a tender understanding of journalistic integrity by leaking to me the confidential details of a Family Court hearing in the lead-up to the '93 elections. They had discovered that a young criminal had been 'rewarded' with a bicycle and other recreational equipment if he promised to go straight and stay out of trouble. Knowing that I would be searching for a few front-page headlines in the last weeks of the election, the editor fed me this information so that I might in turn feed it back to his newspaper. In that way the law might be circumvented and the *Herald-Tribune* duly ran the story for days, finally attracting national media attention. When considered alongside my earlier collaboration with the *Dominion* during the Gang of Twenty affair and many similar private partnerships between politicians and journalists I now dismiss the self-righteous pleadings of independence that often emanate from within the Fourth Estate. Their brushes with politics are similarly corrupting, for they enjoy the role of *agent provocateur* and even of equal partner when hunting political quarry. It was now my turn to be the fleeing prey.

The whole thrust of the media criticism was defused when the Audit Office was asked to review the contract and look into any errors or omissions; I was confident of exoneration given the rationale behind involving my wife's company. The Audit Office duly found that I had transgressed the small print of a 1968 law pertaining to local government and pecuniary interest but it was such a trifling error as to be regarded as 'an honest mistake' and they deemed no further action required. Nevertheless although the breach was technical I promptly paid the $2000 invoice myself and cursed myself for my errant oversight.

Nonetheless the whole incident disturbed me. Two local newspapers, fanned by enemies on the council and also by National MPs in the House, had succeeded in casting public doubt on my civic actions. I had never been motivated by money or material possessions, but the accusation of improbity had wounded — or at least I perceived it to have done so. And that is something else about politics. MPs may develop the legendary hide of a rhinoceros but they also develop cracks of acute vulnerability. At such fissures the skin assumes the fragility of an egg-shell, and on this issue I felt the jab all right — an incision I believed to be manifestly unjust.

At which stage I became aware of a number of personal smears circulating in Hawke's Bay about my private life — deliberately fuelled by Harrison and other ACT sympathisers and gaining a degree of currency in various professional sectors of the community. Paul Sherriff's homosexuality had excited these individuals to proclaim that I too was a 'pooftah' and engaged in a long-term sexual relationship with Paul. Coincidentally I was also supposed to be in the midst of a passionate affair with Louise — plainly, I was a busy boy. That both my alleged paramours had far too refined a taste to ever contemplate such erotic interludes should have been obvious.

Despite the hyperbolic local media treatment of this issue my primary attention at this time was still directed towards my New Zealand First duties and the conversion of Elder and McCardle to the cause. Jack proved no difficulty and I was soon to learn that Ron Mark and Tony Day had also converted to the Peters cause, Mark scathing of Moore's paucity of political will. But I judged McCardle's fondness for detail and his general policy skills to be essential over the coming months; anything to leaven the broad brush of rhetorical bombast that New Zealand First paraded as its considered manifesto. Eventually Peter's resolve cracked, clearly persuaded by his future lack of influence on National's back bench and the prospect of a safe list seat in the new MMP Parliament. As with me, McCardle's new constituency boundaries had suggested a limited half-life beyond the projected November elections.

Distracted by pressing policy and strategy tasks and irritated by previous denunciations of my polling motivations, I became even further annoyed when the signature to the Napier poll was publicly questioned by Harrison and the symbiotic *Hawke's Bay Sun*. Their intention was plain — to cast doubt on the poll's integrity and, by association, mine as well. Even before this issue Harrison and Single had already accused me of corruption and likened my credibility to that of OJ Simpson, while feeding a grateful Prime Minister's office lurid and false information relating to the conduct of the poll. A series of supposedly damaging parliamentary questions were tabled and an old Caucus enemy, Birkenhead MP Ian Revell, led the charge.

It was my perception that this gaggle of enemies was motivated by nothing more than malignant spite and no further public succour should be provided.

The logical leap from that conclusion to my next action defies comprehension. I discussed the issue with a bemused Paul Sherriff, who regarded the attention of the Hawke's Bay press as feverish foolishness and thus enjoyed perpetuating the spoof further — to the extent of developing a mock persona for the absent Antoinette. When it became clear that the issue was developing onto the national stage Paul decided to accept responsibility himself — the accusation by now being that I had signed the report. Suddenly this non-scandal assumed minor *cause célèbre* status because I had wished the issue to evaporate and been prepared to mislead a hostile media to that effect.

The rest, as they say, is history.

By early April I had decided that I must accept culpability and resign from the Napier City Council. I had been a willing party to a minor deception and allowed others to accept responsibility for my ultimate lack of candour. I had also dragged my wife and two good friends into a dirty puddle of private gossip and public innuendo. No matter that I was guilty of but a fraction of the charges being levelled against me — I had been wrong. I could see no honourable exit other than that fabled accountability that I constantly demanded from others.

Still I continued to resist, despite daily evidence that my political enemies were intent on prolonging and exaggerating my personal embarrassment so as to tarnish my newest political associates and New Zealand First's dangerous popular appeal.

By now the issue had become sufficiently serious for me to confront Winston and attempt to justify my behaviour. On more than one occasion I attempted to tell Winston the entire truth but Peters would hold up a hand and stop me in mid-sentence: 'Michael, don't tell me anything. When I look down the barrel of the [television] camera I want to honestly say that I have absolutely no evidence to doubt your public word. Ride it out — it'll go away.'

Peters' later explanation in the House, that no one within the New Zealand First parliamentary offices was responsible for the poll signature, was not based on any assurances provided by me. As was his tendency, Winston had carried the rhetoric one step too far. I listened to the speech in horror — my failures had become the tar baby with which to entrap Peters as well. I had been careful throughout the whole issue not to mislead the House; inadvertently, Winston had done just that.

From that moment my future actions were obvious — at least to me. I proffered my written resignation from the council to a reluctant Alan Dick, drafted a similar note to Winston and went public on television's 'One Network News' with details of my dishonesty. Incredibly I found enough semblance of ego to complete a festival debate in Dannevirke affirming the topic that the town had regressed into the primeval swamp and its hunter-gatherer populace with it — I made these observations with more than a hint of empathy, my political future sliding into the same ooze.

The following Friday afternoon Winston telephoned me in my Taradale office and cautioned me against precipitate action. His manner was both warm and supportive and over the difficult days and weeks that lay ahead it would be Winston's friendship and my family's support that proved critical in weathering my wretched frustration and self-pity. I had determined that my council resignation was not sufficient penance — my actions also reflected on my parliamentary probity and only the sacrifice of my career would be suitable recompense. By now I was submerged way past guilt and had descended beyond remorse — I had let down Karen, my parents, my friends, my staff, my constituents and my new party, and there could be no suitable act of apology or redemption.

Calmly and methodically, in a trance of quiet despair, I even contemplated the ultimate refuge of depression — suicide. It was no mere consideration and Karen must have guessed at my mental state for she barely left my side over that dreadful weekend, forcing my pain to the surface so that I could attempt its articulation. But the liberation of release would not come — I was incapable of grieving or even crying and hovered in a strange netherworld unable to eat or sleep, with every anxiety magnified beyond sanity.

Still Winston refused to accept my resignation and with his typical bluff humour sought to cajole me out of my depression. Karen and I shared dinner with Winston and some of his closest friends the next Saturday evening, Peters insistent that my errors had been atoned for by my council resignation.

'Have you stolen anything? Have you misused your position for personal advancement? Have you maimed or killed anyone?' Winston demanded. 'Look, you stuffed up. So, you're not perfect. Put it behind you and get on with it.'

I shook my head.

'Win. They will use this affair to drag you down — to drag down the party. We're now at twenty-per-cent-plus in the polls. They will manufacture more shit to keep this thing going for weeks, maybe months. It will be the death of a hundred leaks, a thousand cuts.'

I was making no impression. 'It's about guts, Michael — you have to tough it out. I didn't have you join me just to leave.'

At the end of the evening Peters switched tack and drew Karen aside. 'Don't let him resign — this isn't worth it.'

Buoyed by Winston's loyal support and soaked by enough merlot to fong even my deep melancholy I went home and fell into instant sleep. By three in the morning I had returned to my former fitful state and could sleep no more, the darkness amplifying my depression. I stole downstairs, made myself a hot drink topped with whisky and attempted to numb the inevitability of the coming week.

The events of the next 48 hours rushed through my consciousness. A welter of politically motivated charges detonated in the media — each breathlessly reported as if an axe murderer had run amok in a nursing home. Between my parliamentary and council enemies I counted no fewer than five separate complaints — one to the Serious Fraud Office, two to the police, another to the Local Government Commission and now another by Harrison to the Audit Office — the last alleging that I had misused public monies for private ends. A telekinetic smear, primed by any number of ministerial spinners, set out to convince the public that my motivations and actions had passed beyond lack of judgement and into the criminal.

By the Tuesday morning I had decided my fate and informed my Caucus colleagues — each, by now, convinced that there must be some truth to the various rumours circulating through Parliament but content to leave the final decision to Winston. Tau Henare expressed his anger directly, saying that my actions had 'shitted on New Zealand First' and that my resignation was long overdue — ironic comments given his later actions over the Tuku Morgan affair. Still Winston resisted — his loyalty to an old friend blocking out the obvious and expedient course. Finally, I gave him no choice — I would be convening a press conference that afternoon.

The room fell silent. Then, with tears in our eyes, we embraced, shook hands and nodded finality to each other. Not a word passed.

'I'll announce it Michael. You talk to Karen and your family — be with them. Let me look after you for the next 48 hours.' And so he did.

I still held the press conference — I had no option. The House had been stunned by Winston's announcement of my resignation but recovered quickly, with various Government MPs dancing a verbal jig and accusing me of cowardice in not fronting up in the chamber myself. Paul Holmes called and asked if Karen and I might appear on his evening show — reluctantly, we agreed. I reasoned that if I could confine my horror to just the one day then tomorrow would dawn brighter — a forlorn hope as it transpired.

That afternoon all vestiges of self-confidence wholly deserted me as the enormity of my misjudgement sank home. Again, it was not that I had destroyed my political career; there was actually a bizarre relief to that aspect that brightened my day. I was like a junkie who has been told that there will be no more heroin — despite the addictive loss another part of your consciousness embraces the prospect of freedom. Rather it was the shaming of Karen, my family, my friends and my newest political associates. And there was nothing I could do, nothing, to repair the damage.

Later that evening, in private conversation with Winston, I confessed to my dejection. A smile drifted through the cigarette haze.

'I've been on the phone this afternoon, Laws.' We were back to our boarding school camaraderie. 'And I've arranged for you and Karen to fly to Christchurch tomorrow, got a rental car organised and you're off to a small fishing village.'

The idea of a holiday appalled me, and I said as much.

'Holiday?' Winston scoffed. 'Laws, you'll be writing the party's economic policy. I want you to finalise all our election policy over the next few months. Don't worry about wages — I'll make sure your salary is looked after and Louise's as well.'

He leaned closer, that magnetic blend of humour and defiance exquisitely tangible. 'If they think they've beaten us, they've got another think coming. They won't beat me — don't let them beat you.'

Winston proved true to his word. Whatever disagreements we might later share, whatever strategic flaws I might later criticise and condemn, whatever personal characteristics and actions might repel, I would never forget Winston's bracing support and friendship during this troubled time. It made the difference. It would have been easy and expedient to cut me adrift and let me suffer the ignominy on my own, for that failure to be my last imprint upon the political scene. Instinctively he rejected the politic step. I was a friend and I was in trouble; his self-appointed responsibility was to be at my side.

Which was just as well. Because tomorrow did not dawn brighter. A telephone call at just after six disturbed my first decent sleep in weeks. It was Paul Holmes.

'Michael — just thought you should know. Radio New Zealand are leading this morning with a story about the police investigating you for perverting the course of justice.'

My enemies were clearly dissatisfied with my severed head — now they wanted my entrails as well.

Chapter 11

ILLUSION

THE PHOENIX FLAPS

The immediate aftermath of my resignation produced an eclectic range of public responses, but the most overwhelming was an unexpected sympathy. I had readied myself for vilification, particularly in view of the whooping media frenzy and Prime Minister Bolger stooping to denounce me. Jim never believed in hitting a man when he was down — except Michael Laws.

A few querulous journalists vox-popped my electorate and received a nasty shock — there is nothing worse for any reporter than having their prejudices denied. Perhaps the most disagreeable of jolts, though, was reserved for the local *Herald-Tribune* who, ironically, ran an opinion poll on my resignation only to discover that a majority of their readers considered my Roman fool option too drastic a punishment. An even greater number opined that I would be back.

They obviously knew me better than I knew myself for my greatest wish was to slink away into a very deep and private hole and there tend my gaping wounds. Thankfully Winston refused to countenance this wallowing in self-pity and before the week was out I was nestled in a spartan fishing crib near Hinds in South Canterbury, surrounded by various Treasury and Reserve Bank papers, and stoically attempting an economic policy draft that might survive the twin threats of election-year scrutiny and the party's burgeoning xenophobia. It proved a singularly frustrating experience, made even less pleasant as radio reports relayed new allegations against me — now so politically exaggerated that money-laundering, forgery, rigging local-body elections and bribery were being added to the list. Poor Karen had married the Mafia.

The Press Gallery, indeed most of Parliament, found it impossible to accept that any MP could resign for misleading the media — especially over a signature on an inconsequential report. Taking responsibility for one's errors was too jejune; there just had to be a deeper, more sinister reason, and all manner of conspiracy theories rushed around the precincts. The most vile was traced back to an ACT source alleging that my resignation had been forced ahead of imminent child molestation charges — a rumour that detonated the last remnants of self-loathing and reinforced a growing resolve to cower no longer.

However, the media tide began to turn perceptibly as various Government agencies dismissed the claims of wrong-doing, although these denials were never given quite the same prominence as the initial accusations. By month's end my fate had fizzled its way to the back pages although, just to complete my personal misery, I was then served with a $1-million defamation suit courtesy of my old council protagonists Harrison and Single. For the next twenty months the prospect of bankruptcy would sour my horizon, with every dollar of my parliamentary super payout dedicating itself to the legal fees required to muster a defence. I was instantly converted to the ideal of deregulating the legal profession, not so much as a reaction to the fees but to the construction of the law itself — one specifically designed by this quasi-masonic order to resist a layman's interpretation and thus demand their specialist and expensive intervention.

Mind you, my resignation did have one favourable repercussion. It established the date for the general election — Saturday, 12 October 1996 — the Cabinet deciding that a by-election in my vacant constituency seat was an expensive and unnecessary luxury. My one parting legacy — I would be speeding up the advent of MMP by a month. Some epitaph.

Perversely, Winston and New Zealand First would gain public kudos from my resignation; the party had proved their MPs were accountable while Winston was perceived as having sacrificed his closest colleague on the altar of political principle. A further sharp incline in polling support was recorded, with the party now vaulting to a record 29 per cent in various media polls — within touching distance of National's support base and outstripping Labour as the prime Opposition force. Such a spectacular rise was not unprecedented in recent political history — both Social Credit and the Alliance had previously topped the 30-per-cent-plus barrier and equally eclipsed Labour. But the trick would be to sustain these levels — a much grimmer task and one that required a perfect appreciation of the valley floor below. The impact craters of both Bruce Beetham and Jim

Anderton could just be made out from the tightrope.

By month's end I had cheered up sufficiently to return to Wellington, a draft economic policy in tow and named as Winston's 'special advisor' — a title specifically designed to cover a multitude of sins. This return from the dead was by no means universally approved. Both Widerstrom and Heffernan persisted in their quite accurate perceptions that I remained a threat to their respective spheres of influence, most especially with the leader. When I discovered that Widerstrom had secretly contacted my council protagonists in the lead-up to my resignation the breach became total.

Rather than prolong such poisonous inter-office rivalry I insisted that Winston either dismiss the resident grumps or give me the authority to oversee and delegate the unit's primary tasks — to impose some sense of external discipline on the seething mess of internal personal agendas. We were but five months out from a general election — a united parliamentary team with transparent lines of communication was plainly required. Instead Winston would fuss, dither and occasionally rage but come no closer to resolving these impasses. The unit would remain an unholy mess — a failure that could only be ascribed to Winston's legendary disinclination to make any hard decisions where staff were involved. Within weeks I became resigned to this difficulty, and Sarah, Louise and I were required to construct a separate Leader's Unit so we could work around, over or through the rest of the staff.

There were two exceptions to this general chaos — the two parliamentary researchers, Deborah Morris and Ernie Davis. Morris is now a Minister of the Crown, Davis the deputy Prime Minister's Chief-of-Staff. Both would have regarded their present employment as a lager fantasy had the scenario been posited at that time. Morris was an able and enthusiastic young woman straight out of Victoria University; Davis an affable, chain-smoking, ex-high school headmaster in the midst of a midlife conundrum. Ernie's appointment was sheer nepotism. I had recruited him through my wife's family connections, surmising that coping with 800 hormonal teenagers while at the same time handling the attendant gaggle of PPTA members demonstrated superior survival skills, and that these could be used to great advantage in coping with both Winston and the New Zealand First rabble. And so it proved.

Winston had promised that private money would be made available to provide Louise and me with salaries but, just like Godot, the riches never arrived. There were party rumours that Sir Robert Jones had provided $50,000 to the New Zealand First coffers and that this would provide the basis of our pay, but if the money was ever gifted then it detoured elsewhere.

I suspected that Winston's legal fees had proved a more pressing priority, by now mounting ever upwards and into the stratosphere. I had no difficulty with such choices; a destitute party leader was hardly a political selling point and given that Winston was New Zealand First and vice versa then the leader's financial health was an issue. Certainly money worries would hamper Winston during the next few months and place further pressure on his temper, already wound tourniquet tight.

Some of the damage was self-inflicted. Peters was not a wealthy man despite his penchant for good restaurants, better wines and expensive nightclubs, and he was often excessively generous with his credit card, entertaining guests and associates despite their protests. Such generosity also extended to his staff — according to Sarah, Peters had spruced up Widerstrom's wardrobe rather than be trailed at his public appearances by Mr Blobby in a large canvas tent.

Despite such overt liberality Peters' basic MP's salary was no more ornate than any other; neither celebrity nor party leadership provided compensatory largesse. And his recent divorce settlement had proven a singularly expensive transaction, stripping Winston of many formerly shared assets. Add the burgeoning legal bills to those strains and I considered it a miracle of modern banking that Peters kept his financial head anywhere near the surface let alone above water. Certainly the various legal actions taken against Peters by a multitude of aggrieved businessmen had their cumulative financial effect. The Cushing defamation case was the most pressing, and I observed one legal bill that might have purchased a decent residence in one of Wellington's better suburbs.

Facing stiff legal fees myself and cognisant of Peters' delicate position I felt both awkward and ungrateful having to insist on payment for Louise's and my joint endeavours. Always there would be the Winstonian promises of 'Tomorrow', 'It's just around the corner' or the more audacious 'Hasn't it gone in yet?' followed by a storming summons for Sarah. But after two months of non-payment the tether broke — Louise and I packed our papers and asked for any personal mail to be forwarded. Within hours a suitably contrite Winston had telephoned, apologised profusely and admitted that the private money had 'fallen through'. Would I mind looking at the unit's parliamentary budget and finding a path towards payment from that avenue?

Within days this arrangement was finalised, although my weekly salary equalled an annual emolument of something less than $25,000. At least from that point on I was able to boast that no one in the unit, including the secretaries and typists, was being paid less than I, so I could become even more intolerant of any slackness in the ranks. Nevertheless the whole experience unsettled me. If New Zealand First did not have the funds to pay me ... ummm, where was the money coming from for a decent election campaign? In fact, where was the money for any campaign at all?

Here again Winston's fudging proved almost ruinous. The truth was that in the previous three years there had been virtually no campaign fundraising nor strategising nor pre-planning. Again I happened upon this information only after hounding Sarah, Winston and party president Doug Woolerton for evidence of some clear tactical approach. Winston had constructed an elaborate shopfront to advance the party's claims all right, but with neither foundation nor any hint of construction behind the facade. Not for the first time I raged at the incompetence of the New Zealand First party machinery — I could excuse abject non-performance; what I simply could not comprehend was such willing self-deception.

Suddenly the tasks multiplied before me. I was now responsible not only for providing daily direction and media support to the leader, but for co-ordinating policy development, planning the election campaign and somehow trying to divine financial pathways to back this adventure. Oh yes, I had been raised from the flames all right but with my wings so severely clipped that flight must be only the remotest possibility. Once again the fire threatened to consume me.

JUST DO IT

New Zealand First's failure to attract suitable talent to the party over the previous three years was nowhere better illustrated than in its choice of portfolio spokespersons — an unsettling collection of the well-meaning and the gorblimey. They all shared two distinctive characteristics — vaulting personal ambition and a stunning political naïveté — the combination of which rendered most policy drafts hopelessly inadequate. The stream of former Moore conspirators provided Winston with the perfect excuse to reshuffle policy responsibilities but even this exercise proved laboured and imprecise.

It had been intended that I would become the party's finance spokesperson but my resignation now precluded that option. Bernard Downey clearly lacked the political nous and intellectual ability for the role so I persuaded Winston that he should accept the role himself and I would provide the background analysis and grunt. This solution had the added advantage of broadening Winston's public repertoire beyond the staple daily goading of Fay Richwhite and Asian immigrants. It would also deliver me day-to-day control of the party's responses on matters economic and from there it was but a short step to annexing entire responsibility for the party's policy strategy by controlling the spending agendas of all the other shadow portfolios.

I had learned the lesson of Richardson and Treasury: those who control the purse-strings control the policy. With Winston fronting this palace coup I was able to ensure that all draft policy passed over my desk before New Zealand First went completely mad and promised everything to everybody. Sadly, in some areas I was already too late — superannuation and housing being two notable examples.

There was, of course, a method in my megalomaniacal madness. Now that the Democratic Coalition had been aborted it was obvious that New Zealand First must form part of any post-election MMP government. Unlike Winston and the New Zealand First hierarchy I believed the party's polling popularity was marshmallow soft and unlikely to survive the fire of an intense election campaign. Once the experienced party machines of National and Labour cranked themselves into campaigning mode New Zealand First's glaring inadequacies would swiftly become apparent. More importantly, these parties had a range of experienced MPs and candidates to take their party's battle to each constituency — in reality New Zealand First had just Winston.

It became my self-appointed role to plug as many of these gaps as possible before election day, but I was acutely aware of both my and the party's limitations and there were still 30-odd candidates to be selected — the emphasis being very definitely on the 'odd'. If the current spokespersons were this miasma of the bizarre and the banal then I shuddered at the perils that must lurk below.

I was not the only person within the parliamentary precincts who appreciated the enormity of the tasks ahead. Peter McCardle, nominally the party's policy co-ordinator, was similarly horrified by the luxuriant incompetence that dwelt within but found his own unique way of coping with such labyrinthine laxity.

'I just close the door and direct all calls to Winston's office. I don't want to know,' he once confided to me. 'It's the only way.' And then he would exclaim in astonishment, 'Some of these people, Michael, are just plain mad!'

I felt faintly reassured by this observation. It was not just my jaundice after all.

Peter and I agreed that a good election result for New Zealand First would be around 15 per cent of the list vote and similarly concurred that the party was destined to play the junior role in any coalition government. This seemed eminently sensible — we had no wish to see the bedraggled and inexperienced oddfellows that made up a good portion of the party's activists instantly elevated to senior control of the government. Similarly, neither of us accepted Winston's fantastic assumption that New Zealand First would retain and expand its present polling support — miracles do not last that long.

However, our cautions, when sparingly proffered in polite company, were dismissed by the party's various functionaries as having a touch of the jeremiad about them. Fuelled by the leader's rhetoric the Promised Land seemed but a Sunday drive away. Even Winston was displeased at being confronted with such sobriety.

'I don't even want you talking like this in private, Laws,' he would angrily command. 'We're going all the way.'

Having been the first convert to the coming glory Peters was not about to abandon himself to the harsh dictates of reality.

This narcotic vision, that both Winston and his neophytes were destined for greatness, corroded all attempts to create internal order. Confronted with the myriad mundane deeds required to develop a nationwide election campaign, Peters' habitual response was to delay — as if the next few months would flash by and willingly divulge the Holy Grail at its concluded passage. It became my view that Winston loathed detail because the minutiae required application and he lacked the self-discipline to confront the relative boredom this involved.

As the ultimate retail politician, Winston was utterly dependent on those staffers who could digest the wholesale product and then regurgitate it in sufficiently large chunks for his comprehension. It occurred to me at the time that Peters also disliked detail because its examination might expose an academic inadequacy, for he was a man too proud to admit to any personal failing. Of all the Seven Deadly Sins, Winston was only guilty of the one. Pride.

Daughter Rachel — living proof that children need not inherit their parents' failings.

If you want something done properly — give the task to a woman. My brilliant electorate and parliamentary staff of 1993. From left: Louise Sampson, Kathy Leach, Anne Averill, Lisa Futschek and my own US political intern, Alice Keane.
The Daily Telegraph

The wooing commences. Mike Moore and I examining hail-damaged fruit in a Hawke's Bay orchard in early 1994. Both our respective Caucuses perceived us as the bad apples all right.
The Daily Telegraph

The second biggest mistake of my life. Being sworn in as a Napier City councillor late-1995 by Mayor Alan Dick.

A Laws family gathering for my mother's birthday (sorry, not allowed to tell you which one) in August 1995. From left (back): brother-in-law Bruce Gray, wife Karen, sister Diane Gray, brother-in-law Craig Carran; (front): father Keith, mother Helen, me, sister Sue Carran.

Prime Minister Jim Bolger — a mutual loathing from the first instant. New Zealand Herald

Michelle Boag taking the fall for Fay Richwhite during the Winebox hearings. I used the moment shamelessly — Michelle deserved better. New Zealand Herald

'The Kiwi Spirit'; election campaign 1996. Great concept, great bus — and a bloody great drama every day.

Possums after the truck
has roared past. The
first New Zealand First
Caucus in October
1996 besieged by the
Press Gallery gaggle.

With Karen. The lady
is too good for me; too
bad everyone knows it.
New Zealand Listener

But these were the cards New Zealand First had at its collective disposal; the hand must be played out. The analogy was not inappropriate, Peters' gift for the poker stare and the art of bluff proving both invaluable allies and infuriating enemies in the weeks ahead.

The combination of New Zealand First's rise in the polls and the Democratic Coalition debacle had attracted any number of able opportunists to the party's ranks. As a general rule, the calibre of these new recruits lifted both the IQ and the political experience of the party, with MPs Elder and McCardle being joined by Ron Mark, old friend Neil Kirton and Police Association general secretary Graham Harding.

Meanwhile Anglican priest and peace activist Ann Batten, a Labour list candidate, had also been recruited, along with Whakatohea negotiator and former National Party nominee John Delamere — a man with an impeccable résumé but, more importantly from Winston's perspective, a committed self-groomer. The leader's great love of a decent haircut, a smart suit and a bold tie could never be underestimated — there was an agitated neuron within him that constantly equated a decent dress sense with decency full stop.

For some weeks now Winston had signalled his intention to reshuffle the party's spokesperson roles to reflect the arrival of this new talent and to drop those who had previously failed to perform. From my cursory examination of the policy drafts I assumed that virtually everyone would get the bullet. No such luck. Winston wanted to accommodate the new talent without offending the incumbents — a luxury that would prove impossible given the egos on offer. Yet again, Winston dithered; this time for weeks. Again the development of the party's manifesto policies was placed on the backburner — at the precise time when the party's popularity was provoking intense public and media interest.

Finally, after a series of joint lobbying assaults from Neems and me, Peters relented. But it would prove only a partial victory, for the incompetents remained, if at a slightly lower elevation. In particular, the key health role remained with the stunningly inept party vice-president, Jenny Bloxham, and her equally bizarre offsider, Patra de Courdray. I often enquired how either woman had assumed such status within the party but never received a convincing explanation; the dearth of talented women within New Zealand First ranks was never more obvious. It had been suggested that de Courdray's previous employment as a GP's receptionist was considered to provide her with sufficient expertise to be the party's associate health spokesperson. Sadly, such a story had the ring of plausibility. But she was now unemployed and pleading poverty — a matter that would assume appalling relevance in the last days of the campaign.

As for Bloxham, any person who boasts a 'Hickory corsetry diploma' as an educational achievement is always suspect in my book. And despite constant provocation Peters refused to discipline or dismiss Bloxham, instead insisting that the appointment of Neil Kirton as one of her associates would bring order to the portfolio and ensure a properly researched health policy. He was absolutely wrong — the combination proved so toxic that Bloxham would telephone on an almost daily basis and threaten written resignation. Sadly, the note never came.

The reallocation of responsibilities did produce one significant change. Widerstrom and Heffernan were stripped of their respective employment and broadcasting spokesmanships, a clear indication that they no longer enjoyed their leader's confidence. Winston's genuine theory was that all unit staff needed to concentrate their endeavours on supporting the party's efforts in the field — having two senior staffers distracted by their own personal and political priorities weakened this emphasis. I concurred with the logic but considered both men were probably owed an explanation of the rationale behind the reshuffle, or they would perceive it as a personal demotion. In the end they were offered a grudging explanation but guessed at an alternative cause — that demon Laws.

For all the histrionics accompanying the revamping of the party's policy roles the end result proved depressingly familiar. The new policy drafts either ignored the essential issues dwelling within each portfolio or conjured mythical monies from the never-never to satisfy the perceived afflictions of the affected lobby groups. Most meandered their sad way to the document shredder.

The trouble was, once the party stepped outside its familiar rhetoric of either chastising the corporates or railing against foreign ownership then it lacked a core philosophy — a political soul. The bizarre result was that the party had most of its election policy constructed by two of its newest recruits — McCardle and me — frustrated refugees from the status quo. Yet there could be no alternative. We were the only two with sufficient experience and command of detail to complete the task. When I complained at the impossible schedule this must impose on our already inelastic resources Winston slyly suggested that perhaps the original policy drafts were not so calamitous after all. Sure enough he provoked enough apoplectic foaming to negate all my objections.

And then an exasperated Peters issued the ubiquitous Nike command: 'Laws, just do it.'

STEERING THE CENTRE

In drafting New Zealand First's election policy there were two fundamental realities that required daily acknowledgement. First, the policy stood an excellent chance of being implemented so there must be no tarty wish lists; post-election the party's performance would be measured against its manifesto, especially in view of its claim to have Virtue as its attendant handmaiden.

Second, the policy should reflect Winston's centrist aspirations; now that the Democratic Coalition was stillborn New Zealand First had a unique opportunity to play the perennial Free Democrats role — always in power, always the moderating influence. I had coined a phrase when working with Moore — a centre party should be 'economically conservative but socially progressive' — and quickly instilled such sentiments into all Winston's speeches and media statements.

An awkward difficulty was that New Zealand First had already determined various policy positions which often contradicted a centrist prescription. For example, restricting foreign ownership of all New Zealand-based companies to a 24.9-per-cent shareholding flew in the face of economic sanity, as did the party's prescribed immigration levels, which essentially required a number of resident New Zealanders to leave the country each year! In addition, Winston had proposed amending the Reserve Bank Act to ensure that employment was a primary factor in establishing monetary policy settings, while Tau Henare had promised to reduce all state housing rents to just 25 per cent of the tenants' income — a policy with significant fiscal and equity implications. With previous pledges to abolish the superannuation surcharge, introduce universal tertiary student allowances and generally scratch a multitude of itches stacked alongside, the party's economic policy owed more to reactive expediency than considered judgement.

To make matters worse Downey had neither drafted nor even attempted to quantify the party's revenue and expenditure assumptions, or realistically cost the various policy promises. My initial overview showed that the party had already hinted at over $3 billion of extra government spending, with no compensatory increase in taxes or other revenue. Constructing an electoral budget became my first task and to that end I turned to both the political Left and the political Right, employing Wellington economist Brian Easton and the Auckland-based Bankers Trust — the latter to ensure that a mainstream institutional viewpoint was represented. Between us we studied all the various economic projections — both official and unofficial — and I eventually chose an arbitrary figure of $1.6 billion of additional expenditure in the first full financial year as the leash for all future policy promises.

It then became a matter of paring back the grandiose intentions of the various spokespersons and assigning each portfolio area a rough estimate of their likely largesse. Again, with Winston fronting these measures internal opposition was confined to the substrata, and with McCardle similarly preaching restraint even the truly profligate were towed to fiscal safety.

But before New Zealand First could even hazard an attempt at policy credibility the party needed to define its vision and its anticipated future role. Although the party boasted its 'fifteen fundamental principles', a legacy of its fevered launch three years earlier, closer inspection revealed just the one principle and fourteen highly questionable policy assumptions. The party's primary intention to 'put New Zealand and New Zealanders first' hinted at a muddy economic nationalism, but it is an inordinately difficult proposition to wed oneself to this sort of financial jingoism when one lives in an extremely small and minor South Pacific hybrid that is utterly reliant on foreign trade. If anything the Alliance were the true preserve of such sentiments with their support for high tariff barriers, an interventionist Reserve Bank and even a confessed abhorrence of export growth.

I managed to convince Winston that while the 'New Zealand Incorporated' style of economic management was important — and here the successful dairy and pipfruit producer boards would prove invaluable — New Zealand First actually needed to represent a new style of politics — one that stripped effective power from the commercial, political and bureaucratic elites and returned them to the ordinary citizen. If New Zealand First was to suggest a realistic alternative to the status quo then it must alter the very balance of political power.

Thus the party's desired changes to the nation's economic and social management would automatically flow from sharing its decision-making powers and authority with an informed populace — and not by imposing an alternative vision from on high. The only sustainable path to power and thence its retention was to advance and maintain a true populist agenda. And the roots of populism lay not so much in chasing the fleeting prejudice of the moment but in drawing the people into the political process as an effective participant and partner.

I accepted that many of New Zealand First's current imperatives buttressed that ideal — the strike against corporate privilege at the Winebox hearings, the refusal to contemplate further state asset sales, the desire to restrict untrammelled immigration — but we needed to wrap these reactive policies within a defined philosophy that marketed the party as a wholly unique beast. No other party, I told Peters, was willing to go into the general election and truly declare that they were going to share power with the public. We must be that party.

Winston liked the rhetoric — I daresay he even empathised with the sentiment — and I was encouraged to incorporate my ideals within a brief Peters speech billed as 'New Zealand First's Vision'. But Winston was in magpie mode. It sounded bright and shiny — it soon became apparent that it was the glint that attracted and not the substance.

Despite my conspicuous success in urging fiscal caution and a clear party vision I pitifully failed to steer Winston away from promoting a compulsory superannuation savings scheme. Initially I had managed to persuade him to pledge a binding referendum on the entire super issue after canvassing all options via a Royal Commission. In this way the final verdict would be wholly removed from the self-interested squabbling of political parties and the ultimate decision made by the general populace. The solution suited the new vision — the final decision endures because it is 'owned' by the public.

But Peters was soon steeled by all manner of New Zealand First cronies to resist any further erosion of their previous daftness, the party's superannuation spokesman, phlegmatic Wellington lawyer David Stevenson, proving a singular thorn. Winston had decided that the lack of a national savings policy was the inherent source of New Zealand's economic weakness. In addition this policy appealed because Peters envisaged a compulsory scheme offering an alternative capital source and thus repelling the blandishments of foreign investors.

I was less than convinced; to satisfy such economic nationalism these super funds would need to be invested in New Zealand and that could militate against providing equitable returns to the individual investor. Besides, it also had a nasty whiff of Norm Kirk's failed socialist ideal of the mid-seventies; the scheme that launched Hanna Barbera's dancing cossacks across the nation's television screens.

I also contended that New Zealand First's scheme would rob low- and middle-income families of a sizeable percentage of their disposable household income — three per cent in the first year, rising to a maximum of eight per cent as the scheme finally bedded in. The obvious query presented itself: how could ordinary families afford to provide this level of retirement savings when much of their present income was already committed? Most were already paying usurious mortgage interest rates — their first savings priority was to discharge that commitment. Besides, having that much money hoovered out of the public's pockets must have an immediate and negative effect on household expenditure and hence GDP.

These objections never made it off the beach, ruthlessly strafed in the landing craft by a mock-Churchillian Peters adamantly declaring that the price of New Zealand's independence required a good dollop of financial sacrifice on the part of all its citizens. We would fight them with our credit cards, we would fight them with our overdraft — we would never surrender.

'Great,' I retorted sarcastically. 'We'll be the only party at the election promising to make everyone poorer. That's a vote winner!'

Winston appreciated the dilemma but his brain had been super-glued to the spot. The compulsory super policy was inviolate. I changed tack. OK then. What if we linked the second round of tax cuts, proposed by the Government for the 1997/98 financial year, to the commencement of the super policy? In that way people should be no worse off — the theory being that what the public never had, they would not miss. Following that logic I then suggested that New Zealand First could even promote further tax cuts as a pain-free way to match the annual increases needed to reach the 8 per cent savings target. Winston instantly agreed and within 30 seconds the party's economic, superannuation and savings policies had been finalised — rather compelling proof that the instant mandate of a party's election manifesto is not always in the public interest.

The presentation of the party's economic policy at its annual convention in mid-July provided New Zealand First with grudging Press Gallery credibility, but more significantly, it established the party as a centrist force. It had always been my view that New Zealand

First would be required to lay down with either National or Labour in any post-election coalition and the party's earlier extremism therefore required tempering. However, I was concerned if this smoothing were publicised before the conference that Peters might be besieged by contra forces and persuaded to remain true to the original warped vision, such as the compulsory super policy.

Fortunately Winston's passion for secrecy assisted me and even the party's associate finance spokesman was only briefed a matter of minutes before the public presentation. Downey hated the new policy and whined his dissent throughout the entire slide show; on the other hand, Winston loved it. It was detailed enough to satisfy the initial media questioning, conservative enough to establish the party's centrist credentials, and sufficiently innovative to justify a good-sized headline.

I had similarly manoeuvred around the dangerous shoals of previous Winstonian excess by accepting that the Reserve Bank Act required amendment, if only by adding the words 'sustainable economic growth' to the legislative emphasis on price stability. In addition the inflation target of zero to two per cent would be softened to somewhere around three per cent — still at a level lower than that of most of New Zealand's major trading partners. Again, the final words used were intended to convey a sentiment rather than a pledge — they would supply sufficient impetus to amend the inflation target in any post-election negotiations without altering the substance of the Act. The same logic was applied to the party's policy on the Employment Contracts Act and the State Sector Act — sufficient amendments to patch up the obvious flaws without damaging the legislative intent.

However, apart from more stringent foreign investment rules, there remained one major economic policy difference between New Zealand First and its larger political rivals — the party wanted to assist the country's producers beyond a minor tinkering with monetary policy. In the end I was quite proud of the party's export policy, with its emphasis on a practical partnership with the export sector via a relatively inexpensive export credit guarantee scheme, a technology transfer programme, boosted Tradenz funding and financial encouragement of trading-oriented research and development. These fantasies survived the later coalition negotiations but were ironically scuttled by the export lobby groups themselves — conclusive evidence that you can cut off your nose to spite your face.

There were other minor victories. Despite a conspicuous lack of success in propelling Winston away from the compulsory super madness I was more effective in dealing to the insanity that posed as a foreign investment solution. Banning all rural land sales to foreign citizens remained a useful symbol of the party's credo of 'New Zealand for New Zealanders'. But restricting foreign ownership in New Zealand-based companies was more problematic — in most cases there were no alternative indigenous suppliers of investment capital, technology or business expertise.

Surely, I argued, the aim of the policy was to ensure that key New Zealand assets remained in Kiwi hands; who owned a timber processing plant, a food factory or a finance company was irrelevant? Besides, there were a myriad practical difficulties in implementing such a policy, not least that no other political party, including the Alliance, would ever agree to such nonsense. Fortunately, Peters agreed and blamed the now dusty duo of Widerstrom and Heffernan for the policy ever having gained currency.

Whatever my personal views of this pair I raised an eyebrow at the blame being shifted in their direction. It was entirely typical of Peters to accuse others for his own errors of political judgement — a failing that remains to this day. But it is also a flaw that weakens Peters' ability to stop the sword swinging in the reverse direction, and he is easily manipulated into an opposing viewpoint if the new persuader similarly dumps on Winston's fetish decoy and proffers a ready alternative.

I had developed a simple mantra appropriate to these internal debates: 'Last one to talk to Win wins.' The opportunity to apply it was obligingly provided by Sarah Neems, who had a particular knack of knowing Peters' exact whereabouts at any time of the day or night. It also enabled me to discover when Winston was most vulnerable to cogent argument — midstream in the urinal. On the other hand, late-night restaurant rendezvous were a complete loss; Peters would rarely remember any conversation and always sought to distract himself and others by ruminating on an increasingly apocryphal past life.

Despite Winston's nervousness that New Zealand First was being seen publicly to soften its hardline xenophobia, thus drawing immature 'U-turn' screams from the Gallery, I reasoned that the tangible electoral effects would prove minimal. The party retained its strident opposition to state asset sales, foreigners purchasing rural land and current immigration levels. The media criticism also allowed me to draw up a list of 'strategic assets' to which the 24.9-per-cent foreign ownership would apply — utility companies, Telecom, Air New Zealand and the like. In truth, I doubted whether even this reduced list would survive any post-election negotiations but it still allowed New Zealand First to brand its identity for political purposes.

However, things were not sailing so smoothly in other policy areas. I was alerted to a potential catastrophe within the party's health policy, where Bloxham was determined to resist any change to her asinine draft of the previous year. After hasty discussion with Peters a strategy was developed — I would complete the policy with Kirton's assistance; McCardle would administer the verbal Prozac to Bloxham. Again, the usual threats of resignation and public controversy were attempted; again there was universal sadness that the exit never eventuated. Given the widespread antipathy to the party vice-president I suggested that a specific New Zealand First policy that closed Bloxham's home hospital might be effective but, strangely enough, no one was game.

Ultimately the party's health policy was one of its better efforts, clearly stealing the Labour Party's thunder and impressing for its emphasis on abolishing management waste and converting those savings into various health initiatives. This was to be achieved largely by abolishing the four regional health authorities (RHAs) while also reducing the number of crown health enterprises (CHEs) to economic levels. With the addition of an extra $1 billion of new health expenditure over a three-year period New Zealand First also promised to establish minimum waiting times for particular surgical operations; establish multi-disciplinary family health teams for 'at risk' communities; provide free GP visits for all children aged twelve years and under; and introduce a Patient's Charter to guarantee service and communication standards to the general public.

It would not be until I worked as a strategic consultant for Associate Health Minister Kirton that I would realise the policy's depressing inadequacy; namely, that the health reforms had so fragmented the sector that no collective sense of a service ethos remained. But that is the great thing about elections — as long as a policy sounds plausible, then it will be perceived as such. And in politics, perception is reality.

Meanwhile there were screams of anguish coming from Gilbert Myles and other Auckland candidates that the party's promised bribing of state-house tenants was being abandoned. I was less impressed. There was no point in holding on to financially untenable policies given the inevitability of their post-election abandonment. Only the

Alliance could approach the election with a lavish spending agenda, its bizarre declaration that it would not enter any post-election coalition freeing it of the need to be fiscally responsible. If people were stupid enough to vote for a party that promised not to be in a position to implement its policies then they were welcome to farm the imbeciles.

It was my intention not just to ensure a strong New Zealand First representation in the first-ever MMP coalition but, more importantly, to provide Winston with a realistic and relatively detailed policy agenda that could garner him future support at the next general election and beyond. Given that politics is all about gaining power it is also about its retention — the second part of the equation is as important as the first.

Besides, making promises that could never be honoured was the exact antithesis of New Zealand First's supposed philosophy and if the immediate price was the shedding of a few percentage points in the polls this seemed a minor sacrifice when placed beside the party's later integrity. To judge by later events I assume this maxim was taken outside and shot as soon as the polling booths closed.

The forthcoming campaign had now begun to dominate the Leader's Unit which, misleadingly, suggests that there was a moment within our consciousness when it was possible to draw breath and reflect on tasks completed and those to be contemplated. No such luck. For New Zealand First was collapsing in upon itself — the deeper it dived into the electoral unknown the greater the external pressure. Everywhere there was petty conflict, organisational disorder and a dumb naïveté that had long passed beyond negligence. The gloomy depths beckoned.

TRAVERSING THE CREVASSE

Future political historians, studying the rise and fall of the Peters cult, will pinpoint certain dramatic events to justify their analyses: the Maori loans affair, 'Ka Awatea', the National Party expulsion, the Winebox Inquiry, Café Brava, the thoughtful dusting of John Banks' lapels — there will be no shortage of significant signposts. Equally there will be those who properly suggest that Winston's rise was associated with the various moods of an uncertain electorate — shaken by the post-'84 revolution, stirred by various social substrata, dismayed by the arrogance of the parliamentary status quo.

That Winston was an opportunist should never be in doubt. Practical politics is all about opportunities and their skilful exploitation whether for party or personal advantage. To condemn Peters for being good at his work is to misunderstand the nature of the profession. One must gain political power to influence the policy agenda; the route to capturing this power will inherently involve a maze of symbols, stratagems and subterfuges.

But of one thing I remain convinced. It was inevitable that New Zealand First would fall from its mid-1996 polling highs. At the precise moment when the public examined the party and its leadership for evidence of something better than the usual dross, both New Zealand First and Winston Peters proved themselves wholly incapable. The party's flaw was that its policy and personnel were unprepared for the spotlight and now mewed like newborn kittens in the unaccustomed glare. No such excuse could be offered Winston, for he was a fully grown and artful feline who had already lost a life or two along the way.

The Selwyn Cushing case came at the worst possible moment for Peters and the party. Had it been resolved six months earlier the damage might have been repaired. It was not just that Judge Dalmer found for Cushing in the latter's oft-delayed defamation action, and it was not just that he delivered a withering personal assessment of Peters' motives and actions. Rather it was Winston's defiant reaction to this judgement that exposed a spectacularly boorish arrogance, made worse by an associated demand for special favour. From that point on New Zealand First's poll ratings went into a steady fall, compounded by a series of disastrous internal ructions that laid out the party's inexperience, incompetence and indiscipline for all to see. Well, almost all.

It had been the view of Peters and his lawyers that Cushing's defamation action should essentially go uncontested. Peters' argument was that his naming of Cushing as the Business Roundtable intermediary who had sought to bribe him into silence prior to the 1990 election had been made under the protection of parliamentary privilege. Cushing's case was that Peters had indirectly alluded to the bribery allegation in other interviews and based his action on those interviews. Judge Dalmer concurred and awarded Cushing $50,000 in damages and a further $70,000 in legal costs — sums of money I knew Winston did not possess.

When the verdict was made public Winston was in London —

ironically, overseeing the Privy Council appeal of corporate tax dodgers European Pacific against the demands of Winebox commissioner Sir Ronald Davison. The timing was appalling and Winston had been strongly counselled against engaging in this gratuitous junket — his presence was of neither consequential nor convalescent value. A number of competing campaign interests, including the Cushing judgement, were approaching fruition — we could scarce afford the luxury of a leader in London nightclub mode.

The time difference would also present difficulties, the judgement having an uninterrupted twelve hours of negative media coverage before any reverse spinning was possible. Peters had ensured that his legal arrangements were kept quite separate from his parliamentary affairs, and this would prove another instance where Winston's obsessional secrecy worked to his ultimate disadvantage. We could neither decide nor pursue a line of public defence when Winston's legal stratagem had been hidden from our sight.

Incredibly Peters had decided, after legal advice, that he should offer no evidence to the court in his own defence. There are amoebas with hangovers that could have proffered better counsel. For, just months out from a general election, Selwyn Cushing and his Queen's Counsel champion, Mike Camp, were allowed to conduct a series of free courtroom hits, lovingly recorded by a hostile media and breathlessly communicated to an eager public in the throes of taking New Zealand First seriously. Peters was New Zealand First — any damage to his credibility would automatically feed through to the party's ratings. And Cushing hurt Peters bad. Real bad.

Not only was Peters portrayed as a tardy and boozy reprobate but, in the absence of evidence to the contrary, the presiding Judge Dalmer appeared to endorse this value judgement and, just for good measure, added his own virulent censure. By the time I had convinced Winston that damaging denunciation demanded reply, it was too late. Impressions had been made and then permanently cast.

Worse, when Peters finally decided to answer media queries on the matter he sought to portray himself as a haughty defender of Parliament's privilege even though he had essentially been found guilty of wantonly abusing that privilege to libel an innocent man. One public opinion poll recorded an eight-point drop in both Peters' and the party's ratings on the back of the Dalmer savaging.

Fortunately, a former parliamentary colleague charged to a most unexpected rescue. Michelle Boag had been recruited by corporate financiers Fay Richwhite to improve their tawdry reputation in the wake of the Bank of New Zealand and Winebox revelations. But Boag was much more than just a PR supremo; she was the National Party's communications strategist and also a political appointee to the board of Television New Zealand. These links would not have proven unhelpful to the merchant bank and there was a public suggestion that another National Party sympathiser, board chairman Norman Geary, had already misused his influence during a 'Frontline' current affairs investigation into various Winebox dealings in the Cook Islands.

Providing further evidence of the link between intellect, ingenuity and an indurate insensibility, Boag secretly employed a private film crew to record the Winebox hearings, and particularly the evidence of Peters. The Gallery rumour was that this filming would be edited in the form of election campaign 'attack' advertisements, portraying Peters as an unscrupulous McCarthyist dissolving in the witness box under tough cross-examination.

When queried about the crew's authority to record the hearing Boag instinctively misled the media — a folly I inherently appreciated — while also failing to inform Sir Ronald Davison or his staff of the arrangement. As a consequence Fay Richwhite were required to withdraw the film crew and hand over the relevant tapes, and were then found guilty of contempt. Instantly I recognised the symbolic gift we had been proffered and, given Peters' post-Cushing predicament, decided that Michelle's embarrassment must be exaggerated as symptomatic of a wider and darker Government agenda.

It was a decision that should have troubled my conscience; it does now but too late. Without Michelle's intervention some ten years earlier I would not have entered the Hawke's Bay selection contest and my political career may have foundered forever against my lack of courage. In short, I owed Michelle and that debt would not be repaid in setting her up, via Winston, for further public pillory.

Ah, but that is the nature of politics; the demands of the present consume the loyalties of the past. Thus began a very successful New Zealand First campaign to use Boag as a symbol for the Government's duplicitous cronyism, its grimy tendrils of patronage infecting any number of public organisations — from prestigious directorships on SOE boards through to the construction of lotteries committees and charitable trusts. After some fevered research Winston was able to produce a telegenic list of National cronies who had used their political connections for financial favour and by adding this to Michelle's public embarrassment we managed to repair some of the Cushing damage. But only some.

Attempts to resurrect Winston's white charger image were still being systematically undermined by his poisonous relationship with many in the media. Earlier in the year Peters had delivered a speech likening this connection to the fatal competition between a cobra and a mongoose, and clearly fancied himself as the avenging mammal. I had not drafted this speech (in fact office rumours abounded that Bob Jones had played a hand) but suggested the metaphor was unfortunate; the relationship was more symbiotic — say, that of a purging wildebeest and a dung beetle. A blank stare in response. OK. The aim, I reminded Winston, was not to destroy the media but to use them in the same way an ant milks an aphid — farming the Gallery to produce the desired public image. Peters appreciated this metaphor; he just refused to entertain the prospect that the media required anything other than constant snarling and the occasional boot in the bollocks.

Which was the largest single difference between the Winston I had guided prior to 1990 and the Winston I now found myself assisting some six years later. The obsessive secrecy, the late-night partying, the dependence on advisers — all those characteristics had been present within Peters in 1990. Sure, some had evolved in new and frightening ways but the essential characteristics were common and could be deciphered and interpreted without too much difficulty. But this passionate dislike of the media was an entirely novel twist.

If there was one common enemy in all Winston's ravings and rantings then it was the Fourth Estate — in his view a dreadful patchwork of political bias, sloth, incompetence and academic flatulence. And that was just the *Dominion*. He reserved a special hostility for current affairs host Paul Holmes and privately boasted of his enduring boycott of all radio and television programmes to which Holmes was even remotely connected. I was horrified. Apart from hosting the top-rating current affairs TV show the mercurial Aucklander also anchored the influential ZB Newstalk breakfast radio programme. Months out from a general election, Peters needed Holmes far more than the electronic elf would ever require Winston. I set out to negotiate a temporary truce — a feat that probably rivals the Camp David Accord as a diplomatic accomplishment and of which the Nobel Peace Prize committee still remain depressingly unaware.

The basis of this seething hostility all related to one issue — the bloody Winebox. If any editorial writer or news commentator ever advanced the view that Winston's conspiracy accusations were misguided or malicious then they went on an unofficial blacklist. Winston might have difficulty in fully absorbing a detailed election policy brief but you could be assured that any obscure reporter's criticism would be recalled in a flash.

It became imperative that Winston repair these gaping media breaches if New Zealand First was to effectively communicate its election messages and respond to any adverse criticism. By now I was producing and marketing most of Winston's speeches and press releases but I could not continue with these tasks and still finalise policy, initiate and co-ordinate campaign planning and participate in the training and instruction of bewildered candidates and their even more disoriented constituency teams. With Widerstrom on the outer and reassigned to Tau Henare, Winston needed a dedicated press secretary and he needed one now.

I had drawn up a short list of Gallery hacks who might pass Winstonian muster, my aim being to pick up one of the more intelligent journos who had sufficient rapport with their colleagues to compensate for the mad hectoring of their employer. Radio New Zealand political editor Karen Fisher and *New Zealand Herald* senior John Armstrong were the first approached with blandishments of power, fame and riches but both managed to politely decline before gagging. And so on down the totem pole, with such growing desperation that I feared we must eventually recruit from a TOPS life skills course. Fortunately, *National Business Review* reporter Mike Booker nibbled at one row of baits long enough to be hooked by the potential excitement and the prospect of following Winston into the Beehive in some three months' time.

Mike was a tall, well-respected and thoroughly decent print journalist who probably realised his error in the microsecond after confronting the chaos of his new surroundings. It was Booker's primary task to draft the daily press releases, spin the Gallery and write the occasional speech, but pacifying his former colleagues soon began to consume an inordinate amount of his energy. By now Winston had become used to the weird rhythm and quirky cadences of my earlier speech-writing efforts and refused to be weaned. Which was just as well because I was now inserting vast reams of new policy into most of these addresses and the last thing I needed was a dispassionate journo with a background in economics vetting out all the obvious errors. Given that most speeches were concluded literally minutes before the appointed hour of delivery it would have proved impossible to amend them anyway without leaving Winston gulping onstage like a demented goldfish.

But at least progress had been made. Most election policy had been finalised, a press secretary had been appointed, a growing number of candidates were being selected, and Winston's legal distractions had been placed to one side. Yep, things were looking up — the party was stirring itself from negligent slumber in preparation for a general election. In 1997. It was a pity this event was but weeks distant.

THE LIST

Perhaps the best example of New Zealand First's inherent lack of organisation was the chronic constipation it experienced when selecting its candidates — each contest seemed to require so much energy that the party hierarchy slumped and then slumbered after the straining exertion. For some inexplicable reason, the party's constitution decreed that only constituency candidates could appear on the party's list — an effective order of merit required to satisfy the provisions of the Electoral Reform Act and generally advertise the party's personality wares.

But this ranking exercise could not be completed until after the last constituency candidate had been selected. By mid-1996 there were still scores of selection contests in prospect and I became worried, then concerned and finally hyper-agitated that the list's completion must intrude upon the menacing shoals of the campaign proper. Every other major political party had experienced public controversy on the publication of their final list as aggrieved egos clashed head-on with internal expediency. Each candidate instinctively believed they deserved a higher list ranking or, at the very least, a higher ranking than so-and-so — the process reviving all manner of past and petty jealousies.

Such selfish melodrama would also occur within New Zealand First, I argued, and the closer the election the more dangerous the consequences. We might even face piqued candidates pulling out at the last minute, leaving some constituencies without a New Zealand First presence. Peters dismissed my fears, claiming to have a series of 'contingency' candidates tucked away for just such an eventuality, but like most such airy assurances this one's later test would prove its falsity.

This selection sloth could be traced to the usual source — Winston's habitual procrastination. No amount of personal petitioning would jolt his curious inertia and in one fierce exchange I was reminded that my role was strictly confined to matters political — the organisational wing of the party did not require my waspish interference.

In conversation with Peters I gleaned that he was unimpressed with the quality of many potential nominees seeking the party's favour, particularly those for the high-profile Wellington seats for which he was determined to attract celebrity candidates. But the real problem rested with head-office-prescribed electorate membership and financial targets that needed to be met before selections could be made — which made it difficult for a region like Wellington, where the party was in a cryogenic state.

With the exception of that perennial civic aspirant, the eerie Helene Ritchie, no one stepped forward to answer Winston's unspoken plea. In the end he still rejected Ritchie — partly because she demanded a high list ranking and partly because of her metropolitan reputation as a spooky fruitcake. This led to the surreal spectacle of a former deputy mayor, Ritchie, employing a former prime minister, Geoffrey Palmer, to publicly protest the blackball amid claims of political censorship.

Unfortunately, the party's basic problem was that as the election loomed closer and head office began relaxing its qualifications to proceed to selection, individual electorates became ever more desperate in their search for election-day champions. Indeed the contests were now serving as a lightning rod for a whole host of political opportunists, wannabes and nutters — particularly those already rejected by other parties. Winston correctly feared the local ridicule that might attend choosing the spurned suitor of another party or the local busybody eccentric. But given the paucity of contenders a good number of selections presented no ready alternative. I soon became aware of at least three candidates who were wholly dependent on welfare benefits and lacked even private transport to attend local rallies as the New Zealand First representative. In hindsight, a blessing.

In addition the late selection of the party's candidates placed the party at an enormous disadvantage within the various constituencies. They had no focus for their energy, no representative to lobby local voting blocs and no contact for prospective members. When I raged at Woolerton or Neems or anyone else within hailing distance about the calamitous state of the party's selection process, I received bashful reminders that New Zealand First scarcely existed south of Taupo with the exception of the internecine Christchurch factions. Winston had surrounded himself with smiling sycophants at the direct expense of administrative competence. Now he would begin paying for this perverse loyalty.

Perhaps more depressing was that a majority of candidates seemed to assume that New Zealand First would slingshot them into the House no matter how inconsequential their efforts at a local level. It is not unnatural for political candidates to have an exalted opinion of their abilities — it is precisely that kind of foolish optimism that drives them into politics in the first place. But I was now encountering a new phenomenon — the party's polling had convinced large numbers of candidates that their most likely passage to Parliament was via the party's list and not by dint of their hard work and enterprise in their constituency. Many candidates expected a party ranking that equated to their inflated self-image and there would be hell to pay when the reality contradicted their expectations. Indeed, it was now my view that a good number would simply give up the moment the list was published — a fear that would be brutally confirmed by subsequent events.

Mind you, the basic composition of the list remained unresolved, a situation compounded by the executive's neglect of even the most basic arrangements as to its organisation. The party's constitution decreed that candidates were to be democratically ranked by the representative membership comprising the national executive, the regional chairpersons and each of the 65 electorate chairpersons. This electoral college comprised some 85 individuals, with a good number pursuing a vested interest given their joint status as both a candidate and a chairperson.

The political dangers of this arrangement approximated a downhill slalom through a pine forest. One obstacle might be avoided, even the next, but sooner or later the odds favoured the trees. No one within New Zealand First's upper ranks foresaw the danger until the imminence of the party vote was upon them. As soon as I joined the party I had warned Winston that the list must be chosen by a competent inner circle, but Peters steamed onwards professing to trust the wider party. It was by now my heartfelt assessment that trusting this lot to buy an ice cream required a fanatic's faith.

There were any number of political difficulties in allowing the wider membership an opportunity to choose the ranking order. The most obvious was that the voting jury were blissfully ignorant about most of the candidates, a one-page résumé being their only guide. Indeed, many electorate organisations had only just been formed in response to the pressing needs of the campaign so their chairpersons lacked even a rudimentary understanding of New Zealand First let alone the political process.

Second, such uninformed choices could easily produce a list that was politically and publicly unacceptable. The first twenty on the list could well end up being male or middle-aged or Maori or North Islanders — or the entire combination if we were really unlucky. In the new MMP environment a party's electoral list was both a marketing tool and an indication of likely talent. It sent an unequivocal message and that message must be carefully managed.

But perhaps most important was that the list would provide a passage into Parliament for its upper echelon and those individuals would be a tangible three-year advertisement of the party's wares. It was essential that political talent determined the list — not the whims of 85 barely informed individuals who possessed the merest knowledge of the competing candidates.

In fact, there was a simple solution to this list quandary. The party's constitution established a 'selection college' comprising Peters, Henare, Woolerton and two personal choices of the leader. Their task was to prepare 'an ordered list' prior to the final vote, although the rules made no attempt to define the nature of this order. My suggestion was to construct a list reflecting the college's preferred ranking and taking into account all the usual variants of demographics, geographical location, gender, ethnicity and party responsibility. Peters had already indicated his latter preferences in rejigging the shadow portfolio responsibilities — the ordered list would be but an extension of these choices. In this way, I contended, the majority of the voting delegates would be confronted by a preferred ranking and Peters' implicit imprimatur.

Such suggestions proved infertile; Peters wanted the voting list in alphabetical order, with no hint of head office preference. I guessed that this choice was again related to Winston's aggravating refusal to offend personal associates; he had no wish to face the inevitable pleadings of the disappointed or the angry denunciations of the aggrieved.

Instead, Winston decided upon a more creative manoeuvre — he would manage the list's order by not-so-remote control. Initially I recoiled at the prospect of such artful manipulation. Already there were grumbling rumours about a possible administrative challenge — whispers to which David Stevenson's name was attached.

'And this still requires a central list,' I maintained, although how this master copy might procreate itself with quite such stunning dexterity escaped me. I was advised not to trouble myself with such trifling matters and quickly reached the necessary abandoned mental state — there were still one thousand and one other matters that must be settled before election day without concerning myself with all these dubious mechanics. Besides, if there was going to be a central list with which to lobby voting delegates then I was conceited enough to dread its composition were I not involved — we could end up with the sartorial overwhelming the sagacious.

The drafters of New Zealand First's constitution had obviously been frustrated lawyers because their explanations as to how the various delegates' votes should be counted introduced the kind of legalese rarely sighted beyond used-car dealers' yards. In effect, the delegates would be required to rank their preferences from numbers one to 65 in descending order of merit — although the method by which these votes should then be totalled and a ranking list produced invited any number of creative endeavours. In theory, a systematic 'voting plunge' could work should a solid phalanx of delegates all cast their votes in exactly the same order. Given the chaotic state of the party's organisation, and the seething cauldron of inter-personal rivalries enveloping all the various list candidates, then the exercise might be accomplished with a surprisingly small number of primed delegates. Such details were the least of my concerns — I had petitioned for the direct route and been repelled. A central lobbying list was, by far, the lesser of the remaining evils.

Between us Sarah, Winston and I attempted to draw up an initial list of preferred ranking — a careful combination of geography, gender and genetic ability. Strangely this exercise required repeating — this time in the main Caucus room, which had by now been converted into a rudimentary campaign headquarters. Surrounded by the candidates' biographies Winston and I drew up the final party list, numbering those choices from one to 65 — the Peters name at both extremities, with oldest brother Ron eschewing list preference to emphasise his constituency loyalties. Oh that there had been 64 other Ron Peters.

Halfway through this process Tau Henare walked into the room and immediately guessed at our endeavour. Although I was aware that Woolerton, Brian Henry and Sarah had been appraised of the exercise I was unsure if Henare was a part of this inner loop — an unease that magnified when I caught the startled expression on Winston's face. Tau drew a stealthy smile and pressed his advantage.

'As long as Tuku is in the top ten, then the list will be fine by me.' Peters nodded his assent and I drew a line through Tuku Morgan's name, presently hovering in the late teens. A palpable relief attended the rest of our deliberations.

Winston was to display some very direct inclinations during this evening, although on some candidates we were in complete agreement. Now that Deborah Morris had been convinced to stand as the Hutt South candidate, her relative youth, enthusiasm and intelligence were to be marketed extensively. Besides, even though she had but a researcher's experience of Parliament any understanding of these tricky surrounds would prove helpful in acclimatising her prospective colleagues. To that end I suggested that she be the first female candidate registered on the list. Peters was more conservative and determined a ranking just above that of Morgan.

It was also Peters' view that the five Maori candidates were certainties to win their seats — an assessment I supported, although I placed a question mark over Te Tai Tonga's Tu Wyllie. Rolling the veteran Whetu Tirikatene-Sullivan would be no easy task. In fact, Wyllie would owe his seat to the efforts and financial assistance of Tirikatene-Sullivan's mortal enemies, Sir Tipene O'Regan and the Ngai Tahu Maori Trust Board, and his lower list ranking seemed to reflect Peters' view of Wyllie's out-there personality and perhaps this alternative political arrangement. Thus the Maori candidates were scattered through the list, with John Delamere, Rana Waitai and Wyllie ultimately dependent on their constituency support to take their respective places in the House.

Peters had his personal favourites, Ann Batten, Brian Donnelly, Peter Brown and Robyn McDonald all receiving high rankings, with Batten usurping Bloxham as the premier woman candidate. That Bloxham had any prominence at all was due to Winston — if there was going to be a central register based on talent then I contended that the party's vice-president should not be within the top 50. Peters laughed at such bias and made a crack about my alleged Freudian desire for the Timaru tizzy. Yeah, right.

To a certain extent the list chose itself. The recent recruits to the party — Batten, McCardle, Elder, Marks, Kirton and Harding — received due recognition of their value to the cause while most party spokespersons attained rankings commensurate with their policy performances. Former MPs Gilbert Myles, Ian Peters and Ralph Maxwell were granted few favours, although Myles and Ian Peters could still reasonably expect election should New Zealand First's popularity stay around the projected fifteen per cent mark.

Winston's relationship with Ian, at times intense and testy, possibly militated against the latter's higher ranking, with Ian never being properly forgiven for staying with the National Caucus after his younger sibling had been expelled. But Winston also wanted to ensure that New Zealand First was not perceived as some Peters family benefit and that Ian was not advantaged because of his fraternal connection to the leadership.

If there was one group universally advantaged by the list selection it was the female candidates. With the exception of Morris and to a lesser extent Batten, New Zealand First lacked quality female aspirants — in part a general commentary on the continuing gender bias of the demon profession but also a specific reflection of New Zealand First's attraction to potential women candidates. The ironic tyranny of the MMP list is that it imposes on parties an unofficial requirement to promote a quota of female candidates and New Zealand First felt similarly constrained. Thus, senior positions on the party's list were given to women when more able male candidates might have been preferred on the grounds of political talent.

Had a properly constituted selection college been required to prescribe an ordered list then the same strictures would have applied — age, location, gender, ethnicity, experience, talent and the like.

But at the end of an exhausting evening a list numbered from one to 65 had been completed — a list which had been primarily composed by Winston and one which utterly reflected his views of the relative merits of all competing individuals and interests.

A few days later the electoral college cast their votes — at five different locations around the country and at exactly the same time. The papers were then gathered and delivered to the appointed judicial officer, Brian Henry, and a ripple of expectancy swept through the party while the media sharks gathered themselves for an anticipated feeding frenzy. They would not be disappointed.

That Monday evening I was in Auckland, due to meet the party's advertising consultant, Marco Marinkovich, to finalise aspects of the campaign; Jack Elder was beside me as Sarah telephoned through the released list. It exactly matched the list that Winston and I had framed.

Despite my best efforts at congratulation Jack's reaction was less effusive than I had anticipated — his ranking at number seven did not match his recall of an earlier Winston undertaking. I arched an eyebrow. My God, if Jack had problems then I shuddered at the reactions further down the food chain. That evening any number of prospective political careers had been dashed to the floor and mercilessly pummelled into the carpet.

In any subjective evaluation of ability, those judged invariably look beyond their own failings for an explanation and an accompanying excuse. This occasion would be no different — less than five weeks out from the election a solid mass of New Zealand First candidates suddenly put themselves into grief mode. They had followed the TV polls that tracked the party's decline over recent months; they all understood how MMP mathematics worked; and they all knew how to use a pocket calculator. And now they were looking for someone to blame.

Me.

Chapter 12

CAMPAIGN

GHOST TRAIN

When I was a young boy the local A & P Show was the highlight of Wanganui's otherwise moribund entertainment calendar and very much the yearly thrill for all my school classmates. It had nothing to do with the sheepdog trials or the prize bulls or the best-sow competition — these were strictly adult fare, with enough mushy and musty farm odours to repel even the most intrepid of my peers. No, our childish anticipation centred around the garish sideshow attractions with their crooked coconut shies, dodgy dodgems and rigged 'skill' contests — the itinerant stall-owners never above swindling any gullible kid out of their pocket money.

But such entertainments paled beside my singular though frustrated desire to be scared witless by a ride on the show's ghost train. My parents point-blank refused even to contemplate the idea — I was already prone to nightmares and cramming my vexed imagination with a new and vivid provocation would only guarantee further sleepless nights. But I would not be dissuaded and on one particular hot spring afternoon extricated myself from the family group and stealthily backtracked to the entrance to the ghost train.

An age minimum had been imposed but I had the necessary florin in my hand and the Maori operator duly winked at my cheek as I clambered aboard the battered carriage. Brimming with fearful anticipation I readied myself for a bout of sustained horror as the train lurched its noisy way through the swinging metal doors and into the dark and dread unknown.

My parents had been right. The next three minutes of mechanical shock and spectral assault became so amplified over the next few nights that I dared not sleep for fear of inviting macabre reminders of my folly. I had learned an early lesson — there are some experiences best avoided no matter the extent of the anticipatory thrill. White House interns should take note.

So it is with election campaigns. From the outside they look fun — a hurly-burly of colour, energy and excitement. In fact election campaigns are chaotic, ill-disciplined and scary, lurching their adrenal way from mini-crisis to mini-crisis and always threatening to derail, smash and burn like an Indian train crash. The conventional wisdom is that the winning party is the one that blunders the least, although there is a newer school of thought that even wonders whether the mistakes have any effect at all. Sadly, the advent of entertainment-based current-affairs television has made modern elections even more sudorific and superficial. Now every politician is required to ooze a mixture of mock sincerity and outrage within a ten-second electronic envelope presided over by a hyper host who arranges the combat with one eye on their ego and the other on the ratings.

The petty demands of television have also obliged political parties to abandon any attempt at rational and constructive policy debate, and to engage instead in 'presidential-style' campaigns centred on the party leader. Given that New Zealand First's one and only asset was its leader (despite my best attempts at policy revision) this modern state of affairs did not entirely disadvantage us. In fact, the decision of Television New Zealand to provide New Zealand First and the Alliance with equal news and current-affairs coverage to that of the established National and Labour parties ensured a media emphasis not entirely merited by the party's structure.

Following my parliamentary resignation in April 1996 Winston had determined that my role as 'special adviser' should include aspects of campaign planning, assisted by a de facto campaign committee. Neither New Zealand First nor Peters ever formally gazetted this group — it was loosely based on those individuals close enough to Winston to merit his trust and possess a rough appreciation of his idiosyncrasies. An exclusive group by nature.

Over the next few months this committee would comprise Sarah Neems, Brian Henry, Grey Advertising supremo Marco Marinkovich, Peters and me, with the party represented by president Doug Woolerton, treasurer Kay Urlich and secretary Lynne Gill, who also doubled as Brian Henry's law clerk. From time to time the other three MPs would attend, depending on their political and family commitments, although they were generally content to rely on later briefings. In practice, much of the campaign strategy and daily tactical positioning would be drafted by me and thence require Winston's formal approval before its action.

Even this summary suggests a measure of internal order and management that was contradicted by the reality. During the campaign proper (the formal campaign generally being regarded as the four weeks preceding election day) 'Frontline' news reporter Richard Harman sought my permission to film 'a day in the life' of New Zealand First's campaign team for post-election viewing. All other parties acceded to Harman's request but I declined; not on the grounds of secrecy or confidentiality, even if the refusal was dressed in such excuses, but simply because New Zealand First had no formal nor even informal approximation of such a structure.

The party's inexact grasp of organisational order ensured that most campaign arrangements were ad hoc — and as with all such arrangements they extended from inspired to insane, touching precious little in between. However, all modern campaigns are initially determined by their ability to raise money, and this would be New Zealand First's largest hurdle. In short, the party had no money — a fact to which I only became appraised when the campaign was properly under way and only after my campaign strategy had been unanimously agreed by both Winston and the party's executive.

At the start of 1996, in preliminary discussions on the campaign and its likely format, Winston had suggested a sum of one million dollars as the necessary budget and with Woolerton's nodding assent determined that this ambitious fund-raising target would be the party's special responsibility. I had enough experience of New Zealand First to consider such a sum at the outer reaches of possibility — particularly given the acute dependence of modern campaigns on corporate funding.

My old research unit colleague Wayne Eagleson had chaired the National Party's effort in 1993 and his campaign budget had been over three million dollars, with much of that sum being raised through National's sophisticated businesshouse network. By contrast Peters had burned off possible corporate support with all his various parliamentary allegations and lacked influential associates to gain backdoor entry to the Queen Street boardrooms. I was ambivalent about such funding anyway — the corporate dollar has an odour of policy influence and New Zealand First's populist credo was supposed to eschew such privileged sectoral favour.

Nevertheless, the confidence exuded around the party's executive table lulled me into believing that some additional effort would be attempted and Winston's ensuing bravado reinforced that impression.

Two months out from the election I presented a campaign plan to Winston's committee with an estimated price tag of $450,000 — not including any free broadcasting that might be provided by the Electoral Commission. Even then the costs were understated — Marco was donating his expertise for free and I had employed a fresh young public relations company from Wellington, Perceptions, who wanted the New Zealand First election contract as an experiential entrée to other political work. They were a thoroughly pleasant if naive group of individuals, who were about to learn the great lesson of all PR companies and election campaigns. Don't. With the possible exception of the National Party, most political parties impose hellish deadlines and then stretch out their payments to bad-debt status. New Zealand First might be a new party but it had learned all the old tricks.

Thankfully the party's financial arrangements were not my affair, although their general disrepair would seriously intrude upon subsequent planning. This became even more obvious when I was required to draft the party's submission to the Electoral Commission seeking public broadcasting monies. Around $2 million was on offer, to be allocated to all those parties duly registered, and distributed according to arcane legislative criteria that reeked of a National/Labour gerrymander. Incredibly, both parties even provided their own representatives to the allocation committee, David Beatson and Lloyd Falck respectively, and it required a gargantuan leap of faith to assume an impartial Commission hearing.

Still, if we wanted public money there was no other way. All parties were required to divulge various political details including their current number of MPs, past electoral support, indications of current public rating and the holy of holies — the financial membership of their organisation. This last proved particularly problematic for New Zealand First. Peters had repeatedly boasted that New Zealand First now possessed the second largest party membership in the country — outstripped only by National. Like many of Winston's claims this one also exceeded the straitjacket of actuality, and embarrassment loomed should the party's official figures contradict its leader's braggadocio.

A tactical withdrawal was clearly required and Peters decided that such sensitive information should not be provided to the Commission on the grounds that the presence of Beatson and Falck allowed the major parties access to confidential information about their smaller rivals. However, the Electoral Commission called Winston's bluff by producing signed assurances from both men that any information received would remain strictly confidential, while reminding the party that failure to supply the membership information must impact on the Commission's final determination.

Facing the prospect of over $100,000 of free broadcasting time being flushed down the toilet — chiefly to protect Winston's vanity — I angrily petitioned both Peters and Woolerton to render up the necessary information. So what if we were second or third in membership numbers? Was that contest more important than precious free television time? And given that the legislation itself denied parties from purchasing additional television time beyond the Commission's quota, the price being asked to avoid minor embarrassment was clearly excessive.

Woolerton duly provided the party's confidential membership figures to the Commission, although only after checking with me as to that body's ability to demand verifiable proof, and upon the Alliance and Labour's stated numbers. That Woolerton was in a position to supply the Commission with any figures at all was something of a minor miracle given the party's chaotic record-keeping. In addition, the party was being inundated with 'one-dollar memberships' as potential candidates sought to secure their candidacy selection by enrolling family members, the local sports club and the not-so-occasional random phantom. Whether these persons were aware of their new political association was another matter entirely. I suspected that such laxity was not confined to NZ First's organisation as the membership numbers of any political party was a critical determinant in the Commission's final allocation of public broadcasting monies. A broad incentive to cheat is not the kind of temptation any party needs.

Despite the Commission's final hefty allocation, money troubles would continue to plague the party's campaign. This difficulty confronted me directly when the first down-payment was required for the 'Kiwi Spirit' — a luxury tourist bus that had been specially converted to act as Winston's mobile campaign headquarters, spectacularly liveried in the party's colours. The total cost of the 'Kiwi Spirit' campaign was near $250,000, which included associated advertising, public rallies and the nationwide distribution of various propaganda pamphlets. Perceptions, the PR company, had organised the bus but required a $50,000 deposit to satisfy the tourism company from which it had been leased. I duly passed this request over to Sarah Neems and thought no more of it.

But days turned into weeks and despite constant reminders the invoice remained unpaid. On the eve of the party's campaign launch, at which the 'Kiwi Spirit' was to play a starring role, the bus company threatened to pull the plug. And I did not blame them. Finally, after a flurry of telephone calls and a frenetic display of internal duck-shoving the truth was revealed to me — the party could muster just $39,000 towards the deposit. The remaining $11,000 was finally scrambled through a series of personal loans from associates of Winston but such generosity only forestalled the inevitable. Where was the other $400,000 for the campaign going to come from? This could be the shortest party campaign in general election history.

Each time I attempted to gain some clarity about the matter I was forcefully reminded that my responsibility was campaign strategy — others would attend to its financing. At which point I would close my eyes, draw several deep breaths and fight for internal calm — to absolutely no effect. The parliamentary offices would daily reverberate with my frustration. There were eight words I particularly came to fear — usually uttered in an apologetic tone by a retreating Sarah but always portending disaster.

' Michael...' Pause. 'You're not going to like this but...'

My fears over the campaign finances remained with me until election day. I was never sure when one of the aggrieved creditors would simply demand instant payment and then pull the plug. Then the New Zealand First illusion would simply shimmer away under the baleful glare of the smug media.

Noting Woolerton's floundering efforts, I suggested that a pre-election tithing pledge from the likely influx of New Zealand First MPs might convince some financial institutions to advance credit — which led to a fevered burst of activity as Woolerton and Peters sought to convince well-endowed list candidates to share their prospective plenty. But the very fact that my proposal had been acted upon scared me even more, for it had further exposed the complete absence of financial forethought.

I was back on the ghost train.

INTENTIONS

If political commentators were confused as to the direction of New Zealand First's election campaign they had every right to be. So was New Zealand First.

At no stage did the campaign committee, or even Winston and I in private discussion, decide on the campaign's key objectives. Such were the demands of the daily pressures that they consumed the construction of a proper strategic overview. As the saying goes — 'When you're up to your arse in alligators, you tend to forget that you went there to drain the swamp.'

In many ways that was my fault. I had allowed myself to be distracted by the minutiae of campaign planning and policy, while my speech-writing role for Winston delivered daily and then almost hourly ultimatums. My strategic vision thus took on an air of opportunistic spontaneity. In defence I had no real choice — the paucity of political organisation demanded my instant attention, but such immediacy militated against a proper sense of professional detachment. Under pressure it is only human to err but under campaign pressure then errors are almost mandatory; the trick is to distract the media and the public long enough to repair the more obvious damage and hope you have second-guessed the next crisis point before the media get there.

In truth, though, Winston and I also had conflicting objectives. In fact, Winston had conflicting objectives — as would become plain at the height of the battle. My general aim was simple: to ensure that New Zealand First held the balance of power on election night and that neither National nor Labour could form a government without us. To this end I surmised that New Zealand First must gain around fifteen per cent of the list vote and secure the third-place ranking in popular preference behind the two major parties. We needed to beat the Alliance to hold MMP's first 'balance of responsibility'.

Winston's objectives were much grander. He genuinely wanted to win the preference ranking and gain 30-per-cent-plus of the party vote, believing this outcome achievable despite the Cushing affair, the general paucity of party organisational skills and a stunning lack of campaign capital. Although I regarded such thinking as delusional it was important for me to at least divine Peters' intent, for it suggested Winston wanted to maximise New Zealand First's list vote — which would require a quite different strategic plan from my own hasty stratagem.

To win fifteen per cent of the vote Winston and New Zealand First must recapture their supporters from three years ago and then embolden sufficient disaffected former Labour and Alliance supporters to cast their vote in the party's favour. However, if the party really wanted to chase Winston's dream, then New Zealand First needed to spread its wings beyond anti-National voters and reach into the Centre-Right support base as well. One was a conservative policy — the other expansionist. Unwittingly the party adopted a little of each and fell between the two stools.

To appeal to Centre-Right voters New Zealand First needed to target National's soft underbelly — provincial New Zealand. And yet with the exception of Tauranga and the Far North the party structure lacked the necessary substance to provide on-the-ground support for these regional efforts. Weaning the farmers themselves from National's dry teat would take years of moist overtures and, ironically, the virulently *laissez faire* ACT were more attractive preachers. My pragmatic view was that if the agricultural community had chosen the arrogant and arid Federated Farmers to be their major lobby group then they deserved everything they got.

However, in the rural servicing towns and provincial cities there existed potential New Zealand First support. But how to reach and motivate these voters, particularly when our candidates lacked even the barest political nous or the requisite funds to run effective local campaigns?

For a number of weeks I had been toying with the idea that New Zealand First should compensate for its lack of resources by running a campaign that was demonstrably different — one that obviously contrasted with that of its well-endowed rivals. Of course I did not have much choice — New Zealand First could not compete with the money of National, the networks of Labour or the activist passion of the Alliance. The risk was that any departure from the campaigning norm would come up against the various rigidities of the media, and particularly the demands of television. Given that the electronic media are inherently selfish, pompous and lazy, then New Zealand First stood a good chance of offending their collective sense of self-worth if it attempted activities outside the mainstream. Which was a matter quickly appreciated by the major party leaders, who geared their campaigns around television with low-risk photo opportunities, staged audiences and a clear distaste for public contact. But I reasoned that the risk of offending the networks was worth it. Screw the media —

where we went over the last four weeks of the campaign they would be obliged to follow.

So was born the 'Kiwi Spirit' bus tour — an attempt to barnstorm through heartland New Zealand while cynically noting that the nostalgic images created would also be telecast into metropolitan homes. It was not an original concept — I had flogged it from the Clinton/Gore US presidential campaign of 1992, while even their basic modus operandi owed its origins to the old-style whistle-stop tours during which aspiring candidates would crisscross the nation in search of every last vote rather than rely upon the omnipotent six o'clock news. The potential advantages of this political road trip were considerable — we could ascend above the media ruck in delivering the message direct to the people, and Winston was always at his best when confronted with live audiences. And, with a bit of luck, New Zealand First's old-style campaign would be viewed as an obvious contrast to the fly-in/pose/fly-out slickness of the other major parties.

One spring evening I laid out a huge map of New Zealand in the Caucus room and attempted to devise an itinerary that would send the 'Kiwi Spirit' from Whangarei to the Bluff and most points in between. I half hoped that the task would prove impossible — keeping Peters constantly on the move had its own risks, including loss of direct contact and thence of control — but, dammit, the logistics defeated me. Provided this new super-duper luxury coach remained roadworthy Winston could indeed cover the country in four weeks, by starting in Auckland, ploughing down the western side of the North Island, touring the entire South Island, and concluding the journey by a more leisurely haul up the North Island's east coast before spending a weekend in Tauranga and thence concluding the campaign in Auckland and the Far North. A few alterations were then ordered to the coach's internal configuration, with sleeping quarters and a decent bathroom installed for the leader along with a state-of-the-art public address system for the open-air meetings in smaller provincial towns and hamlets.

For all the symbolism of the 'Kiwi Spirit' road tour there were many glaring disadvantages. Like it or not, television was still the most important news medium and there would be days and evenings when Winston's routine would clearly defy the pre-planned coverage of the major networks. In addition, the four-week tour would set a punishing personal schedule for Winston, despite his legendary stamina and his great love of informal speeches. Crowds energised Winston — they must recharge him where sleep would not.

In fact, the greatest battle during this period was in disciplining Peters to get adequate rest. In the end I was forced to assign Ernie Davis to act as Winston's personal minder, once it became obvious that Mike Booker lacked sufficient influence to point Peters to bed. Instead, Winston would complete his evening engagements and thence entertain the accompanying journalists over a late meal, a few whiskies and much reminiscence. One television journalist would spend just three days on the 'Kiwi Spirit' and bale out, exhausted from attempting to keep up with Peters' late-night antics. I seethed in frustration. Clearly Ernie was not as effective as I had anticipated, and we tetchily discussed Peters' post-event carousing and its unfortunate effect on his early-morning exchanges with the media. Ernie raised his shoulders and offered a look of pure resignation.

' Michael,' he challenged. 'You try. He's impossible.'

I gloomily accepted the challenge and a stormy showdown was attempted with my errant chief. The early-morning media stories set the tone for the entire day, I argued. Stuff them up and you are fighting to recover that impression instead of selling your own message. Peters would concur with this observation but then blame individual reporters for deliberately misinterpreting his unguarded comments. Remonstrating with Winston at such times was always tough — it was like scolding a five-year-old with attention-deficit syndrome.

353

'OK Laws,' he would scowl in his best approximation of undeserved rebuke, 'I'll get an early night tonight.'

But such intentions, sincere or managed, would always founder upon the spontaneity of the hour. It would have been easier to surrender and admit defeat, but I would not. It was a purely selfish rearguard action on my part. Having invested such emotional and mental energy in planning and executing the campaign I was not prepared to let any bastard stuff it around — least of all the leader. Scarcely a day of the campaign would pass without my admonishing Peters for his irregular attempts at nightly rest and consequent verbal indiscipline.

Virtually every gaffe Peters made on the election campaign trail — either in publicly attacking an elderly New Zealand First supporter in Hawke's Bay as 'a National Party plant' or in angrily rising to the bait of hecklers at a Wellington midday rally — was attributable to fatigue. Towards the end of the campaign the folly of our overreliance on the 'Spirit' became obvious — Winston's weary demeanour now began to affect the quality of his television performances. His eyelids fluttered against the glare of the studio lights like a tipsy fantail, while his usually sharp commentary lacked snap and vigour. Yet whenever Sarah and I decided that a minor scheduled meeting should be cancelled to allow Winston the necessary rest before an important TV debate or function, a solid wall of protest from party functionaries would persuade Peters to fulfil their local expectations — even to the point where Winston would change the driver's daily instructions to accommodate such entreaties. Trying to impose campaign discipline from Wellington would prove an utterly futile exercise — if the leader was not going to discipline himself then I had precious little chance of imposing a collective sense of order on the rest of the rabble that posed as party activists.

In the main the candidates themselves proved more proficient than I expected. They were the usual party political mixture of the flashy and the feeble, the flocculent and the fluent. Fortunately most of them also accepted the aphoristic wisdom that it is better to keep quiet and be thought a fool than to speak and remove all doubt. Those who were not convinced only needed to watch the series of electorate debates on Wellington's local TV station, hosted by Mike Hosking of 'Morning Report' and featuring candidates from each of the contesting parties. Initially McCardle and I would gaze in stunned horror at our candidates' truly awful performances but we soon appreciated the unwitting humour of the situation and contented ourselves with the knowledge that the equally appalling TV ratings that attended these debates should preclude too much public damage.

Equally, the party's education and health spokespersons, Brian Donnelly and Neil Kirton, spooked themselves senseless when appearing on the more prestigious TVNZ issues-based election debates chaired by Ian Fraser — despite a prior weekend of media training. Both appeared to be suffering from some mutant form of catatonic shock — I had witnessed zombie extras from *Invasion of the Bodysnatchers* demonstrating a better awareness of their surroundings.

Yet it was difficult to truly attribute blame to any particular candidate — most were untrained, politically naive and depressingly gullible, and local campaign efforts must always founder if national responsibility was placed upon their inexperienced shoulders. I attempted to circumvent some of this difficulty by publishing a 'Candidate's Handbook' — a basic 'how to stay out of the shit' electioneering guide — supplemented with the occasional regional seminar. But even this effort required some degree of local finance to properly implement and a good many electorates were struggling even to find their candidate's deposit.

The closer the election drew the more obvious it became that the party was suffering from a kind of collective tarantism, and I was not immune from such hysteria. In the end I decided that rather than inflict myself and my growing frustration on the parliamentary staff I would set up my own campaign centre in my home, complete with PC, fax, Internet and e-mail communications and three separate telephone lines. In that way I could simultaneously monitor the progress of 'Kiwi Spirit' and the campaigns of the other parties; draft, print and electronically distribute Winston's daily speeches and media releases; supervise the parliamentary operations via Sarah and Louise; handle panicky distress calls from local candidates (which usually consisted of repeating my father's dodgy advice that they 'should get a good night's sleep'); work with Marco in devising and implementing the party's advertising and television campaign; generally screen out those media enquiries that could not simply be answered with a monosyllabic grunt; and, finally, monitor the Perceptions lads and their growing and onerous propaganda duties.

Karen would silently deliver my meals and then clear away the dirty dishes — for the last three weeks of the campaign I existed in a small triangle framed by the bathroom, the PC and my bed.

All this time I was keeping an increasingly anxious eye on the public opinion polls and praying that election day would rush its way to the rescue — for Labour had easily reclaimed second place and New Zealand First was now in free fall. The searing intensity of the campaign had properly exposed the New Zealand First chimera as its soft edges shimmered into the background, with great chunks of anti-National voters returning to their former Labour and Alliance homes. The party was facing a meltdown in its popular backing — just holding it together until election day would require either superhuman endeavour or the greatest sprinkling of good fortune. Most probably both.

THE GAFFE EXPRESS

The 1996 election always possessed a slightly phoney ambience — as if the public had all drawn different horses in some exotic sweepstake but the winner was going to be determined by random chance. Which nag crossed the line first would be irrelevant — MMP's quaint mathematics had rendered such contests virtually obsolete.

National and Labour possessed the same objective — to be the senior party in any post-election coalition. To that end both parties could run their usual pluralist campaigns and try to retain their former broad gathering of disparate interests. But the lesser parties had a more refined target — they needed enough votes to make or unmake any prospective government. In some ways their task was slightly easier — find a niche in the market and then exploit it.

Curiously, the Alliance had decided that even this competition was too reactionary for their tastes. Their bizarre decision to become the new MMP parliament's non-contact conscience suggested that all their potential partners had a nasty whiff of leprosy about them. It was a particularly dumb tactical ploy for it broadcast an air of isolationist ambivalence about the whole political process — as if it was all too sordid to risk the embrace. They might have been morally right but elections are not about morals; this was politics, where the end pursuit is always power. Anderton's strategy thus had the consequence of promoting other parties to the Alliance's ultimate electoral disadvantage. If voters wanted to change the world — or even confirm its current status — then a vote for Jim Anderton's 'rainbow coalition' would be an act of political masturbation.

Essentially this left the kingmaker role to New Zealand First. In fact, looking back I wonder if the whole campaign was not some completely unnecessary charade. Given that neither National nor Labour had the electoral support to win the election outright, and that the Alliance was making whoopee with its own five constituent digits, then New Zealand First was always destined to cast the winner's laurel. There was an important rider to this observation: provided New Zealand First gained sufficient seats to properly bestow Excalibur.

There were irritants to this analysis. National had reached the same strategic conclusion and was trying to encourage, cajole, sweeten and thence embrace a plethora of minor parties to cobble together a post-election coalition of its own. In the Ohariu-Belmont seat this would result in National withdrawing from the constituency contest in favour of United's Peter Dunne, thus assuring that party of parliamentary representation. Similarly, Prime Minister Bolger coolly kneecapped National's Wellington Central candidate, Mark Thomas, to give voters the message that Richard Prebble's ACT deserved special consideration. Meanwhile former National minister Graeme Lee had been provided with every encouragement to build his decidedly unchristian Christian Democrat/Christian Heritage conglomerate past the five per cent MMP threshold — despite the anguish of the gay lobby within the National Party. National's plan was obvious. They hoped to organise enough political pygmies into a pyramid and thence vault over the fence.

To counterpoint this stratagem Bolger's speech-writers coined a pejorative term for their larger political opponents. Labour, New Zealand First and the Alliance were the 'gloom gang' — poised to roll back the 'more market' economy and return New Zealand to the bad old days of intervention, profligacy and the nanny state. The delicious irony, that this Stalinist oppression had been created by a National Cabinet of which Prime Minister Bolger and Finance Minister Birch were principal players, wholly escaped the Nats.

In turn I devised a suitable retort. National, ACT and the Christian Coalition were politics' 'toxic trio' — illiberal, insensitive and infelicitous — and I worked the insult into all of Winston's campaign speeches. It was a phrase with real media bite and soon assumed a currency well beyond its immediate surroundings. Journalists now portrayed the first-ever MMP election as a contest between the Left's gloom gang and the Right's toxic trio — in essence reverting to the two-party symbolism of the old electoral system.

Certainly the Nats' electioneering attempted to reinforce such a match-up, with 'attack' advertisements against the spending policies of the Labour/New Zealand First/Alliance triumvirate and an offensive in the rural heartland against the same 'left-wing coalition'. Electors were warned that a vote for any one party within the gloom gang was automatically a vote for the others as well — with the nuttier extremities of each party being mercilessly caricatured as the likely mainstream policy imperatives for any such post-election coalition.

But National did not confine their attacks on New Zealand First to associative denigration. Their research unit recycled a quote from a Tau Henare interview in the Christchurch *Press* of the previous year in which the deputy leader had injudiciously suggested that all Crown land be returned to Maori in satisfaction of outstanding Treaty claims. In addition, radio talkbacks were flooded with primed callers linking Henare and thence New Zealand First to a radical Maori separatism — a claim that had its clear effect on a surprising number of talkback hosts and sent spasms of terror through the party's elderly Pakeha support base.

But Henare's rhetoric was also proving a present embarrassment to the campaign. Having already declared that he would refuse to serve in any coalition Cabinet of which Jenny Shipley was a member, he now extended this personal blackball to Jim Bolger and Bill Birch as well. In fact, Henare emphasised — now intoxicated with an infusion of *Once Were Warriors* insouciance and rising to the provocation of John Banks at an Auckland public forum — he would not take executive responsibility in any government that included the dastardly Nats. Peters was furious and the resultant telephone call was captured and then replayed by an appreciative TVNZ news crew. I could handle Henare being goaded into an injudicious remark, but allowing a film crew to capture Peters' scolding reaction was inexcusable.

Winston's primary concern was that New Zealand First should position itself as the responsible centre party during the coming campaign, with the ability to move left or right depending on the outcome of post-election negotiations. Henare was unwittingly entrapping Peters and New Zealand First within the Alliance/Labour embrace, and providing credence to National's claims that New Zealand First was indeed a close cousin of the Left.

In addition, the party's populist campaign must founder if New Zealand First assumed the public demeanour of a left-wing Maori party, and Henare's repeated outbursts were reinforcing that unfortunate impression. Initially I made the mistake of dismissing Peters' concerns, if only because of a gut feeling that the influential days of activist talkback radio were over and that most listeners were drawn from a lessening pool of hardened malcontents. Of course that pool included a goodly number of Peters supporters so my analysis, though probably correct, possessed an obvious strategic flaw.

My tactical hesitation in covering the Henare blunders and the separatist smear proved a mistake. During any election campaign there will be rumours that career their way through an excited media and into the wider community. Most can safely be ignored as the next new rumour wipes out the previous one. But there are also those subterranean impressions that insidiously work their way into the public consciousness, especially if fanned by one's opponents. Then a party has just two options: confront and deny, and run the risk of widening the damage, or continue to ignore and evade.

A week into the campaign Winston and I jointly decided that confrontation was the more viable option. Besides, it suited our personalities. I drafted a speech slamming Maori radicals for their 'hymn of hate', while rejecting the 'creepy creed of radical separatism' that underlined their motivations. Fate then played its hand — the 'Kiwi Spirit' was to pass through Wanganui, the scene of the divisive Moutoa Gardens occupation. Perfect timing. Better still, leading Moutoa protester and Labour list candidate Tariana Turia strayed into the assembled audience, listened to Peters' condemnation and pronounced herself disgusted with Winston's 'Maori-bashing'. This verdict was then prominently relayed on that evening's television news, accompanied by much celebration from the New Zealand First troops. Playing the Maori separatist card at Peters suddenly became unfashionable. But, just in case, Henare's campaigning efforts were to be confined to the Maori constituency seats where he could do the least verbal damage.

Henare's unfortunate collision with diplomacy and the inevitable fallout from the party's newly published list rankings had coincided to deliver the worst possible campaigning start for New Zealand First. Both events overshadowed the campaign's launch, which was held outdoors at the bottom of Auckland's Queen Street, our collective anxieties further heightened by a forecast of torrential rain. But nature took pity on us, perhaps reasoning that this much self-inflicted damage required no climatic exclamation.

Widerstrom and Stevenson publicly bemoaned their lowly list rankings — somewhere in the mid-twenties — and then, encouraged by the media's interest, escalated the rhetoric and began ululating wildly at the injustice of it all. Fortunately most reporters interpreted their display as selfish petulance or unrequited personal ambition or possibly both, and despite their initial clatter the issue quickly subsided. Both Peters and Woolerton took the non-apologetic high road; the party's democratic will had prevailed and if disappointed candidates did not like democracy in action then they had clearly joined the wrong party. Within days both men had resigned as the party's candidates, although with little public or party sympathy, their motivations seemingly transparent. Nevertheless, the whole affair had again distracted media focus from any attempt by New Zealand First to be proactive, while also inducing an entirely unproductive 48 hours within the Leader's Unit. Which is usually the way. Political embarrassments rarely linger but they do distract. And in that distraction the real blunders occur.

HUNTED BY THE SNARK

The greatest problem for any centrist party is that one automatically assumes political enemies from both the political Left and the political Right. The Left will accuse you of being uncaring, the Right of being unthinking. Both will lay siege to your motivation. Being middle of the road is always an invitation to be mown down by the passing traffic.

It had long been Peters' intention that such political ambivalence should remain a key part of New Zealand First's campaigning stratagem — the supposed rationale that casting a Janus-like image maximised the party's electoral appeal. However, such positioning created tactical tensions between Winston and me, in part based on our differing perceptions as to New Zealand First's likely level of voter support. My concern was that in seeking to pursue pluralist ends we would be in danger of losing our primary focus on the twin themes of economic nationalism and a radical political accountability.

This latter theme had been further developed in the party's Democracy Policy — admittedly something of a personal policy lust, now that New Zealand First seemed capable of transforming my 'direct democracy' concepts into post-election reality. But such ambition quieted normal caution and I now embarked upon a doomed plan to draft Mike Moore away from Labour's campaigning embrace. Clearly my general exhaustion affected my judgement, despite initial success in convincing Winston to publicly offer Moore the trade portfolio in any New Zealand First-led coalition Cabinet. Given that Helen Clark had yet to woo the former leader back to Labour's front bench I anticipated that such an audacious offer might well sow further discord — particularly if Moore were to accept.

This stratagem was wrapped within another of my perennial favourites — a 'Ministry of All Talents'. As part of the reformist agenda I had also persuaded Winston to the view that the new MMP Parliament must find innovative ways in which to break down the inherited division of the now discredited Westminster parliamentary system. One such method would be to draw the Cabinet from Parliament itself rather than from just the victorious Government parties. There were any number of non-partisan portfolios that could benefit from a more co-operative legislative approach, and the trade portfolio was one example. Why not appoint an Opposition MP as a Minister of the Crown if they happened to be the best qualified parliamentarian for that portfolio?

I duly wrote the speech — Winston duly delivered it — and Mike Moore duly refused. Worse. Moore chose exactly the same timing to repatriate himself to Labour's front bench. An odour of double-cross twinkled Winston's nostrils. Prior to the 'Ministry of All Talents' speech I had sounded out Moore's likely reaction to the offer and been generously advised of his imminent public make-up with Clark. Scratch that idea. OK then, but what about this idea of non-partisan portfolios? Great idea, Moore enthused. Or at least that was my interpretation of our conversation, an interpretation reinforced by Moore's later apology to me for the ungracious media coverage that attended his rejection. Certainly the whole incident left Peters with a nasty taste, an experience he would later recall during the coalition negotiations.

Nevertheless, most of Winston's campaign speeches had set up the National Government as the rhetorical target: their social policies panned for a lack of focus and integration; their economic policies slammed for their dependence on the Reserve Bank. It was clear from these speeches, and from the party's election manifesto, that New Zealand First regarded Labour as a closer political cousin than the incumbent administration. Publicly admitting to such a reality reinforced my general view that New Zealand First should be attempting to mop up disaffected Labour and Alliance supporters rather than plough fresh furrows elsewhere. Winston demurred. There was to be no public or even off-the-record indication of likely coalition partners. He intended to play the game straight: vote first, negotiate later.

Within days of the various parties' formal campaign openings my concerns about this positioning stance had been confirmed. The real issue of the 1996 general election now emerged with a vengeance, and it had nothing to do with hospital waiting lists, overseas investment or Maori separatism. The question on every commentator's lips was the same: Who, in the post-election courting, would sleep with whom?

Clark had already spurned Bolger's previous advances, although by now ACT and the Christian Coalition were hyperventilating at the mere prospect of post-election coitus with the Nats. The Alliance steadfastly professed abstinence, but seemed prepared to refrain from converting other parties to this bizarre 'just say no' mentality. Should Labour need to satisfy their baser desires and shack up with some other party then the Alliance would offer an uneasy approval — an acceptance similar to letting one's daughter go mixed flatting. In turn, Helen Clark hinted that New Zealand First might indeed get lucky, depending on the quality of the foreplay. Typically the media just wanted to fast forward the whole election video and get right down to the nitty gritty. Equally typically, Winston refused to divulge any prospective thinking — by now as much in reaction to the Press Gallery's incessant prying as to any latent strategy.

'No-one plays their cards before they are dealt,' Winston would maintain. Let the people vote for the party that best represents their views and then leave the post-election coupling to look after itself. With the lights out. It was a deeply unsatisfying reply and clearly dismayed a wider sector of the community than just the prurient media. The practicality of campaigning in an MMP environment required a degree of forethought as to one's potential allies as well as to one's enemies. I had attempted to sabotage Winston's Swiss resolve by coining the 'toxic trio' criticism, but Winston's equivocation was now undermining its original impact.

Both Labour and the Alliance perceived their opportunity in the same instant. New Zealand First's stunning rise had damaged the support base of both parties; attacking Peters for refusing to give centre-left voters an unqualified assurance as to post-election arrangements made good tactical sense. The subtext — that Peters could not be trusted — especially irritated Winston, and in response he would launch into an emotional history of all his political, financial and legal battles with the National Party. Yet when subsequently pressed by assorted media to clarify his post-election preference the vague waffle would return.

On the back of such public indecision, and allied with all the other various gaffes of the moment, New Zealand First's polling support plummeted further. Now even the fifteen per cent scenario was in grave danger, with some media polls reporting that the Alliance had reclaimed past voting support and surged into third spot behind National and Labour respectively. Things were starting to look grim — we may not be in a position to award the laurel wreath after all.

Part of the problem was that New Zealand First had been unable to afford any polling or attitudinal research prior to the campaign; no commissioned overview, no focus groups, no random telephone polling — nothing. In a perfect world the party's election strategy and advertising agenda would have been privately trialled, but again the party's chronic lack of pre-planning led to last-minute snap judgements followed by equally feverish execution. As a consequence there was a slightly self-indulgent air to the party's advertising campaign. Marco Marinkovich's black-and-white silent movie stills were visually clever but lacked the visceral grunt to make the necessary emotional connection. Even the party's spectacular Auckland billboard, 'Shipley's List', highlighting burgeoning public health queues, proved needlessly controversial, the Jewish lobby outraged at the pun. The campaign's populist focus, which the 'Kiwi Spirit' bus tour had been designed to emphasise, was now being diverted by a series of foreseeable crises requiring considerable reactive energy.

In an atmosphere of regret, and with an acute awareness of the falling media polls, a Sunday afternoon crisis meeting was hastily convened, linking all the party's principals by telephone conference call — Peters, Woolerton, Neems, Marinkovich, Brian Henry and me. It would be the only campaign committee meeting of that entire last month — again a commentary on our haphazard personalities. Earlier that Sunday I had faxed Winston a four-page memo establishing my concerns over the party's coalition stance and proposing that New Zealand First declare the Labour Party its preferred early option. My rationale was that this would cease the damaging speculation about New Zealand First's post-election trustworthiness while also allowing the party to raid the Alliance's support base. I continued:

Similarly, we could appeal to rural/provincial Nats to get us [sic] to keep Labour honest ... and support our export-led economic and trade policies.

'The danger of our current position is —
- anti-Right forces distrust our intentions;
- pro-Right forces condemn us as 'Left' anyway & have other options.

'NZ First rose in the polls on the back of anti-National sentiment — we picked support off Labour and the Alliance rather than from National.

I also proffered the advice that New Zealand First must emphasise its 'new style of politics' over the remaining fortnight by presenting an indicative outline of the political reforms that would be demanded as the price of prospective partnership. In that way New Zealand First could receive the post-election credit for empowering the public — credit that would have implications for voting behaviour in 1999.

In the end I was a distinct minority of one. Winston delivered one of his usual 'we must tough this out' homilies and appealed to our panicky little gathering to trust in his superior judgement. The poker analogy was flourished once more — you do not play cards you do not have. Still I persisted — still Winston resisted. I changed tack. Could we not, at least, hint our direction? No.

By the end of the conference call I had become convinced of two things. First, that we would need a spectacular last fortnight for New Zealand First to attain even my conservative predictions. Second, Winston had already chosen his post-election partner. And the audacity of that choice stunned me.

THE MEDIA TURN

I have said it elsewhere in this book but it bears repeating. Only one other profession is distrusted by the New Zealand public as much as politics. The media.

Despite an undergraduate wish to train as a journalist, and despite a subterranean stint as a Sunday tabloid freelance while working as an Opposition researcher, I profess no great affinity for, nor even understanding of, the Fourth Estate. That I have acquired a reputation as a premier spin doctor bemuses me, because my endeavours on behalf of others just seem to be a common-sense mixture of fawning in-gratiation and outraged displeasure, with very little in between. That it works is even more disturbing.

The problem with the modern media is their deliberate accent on hyperbole. Every budding young reporter is taught to write their copy with a 'hook'— a crude stylistic shorthand that sacrifices the drab for the dramatic. As a consequence a skewed reality is presented, provoking many New Zealanders to doubt the ability and accuracy of the profession itself. An additional problem with the 'hook' mentality is that it forces the individual journalist to make a snap value judgement, and snap judgements draw more upon emotion than they do on reason.

In all my years in practical politics I have only ever encountered a bare handful of journalists who did not portray a personal bias or prejudice in their reporting of news events. The trick is to learn which journalist possesses which predisposition, and then to mercilessly feed their jaundice. In such ways are the media manipulated — not by devious spin doctors but by their own weaknesses.

The parliamentary Press Gallery generally regard themselves as the cream of the journalistic crop, so any good press secretary quickly appreciates that not all the egos are confined to the House debating chamber. This is especially true of television journalists, a voluble and opinionated lot who desire a measure of public celebrity to sweeten their salaries. In their defence, such vanity goes with the territory. Cabinet ministers, MPs, press secretaries, researchers and lobbyists will daily drool at their office door for special favour, brimming with gaudy trinkets in the hope that a benevolent eye might fall sympathetically on their dubious wares.

There is also a strict hierarchy within the Gallery that each spinner must observe: first choice must always go to the television networks, and especially to Television New Zealand. However, the timing of any story seeding is critical — television journalists tend to turn their noses up at anything that has previously been reported in the print media, unless the story is too large to ignore. Equally, if a story is purposefully seeded for evening news coverage, then metropolitan dailies can get very sniffy at the merest hint of preferential treatment. A good press secretary will generally share their stories around, although always reserving the most favourable for the mass audience that is delivered by television.

Fortunately, most New Zealand media outlets accept that political parties should receive roughly similar coverage during election campaigns — the quality of that quantity being an entirely separate issue. And therein is waged a daily battle to ensure that one's favoured party receives its fair share of positive reportage; even something as basic as a bad camera angle or inadequate lighting has the ability to sour the most impressive sound bite.

Within New Zealand First circles there was a pronounced view that many media outlets wore their political colours in much brighter hues for the 1996 election campaign than in previous contests. As a general rule I thought each of the major parties was equally ill-served, although there could be no question that Helen Clark gained a wholesome degree of empathy from many of the Gallery's female staff.

On the other hand, the three daily metropolitan newspapers, the *New Zealand Herald*, the *Dominion* and the Christchurch *Press*, displayed a strong editorial partiality for the National Party, the *Dominion* allowing some of that bias to intrude in its general political coverage. Winston had been engaged in a lengthy running verbal war with the editor, Richard Long, particularly with regard to the Winebox transactions and connected events, while the Gallery reporter assigned to cover New Zealand First's campaign, Graeme Speden, made no apologies for his dislike of both the party and its leader. When I tackled him over this scarcely concealed hostility, adding a stern lecture on media impartiality for good measure, Speden curled his back like a cornered cat and hissed : 'You're just a pack of bullshitters.'

'Ummm,' — I glanced sideways at this curious defiance — 'this is politics, Graeme. What do you expect?' He remained stoically unpacified, particularly when Winston began to derive a peculiar amusement from baiting the *Dominion* at every opportunity. But Speden was not alone in venturing his personal opinion about New Zealand First's intrinsic worth. *New Zealand Herald* Gallery reporter Audrey Young gleefully informed me that she was looking forward to accompanying Winston on the 'Kiwi Spirit' because 'there'll be a stuff-up every day. It'll make great news.' By the end of the campaign

Audrey ruefully admitted that Peters had been a little more disciplined than she had anticipated — I assumed that she had expected the New Zealand First road-show to breeze through the provinces like the US ice hockey team.

There would be only one real media blot on the 1996 election campaign, but it would prove so influential that it affected coverage of the entire campaign. The TVNZ 'worm'.

It was the general wisdom of all the various campaign teams that the televised Leaders' Debate series would prove critical to the various parties' chances. Winston performed poorly in both TVNZ contests, betraying an unattractive scowl when placed under pressure — a manifestation of tiredness rather than character. One of the great lessons I had learned from my time as an MP is that the viewing public loathe an evasive politician; in fact, they will swallow an obvious lie rather than accept equivocation. There is one important qualification to this rule — audiences will admire a clever politician under attack from an aggressive or intrusive interviewer. Then they allow themselves to admire the dexterous verbal skills if the hunted politician niftily avoids all the pursuer's traps. But election debates are different. The emphasis changes from a one-on-one verbal contest between two equally despised professional shit-stirrers to the direct imparting of information from the politician to the viewer, albeit via the compressed and artificial filter of a quasi-gameshow. In reality they are not debates at all — they are verbal beauty contests.

Only Labour's Helen Clark fully accepted this subtle shift in televisual emphasis — a tribute to the remorseless grooming provided by experienced TV professionals, husband and wife team Brian Edwards and Judy Callingham. It was a measure of Clark's intelligence and humility that she was prepared to accept pre-election marketing advice that her hair looked as if it had died of fright, her speaking style smacked of a lesbian body-builder on steroids, and that some corpses in funeral parlours had livelier facial complexions. The contrast between the pre-Edwards/Callingham Clark and the post-makeover Labour leader was more than striking; it was endearing — the kind of gooey transformation that made *Muriel's Wedding* such a sentimental hit.

The electronic 'worm' went mad in appreciation — itself a bizarre device often used by advertising agencies to plot the instant reactions of particular focus groups to experimental stimuli. Television New Zealand had decided to apply the same technology to a group of supposedly non-committed voters — although my enquiry to the programme's producers as to how this allegedly impartial group were selected was never properly answered. Whatever the bias, the 'worm' stood to attention whenever Clark spoke and generally sagged or lay dormant whenever Anderton, Bolger or Peters attempted their 60-second sound bite. There was clearly more than one explanation for the worm's frenzied activity, but the Press Gallery reached their own less sensual conclusion. Helen Clark was a winner, and they wrote it up as if the election had already been decided. From that moment on it was the media perception that Clark could do no wrong — the more cynical among us suggesting that she was never in public view long enough to even hazard the opportunity.

The remaining fortnight of the campaign staggered to its conclusion: Prime Minister Bolger caught the New Zealand First disease and took over the gaffe commentary; Clark continued to smile sweetly and mouth endless soporifics; Anderton kept trying to explain to his Alliance supporters why he still required their vote having decided to be a parliamentary spectator; and, wonder of wonders, the 'Kiwi Spirit' tour concept finally began to work, with Peters drawing larger public audiences then any of the other major contenders and garnering superb provincial media coverage.

By the last week of the campaign Peters' exhaustion was at least matched by his contemporaries'. The public were equally weary of the whole exercise and acutely pissed off that their letter boxes were being used as a recycling collection point. There were still the daily dramas — New Zealand First's second promotional pamphlet remained locked in a printer's warehouse because the party had run out of money for its distribution, although it masked this potential embarrassment by picking a legal battle with the distribution firm. A vengeful creditor began parading a recent court summons and judgement against Patra de Courdray on the eve of Winston's final-week visit to her electorate; fortunately TV3's Sean Plunket provided the tip-off and I arranged for the issue to be legally postponed until after election day. Widerstrom and Stevenson were still doing their mischievous best to interest the Electoral Commission in an investigation of the party's list, and thoughtfully alerted the media each time any of the principal parties even hinted at a bowel movement. A myriad similar mini-crises invaded my remaining sentience as I continued to churn out Peters' speeches and plot daily strategy.

And still I could not persuade Winston to modify his damaging ambivalence upon the issue of post-election negotiations. By now I was utterly convinced that Peters had come to loathe Labour more than National, if only because he had hoped that New Zealand First might supplant that party as the Government's prime opponent. But there was something else; in my constant daily discussions and debates with Peters I came to realise that his age-old distrust of the Labour Party had never lessened, and again we talked of his first entry into Parliament in 1979 and the jeering and booing from the Opposition benches that had greeted this proud moment. Of one other thing I was certain — Winston loathed the whole idea of playing the deputy to New Zealand's first-ever woman prime minister. As I watched Clark's foolishly grand performance on election night, swamped by simpering journalists seeking her reaction to this historic role, I knew Winston well enough to be certain he would seethe at Clark's presumption. I could feel the rage from five hundred miles away.

ELECTION NIGHT

On the eve of the election Sarah Neems and I scribbled our best guesstimates of the next day's results and secretly hoped that our conservative predictions would prove untrue. Despite the past favourable fortnight New Zealand First had refused to grapple with the only real issue of the campaign, and my last-ditch efforts to tighten Winston's rhetoric continued to smash against his stronger obstinacy.

That Friday evening I telephoned my old friend Neil Kirton in Hamilton and wished him all the best luck that I could muster. His fourteenth ranking on the party's list would ensure him a nervy election night, with his prospects dependent on not just the final party vote but also whether any higher-ranked candidates won their constituencies. By now my political intelligence suggested a clean New Zealand First sweep of the Maori seats, with Delamere, Waitai and Wyllie occupying lower list rungs.

The party's major election night function was to be hosted in Tauranga, but my exhaustion, twinned with exasperation at Winston's general conduct, meant I chose instead to attend a small gathering of the parliamentary staff and Wellington candidates. TVNZ's election night coverage was to include commentary from the various party strategists, so at least if I wanted to publicly criticise Peters or anyone else then I was well out of grab distance. Bolger's chief press secretary,

Richard Griffin, had no such qualms, and that evening used his 30 seconds of fame to chastise Bolger for his efforts of the past month. As my colleagues gasped at this daring admonition I could only mutter, 'I know where you're coming from, mate.'

I had also decided — partway through the campaign — that I would officially 'retire' from politics once the post-election negotiations were completed. If anything the campaign had reinforced the emotional reaction to my resignation — I must be either totally committed to the process or not at all. In a year or so I would be 40 — my midlife crisis was already upon me and the red Mustang with the obligatory blonde bimbo was starting to look good. Politics was not part of that equation. I had written the party's policy, persuaded Peters to support a radical revamp of the country's democratic structure, and satiated my own desire for political influence. And there was something else — a quirk that rose from childhood: I found the journey more interesting than the destination.

As I entered the Wellington gathering a youngish journalist introduced himself and thrust at me a TVNZ poll taken from the previous evening. There was a hint of knowing sneer in his demeanour and I soon appreciated why — National and Labour were locked together in the low thirties, with the Alliance at fifteen and New Zealand First at eleven. Just to cap the disaster, the ACT party also breached the five per cent threshold. If this poll was going to be matched by the results then it was going to be a long, long night. I did the only sensible thing possible and headed for the drinks cabinet.

In fact the night was a near-complete triumph. The only dampener was that ACT had struggled past the threshold — further proof that you can fool some of the people all of the time. National's vote had held up surprisingly well, almost reaching its support level of three years before, while, despite most commentators' glowing commendations, Labour remained a clear runner-up with just 28 per cent of the list vote — its worst result in over 60 years.

New Zealand First eclipsed my election-eve prediction and polled just over thirteen per cent, also sweeping all five Maori constituency seats — a remarkable result considering that just about everything that could go wrong with an election campaign actually had. By the middle of the evening it became apparent that provincial New Zealand had accepted a measure of the party's economic nationalism and viewed Winston as a ready anti-National alternative to both

Labour and the Alliance. A strong 'if only' invaded my horizon — Labour had clearly been ready to be plucked.

Clearly the biggest loser on the evening was the Alliance — they near halved their support from the '93 election but still inherited Alamein Kopu. Sometimes politics is cruel.

As the assorted journalists sought my reaction I purred a benign contentment. Yes, this had been my objective — New Zealand First with the balance of responsibility; neither major party could form a government without us. This superficial overview mollified the networks — I was now more interested in the press and public reaction to Peters' election-night address.

I had written the speech that afternoon — I would later claim a touch of prescience as to the evening's conclusion. And yet it was an eminently obvious result. Even had Labour performed better, even if the Alliance had fulfilled TVNZ's last-minute polling prediction, New Zealand First would still have been in the position of kingmaker. It would have required a miracle for National and ACT to breach the 50-per-cent barrier, and in politics there are no miracles. Sleights of hand, illusions, the occasional magical puff — yes; but bona fide miracles? Never.

Peters added an uncomfortable Maori proverb to my speech — something about seagulls and rocks and oceans — wholly gratuitous and wholly inappropriate, but plainly some pub patron's bullshit homily had impressed him earlier that day. I included the proverb in Winston's original but deleted it from the media copy faxed out later that evening: if Peters was going to play the statesman's role then the script needed to be entirely professional. Journalists would scour the text for weeks in the hope of discovering some weird Winstonian mathematical code; it was my aim not to have them diverted by extraneous matters. Vain hope.

Slightly before midnight I drove home and Karen greeted me at the door, her face betraying a knowing relief rather than any exultant excitement.

'Is this what you wanted, Michael? Winston with all that power?'

I snorted a grudging understanding and wondered why God had gifted women with all the best insights. Of all the questions Karen has ever asked me in our marriage this would prove the hardest.

'I don't know darling,' I lied. 'I'll tell you in the morning.'

Chapter 13

POWER

SELF-IMMOLATION

The answer was yes — and no. Yes, if I was to stay with Peters as a strategic aide; no, if I was to fulfil my resolve to quit. Too simplistic — bear with me.

Yes, if all those pre-election pledges to radically reform the country's political structure were to be implemented. Peters stood at the portal of constitutional immortality, possessing the ability to manipulate the coalition negotiations to almost any outcome of his choosing, and if that meant implementing the underlying rationale of the Democracy Policy then my job was complete. Find a beach, Michael, get completely blotto and then reinvent your past. There was no need to carry on. It was the journey and the destination analogy all over again, the frontier and the settling — I did not need a tangible sense of conclusion to my previous endeavours. Leave the boring details (and plush salaries) to others.

If the spiritualists are right and each of us is gifted a spirit guide — updated these days to suggest that some benign angel flutters through our subconscious in place of a sentient conscience — then God knows where mine had gone at this juncture. Smacked up, shacked up and generally stupefied, I would hazard. Because all these post-election New Age feelings of personal completeness were complete all right — complete crap.

I had known Winston for almost a decade, been friends with him for most of that ten years, and played just about every supporting role from Ivanhoe to Iago. If I had gleaned one insight into Winston's character it was that this was a man who needed to be protected from himself. His first instincts were often wrong, and his pouting pride had the ugly ability to warp his perceptions in the twinkling of a frown. He could mutate from Mary Poppins to Mussolini and back again, depending entirely on the external stimuli. But now he was dog tired from the exertions of the past year, and those internal character transformations were becoming quicker and quirkier.

Such failings are not uncommon in politics — stress provokes chemical imbalances at the worst of times. But suddenly assume a historical responsibility for the nation's future and one's mind virtually invites Du Pont to dump their entire stock of use-by pollutants into one's cranium.

For Winston now had power. Real power. Thumping-the-table, do-as-I-say, stuff-what-the-neighbours-think power. Faustian stuff. With that undiluted, unadulterated influence combined with Winston's usual lack of strategic focus it was clearly my job, my role — hell, my absolute responsibility — to continue playing the nagging, scolding, cajoling political conscience.

Instead, I walked away. The worst part is that I walked away suspecting that Peters was about to make the biggest mistake of his entire political life.

Looking back now I can rationalise my feelings. I was in a peculiar state of self-immolation that continued to attend the aftermath of my resignation and was now rarefied by the mental exhaustion of the previous four months. Trying to provide the New Zealand First campaign with a sense of strategic and intellectual coherence had been a not inconsiderable exertion. But it is no excuse. I sensed Peters' danger and I turned away.

It is debatable whether I could have forestalled the disaster anyway. I had failed to alter Peters' post-election direction even during the white-hot intensity of the election campaign, despite the falling polls and despite a sense of crisis. Winston had not been immune to these pressures but, entirely conscious of the political and electoral costs, remained true to his preferred course. He wanted to hit the iceberg. But I should have tried — noble failure is always better than ignoble observation.

The truth was that Peters was always going to lie down with National. Every fragment of conversation, of body language, of facial expression displayed a personal distaste for the Labour option. Whatever the Nats had done to him, whatever the humiliations, the attacks and the malicious gossip, Winston regarded his former colleagues with a peculiar sense of familial longing — a connection that refused to be excised or exorcised. And Lord knows, I had done my best.

In Winston's defence, his predisposition was matched by the

electoral algebra, something still grossly underappreciated by either the media or the smarty-pants set that loiter in all the best political science departments and wish they were even half as important as their blighted egos demand.

The Centre-Left had performed poorly in the general election — Labour had shed over a fifth of its 1993 support, the Alliance nearly half. In contrast the 'toxic trio' had polled over 44 per cent of the popular vote. Even that result could be counterbalanced by the fact that a good proportion of New Zealand First's final 13 per cent possessed a general Centre-Left predisposition but, mathematically at least, there still existed no obvious mandate to embrace the Left.

But that was not the real flaw. The Alliance's decision to remain outside any coalition government emphasised the curious dependence that any Labour/New Zealand First combination must have upon Jim Anderton and his clearly unstable Caucus. In a surreal sideshow, Labour and the Alliance decided to conduct their own post-election talks and effected a meaningless understanding as to the measure of Anderton's trustworthiness. Clark would eventually emerge from this huddle, Neville Chamberlain in drag, and wave the Alliance's tacit consent. But Winston was wholly unconvinced; he loathed Anderton and had lathered up a good dislike of Helen Clark — any progeny these two created would only provoke Peters' sneering derision. In fact, he would actually brandish the Labour/Alliance document at his Caucus as conclusive evidence of National's greater charms.

But those events were in the future. New Zealand First had still to enter the negotiations, let alone survive them. In an attempt to distract myself from my election-day anxiety I had penned Winston a cautionary and confidential memorandum on the MMP negotiations and related issues — rudimentary advice on the composition of the negotiating team, the public persona to adopt over succeeding days, and the conduct of the new Caucus.

Much of this counsel was endorsed and later implemented, but the memo also contained an emphatic warning that would be blithely ignored, the gist being that the election was the easy part — it would be how New Zealand First conducted itself both during and immediately after the MMP negotiations that would secure its public reputation. Perhaps I misread Winston — or perhaps he understood my watchful advice perfectly but was intent on living out some Gothic death wish. But I doubt it.

For Winston became fully intoxicated with his new status. The fawning respect from National and Labour intermediaries; the sudden congratulations from a Press Gallery that had made an art form of its covert disrespect; the requests for exclusive interviews from the international media and powerful lobby groups — all these coagulated to block Winston's sense of perspective. There was only one celebrity in New Zealand this day, this week, this month and it was Winston Peters. Each day merely intensified that status, and I discerned Peters' pride evolving into something that reeked of a prurient vanity.

A frosty atmosphere enveloped our first face-to-face meeting on the post-election Monday afternoon, Peters furious that Mike Moore had leaked to the *New Zealand Herald* details of a private conversation I had shared with the Labour MP the previous day. I was similarly displeased — Moore's attempt to inflate the public impression of his political value left me cold. In fact, I misjudged Mike; he was attempting to emphasise his value to his Labour colleagues rather than the Gallery, an indication of his remaining isolation despite the show repatriation of the campaign.

And there was worse. A cartoon in that morning's *Dominion* had added to Peters' displeasure, the cartoonist having portrayed Winston mouthing worthy thoughts to an assorted battery of cameras, while I sat behind his overlarge chair directly spoon-feeding him statesmanlike rhetoric.

'I don't want to see any more of this sort of stuff, Laws,' he said as he thrust the newspaper at me.

'Well, you'll have to start thinking for yourself then,' I bristled in reply. I was about to add, '...you ungrateful little shit', but Sarah's warning glance suggested Peters was on a short fuse. Instead I turned his attention to an advisory paper I had drafted the previous day outlining my preferred role for Winston in any post-election coalition: the position of Treasurer.

My reasoning was wholly unsophisticated. There were only two positions that had a direct command over the policy tiller — Prime Minister and Minister of Finance. I surmised correctly that both National and Labour would want to retain both these premier roles — their arrogant mentality would only admit New Zealand First as an equal partner for the duration of the negotiations. The new party would be in the greatest peril after the coalition agreement had been signed. The larger party would inevitably outnumber the smaller in the executive seats, and the latter risked being outvoted at every Cabinet meeting.

Treasury ran the bureaucratic show, I argued. Winston should thus run Treasury. In that way the policy process could be manipulated long before the Cabinet face-down.

Peters proved ambivalent. Until the Saturday night he had still harboured thoughts of being Prime Minister-elect come Monday morning. We discussed other portfolios, and the only other possibility appeared to be Foreign Affairs, following the German Free Democrat example. Oodles of favourable publicity, a great deal of overseas travel, and a one-step removal in the public perception from government association.

Finally Peters concluded that his fresh young Caucus required constant guidance, and that leaving them in the occasional embrace of Tau Henare might prove excessively negligent. Besides, he postulated, what challenge was there in getting rat-faced half a world away when you could get rat-faced at home and still have a goodly measure of control over government policy? There was no answer to that.

My advisory paper also contained a salutary warning and a prescience that makes me now wonder if my spirit guide had not returned from the never-never and mistakenly tweaked the wrong astral channel. For I warned Peters that if he was to take on the Treasurer's role there were two critical provisos:

> CCMAU (Crown Company Monitoring Advisory Unit) — these are the bastards that do all the work with regards to the CHEs, CRIs, SOEs, etc. They are very powerful fiscal Jesuits and you need control over them...
>
> You must have the ability to access independent economic and financial advice (eg BT) [Bankers Trust] OUTSIDE of Treasury. They will kick against it but sometimes that might include advice on confidential Treasury papers. In this way you can check on Treasury and ensure that you are not the victim of "information capture".

To buttress this advice I suggested that Peters convoke his own financial advisory team — to sift various Treasury papers and information and provide him with other policy options. Initially Winston approved the whole idea and spoke of the public kudos that might be gained in being viewed as Treasury's master and not its mistress. In the event CCMAU ended up under Bill Birch's gentle hand and Winston ended up as Treasury's downstairs chambermaid — rather fulfilling all my post-election fears.

It had been my intention to be part of the emergency medical team that would be required to nurse New Zealand First through the coalition discussions. But each conversation with Peters convinced me that the partner decision had already been made — at least in Winston's mind. There would be negotiations with Labour all right, but they would be for a distinct purpose — to act as the ratchet that forced further National concessions. Ironically, Peters' first job was to persuade the Nats that they actually had the chance to coalesce — much of their back bench surmising that the ratchet roles had been reversed, National only being there to indirectly pressure Labour.

From the first moment of the negotiations Labour misunderstood Winston's intentions. They assumed he had no real choice — that it was them or no-one. Incredibly, most of the Press Gallery shared this assumption and were stupid enough to commit it to paper — a lingering reminder to their employers that the Gallery's very closeness to the political fray blinds it to dispassionate observation. Labour also suffered because their objectives were confused; in contrast, the Nats, and particularly Jim Bolger, knew exactly what they wanted. They wanted to be in government — and they wanted it more than Labour. Or rather, they did not want to lose power.

I only appreciated this distinction and the compelling aggression that accompanied it when I compared my personal election performance in 1990 with that of 1993. Both times I wanted to win the Hawke's Bay seat, but the intensity was much greater for the 1993 struggle simply because I would lose my livelihood, my status and my local influence if I was defeated. In 1990, as the challenger, these sacrifices were never apparent.

So it was with Bolger and National in late 1996. They stood to lose control of their portfolios, their six-figure salaries, a refined pomposity and their own dining room — the stakes were much more personal. And Bolger stood to lose something else — both his role as Prime Minister and that of National Party Leader. I could already hear the Caucus leather being stropped from my distant vantage point.

There is something else about National that forcibly contrasts with the Labour experience. The Nats are instinctively pragmatic — their party was actually formed in 1935 with no higher purpose than to oppose Labour. In contrast, Labour prefers the 'Braveheart' role — the mad, crashing, doomed sprint against insuperable odds. This is not to suggest that Labour's politicians are not arrogant — indeed, it would be the imperious superiority of deputy Michael Cullen that would so infuriate the New Zealand First negotiators. But it is an arrogance borne of assumed moral rectitude — Labour automatically accept that their ends are noble, and thus arm themselves with an ugly self-esteem. It is a little like teaching a Mongrel Mob member pride in his Maori culture — giving these thugs any further excuse for personal swagger seems self-defeating. So it is with Labour — they feel a need to cloak their tribal mentality with some inverted higher purpose.

To Bolger such reasoning was just an academic wank — staying in power was the name of the game, and stuff all the window dressing. Winston knew this; so did I. We had been in National's Caucus. We had witnessed the Bolger international-statesman preen — long-winded, pompous travelogues supplemented by fantastic tales of Jimbo's Versailles-like diplomatic skills. In these flights Bolger could never quite distinguish between his own personal greatness and the build-up of rectal gas.

But Peters was not alone in his fondness for the devil he knew. Peter McCardle privately shuddered at the prospect of sitting alongside Helen Clark, Lianne Dalziel and other leading Labour lights on the Government front benches. Equally, Jack Elder made no secret of the fact that having just escaped from the contempt of his former colleagues he possessed no great desire to be so hastily reunited.

Three days after the first-ever MMP election New Zealand First's three most senior MPs had already privately declared their personal preferences as to the coalition choice. The die was cast.

So even if I had stayed, the odds would have been stacked against me. I knew the MMP arithmetic; I appreciated that Labour were no better than National; I accepted the Alliance's preference for playing the daily joker — but those were just new challenges that must be confronted and properly managed. For New Zealand First's support base loathed National — they disliked its leadership, its legacy and its loopy friends. The overwhelming majority of New Zealand First's electors had voted for change, and Peters battling anti-authoritarianism personified their ambition. Embracing the enemy would always signify a betrayal of those voters, dooming New Zealand First to only temporary power when the greater prospect of permanent influence was on direct offer.

On the Tuesday after the election I greeted the new swag of New Zealand First list MPs, readied the Caucus room for their arrival and arranged the media ruck that burst out to assault them. Most reacted as if electrodes had been attached to their genitals, with popping eyes, flushed faces and a nasty inner feeling that some great harm was about to be perpetrated. They resembled nothing so much as the proverbial possum in the headlights — except this time it had already been run down, although the shock was still attempting to make its way through to the crushed cortex.

At the time I felt an overwhelming sense of both vicarious pleasure and paternal concern flash through me — mixed, in truth, with a tinge of personal regret. The exhilaration of election is a very powerful narcotic, but this would be the first Caucus in modern history that must immediately confront its own peril and yet be so spectacularly ill-equipped to cope. It was like waving away raw soldiers at the wharf as they decamped to foreign climes — you were proud of their brave optimism but you just knew that most would never return.

IMPOTENCE

Four days after the general election — with Parliament so pregnant with anticipation that drip trays were issued in readiness for the waters breaking — I resigned.

It was much easier than I had expected, but then the immediate act often is. It's the aftershock that cripples. I penned a terse and official confirmation of my intentions, drove home and took the telephone off the hook. The next morning, when I bothered to check the answerphone, there were five increasingly frantic messages from Winston openly wondering at my mental state. The next day I called him and explained my departure with a series of half-truths — I was burned out, had served my political time and wished to start afresh. Winston's tone signalled a general disbelief but little more. We knew each other well enough not to probe the more obvious minefields.

That afternoon Mike Booker issued a media release from Winston's office announcing my retirement from politics, officially thanking me for my contribution and crediting me with being one of the original architects of MMP. This was a very personal remark — disbelieved by the Gallery but redolent of past intimacy when Winston and I would consume one glass of wine too many and proclaim ourselves the only true political reformers within Parliament. That he even remembered those evenings touched my hopeless vein of sentimentality.

Later that day I literally bumped into Radio New Zealand's political editor, Karen Fisher, who informed me that the Gallery was agog with speculation over my resignation, the pushed-or-fell dichotomy provoking the usual riot of rumour-mongering. I swore her to secrecy and, remembering past treatment and respecting her innate professionalism, confessed my reasons. New Zealand First were about to copulate with National — I had no intention of hanging around for the cuckolding. Incredibly, Fisher kept her end of the bargain, although she would often call during the negotiations just to check that my predictive abilities were being confirmed by further intelligence from New Zealand First sources.

Of course they were. Neil Kirton was staying at my Wellington home, and both Robyn McDonald and Deborah Morris had asked me to draft their maiden speeches. In addition, Louise Sampson had been recruited as Doug Woolerton's executive secretary, and I continued to enjoy convivial relations with most of the Caucus, Winston included. It was thus fascinating to observe the manipulation of the fledgling Caucus by Peters, while also noting Tau Henare's distancing from the rest of the New Zealand First negotiating team. Henare's preference was plain — Labour was his partner of choice — and its negotiators assumed that he would actively champion their cause with his colleagues.

There were two flaws to this assumption. First, Tau possessed insufficient Caucus credibility to lobby any MPs other than those from the Maori seats. Second, he was lazy, playing only a minor role in the negotiations and finding much of the policy detail beyond his academic grasp. Winston had chosen his negotiating team wisely — his brother Wayne, chosen for his fraternal loyalty as much as his provincial legal skills; president Doug Woolerton, who would have voided his bowels in public had Winston ever commanded him to do so; Peter McCardle, for his appreciation of detail (as well as his pro-National sensibilities), and Tau Henare. That Labour considered Henare their inside trump card was like trusting the Ingham twins with a shipload of friendly sailors.

During the next week I set out to cure the worst effects of sleep deprivation, rediscovered a sense of self-perspective, and batted away most media requests for insightful interviews. The Gallery had now whipped itself beyond frenzy, and some sportive remarks on Ian Fraser's 'Meet the Press' brought on a further spasm of speculation. Only the *Dominion* managed to decipher the deliberately enigmatic encounter and reasoned that I was predicting a National/New Zealand First coalition.

I believed I owed it to Winston and my former colleagues to remain silent — the choice was theirs to make, and they might yet prove me wrong. The editor of Wellington's *Evening Post*, Suzanne Carty, had invited me to begin a fortnightly column in her newspaper, and I took the liberty of using this opportunity to send the various negotiating parties a series of Lawsian smoke signals. Meanwhile, Mike Moore would regularly telephone for any insights on the New Zealand First position, and I would relay the best advice I could.

Both articles and advice posited two simple theories. First, it was politically smarter for New Zealand First to choose the Labour option; second, that the party that offered Winston the role of Treasurer must have the inside running. Moore repeatedly affirmed that Labour had no intention of surrendering the key finance portfolio. From our conversations it became clear that Labour's negotiating team appeared to have conflicting objectives — they were already dividing up the portfolio spoils, before they had secured the necessary agreement with New Zealand First.

Each evening Neil Kirton would arrive home and brief me on his activities; he was now heading New Zealand First's discussions with both major parties on the key health portfolio. These conversations were generally one-on-one encounters with National's Health Minister, Jenny Shipley, and Labour's health spokesperson, Lianne Dalziel, and while he found Shipley a consummate professional, Dalziel proved brittle and fractious even though her party's policy more closely mirrored the New Zealand First position. This subtle contest between policy and personality was being repeated elsewhere in the negotiations, Brian Donnelly confessing to a similar dichotomy during his education policy talks.

Within days Neil had asked me for formal strategic assistance, and I was soon able to appreciate Shipley's plan better. Taking advantage of Kirton's naïveté amid the involved and often contradictory jargon of central government, Shipley was aiming to entrap New Zealand First within a series of generalities that would, in essence, preserve National's health reforms. Often Neil would exclaim excitedly in response to a perceived Nat concession, only to resile when the true implications were sifted from the diplomacy. It was hardly Kirton's fault — Winston had thrust him into the arena untrained, unarmed and matched against an experienced and skilled political operator who could command the vast resources of a major department. That he would eventually emerge with the most detailed of all the Coalition policy settlements was a tribute to his terrier graft — although it would provoke Shipley's successor, Bill English, to sabotage the agreement from his first day in ministerial office.

In the midst of the negotiations Winston telephoned and suggested a private dinner at one of Wellington's better restaurants, Il Casino. That same afternoon Moore sought my assistance in summarising New Zealand First's Democracy Policy, and asked me to develop further some of the concepts contained therein — the aim being to dangle such reforms before Winston in the coming days. In the course of our conversation I mentioned that Karen and I would be dining with Winston that evening, and a plan was duly hatched to contrive a fortuitous meeting — Moore having extended a similar invitation to Wayne Peters, the venue as yet undecided.

So began, surely, one of the most surreal encounters of the MMP negotiations, the entire night a carnal metaphor. The 'accidental' merging of the parties duly occurred, with Winston gaining his usual post-10pm wind; Moore machine-gunning the English language; Wayne Peters his usual wary, watchful self — a demeanour more suited to a humble undertaker than a political wheeler-dealer; Karen enjoying the company of fellow chain-smokers; and I, vainly, attempting to inject a touch of politics into the proceedings. By the end of a convivial evening of good wine, great food and humorous lies both Karen and Wayne could foresee further late-night antics and sensibly cried off. I had imbibed sufficiently to assume that typical Kiwi middle-aged bombed-male demeanour which lent the world the appearance of one great boisterous party with me its leering centre. When Winston suggested adjourning to a nightclub for a post-dinner nightcap I leapt at the idea, while Moore steadfastly trailed along just to keep the two of us out of obvious trouble — the Café Brava bust-up a far too recent memory.

We ended up at one of the capital's premier singles bars, The Big Easy, facetiously known to most Wellingtonians as The Big Sleazy — its clientele a willing mixture of young shop assistants, stockbrokers and hairdressers, all in search of abandoned oblivion. That Winston Peters, Mike Moore and Michael Laws had entered the pond scarcely raised a flicker — if wonder was occasioned in any of the clientele it was more likely to have been over why three middle-aged suits were slumming it. Frankly, I loved the place, the concentrated and abandoned adolescent pheromones lunging at my nostalgic libido.

The proprietor was suitably pleased to see us and hailed Winston

382

like a long-lost Slavic relative. Before long we were propped against the bar being plied with an endless supply of complimentary depth charges — a fatal mixture of liqueur and lager — while trying to make ourselves heard above the throbbing dance music. Somehow Moore and Peters achieved this feat — I turned away and imbibed the surroundings, a particularly flirtatious brunette in yellow, barely a metre away, returning my unhealthy interest. At which point Moore dragged me back into the conversation and ensured my participation by raising the issue of parliamentary reform — Labour were getting their money's worth from their former leader that night.

After that exchange had run its course I turned back to my pathetic visual pursuit of the yellow brunette. Plainly my guardian angel had been at work. The brunette was now being fondled beneath her summer dress by a male version of herself — a heaving mass of late-night licentiousness — and as I watched the embraces grew ever closer, ever more intimate, ever more passionate. Around them various of the patrons were exchanging glances of excited embarrassment while doing their surreptitious best to examine the carnal plumbing that was now occurring, as the girl arched her derriere, wholly oblivious to anything other than the sensual friction being created.

I glanced back at my companions — the music still throbbed with a sympathetic intensity, several other couples were entangled in not dissimilar sport, and just two metres from the main event Winston Peters and Mike Moore, oblivious to their surroundings, cradled their whiskies and discussed their unlikely memoirs. A certain mocking by the gods could be discerned. Sure, a potential government may be in the offing, but a vigorous proportion of the population did not give a toss. Their energy was being directed elsewhere.

SKY'S THE LIMIT

By early December an air of inevitability had permeated the New Zealand First Caucus, John Delamere having exited the Maori bloc and even liberals like Deborah Morris resigning themselves to National's embrace. In addition, Bolger had refined his whisky diplomacy to properly entreat Winston's hand — harking back no doubt to the lessons he had learned from Rob Muldoon and his courtship of FOL chief Tom Skinner. Against such matey comradeship Helen Clark was always destined to fail. Maybe if she had worn a Wonderbra...

James Margach, one of Britain's better political journalists, perhaps best summarised the dynamics of such moments. 'Politics is about power. Power is about people. People are personalities.' The parable of the prodigal son was being updated — a quasi-emotional reconciliation that spectacularly complemented the political instincts of both leaders.

Two days before the fateful Caucus meeting Winston telephoned again to seek a last favour, one whose boundaries would definitely stretch over the next week. Would I meet with Wayne Peters, Ernie Davis and Sarah Neems and construct a suitable speech for the coalition announcement?

I may have retired but my ego was alive and well and tempted beyond endurance — writing the words to announce this historical choice had a hint of vicarious immortality. It seemed I was still sufficiently possessed by the demon profession to appreciate the moment and accept the privilege fate offered.

Kirton's earlier indications were now confirmed, as Winston's brother and his two closest aides taxied to my Khandallah home and mapped out their expectations for the next day's speech. All three accepted my caution that no matter how clever, how forceful, how dramatic the coalition announcement, a massive marketing campaign would be required, pre-Christmas, to properly explain Caucus's decision. The choice might be crystal clear to New Zealand First insiders — that would not be its supporters' perception.

I also suggested that if Winston was going to play this piece of theatre effectively then each move must be scripted — each utterance must be linked to the prime theme that New Zealand First's choice had been based upon the mandate of its election policy. To that end Peters asked me to prepare a script for Tuesday's fateful Caucus — a speech that would be publicly released as proof that Peters had not influenced his colleagues' collective decision. I appreciated the sophistry behind such daring audacity and began Peters' homily with the reminder that 'New Zealand First was a party formed to restore integrity and accountability to New Zealand politics'.

I was quite sure the irony would be lost on all gathered within the Caucus room. And so it proved.

That evening Winston would touch the heavens — in more ways than one. As a piece of theatre the coalition announcement was one of his finest performances, carried live on national television and radio, with the whole country literally perched on the edge of their living-room seats, political Lotto tickets at the ready. Peters had requested that in writing the speech I should leave the announcement of the decision to the last possible moment — its impact bringing the speech to a climactic conclusion. But still the announcement relied on Winston's sense of on-stage timing and he did not disappoint, the cadence and rhythm almost perfect. At that instant he reached the apogee of his entire political career and there seemed enough self-awareness in him to appreciate that no matter what came after, it would struggle to match up against that moment. As an old friend I appreciated his sense of triumph all the more because it carried such bitter hints of past disappointment, and the certainty of future fall.

For Winston still lacked the necessary caution to avert even the most obvious of political dangers. By fortuitous mischance I had interrupted a conversation between Doug Woolerton and Peters as they hatched a disastrous plan to sell Winston's coalition announcement to the Sky television channel; apparently Sky had approached the party with a healthy financial incentive for a televised exclusive. I ranted at both men that they were utterly mad for even contemplating such an offer, and eventually the logic of my protests was recognised — the winning argument being that any party professing a populist philosophy should not restrict access to its critical announcements to those able to afford pay television. That neither man could instantly see the absurdity of the idea banished any lingering misgivings I had about my earlier resignation. Spending the next three years baling them out of such madness was not my idea of a sane career choice.

Nevertheless, a pre-announcement interview with Peters was still conducted by Sky's Leighton Smith, although it was telecast only after the public announcement. In reply to suspicious Gallery queries I invented the excuse that Winston had wished to reassure jittery international markets about the country's economic direction and stability. The incident proved a portent, with neither Neems, Davis nor Woolerton able to restrain Winston's strategic outbursts. It was going to be a long three years.

That night Winston hosted one of Parliament's great piss-ups, attended by virtually every political and media luminary, each paying homage to the man of the hour. Jim Bolger tested the waters by sending an advance guard of Bill Birch and Rob Eaddy then, confident that no great mischief was at hand, beamed into Peters' Bowen House suite mightily relieved. We attempted to exchange pleasantries but soon abandoned the pretence — there were some experiences that no amount of diplomacy could overcome.

During the evening various reports from the Gallery filtered into the party, including that of two prominent female journalists openly sobbing at Peters' announcement and exchanging commiserations with their Labour contacts. I had the nastiest of feelings that the story was true — any number of Gallery reporters had just been made to appear complete fools, after falsely and loudly predicting the reverse outcome to their readers. There would be no political honeymoon from that quarter. Not even a Christmas card.

A cursory examination of the Coalition Agreement suggested major New Zealand First policy gains, with Winston's succession to the new role of Treasurer the obvious achievement. Apart from noting the Agreement's lamentable approximation of the English language, I also deciphered a revealing contradiction in the document. In its preparatory preamble the Coalition was confined to an additional $5 billion of government expenditure over the next three financial years — in reality a much lesser sum if inflation and demographic growth were taken into account. However, as I skimmed over the various portfolio subheadings it soon became clear that the total policy programme easily exceeded the gazetted $5 billion.

Plainly there were a series of policy battles yet to be fought. Jenny Shipley's strategy had been successfully pursued by other National negotiators — a series of 'we'll do our best' platitudes had been framed, rather than any definitive blueprint. New Zealand First's war with National was not over. It had just begun.

FIRST SHOTS

Content that my temporary role had been completed, and contemplating the prospect of Christmas shopping, I was surprised to be woken early on Saturday morning by an agitated Winston — this time seeking counsel over the newly created but undefined role of Treasurer. Did I know how the Australian experience worked?

Apparently the Treasury elves had laboured to produce a recommendatory paper that split the current finance portfolio equally between the new Treasurer and the existing Minister of Finance. Indeed, on closer inspection of this document, I surmised that the Minister of Finance actually appeared to hold the senior responsibilities.

Winston's antennae tweaked at this obvious anomaly, and he had reached the not impossible conclusion that Treasury was attempting to inhibit his influence by ensuring that the house-trained Bill Birch would act as the resident Beehive nanny. According to Winston, both Bolger and Treasury had suggested that Treasury's projected division of labour should mirror the Australian example — hence his telephone call to me.

One bluff always deserves another, and I armed Winston with his own paper — a strategic riposte declaring that the Australian experience clearly demarcated the Treasurer as the senior position, with the Minister of Finance little more than a book-keeper. A weekend of unseemly haggling ensued, Treasury obviously petrified that Peters was in a position to undo all their more obvious mischief of the past twelve years. I shared their assumption, although subsequent events would prove us both horribly wrong: not only would Winston respond to The Terrace whistle (disproving the theorem that you cannot teach an old dog new tricks) but the mooted and independent economic advisory team would never be activated, thus ensuring Peters' complete capture.

At this time Winston's attention was also on the imminent nomination of his party's representatives on the National/New Zealand First Coalition Cabinet, and I ended up working the entire weekend on both these matters. Foolishly, I misunderstood Winston's intent with regard to the position of Treasurer — he wanted the mana associated with the senior role rather than the role itself. It would only take Treasury a matter of weeks to appreciate this distinction and regain their vice-like grip on the Government's policy throat.

Even on the following Monday, with the Coalition ministers due to be sworn in by the Governor-General at Government House, Peters was still debating the Treasurer's responsibilities with Bolger and Birch. He told me later that only his threat to cancel the swearing-in ceremony overcame National's final objections to his clear supremacy — something of a pyrrhic victory given later events.

The selection of New Zealand First's ministers was less problematic, though once again I was astounded at Winston's lack of application to this quandary; that he had requested my assistance at all was a clear act of desperation. My first success was in convincing Peters that New Zealand First must have the police portfolio, given the party's pre-election emphasis on law and order and the Coalition Agreement's promises to increase police resources. I assumed these to be categoric;

on later analysis I would come to appreciate the fine print — another victory to National's negotiators.

Sure, the police would get additional sworn staff, but from what starting date? The difference of just one year could mean an actual reduction in personnel strength as police headquarters slashed staff to compensate for yet another failed public sector attempt at introducing information technology. But managed properly, the portfolio was a potential vote winner, able to be identified as a particular New Zealand First strength over the next three years.

Christchurch list candidate Ron Mark was the obvious choice although, understandably, Peters considered Mark too junior for the role. I telephoned Peter McCardle at his Upper Hutt home and offered him the portfolio, stressing its likely prominent profile and reminding him of how John Banks had become the force's darling by delivering an extra nine hundred cops. McCardle would not have a bar of it; there was only one portfolio he wanted and only one he would accept — the legendary blinkers at their insistent best. A back-up call to an excited Jack Elder and the deal was done.

In the end Winston drew up his Cabinet with roughly the same degree of forethought that accompanied his construction of the party's pre-election list. Peters, Henare, McCardle and Elder were the four automatic choices. Now, who for the final allotted Cabinet slot, and which four lucky first-time MPs would assume ministerial roles outside Cabinet?

In earlier briefings I had persuaded Winston that he must have a New Zealand First associate to assist him with his Treasurer's portfolio. Noting Peters' loathing for detail, it was absolutely critical that he had someone who would sift the Treasury advice and generally spot a crock of the proverbial when they saw it. It was my view that McCardle was the obvious candidate and that his pleas to be left alone with his inconsequential, almost clerical, ministerial duties should be ignored. In addition, Peters could easily find himself bogged down by the onerous responsibilities of being both deputy Prime Minister and coalition party leader; he needed someone else from the New Zealand First ranks to handle the detail, rather than allow Bill Birch to perform this role for him.

'Tell Peter,' I urged Winston, 'if he wants employment, then he'll have to take associate finance as well. Or it's nothing.'

I knew McCardle well enough to predict minor grumbling but a final relenting — he could be diplomatically bullied to most conclusions,

THE MOST POPULAR TOY THIS CHRISTMAS - THE 'TICKLE ME WINSTON/TICKLE ME JIM ' DOUBLE PUPPET DOLL PICTURED HERE WITH ITS CREATOR...

provided his grand employment vision was not obviously compromised. Besides, being that close to the money was an obvious incentive for any spending minister.

Over the years I had come to appreciate Winston's private code — a mixture of mannerisms, eye movement and revealing sighs that unconsciously signalled his inner thought processes. This insight was not confined solely to me; Sarah Neems was the resident expert interpreter, while one or two of Winston's past secretarial staff had also a pidgin understanding of the facial tics and body shrugs that made up their boss's secret language. That weekend each Peters code signal seemed suddenly exaggerated — perhaps an indication of the man's near-total exhaustion.

Thus, very early on in our conversations I was able to decipher which counsel would be enacted and which scorned — the police/ Elder advice being accepted, McCardle as Associate Finance Minister being rejected. Winston clearly had someone else in mind for the position — a view that was reinforced when my suggestion of Deborah Morris as the fifth Cabinet minister was categorically rejected. When it became apparent that John (Tuariki) Delamere was Peters' preferred appointment to both roles I blanched: an extensive curriculum vitae does not make an effective minister, even if to Winston it automatically suggests unimpeachable expertise. It had always been my view that the more detailed the references, the greater the rogue.

Besides, Delamere was an obvious Nat-in-drag and not a very bright one at that — suitably lobotomised for Treasury purposes and the direct antithesis of the protector role required.

Donnelly and Kirton picked themselves — associates to the education and health portfolios — although only Kirton would actually seek to implement the Coalition Agreement. Donnelly would become Wyatt Creech's little helper, easily satisfied by a weekly gold star in his parliamentary notebook. Deborah Morris's parliamentary experience, vitality and body-piercing expertise made her the obvious ministerial choice for youth affairs, if a bloody nuisance for international airport security, but the last ministerial position proved a toss-up, Winston being pushed between the competing interests of Ron Mark, Doug Woolerton, Peter Brown and Robyn McDonald. That McDonald assumed the role was entirely due to her gender although, ironically, the most vicious private criticism of this appointment would emanate from Jenny Bloxham.

'I knew I didn't stand a chance,' she told one newspaper, 'when I saw Michael Laws with Winston over the weekend.'

Like Bolger, Bloxham appeared to believe that any personal evil emanating from Winston could only have been injected by myself.

But Bloxham's self-deception proved the least of the reactions to Winston's ministerial choices. The Maori members were particularly incensed, Tau Henare and Tuku Morgan leading the verbal assault in the next New Zealand First Caucus and reducing both Morris and McDonald to helpless tears. Both women were supposedly bumbling and vacuous nonentities compared to the superior mana and experience of Morgan, Waitai and Wyllie — Wyllie organising a 'fax attack' upon the leader's parliamentary office demanding appointment as Minister of Fisheries. Henare's Maori Caucus now had its necessary cohesive focus — a grievance. Little wonder that there would be mixed feelings within the wider Caucus when the Aotearoa Television affair scorched its way into the political lexicon.

Fortunately Peters was able to avert a wider meltdown with the promise of further ministerial slots being available in October 1998, when the Coalition Agreement promised New Zealand First three new Cabinet postings and three further ministerial appointments. The hint was obvious — keep your nose clean over the next eighteen months and the ministerial limousine will be yours. Only the truly stupid and the truly gullible bought this proposition; fortunately both subsets had recently merged within the Caucus. Even after the resignation of Associate Health Minister Neil Kirton and his effective non-replacement (indeed, Tuariki Delamere assumed his portfolio responsibilities emphasising the ephemeral nature of this exchange), the mouldy bait still cast its disciplinary spell. It is true then, there is a sucker born every minute — but who would have thought they would have chosen the New Zealand First Caucus in which to hold their reunion?

The swearing-in of the new Cabinet proved a marked contrast to the last time Winston had journeyed to Government House with Jim Bolger. Six years earlier Peters had publicly scowled his displeasure throughout the entire ceremony, insulted by both his low Cabinet ranking and his sole portfolio of Maori affairs. This time he was at Bolger's side, almost an equal — deputy Prime Minister, Treasurer, and supported by seven other New Zealand First ministers who directly owed him their position and their status. Such symmetry would also have its sting. For both Prime Minister and deputy were now dependent on each other's fortunes — the most unlikely of Siamese twins, drawn together by equal measures of ego, ambition and necessity. The failure of one would mean the eclipse of the other — their partnership a stunning volte-face that both amazed and horrified.

As I beat my retreat back into retirement and a new business — an unsatisfying and dubious mix of political and corporate consultancy — I shared a last Christmas drink with Winston and ruminated over past years, events and personalities.

'That's all in the past, Laws,' Peters noted impatiently, his usual nostalgic instinct overtaken by more pressing considerations. 'There are fresh challenges ahead...' — his eyes misting towards the horizon.

A puzzled thought dithered behind my smile — maybe I was wrong; maybe Winston had a vision after all.

'Yep, Laws.' Winston's tracer smile darted across at me, his mouth now wider and grinning in celebration. 'This government isn't just about getting to 1998 or even the next election. We'll carry on past that — we're going to be a real coalition.'

I understood his emphasis — he meant the kind of coalition in which parties merged forever but appealed to differing voter segments, the Liberal/Country accommodation of Australia being the obvious example. I groaned inwardly at his abandonment of the German Free Democrat prototype that had been our model. Plainly this coupling with the Nats was no one-night stand. Winston seemed to want the whole marital performance — the kids and the mortgage too. How depressing.

We shook hands, indifferently enquired after each other's families, and wished each other a relaxing Christmas. The partnership was now officially over, although without regret. Winston had new friends and fresh adventures in prospect; I had wounds to heal before I ventured forth on further enterprises.

But of one thing I was assured — the demon profession had finally relinquished its possession and I was now free of its thrall. A new batch of parliamentary recruits had just been sacrificed to feed its hunger.

Temptation was already hurtling their way.

EPILOGUE

MICHAEL LAWS did not quite make the break from politics that he would have wished. Suffering a relapse of the possession (although utilising the justification that he was 'just helping a friend') Laws would work as Hon. Neil Kirton's part-time strategic adviser — building Kirton's political reputation as a 'straight arrow' and guiding him through New Zealand First's only notable policy successes — a publicly funded cardiac unit for Christchurch, free healthcare for children aged six and under, and a Customs crackdown on 'clocked' Japanese car imports.

Laws' involvement with Kirton would excite, anger and otherwise drive Beehive strategists and press secretaries to distraction.

In turn, NEIL KIRTON would be sacked as an Associate Health Minister after an acrimonious and long-standing feud with Health Minister Bill English over the role of the private sector in the public health system. Kirton would immediately resign his customs portfolio and become the leading dissident in New Zealand First's Caucus. Rumours abound that he will contest the Napier mayoralty later this year.

Laws would publicly slam his former boss Winston Peters for a lack of political nous and courage in siding with Jim Bolger and Bill English against Kirton. New Zealand First Caucus reaction was strangely muted — their collective tongues stilled with anticipation of Kirton's replacement. No replacement was made — the portfolios being distributed to Associate Finance Minister Tuariki Delamere, who immediately canned the internal customs inquiry and assented to further private sector participation in the provision of taxpayer-funded health services.

GILBERT MYLES is next on the New Zealand First party list and would automatically return to Parliament should any current New

Zealand First list MP expire or retire prior to the 1999 general election.

WINSTON PETERS would become one of the most unpopular politicians in recent history and his New Zealand First party would scarcely register in public opinion polls. Commentators suggest that the party's spectacular demise is linked to the widely held public perception that New Zealand First have betrayed many of their key pre-election promises and that Peters himself has rejected the tenets of political accountability that were his populist rallying cry in Opposition.

The New Zealand First leader would suffer further political humiliation in September 1997 when an overwhelming 92 per cent of New Zealanders would reject a Treasury-designed compulsory superannuation scheme in a nationwide postal referendum.

Despite Laws' devastating public commentary upon current New Zealand First strategy and actions both he and Peters retain social contact to this day. 'We reminisce about the good old days. The past may be another country but it's a lot safer there,' says Laws.

Prime Minister JIM BOLGER would be the victim of a brilliantly executed leadership coup in October 1997, staged by former Social Welfare minister JENNY SHIPLEY. Ironically, it would be the Prime Minister's closeness to Winston Peters that would provoke widespread Caucus and party resentment and precipitate his own demise. Bolger would resign from Parliament in 1998 and be posted to Washington DC as New Zealand's ambassador to the United States.

JENNY SHIPLEY would become New Zealand's first woman Prime Minister.

Close Shipley confidante and former National Finance minister RUTH RICHARDSON would actively campaign for the right-wing ACT Party in the ensuing Taranaki/King Country by-election.

MIKE MOORE would remain a leading Labour Opposition frontbencher, while continuing his self-appointed role as the nemesis of political correctness. In mid-1997 he would accompany Winston Peters to the Hong Kong handover and observe first-hand Peters' wooing of the former British colony's new Chinese landlords.

TUKU MORGAN and his brother-in-law TAU HENARE would become intimately involved in the Aotearoa television affair. Morgan would face extensive public criticism for alleged profligate spending of Aotearoa monies and Henare for his role in the company's later demise. Both men would bring a warrior aggression to New Zealand First Caucus meetings and engage in bitter private battles with

Winston Peters and party president Doug Woolerton.

DAVID STEVENSON and REX WIDERSTROM would fail in their legal action against the New Zealand First party over the construction of that party's 1996 election list. The case would be dismissed on a technicality — neither Stevenson nor Widerstrom being financial members of the party when they lodged their action.

The WINEBOX INQUIRY would finally end and former Chief Justice Sir Ronald Davison deliver his judgement that both the Serious Fraud Office and the Inland Revenue were innocent of any criminal or negligent conduct. Davison would reserve his harshest comments for Winston Peters and Peters' legal counsel, Brian Henry. Despite a failed High Court attempt to overturn the Davison findings Peters has vowed to take the issue to the Privy Council.

The MMP ELECTORAL SYSTEM would plummet in public esteem and a variety of conservative forces are seeking its overthrow in favour of less proportionate electoral systems. A petition to reduce the number of MPs from 120 to 100 would draw strong public and parliamentary support, with new Prime Minister Jenny Shipley floating the possibility of a national referendum on the issue.

In December 1997 Michael Laws would successfully represent himself in the $1 million High Court defamation action lodged against him by former Council adversaries JOHN HARRISON and KERRY SINGLE. Ironically, the plaintiffs would be represented by MIKE CAMP QC — SELWYN CUSHING's barrister in Cushing's successful defamation action against Winston Peters.

ROSS MEURANT is still missing.